Lecture Notes in Computer Science 8902

More information about this series at http://www.springer.com/series/7407

Matteo Maffei · Emilio Tuosto (Eds.)

Trustworthy Global Computing

9th International Symposium, TGC 2014
Rome, Italy, September 5–6, 2014
Revised Selected Papers

Springer

Editors
Matteo Maffei
Department of Computer Science
Saarland University
Saarbrücken
Germany

Emilio Tuosto
Computer Science
University of Leicester
Leicester
United Kingdom

ISSN 0302-9743 ISSN 1611-3349 (electronic)
Lecture Notes in Computer Science
ISBN 978-3-662-45916-4 ISBN 978-3-662-45917-1 (eBook)
DOI 10.1007/978-3-662-45917-1

Library of Congress Control Number: 2014959178

LNCS Sublibrary: SL1 – Theoretical Computer Science and General Issues

Springer Heidelberg New York Dordrecht London

Printed on acid-free paper

Springer-Verlag GmbH Berlin Heidelberg is part of Springer Science+Business Media
(www.springer.com)

Preface

This volume contains the proceedings of TGC 2014, the Ninth International Symposium on Trustworthy Global Computing. The symposium was held in Rome, Italy, during September 5–6, 2014. It was colocated with the CONCUR and IFIP-TCS. Informal pre-proceedings were made available in electronic form to the participants. The papers in this volume were further improved by the authors, in response to helpful feedback received at the symposium.

The Symposium on Trustworthy Global Computing is an international annual venue dedicated to safe and reliable computation in the so-called global computers, i.e., those computational abstractions emerging in large-scale infrastructures such as service-oriented architectures, autonomic systems, and cloud computing systems. It focuses on frameworks, tools, algorithms, and protocols for open-ended, large-scale systems and applications, and on rigorous reasoning about their behavior and properties. The underlying models of computation incorporate code and data mobility over distributed networks that connect heterogeneous devices, often with dynamically changing topologies. In this context, TGC 2014 focused on secure and reliable computation.

The first TGC event took place in Edinburgh in 2005, with the co-sponsorship of IFIP TC-2, as part of ETAPS 2005. TGC 2005 was the evolution of the previous Global Computing I workshops held in Rovereto in 2003 and 2004 (see LNCS vol. 2874) as well as of the workshops on Foundation of Global Computing held as satellite events of ICALP and CONCUR (see ENTCS vol. 85). Four editions of TGC were co-located with the reviews of the EU-funded projects AEOLUS, MOBIUS, and SENSORIA within the FP6 initiative. They were held in Lucca, Italy (TGC 2006, LNCS vol. 4661); in Sophia Antipolis, France (TGC 2007, LNCS vol. 4912); in Barcelona, Spain (TGC 2008, LNCS vol. 5474); and in Munich, Germany (TGC 2010, LNCS vol. 6084). Further editions of TGC were held in Aachen, Germany (TGC 2011, LNCS vol. 7173) and in Newcastle upon Tyne, UK (TGC 2012, LNCS vol. 8191). In 2013, TGC was held in Buenos Aires (LNCS vol. 8358).

TGC 2014 solicited contributions in all areas of global computing, including (but not limited to) theories, languages, models, and algorithms; language concepts and abstraction mechanisms; security, trust, privacy, and reliability; resource usage and information flow policies; software development and software principles; model checkers, theorem provers, and static analyzers.

The fruitful collaboration with CONCUR, initiated in 2013, was continued this year allowing concurrent submissions to CONCUR and TGC, with the reviewing schedule of TGC slightly delayed with respect to that of CONCUR and submissions accepted by CONCUR were automatically withdrawn from TGC. This year there were 5 papers concurrently submitted to TGC and CONCUR and 15 papers were submitted only to TGC (a paper initially submitted was later withdrawn). This time, the papers submitted at CONCUR and TGC were also reviewed by the Program Committee of TGC, praiseworthy for the effort put in the thorough revision process and the accurate discussion.

The Program Committee selected 12 papers to be included in this volume and to be presented at the symposium (2 of which were conditionally accepted in the first instance). The program was structured in sessions named "Theory" (chaired by Michele Loreti), "Session Types" (chaired by Massimo Bartoletti and Stephanie Delaune), "Security" (chaired by Peter Thiemann), "Cryptographic Protocol Analysis" (chaired by Matteo Maffei). Also, a session on "Brief Announcements" (chaired by Emilio Tuosto) gave the possibility to participants to present (on-going) work not included in this proceedings. Finally, TGC's program had invited lectures of Véronique Cortier (CNRS, France) and, jointly with CONCUR, of Catuscia Palamidessi (Inria Saclay and LIX, France).

We would like to thank the Steering Committee of TGC for inviting us to chair the conference; the members of the Program Committee and external referees for their detailed reports and the stimulating discussions during the review phase; the authors of submitted papers, the invited speakers, the session chairs, and the attendees for contributing to the success of the event. We are also grateful to Paolo Baldan and Daniele Gorla, the chairs of CONCUR 2014, with whom we had the opportunity to collaborate. Finally, we thank the providers of the EasyChair system, which was used to manage the submissions.

November 2014

Matteo Maffei
Emilio Tuosto

Organization

Program Committee

Stephen Chong	Harvard University, USA
Anupam Datta	CMU, USA
Stephanie Delaune	CNRS, LSV, France
Mariangiola Dezani-Ciancaglini	Università di Torino, Italy
Fabio Gadducci	Università di Pisa, Italy
Dan Ghica	University of Birmingham, UK
Andrew D. Gordon	Microsoft Research and University of Edinburgh, UK
Joshua Guttman	Worcester Polytechnic Institute, USA
Daniel Hirschkoff	ENS Lyon, France
Christos Kaklamanis	University of Patras and CTI, Greece
Boris Köpf	IMDEA Software Institute, Spain
Alberto Lluch Lafuente	IMT Institute for Advanced Studies Lucca, Italy
Michele Loreti	Università degli Studi di Firenze, Italy
Matteo Maffei	Informatik, Saarland University, Germany
Sergio Maffeis	Imperial College London, UK
Hernan Melgratti	Universidad de Buenos Aires, Argentina
António Ravara	Universidade Nova de Lisboa, Portugal
Alejandro Russo	Chalmers University of Technology, Sweden
Andrey Rybalchenko	TUM, Germany
Emilio Tuosto	University of Leicester, UK
Björn Victor	Uppsala University, Sweden
Roberto Zunino	Università degli Studi di Trento, Italy

Additional Reviewers

Barbanera, Franco
Capecchi, Sara
Castellani, Ilaria
Celestini, Alessandro
Coppo, Mario
Crafa, Silvia
Giunti, Marco
Grossi, Roberto
Knowles, Kenneth
Lozes, Etienne
Mostrous, Dimitris
Santini, Francesco
Tinacci, Marco
Vigliotti, Maria Grazia
Weber, Tjark

Abstracts

Generalized Bisimulation Metrics

Konstantinos Chatzikokolakis[1,2], Daniel Gebler[3], Catuscia Palamidessi[4,2], and Lili Xu[2,5]

[1] CNRS
[2] LIX, Ecole Polytechnique
[3] VU University Amsterdam
[4] INRIA
[5] Institute of Software, Chinese Academy of Science

Abstract

Originally proposed in the seminal works of van Breugel and Worrel [2,3] and of Desharnais et al. [6,7], the pseudometric based on the Kantorovich lifting has become very popular in the process algebra community. One reason for its success is that, when dealing with probabilistic processes, distances are more suitable than equivalences, since the latter are not robust wrt small variation of probabilities. Another important reason is that, thanks to the dual presentation of the Kantorovich lifting in terms of the mass transportation problem, the distance can be efficiently computed using linear programming algorithms [1,2]. Furthermore, this pseudometric is an extension of probabilistic bisimilarity, in the sense that two states have distance distance 0 if and only if they are bisimilar. Furthermore, it is defined as the greatest fixpoint of a transformation that has the same structure as the one used for bisimilarity. This allows to transfer some of the concepts and methods that have been extensively explored in process algebra, and to use lines of reasoning which the process algebra community is familiar with. Along the same lines, a nice property of this pseudometric is that the standard operators of process algebra are non-expansive wrt it. This generalizes the result that bisimulation is a congruence, and can be used in a similar way, for compositional reasoning and verification.

Last but not least, the Kantorovich bisimilarity metric provides a bound on the corresponding distance on probabilistic traces [5] (corresponding in the sense that the definition is based on the same Kantorovich lifting). This means that it can be used to verify certain probabilistic properties on traces. More specifically, it can be used to verify properties that are expressed in terms of difference between probabilities of sets of traces. These properties are linear, in the sense that the difference increases linearly wrt variations on the distributions.

Many properties, however, such as several privacy and security ones, are not linear. This is the case of the popular property of differential privacy [8], which is expressed in terms of ratios of probabilities. In fact, there are processes that have small Kantorovich distance, and which are not ϵ-differentially private for any finite ϵ. Another example are

This work has been partially supported by the project ANR-12-IS02-001 PACE, the project ANR-11-IS02-0002 LOCALI, the INRIA Equipe Associée PRINCESS, the INRIA Large Scale Initiative CAPPRIS, and the EU grant 295261 MEALS.

the properties used in quantitative information flow, which involve logarithmic functions on probabilities.

An interesting line of research, therefore, is to generalize the Kantorovich lifting to obtain a family of pseudometrics suitable for the verification of a wide class of properties, following the principles that:

i. the members of this family should depend on a parameter related to the class of properties (on traces) that we wish to verify,
ii. each member should provide a bound on the corresponding distance on trace distributions,
iii. the kernel of each member should correspond to probabilistic bisimilarity,
iv. the general construction should be coinductive,
v. the typical process-algebra operators should be non-expansive,
vi. each member should be feasible to compute.

In a recent work [4], we have achieved the first four desiderata. Regarding the last two, so far we have studied a particular case (hereafter called multiplicative variant of the Kantorovich lifting) based on the notion of distance used in the definition of differential privacy. We were able to find a dual form of the lifting, which allows to reduce the problem of its computation to a linear optimization problem solvable with standard algorithms. We have also proved that several typical process-algebra operators are non-expansive, and we have given explicitly the expression of the bound. As an example of application of our framework, we have shown how to instantiate our construction to obtain the multiplicative variant of the Kantorovich pseudometric, and how to use it to verify the property of differential privacy.

References

1. Bacci, G., Bacci, G., Larsen, K.G., Mardare, R.: On-the-fly exact computation of bisimilarity distances. In: TACAS. LNCS, vol. 7795, pp. 1–15. Springer (2013)
2. van Breugel, F., Worrell, J.: An algorithm for quantitative verification of probabilistic transition systems. In: Proc. of CONCUR'01. pp. 336–350. Springer (2001)
3. van Breugel, F., Worrell, J.: Towards quantitative verification of probabilistic transition systems. In: Proc. of ICALP. LNCS, vol. 2076, pp. 421–432. Springer (2001)
4. Chatzikokolakis, K., Gebler, D., Palamidessi, C., Xu, L.: Generalized bisimulation metrics. In: Proc. of CONCUR. LNCS, vol. 8704, pp. 32–46. Springer (2014)
5. Chen, D., van Breugel, F., Worrell, J.: On the complexity of computing probabilistic bisimilarity. In: FOSSACS. LNCS, vol. 7213, pp. 437–451. Springer (2012)
6. Desharnais, J., Gupta, V., Jagadeesan, R., Panangaden, P.: Metrics for labeled markov systems. In: Proc. of CONCUR. LNCS, vol. 1664, pp. 258–273. Springer (1999)
7. Desharnais, J., Jagadeesan, R., Gupta, V., Panangaden, P.: The metric analogue of weak bisimulation for probabilistic processes. In: Proc. of LICS. pp. 413–422. IEEE (2002)
8. Dwork, C.: Differential privacy. In: Proc. of ICALP. LNCS, vol. 4052, pp. 1–12. Springer (2006)

Electronic Voting: How to Ensure Privacy and Verifiability

Véronique Cortier

LORIA - CNRS, France

Electronic voting is now used in many countries such as Estonia, United States, Norway, Canada, or France. It provides a convenient way to tally the votes and enables voters to vote from their home. However, it also raises controversy about the security and transparency of the election. How to make sure each vote is counted as intended? How to protect vote privacy? Therefore, several countries like Germany, Netherlands, or the United Kingdom have stopped electronic voting, at least momentarily [5].

Electronic should offer at least the same guarantees than traditional paper-based voting systems. Namely, it should ensure both ballot privacy (no one should know my vote) and verifiability (the result of the election corresponds to the votes casted by voters). Even stronger than ballot privacy is receipt-freeness or coercion-resistance: each vote should remain private even when a voter is willing to tell how he voted. This is to protect against vote buying and coercion. These properties are antagonist: a voter should not be able to prove how he voted, yet he should be able to check that his vote has been counted. Designing a secure e-voting protocol therefore requires a fine tuning between these two properties.

The two main academic Internet voting protocols are Civitas [2] and Helios [1]. We refer the reader to [3] for a short survey on other electronic voting systems. Civitas offers the best security guarantees: coercion-resistance and full verifiability. It might however be difficult to use in practice. Helios is not coercion-resistant but offers ballot privacy and verifiability except for voter eligibility. The fact that Helios does not cover eligibility verifiability means that a compromised ballot box may add ballots. This is fixed by a variant of Helios, named Belenios [4].

Formal methods have been successful in the analysis of standard security protocols such as key exchange or authentication protocols. Electronic voting however challenges the current techniques. First, electronic voting systems often make use of more subtle cryptographic primitives that include blind signatures, homomorphic encryption, or zero-knowledge proofs. Most existing tools cannot yet handle these primitives, or at least not all of them. Moreover, most verification techniques for security protocols are dedicated to trace properties such as authentication or confidentiality. However, ballot privacy is typically expressed as a behavioral equivalence. Decision procedures for equivalence-based properties are yet under development. Another challenge in the context of electronic voting is to identify and model security properties. What is a good electronic voting system? This question is yet to be answered. Even the definition of a key property like ballot privacy has a lot of variants and is still under study. We refer

The research leading to these results has received funding from the European Research Council under the European Union's Seventh Framework Programme (FP7/2007-2013) / ERC grant agreement no 258865, project ProSecure.

the reader to [4] for a more detailed survey on existing techniques for the analysis of e-voting systems.

References

1. Ben Adida, Olivier de Marneffe, Oliver Pereira, and Jean-Jacques Quisquater. Electing a university president using open-audit voting: Analysis of real-world use of Helios. In *Proceedings of the 2009 conference on Electronic voting technology/workshop on trustworthy elections*, 2009.
2. Michael R. Clarkson, Stephen Chong, and Andrew C. Myers. Civitas: Toward a secure voting system. In *Proc. IEEE Symposium on Security and Privacy*, pages 354–368, 2008.
3. Véronique Cortier. Electronic voting: How logic can help. In *Proceegings of the 12th International Joint Conference on Automated Reasoning (IJCAR 2014)*, volume 8562 of *LNAI*, pages 16–26, Vienna, Austria, 2014.
4. Véronique Cortier, David Galindo, Stéphane Glondu, and Malika Izabachene. Election verifiability for helios under weaker trust assumptions. In *Proceedings of the 19th European Symposium on Research in Computer Security (ESORICS'14)*, LNCS, Wroclaw, Poland, September 2014. Springer.
5. Jordi Barrat i Esteve, Ben Goldsmith, and John Turner. International experience with e-voting. Technical report, Norwegian E-Vote Project, 2012.

Contents

An Information Flow Monitor for a Core of DOM

Introducing References and Live Primitives

Ana Almeida-Matos[1,2], José Fragoso Santos[3(✉)], and Tamara Rezk[3]

[1] SQIG–Instituto de Telecomunicações, Lisbon, Portugal
[2] Instituto Superior Técnico, Universidade de Lisboa, Lisbon, Portugal
[3] Inria, Sophia Antipolis, France
jose.santos@inria.fr

Abstract. We propose and prove sound a novel, purely dynamic, flow-sensitive monitor for securing information flow in an imperative language extended with DOM-like tree operations, that we call Core DOM. In Core DOM, as in the DOM API, tree nodes are treated as first-class values. We take advantage of this feature in order to implement an information flow control mechanism that is finer-grained than previous approaches in the literature. Furthermore, we extend Core DOM with additional constructs to model the behavior of *live collections* in the DOM Core Level 1 API. We show that this kind of construct effectively augments the observational power of an attacker and we modify the proposed monitor so as to tackle newly introduced forms of information leaks.

1 Introduction

Interaction between client-side JavaScript programs and the HTML document is done *via* the DOM API [11]. In contrast to the ECMA Standard [1] that specifies in full detail the internals of objects created during the execution, the DOM API only specifies the behavior that DOM interfaces are supposed to exhibit when a program interacts with them. Hence, browser vendors are free to implement the DOM API as they see fit. In fact, in all major browsers, the DOM is not managed by the JavaScript engine but by a separate engine whose role is to do so. Therefore, the design of an information flow monitor for client-side JavaScript Web applications must take into account the DOM API.

Russo et al. [13] first studied the problem of information flow control in dynamic tree structures, for a model where programs are assumed to operate on a single current working node. However, in real client-side JavaScript, tree nodes are first-class values, which means that a program can store in memory several references to different nodes in the DOM forest at the same time. We present a flow-sensitive monitor for tracking information flow in a DOM-like language, that we call Core DOM. In Core DOM, tree nodes are treated as first-class values and thus they support all operations available to other types of values, such as assignment to variables. Interestingly, this language design feature enables us

M. Maffei and E. Tuosto (Eds.): TGC 2014, LNCS 8902, pp. 1–16, 2014.
DOI: 10.1007/978-3-662-45917-1_1

to implement a more fine-grained information flow control mechanism, since it becomes possible to distinguish the security level of the node itself from both the security level of the value that is stored in the node and from the level of its position in the DOM forest. We prove that the proposed monitor is sound with respect to a standard definition of noninterference.

Live collections are a special kind of data structure featured in the DOM API that automatically reflects the changes that occur in the document. There are several types of live collections. For instance, the method `getElementsByTagName` returns a live collection containing the DOM nodes that match a given *tag*. In the following example, after retrieving the initial collection of DIV nodes, the program iterates over the *current* size of this collection, while introducing a new DIV node at each step:

```
divs = document.getElementsByTagName("DIV"); i = 0;
while(i <= divs.length){
  document.appendChild(document.createElement("DIV")); i++; }
```

Every time a new DIV node is inserted in the `document` (no matter where in its structure), it is also inserted in the live collection bound to `divs`. Due to the live update of the loop condition, if the initial `document` contains at least one DIV node, the program does not terminate.

Live collections can be exploited to encode new types of information leaks. Therefore, we extend Core DOM with two additional constructs that model the behavior of `getElementsByTagName` in the DOM API. We demonstrate that these constructs effectively augment the observational power of an attacker and we show how to modify the proposed monitor so as to tackle this issue.

In the remainder of the paper, we start by formally introducing the target language Core DOM (Section 2). We then present a mechanism that controls information flows by means of a flow-sensitive monitor (Section 3). The scenario is then extended with live collections, for which we propose a modified mechanism (Section 4). Finally, we discuss related work and conclude. Due to space restrictions, proofs are presented in the article's full version [2].

2 Core DOM

We now present Core DOM – a simple imperative language extended with primitives for operating on tree structures. Its syntax is given by the following:

$e ::= v$	literal value	|	$\underline{v}$	runtime value
| x	identifier	|	$\mathsf{if}(e_0)\{e_1\}\ \mathsf{else}\ \{e_2\}$	conditional
| $\mathsf{while}(e_0)\{e_1\}$	loop	|	$\mathsf{while}^{e_0}(e_1)\{e_2\}$	internal loop
| $e_0; e_1$	sequence	|	$\mathsf{move}_\uparrow(e)$	move upward
| $\mathsf{move}_\downarrow(e, e)$	move downward	|	$\mathsf{remove}(e, e)$	remove node
| $\mathsf{insert}(e, e, e)$	insert node	|	$\mathsf{new}^{\sigma_0,\sigma_1,\sigma_2}(e)$	new node
| $\mathsf{value}(e)$	node value	|	$\mathsf{store}(e, e)$	store value
| $\mathsf{len}(e)$	node length	|	$\mathsf{end}(e)$	end

Every tree node has a type, called its *tag* (for instance, DIV) and can store a single value taken from a set $\mathcal{P}rim$ containing integers, strings, booleans, and a special value *null*. All the nodes in memory form a *forest*, meaning that every node has a possibly empty list of *children* and at most a single *parent*. We define the *index* of a node as the position it occupies in the list of children of its parent.

New nodes are created using the primitive new, which expects as input the tag of the node to be created and is annotated with three security levels that are explained later. When given a node as input, the primitive $\mathsf{move}_\uparrow$ evaluates to its parent in the DOM forest. Complementarily, the primitive $\mathsf{move}_\downarrow$ expects as input a node n and an integer i and evaluates to the ith child of n. The primitive insert is used for inserting an *orphan node* (that is, a node with no parent) in the list of children of another node, whereas the primitive remove is used for removing a node from the list of children of its parent. Concretely, insert expects as input two nodes n_0 and n_1 and an integer i and inserts n_1 in the ith position of the list of children of n_0 right-shifting by one all the children of n_0 whose indexes are greater than or equal to i. The primitive remove expects as input a node n and an integer i and removes the ith child of n from its list of children left-shifting the right siblings of the removed node by one position. When given as input a node, the keyword len evaluates to its number of children. The keyword value expects as input a node and evaluates to the value that it stores, whereas the keyword store expects as input a node n and a value v and stores v in n. Finally, the syntax of Core DOM includes two special primitives: (1) end [12,14] (not available for the programmer) that is used by the semantics to signal the end of a structure block and (2) an internal while primitive used by the semantics for bookkeeping the guard of the loop currently executing.

We model a DOM forest $f : \mathcal{R}ef \rightarrow \mathcal{N}$ as a partial mapping from a set of references to the set of DOM nodes. A DOM node is a tuple of the form: $\langle m, \underline{v}, r, \omega \rangle$, where: (1) m is the node's tag, (2) $\underline{v}$ the runtime value that it stores, (3) r the reference pointing to its parent, and (4) ω its list of children. For simplicity, given a DOM node n, we denote by n.tag, n.value, n.parent, and n.children its tag, value, parent, and list of children, respectively. The semantics of Core DOM makes use of a semantic function $\mathcal{R}_{Ancestor}$ that, given a forest f, outputs a binary relation in $\mathcal{R}ef \times \mathcal{R}ef$ such that $\langle r_0, r_1 \rangle \in \mathcal{R}_{Ancestor}(f)$ iff the node pointed to by r_0 is an ancestor of that pointed to by r_1. The set V_F contains the runtime values that cause the guard of a conditional or loop to fail.

Figures 1 and 2 present the small-step semantics of Core DOM. Configurations have the form: $\langle \mu, f, e \rangle$, where μ is a mapping from variables to values, f a DOM forest, and e the expression to evaluate. References can be viewed as pointers to nodes, in the sense that the creation of a node yields a new reference that points to it. As in [6], the semantics makes use of a *parametric allocator*, *fresh*, that given a DOM forest f and a security level σ, generates a new reference r, such that $r \notin dom(f)$. The semantic transitions are annotated with *internal events* [12] to be used by the monitored semantics.

The evaluation order is specified by writing expressions using *evaluation contexts*. We write $E[e]$ to denote the expression obtained by replacing the occurrence of $[]$ in the context E with e. The syntax of evaluation contexts is given by:

Identifier
$$\langle \mu, f, x\rangle \xrightarrow{\mathsf{var}(x)} \langle \mu, f, \mu(x)\rangle$$

Assignment
$$\langle \mu, f, x = \underline{v}\rangle \xrightarrow{\mathsf{assign}(x)} \langle \mu\,[x \mapsto \underline{v}]\,, f, \underline{v}\rangle$$

Sequence
$$\langle \mu, f, \underline{v}; e_0\rangle \xrightarrow{\bullet} \langle \mu, f, e_0\rangle$$

End
$$\langle \mu, f, \mathsf{end}(\underline{v})\rangle \xrightarrow{\succ} \langle \mu, f, \underline{v}\rangle$$

Value
$$\langle \mu, f, v\rangle \xrightarrow{\mathsf{pval}} \langle \mu, f, \underline{v}\rangle$$

Loop
$$\langle \mu, f, \mathsf{while}(e_0)\{e_1\}\rangle \xrightarrow{\circ} \langle \mu, f, \mathsf{while}^{e_0}(e_0)\{e_1\}\rangle$$

Loop - True
$$\frac{\underline{v} \notin V_F \qquad e' = \mathsf{end}(e_1; \mathsf{while}(e_0)\{e_1\})}{\langle \mu, f, \mathsf{while}^{e_0}(\underline{v})\{e_1\}\rangle \xrightarrow{\mathsf{branch}} \langle \mu, f, e'\rangle}$$

Loop - False
$$\frac{\underline{v} \notin V_F \qquad e' = \mathsf{end}(v)}{\langle \mu, f, \mathsf{while}^{e_0}(\underline{v})\{e_1\}\rangle \xrightarrow{\mathsf{branch}} \langle \mu, f, e'\rangle}$$

Conditional
$$\frac{\underline{v} \notin V_F \Rightarrow i = 0 \qquad \underline{v} \in V_F \Rightarrow i = 1}{\langle \mu, f, \mathsf{if}(\underline{v})\{e_0\}\ \mathsf{else}\ \{e_1\}\rangle \xrightarrow{\mathsf{branch}} \langle \mu, f, \mathsf{end}(e_i)\rangle}$$

Context Composition
$$\frac{\langle \mu, f, e\rangle \xrightarrow{\alpha} \langle \mu', f', e'\rangle}{\langle \mu, f, E[e]\rangle \xrightarrow{\alpha} \langle \mu', f', E[e']\rangle}$$

Fig. 1. Core DOM Semantics - Imperative Fragment

Move Upward
$$\frac{f(r).\mathsf{parent} = r'}{\langle \mu, f, \mathsf{move}_{\uparrow}(r)\rangle \xrightarrow{\uparrow(r)} \langle \mu, f, r'\rangle}$$

Move Downward
$$\frac{f(r).\mathsf{children}(i) = r'}{\langle \mu, f, \mathsf{move}_{\downarrow}(r, i)\rangle \xrightarrow{\downarrow(r')} \langle \mu, f, r'\rangle}$$

New
$$\frac{r = fresh(f, \sigma_0) \qquad f' = f\,[r \mapsto \langle m, null, null, \epsilon\rangle]}{\langle \mu, f, \mathsf{new}^{\sigma_0,\sigma_1,\sigma_2}(m)\rangle \xrightarrow{\mathsf{new}(r,\sigma_0,\sigma_1,\sigma_2)} \langle \mu, f', r\rangle}$$

Remove
$$\frac{\begin{array}{cc} f(r) = \langle m, \underline{v}, \hat{r}, \omega\rangle & f(\omega(i)) = \langle m', \underline{v}', r, \omega'\rangle \\ r' = \omega(i) & f' = f\begin{bmatrix} r \mapsto \langle m, \underline{v}, \hat{r}, Shift_L(\omega, i)\rangle, \\ r' \mapsto \langle m', \underline{v}', null, \omega'\rangle \end{bmatrix}\end{array}}{\langle \mu, f, \mathsf{remove}(r, i)\rangle \xrightarrow{-(r,r')} \langle \mu, f', r'\rangle}$$

Insert
$$\frac{\begin{array}{c}\langle r', r\rangle \notin \mathcal{R}_{Ancestor}(f) \qquad f(r) = \langle m, \underline{v}, \hat{r}, \omega\rangle \qquad f(r') = \langle m', \underline{v}', null, \omega'\rangle \\ f' = f\,[r \mapsto \langle m, \underline{v}, \hat{r}, Shift_R(\omega, i, r')\rangle, r' \mapsto \langle m', \underline{v}', r, \omega'\rangle]\end{array}}{\langle \mu, f, \mathsf{insert}(r, r', i)\rangle \xrightarrow{+(r,r',\omega(i))} \langle \mu, f', r'\rangle}$$

Length
$$\frac{i = |f(r).\mathsf{children}|}{\langle \mu, f, \mathsf{len}(r)\rangle \xrightarrow{\mathsf{len}(r)} \langle \mu, f, i\rangle}$$

Value
$$\frac{f(r).\mathsf{value} = \underline{v}}{\langle \mu, f, \mathsf{value}(r)\rangle \xrightarrow{\mathsf{val}(r)} \langle \mu, f, \underline{v}\rangle}$$

Store
$$\frac{f(r) = \langle m, \underline{v}, \hat{r}, \omega\rangle \qquad f' = f\,[r \mapsto \langle m, \underline{v}', \hat{r}, \omega\rangle]}{\langle \mu, f, \mathsf{store}(r, \underline{v}')\rangle \xrightarrow{\mathsf{store}(r)} \langle \mu, f', \underline{v}'\rangle}$$

Fig. 2. Core DOM Semantics - Primitives for Tree Operations

$$\begin{array}{l} E ::= [\,] \mid x = E \mid \mathsf{if}(E)\{e\}\ \mathsf{else}\ \{e\} \mid \mathsf{while}^{e}(E)\{e\} \mid E; e \mid \mathsf{end}(E) \mid \mathsf{len}(E) \mid \mathsf{value}(E) \\ \quad \mid \mathsf{move}_{\uparrow}(E) \mid \mathsf{move}_{\downarrow}(E, e) \mid \mathsf{move}_{\downarrow}(\underline{v}, E) \mid \mathsf{remove}(E, \underline{v}) \mid \mathsf{remove}(\underline{v}, E) \mid \mathsf{insert}(\underline{v}, E, e) \\ \quad \mid \mathsf{insert}(E, e, e) \mid \mathsf{insert}(\underline{v}, \underline{v}, E) \mid \mathsf{new}^{\sigma_0,\sigma_1,\sigma_2}(E) \mid \mathsf{store}(E, e) \mid \mathsf{store}(\underline{v}, E) \end{array}$$

Given a list ω, an integer i, and an arbitrary element a, we denote by: (1) $\omega(i)$ the ith element of ω if it is defined and $null$ otherwise, (2) $|\omega|$ the number of elements of ω, (3) ϵ the empty list, (4) $Shift_L(\omega, i)$ the list obtained by removing from ω its ith element (provided that it is defined), (5) $Shift_R(\omega, a, i)$ the list obtained by inserting a in the ith position of ω (provided that i is smaller than or equal to the number of elements of ω), (6) $\omega :: a$ the list obtained by appending a to ω, and (7) $\omega_0 \oplus \omega_1$ the concatenation of ω_0 and ω_1. We use the notation $f[a \mapsto b]$ for the function that coincides with f everywhere except in a that it maps to b.

3 Dynamic IFC in Core DOM

Before proceeding to describe the monitor for securing information flow in Core DOM, we discuss the main challenges imposed by the particular features of this API and how we propose to tackle them. As usual, the specification of security policies relies on a lattice $\mathcal{L}$ of security levels and a labeling that maps resources to security levels. In examples and informal explanations, we use $\mathcal{L} = \{H, L\}$ with $L \sqsubseteq H$, meaning that resources labeled L (*low*, *visible*) are less confidential than those labeled H (*high*, *invisible*). Hence, H-labeled resources can depend on L-labeled resources, but not the contrary, as that would entail a *security leak*.

3.1 Challenges for IFC in Core DOM

The range of tree operations offered by Core DOM allows information to be stored and inspected from arbitrary nodes in several ways: (1) A node can be created and its existence tested; (2) A value can be stored and read from a node; (3) A child node can be inserted at/removed from a certain position, and both the number of children and their positions can be retrieved. (The *position* of a node can be understood as the pair consisting of its parent in the DOM forest and its index.) These operations can be used to encode security leaks via the different information components that are associated with every node. We now examine these leaks and introduce the formal techniques we use for tackling them. In the examples, we assume three initial nodes, div_0, div_1 and div_2, created as follows:

$$div_0 = \mathsf{new}(\text{"DIV"});\ div_1 = \mathsf{new}(\text{"DIV"});\ div_2 = \mathsf{new}(\text{"DIV"}) \tag{1}$$

Differentiating information components. Each node in a DOM forest can be seen to carry four main information components: its existence, its value, its position and its number of children. To some degree, these components can be manipulated separately, and there is value in treating them separately by the security analysis. For instance, in the following program, the final position of div_2 carries *high* information (because it is inserted in a *high* context), despite the fact that it contains the *low* level value l_0:

$$\mathsf{store}(div_2, l_0);\ \mathsf{if}(h)\{\mathsf{insert}(div_0, div_2, 0)\}\ \mathsf{else}\ \{\mathsf{insert}(div_1, div_2, 0)\} \tag{2}$$

After the execution of this program, the position of div_2 should not be revealed to a low observer. Its value, however, can be made public. Hence, while the evaluation of $\mathsf{move}_{\uparrow}(div_2)$ should yield a high value, the evaluation of the expression $\mathsf{value}(div_2)$ in the final memory can yield a low value. Similarly, there is no reason why the position of a node that stores a secret value should not be public.

By treating tree nodes as first-class values, we can naturally differentiate the security levels that are associated to each of the node's information components. We propose to associate every tree node with four security levels. The *value level* of a node is the level of the value that it stores. The *position level* of a node is the level of its position in the DOM forest. Hence, the position level of a node constitutes an upper bound on the levels of the contexts in which its position in the DOM forest can change (such as by its insertion/removal). The *structure security level* [10] of a node is associated to the node's number of children. It serves as an upper bound on the levels of the contexts in which the number of children of a node can be changed (such as by insertion/removal of nodes in/from its list of children). Finally, the *node level* is the level associated to information about the existence of the node itself. It is used as an upper bound on the levels of the contexts in which the node can be created or a lower bound on its own value and structure level, and on its children's position levels.

New forms of security leaks. When inserting/removing a node in/from the list of children of a given node, the indexes of its right siblings change, thereby entailing a new kind of implicit flow. Consider the following example:

$$\mathsf{insert}(div_0, div_1, 0);\ \mathsf{if}(h)\{\mathsf{insert}(div_0, div_2, 0)\}\ \mathsf{else}\ \{null\};\ l_0 = \mathsf{move}_{\downarrow}(div_0, 0) \quad (3)$$

The program above prepends div_1 to the list of children of div_0 (which is originally empty). Then, depending on the value of h, the program prepends div_2 to the list of children of div_0. Hence, depending on the value of h, the program assigns either div_1 or div_2 to the *low* variable l_0. We refer to these forms of security leaks as *order leaks*, as they leverage information about the order of the nodes in the list of children. Order leaks can also be obtained by removing a child node when a second sibling node of higher index exists. Program 3 shows that, when changing the position of a node in the DOM forest, the positions of its right siblings also change. Therefore, the monitor enforces the position levels of the right siblings of a given node to be equal to or higher than its own position level. Furthermore, when moving from one node to another information about the position of the child node is leaked. For instance, for Program 3 to be legal, the position levels of div_1 and div_2 must be H. Therefore, the value associated with the evaluation of the instruction $\mathsf{move}_{\downarrow}(div_0, 0)$ is H.

The fact that a program can inspect the number of children of a given node can be exploited to encode implicit information flows. If we add the low assignment $l_1 = \mathsf{len}(div_0)$ to the end of Program 3, the value of l_1 will be set to 2 or 1 depending on the value of the *high* variable h. The *structure security level* is meant to control this kind of leaks. If a node has *low* structure security level, one cannot insert/remove nodes in/from its list of children in *high* contexts. Therefore, the level associated with looking-up the number of children of a given node corresponds to its structure security level. For instance, for Program 3 to be legal, the structure security level of div_0 must be H. Hence, the level associated with the evaluation of $\mathsf{len}(div_0)$ is H independently of the original value of h.

Flow-sensitive versus flow-insensitive IF monitoring. The *no-sensitive-upgrade* discipline [3] has been widely used in the design of *purely dynamic monitors*. This discipline establishes that visible resources cannot be upgraded in invisible contexts, since such upgrades cause the visible domain of a program to change depending on secret values. Hence, flow-sensitive monitors that implement the no-sensitive-upgrade discipline abort executions that encode illegal implicit flows. Since both the structure security level and the position level of a node are used to control the implicit flows that can be encoded by inserting/removing nodes in/from the DOM forest, these levels cannot be upgraded. This point is illustrated in the following table, which represents four monitored executions of a program (represented on the left) in two distinct memories, by showing how the variable labeling Γ and the node labeling Σ evolve during each execution. The initial memories are such that div_0 and div_1 each bind an orphan node with *low* structure security level, and are pointed to by r_0 and r_1, respectively, but differ in the value of *high* variable h.

While the monitor following the *naive approach* raises the structure security level of div_0 to H (allowing the execution to go through), the monitor following the *no-sensitive-upgrade* discipline blocks the execution when the program tries to add div_1 to the list of children of div_0 in a *high* context. The case regarding the position level can be seen by replacing the test of the second `if` instruction with $\mathsf{move}_{\uparrow}(div_1) == div_0$, assuming that the original position level of div_1 is *low*. In contrast to the position level and to the structure security level, the value level of a node can be upgraded, as the value stored in a node is set explicitly. However, such upgrades cannot be caused by implicit information flows.

	Both Approaches	*Naive Approach*	*No-Sensitive-Upgrade*
Initial High Memory:	$h = \mathsf{false}$	$h = \mathsf{true}$	$h = \mathsf{true}$
$l = \mathsf{true}$	$\Gamma(l) := L$	$\Gamma(l) := L$	$\Gamma(l) := L$
$\mathsf{if}(h)$	branch not taken	branch taken	branch taken
$\mathsf{insert}(div_0, div_1, 0)$	—	$\Sigma(r_0).\mathsf{struct} := H$	*stuck*
$\mathsf{if}(\mathsf{len}(div_0) == 0)$	branch taken	branch not taken	—
$l = \mathsf{false}$	$\Gamma(l) := L$	—	—
Final Low Memory:	$l = \mathsf{false}$	$l = \mathsf{true}$	—

3.2 The Attacker Model

We assume a generic lattice $\mathcal{L}$ of security levels, and use $\sqcup$, $\sqcap$, $\bot$, and $\top$ for the greatest lower bound, the least upper bound, the *bottom* level, and the *top* level, respectively. We consider two types of labelings: *variable labelings* and *node labelings*. While a variable labeling $\Gamma : \mathcal{V}ar \to \mathcal{L}$ maps each variable to a single security level, a node labeling $\Sigma : \mathcal{R}ef \to \mathcal{L}^4$ associates each reference with a tuple of four security levels. Hence, given a reference r and a labeling Σ, $\Sigma(r) = \langle \sigma_n, \sigma_v, \sigma_e, \sigma_s \rangle$, where: (1) σ_n is the node level, (2) σ_v is the value level, (3) σ_e is the the position level, and (4) σ_s is the structure security level. For clarity, given a node n pointed to by a reference r and a labeling Σ, we denote by $\Sigma(r).\mathsf{node}$, $\Sigma(r).\mathsf{value}$, $\Sigma(r).\mathsf{pos}$, and $\Sigma(r).\mathsf{struct}$ its node level, value level, position level, and structure security level, respectively. For simplicity, we impose four restrictions on the levels assigned to a given node. First, one cannot store a visible value in an invisible node. Second, an invisible node cannot have a visible position. Third, an invisible node cannot have a visible number of children. Fourth, an invisible node cannot have a visible node in its list of children (in practice, this means that we cannot insert a visible node in an invisible node). Formally, for every reference $r \in dom(\Sigma)$, it holds that: $\Sigma(r).\mathsf{node} \sqsubseteq \Sigma(r).\mathsf{value} \sqcap \Sigma(r).\mathsf{pos} \sqcap \Sigma(r).\mathsf{struct}$. Additionally, for every two references r and

r' in a forest f such that: $r, r' \in dom(\Sigma)$ and $f(r).\mathsf{children}(i) = r'$ for some integer i, it holds that $\Sigma(r).\mathsf{node} \sqsubseteq \Sigma(r').\mathsf{node}$.

In order to formally characterize the observational power of an attacker, we take the standard approach of defining a notion of *low-projection* of a memory/forest at a given level σ, which corresponds to the part of the memory/forest that an attacker at level σ can observe. The low-projection of a memory μ with respect to a variable labeling Γ at level σ is simply given by: $\mu \restriction^{\Gamma,\sigma} = \{(x, \mu(x), \Gamma(x)) \mid x \in dom(\Gamma) \wedge \Gamma(x) \sqsubseteq \sigma\}$. Accordingly, two memories μ_0 and μ_1, respectively labeled by Γ_0 and Γ_1 are said to be *low-equal* at security level σ, written $\mu_0, \Gamma_0 \sim_\sigma \mu_1, \Gamma_1$, if they coincide in their respective low-projections, $\mu_0 \restriction^{\Gamma_0,\sigma} = \mu_1 \restriction^{\Gamma_1,\sigma}$. Definition 1 extends the notion of low-projection to forests. Informally, an attacker at level σ can see: **(1)** the references whose corresponding nodes are associated with levels $\sqsubseteq \sigma$ as well as their tags, **(2)** the values stored in visible nodes whose value level is $\sqsubseteq \sigma$, **(3)** the positions of visible nodes (with visible parents) whose levels are $\sqsubseteq \sigma$, and **(4)** the number of children of visible nodes whose structure security level is $\sqsubseteq \sigma$.

Definition 1 (Low-Projection and Low-Equality). *The low-projection of a forest f w.r.t. a security level σ and a labeling Σ is given by:*

$$
\begin{aligned}
f \restriction^{\Sigma,\sigma} = \ & \{(r, f(r).\mathsf{tag}, \Sigma(r).\mathsf{node}, \Sigma(r).\mathsf{pos}, \Sigma(r).\mathsf{struct}) \mid \Sigma(r).\mathsf{node} \sqsubseteq \sigma\} \\
\cup \ & \{(r, f(r).\mathsf{value}, \Sigma(r).\mathsf{value}) \mid \ \Sigma(r).\mathsf{value} \sqsubseteq \sigma\} \\
\cup \ & \{(r, i, r') \mid \ f(r).\mathsf{children}(i) = r' \ \wedge \ \Sigma(r').\mathsf{pos} \sqsubseteq \sigma\} \\
\cup \ & \{(r, null) \mid \ f(r).\mathsf{parent} = null \ \wedge \ \Sigma(r).\mathsf{pos} \sqsubseteq \sigma\} \\
\cup \ & \{(r, |f(r).\mathsf{children}|) \mid \ \Sigma(r).\mathsf{struct} \sqsubseteq \sigma\}
\end{aligned}
$$

Two forests f_0 and f_1, respectively labeled by Σ_0 and Σ_1 are said to be low-equal at security level σ, written $f_0, \Sigma_0 \sim_\sigma f_1, \Sigma_1$, if $f_0 \restriction^{\Sigma_0,\sigma} = f_1 \restriction^{\Sigma_1,\sigma}$.

In the following figures, **a)** and **b)** represent the final forests obtained from the execution of Program 3 in two distinct memories that initially map the *high* variable h to 1 and to 0, respectively. Forest **c)** represents their (coinciding) low-projection. Nodes are labeled with their node level and structure security level, while edges are labeled with the child's position level. The position levels of div_1 and div_2 as well as the structure security level of div_0 are assumed to be originally *high*. All other levels are assumed to be originally *low*.

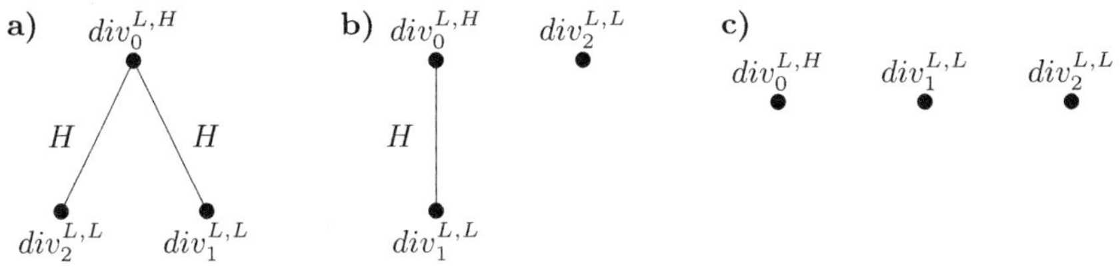

3.3 Enforcement

We define a monitored semantics in the style of Russo et al. [12,14]. A configuration of the monitored semantics is obtained by pairing up a configuration

IDENTIFIER
$$\frac{\sigma = level(o) \sqcup \Gamma(x)}{\langle \Gamma, \Sigma, o, \zeta \rangle \overset{\mathsf{var}(x)}{\rightarrow} \langle \Gamma, \Sigma, o, \zeta :: \sigma \rangle}$$

ASSIGNMENT
$$\frac{level(o) \sqsubseteq \Gamma(x) \qquad \sigma' = level(o) \sqcup \sigma}{\langle \Gamma, \Sigma, o, \zeta :: \sigma \rangle \overset{\mathsf{assign}(x)}{\rightarrow} \langle \Gamma\left[x \mapsto \sigma'\right], \Sigma, o, \zeta :: \sigma' \rangle}$$

LITERAL VALUE
$$\langle \Gamma, \Sigma, o, \zeta \rangle \overset{\mathsf{pval}}{\rightarrow} \langle \Gamma, \Sigma, o, \zeta :: level(o) \rangle$$

BRANCH
$$\langle \Gamma, \Sigma, o, \zeta :: \sigma \rangle \overset{\mathsf{branch}}{\rightarrow} \langle \Gamma, \Sigma, o :: \sigma, \zeta \rangle$$

END
$$\langle \Gamma, \Sigma, o :: \sigma, \zeta \rangle \overset{\curlyvee}{\rightarrow} \langle \Gamma, \Sigma, o, \zeta \rangle$$

DISCHARGE
$$\langle \Gamma, \Sigma, o, \zeta :: \sigma \rangle \overset{\bullet}{\rightarrow} \langle \Gamma, \Sigma, o, \zeta \rangle$$

EMPTY
$$\langle \Gamma, \Sigma, o, \zeta \rangle \overset{\circ}{\rightarrow} \langle \Gamma, \Sigma, o, \zeta \rangle$$

Fig. 3. Core DOM Monitor - Imperative Fragment

of the unmonitored semantics with a configuration of the security monitor. At each computation step, the security monitor uses the internal event generated by the unmonitored semantics to determine its corresponding transition. Hence, the transitions of the monitored semantics are defined as follows:

$$\frac{\langle \mu, f, e \rangle \overset{\alpha}{\rightarrow} \langle \mu', f', e' \rangle \quad \langle \Gamma, \Sigma, o, \zeta \rangle \overset{\alpha}{\rightarrow} \langle \Gamma', \Sigma', o', \zeta' \rangle}{\langle \langle \mu, f, e \rangle, \langle \Gamma, \Sigma, o, \zeta \rangle \rangle \rightarrow \langle \langle \mu', f', e' \rangle, \langle \Gamma', \Sigma', o', \zeta' \rangle \rangle}$$

The arrow $\rightarrow$ denotes the transition relation (whilst $\rightarrow^*$ its reflexive-transitive closure), and the configurations of the security monitor have the form $\langle \Gamma, \Sigma, o, \zeta \rangle$, where: (1) Γ is the variable labeling, (2) Σ is the node labeling, (3) o is the *control context*, that is, a list containing the levels of the expressions on which the program branched in order to reach the expression that is currently executing, and (4) ζ is the *expression context*, that is, a list consisting of the levels of the expressions of the current evaluation context that were already computed. The control context and the expression context lists are used as stacks. Concretely, each time the evaluation enters the body of an `if` or a `while` expression, the level of the expression that was tested is appended to the control context. Conversely, when the control flow leaves the body of an `if` or a `while` expression, the monitor removes the last element of the control context. Similarly, after the evaluation of an expression that is nested inside another expression, its level is appended to the expression context and, whenever an expression is no longer nested inside another expression, its level is removed from the expression context. The transitions of the monitor are presented in Figures 3 and 4. We are only concerned with monitored executions beginning with $\langle \Gamma_0, \Sigma_0, \epsilon, \epsilon \rangle$, where Γ_0 and Σ_0 are the original variable and node labelings. Furthermore, letting μ_0 and f_0 be the initial memory and the initial forest, we require that: $dom(\mu_0) = dom(\Gamma_0)$ and $dom(f_0) = dom(\Sigma_0)$. Given a list ω, we use the $level(\omega)$ as an abbreviation for $\sqcup\{\omega(i) \mid 0 \leq i < |\omega|\}$.

Let us briefly explain the rules of the proposed information flow monitor. Rules [MOVE UPWARD] and [MOVE DOWNWARD] update the expression context ζ with the levels of the current expression's subexpression(s) (that are retrieved from ζ), of the program counter, and of the departing/arriving node's position. Observe that the levels of the nodes that the traversed edge connects are ignored,

$$\text{Move Upward}\quad \frac{\sigma' = level(o) \sqcup \Sigma(r).\mathsf{pos} \sqcup \sigma}{\langle \Gamma, \Sigma, o, \zeta :: \sigma \rangle \overset{\uparrow(r)}{\rightarrow} \langle \Gamma, \Sigma, o, \zeta :: \sigma' \rangle}$$

$$\text{Move Downward}\quad \frac{\sigma' = level(o) \sqcup \Sigma(r).\mathsf{pos} \sqcup \sigma_0 \sqcup \sigma_1}{\langle \Gamma, \Sigma, o, \zeta :: \sigma_0 :: \sigma_1 \rangle \overset{\downarrow(r)}{\rightarrow} \langle \Gamma, \Sigma, o, \zeta :: \sigma' \rangle}$$

$$\text{Length}\quad \frac{\sigma' = \sigma \sqcup level(o) \sqcup \Sigma(r).\mathsf{struct}}{\langle \Gamma, \Sigma, o, \zeta :: \sigma \rangle \overset{\mathsf{len}(r)}{\rightarrow} \langle \Gamma, \Sigma, o, \zeta :: \sigma' \rangle}$$

$$\text{Remove}\quad \frac{level(o) \sqcup \sigma_0 \sqcup \sigma_1 \sqsubseteq \Sigma(r).\mathsf{struct} \sqcap \Sigma(r').\mathsf{pos}}{\langle \Gamma, \Sigma, o, \zeta :: \sigma_0 :: \sigma_1 \rangle \overset{-(r,r')}{\rightarrow} \langle \Gamma, \Sigma, o, \zeta :: \Sigma(r').\mathsf{pos} \rangle}$$

$$\text{Insert}\quad \frac{\begin{array}{c} r'' = null \lor \Sigma(r').\mathsf{pos} \sqsubseteq \Sigma(r'').\mathsf{pos} \\ level(o) \sqcup \sigma_0 \sqcup \sigma_1 \sqcup \sigma_2 \sqsubseteq \Sigma(r).\mathsf{struct} \sqcap \Sigma(r').\mathsf{pos} \end{array}}{\langle \Gamma, \Sigma, o, \zeta :: \sigma_0 :: \sigma_1 :: \sigma_2 \rangle \overset{+(r,r',r'')}{\rightarrow} \langle \Gamma, \Sigma, o, \zeta :: \Sigma(r').\mathsf{pos} \rangle}$$

$$\text{Value}\quad \frac{\sigma' = \sigma \sqcup \Sigma(r).\mathsf{value}}{\langle \Gamma, \Sigma, o, \zeta :: \sigma \rangle \overset{\mathsf{val}(r)}{\rightarrow} \langle \Gamma, \Sigma, o, \zeta :: \sigma' \rangle}$$

$$\text{Store}\quad \frac{\begin{array}{c} \sigma = level(o) \sqcup \sigma_0 \sqcup \sigma_1 \sqcup \Sigma(r).\mathsf{node} \\ level(o) \sqcup \sigma_0 \sqsubseteq \Sigma(r).\mathsf{value} \\ \Sigma' = \Sigma\,[r \mapsto \langle \Sigma(r).\mathsf{node}, \sigma, \Sigma(r).\mathsf{pos}, \Sigma(r).\mathsf{struct} \rangle] \end{array}}{\langle \Gamma, \Sigma, o, \zeta :: \sigma_0 :: \sigma_1 \rangle \overset{\mathsf{store}(r)}{\rightarrow} \langle \Gamma, \Sigma', o, \zeta :: \sigma_1 \rangle}$$

$$\text{New}\quad \frac{\begin{array}{c} level(o) \sqcup \sigma \sqsubseteq \sigma_0 \sqsubseteq \sigma_1 \sqcap \sigma_2 \\ \Sigma' = \Sigma\,[r \mapsto \langle \sigma_0, \sigma_0, \sigma_1, \sigma_2 \rangle] \end{array}}{\langle \Gamma, \Sigma, o, \zeta :: \sigma \rangle \overset{\mathsf{new}(r,\sigma_0,\sigma_1,\sigma_2)}{\rightarrow} \langle \Gamma, \Sigma', o, \zeta :: \sigma_0 \rangle}$$

Fig. 4. Core DOM Monitor - Primitives for Tree Operations

as they are assumed to be lower than or equal to the child's position level. Analogously, rule [Length] updates the expression context ζ with the levels of the current expression's subexpression, of the program counter, and of the structure security level of the node whose number of children is being inspected. Rules [Remove] and [Insert] prevent the removal/insertion of a node with a visible position in an invisible context. Furthermore, they prevent the semantics from inserting/removing a node in/from a node with a visible number of children in an invisible context. Since changing the position of a node causes the position of its right siblings to change, Rule [Insert] ensures that the position levels of the children of every DOM node are always in increasing order. Finally, rules [Store] and [Assignment] update the security level of the corresponding value, provided that it does not constitute a sensitive-upgrade. Hence, updates of visible values in invisible contexts cause the execution to abort.

Informally, a monitor is said to be *noninterferent* (NI) if, whenever the monitored execution of a program on two low-equal memories/forests terminates successfully, it also produces two low-equal memories/forests. Hence, an attacker cannot use the monitored execution of a program as a means to disclose information about the confidential contents of a memory. Theorem 1 states that the monitored successfully-terminating execution of a program on two low-equal memories/forests always yields two low-equal memories/forests.

Theorem 1 (Noninterference). *For any expression e, memories μ_0 and μ_1, forests f_0 and f_1, variable labelings Γ_0 and Γ_1, node labelings Σ_0 and Σ_1, and security level σ such that $\mu_0, \Gamma_0 \sim_\sigma \mu_1, \Gamma_1$ and $f_0, \Sigma_0 \sim_\sigma f_1, \Sigma_1$, and also:*

- $\langle\langle\mu_0, f_0, e\rangle, \langle\Gamma_0, \Sigma_0, \epsilon, \epsilon\rangle\rangle \rightarrow^* \langle\langle\mu'_0, f'_0, v_0\rangle, \langle\Gamma'_0, \Sigma'_0, \epsilon, \epsilon :: \sigma_0\rangle\rangle$
- $\langle\langle\mu_1, f_1, e\rangle, \langle\Gamma_1, \Sigma_1, \epsilon, \epsilon\rangle\rangle \rightarrow^* \langle\langle\mu'_1, f'_1, v_1\rangle, \langle\Gamma'_1, \Sigma'_1, \epsilon, \epsilon :: \sigma_1\rangle\rangle$

It holds that: $\mu'_0, \Gamma'_0 \sim_\sigma \mu'_1, \Gamma'_1$ *and* $f'_0, \Sigma'_0 \sim_\sigma f'_1, \Sigma'_1$. *Furthermore, if either* $\sigma_0 \sqsubseteq \sigma$ *or* $\sigma_1 \sqsubseteq \sigma$*, then:* $\sigma_0 \sqcup \sigma_1 \sqsubseteq \sigma$ *and* $v_0 = v_1$.

4 Extension to Live Primitives

The DOM API includes several methods that return live collections. For instance, the method `getElementsByTagName` returns a live collection containing all the nodes in the document tree whose tag matches the string given as input. The distinctive feature of live collections is that they automatically reflect modifications to the document. Hence, every time a node matching the query that generated a given live collection is inserted/removed in/from the document, it is also automatically inserted/removed in/from the corresponding live collection. Therefore, a live collection is in fact a dynamic query to the document.

4.1 Formal Syntax and Semantics

The nodes of a live collection are always arranged in *document order*. The document order is an ordering $\leq$ on the nodes of the DOM forest such that for every two nodes n_0 and n_1 in the same DOM tree, $n_0 \leq n_1$ if and only if n_0 is found before n_1 in a depth-first left-to-right search starting from the root of the tree. In order to model the live collections returned by the method `getElementsByTagName`, we extend Core DOM with two additional constructs:

$$e ::= \ldots \mid \mathsf{move}_{\lightning}(e, e, e) \mid \mathsf{len}_{\lightning}(e, e)$$

The *live move* primitive receives as input a node n, a tag name m, and an integer i and evaluates to the ith node with tag m in the tree rooted at n when traversed in document order. The *live length* primitive receives as input a node n and a tag name m and evaluates to the number of nodes with tag m in the tree rooted at n. The example given in Section 1 can be rewritten in Core DOM as:

$$i = 0;\ \mathsf{while}(i < \mathsf{len}_{\lightning}(\mathsf{doc}, \text{“}\mathit{DIV}\text{”}))\{\mathsf{insert}(\mathsf{doc}, \mathsf{new}(\text{“}\mathit{DIV}\text{”}), \mathsf{len}(\mathsf{doc}));\ i = i + 1\} \quad (4)$$

where doc is assumed to be a special identifier bound to the root of the *document*. The syntax of the evaluation contexts is extended to take into account the new syntactic constructs:

$$E ::= \ldots \mid \mathsf{move}_{\lightning}(E, e, e) \mid \mathsf{move}_{\lightning}(\underline{v}, E, e) \mid \mathsf{move}_{\lightning}(\underline{v}, \underline{v}, E) \mid \mathsf{len}_{\lightning}(E, e) \mid \mathsf{len}_{\lightning}(\underline{v}, E)$$

The extension of the semantics to live primitives is presented in Figure 5. The semantics makes use of a search predicate of the form $f \vdash r \rightsquigarrow_m \omega$ (given in appendix), that formalizes the search for the nodes matching a given tag in a tree. Intuitively, given a forest f, a reference to a node r, a tag name m, and a list of DOM references ω, $f \vdash r \rightsquigarrow_m \omega$ holds iff ω is the list of all the nodes with tag m found when traversing the tree of f rooted at r in document order.

Live Move

$$\frac{f \vdash r \leadsto_m \omega \qquad \omega(i) = r'}{\langle \mu, f, \mathsf{move}_{\lightning}(r, m, i)\rangle \stackrel{\lightning(f,r')}{\rightarrow} \langle \mu, f, r'\rangle}$$

Live Length

$$\frac{f \vdash r \leadsto_m \omega}{\langle \mu, f, \mathsf{len}_{\lightning}(r, m)\rangle \stackrel{\mathsf{len}_{\lightning}(f,r,m)}{\rightarrow} \langle \mu, f, |w|\rangle}$$

Fig. 5. Extension of the Semantics to Live Primitives

4.2 Information Leaks Due to Live Primitives

The *live* constructs introduced in this section can be exploited to encode new types of information leaks.

Leaks via $\mathsf{len}_{\lightning}$**.** Consider the program below, which is to be executed in a forest that originally contains five orphan DIV nodes respectively bound to the variables: div_0, div_1, div_2, div_3, and div_4.

$$\begin{array}{l}\mathsf{insert}(div_0, div_1, 0);\ \mathsf{insert}(div_0, div_2, 1);\ \mathsf{insert}(div_0, div_3, 2);\\ \mathsf{if}(h)\{\mathsf{insert}(div_1, div_4, 0)\}\ \mathsf{else}\ \{null\};\ l = \mathsf{len}_{\lightning}(div_0)\end{array} \quad (5)$$

Depending on the value of h, l may be set either to 4 or 5. In order to tackle this type of leak, we require the programmer to pre-establish for each possible tag name m an upper bound on the position levels of the nodes with that tag name, that we denote by σ_m and call *global position level.* For instance, $\sigma_{\mathbf{DIV}}$ corresponds to the pre-established upper bound on the position levels of DIV nodes. In order to allow the execution of $\mathsf{len}_{\lightning}$ to go through, the monitor checks whether the position levels of all nodes in the forest are lower than or equal to the global position level, in which case the level associated with the expression is the global position level. Therefore, for Program 5 to be legal $\sigma_{\mathbf{DIV}}$ must be set to H. Accordingly, the expression $\mathsf{len}_{\lightning}(div_0)$ yields a value of level H.

Leaks via $\mathsf{move}_{\lightning}$**.** As the primitive $\mathsf{move}_{\lightning}$ traverses the tree in document order, it can be used to encode a new type of *order leak.* Let us modify Program 5 by replacing the last instruction with $l = \mathsf{move}_{\lightning}(div_0, \text{“}\mathit{DIV}\text{”}, 3)$. Then, depending on the value of the *high* variable h, l is assigned to div_3 or div_2. A NI monitor must detect this information flow and raise the level of the originally *low* variable l to H. In particular, for this program to be legal (according to the current enforcement mechanism), the position level of div_4 as well as the structure security level of div_1 must be *high.* All other levels can be set to L. In the following figures, **a)** and **b)** represent the final forests obtained from the execution of this program in two distinct memories that initially map the h to 0 and to 1, respectively. Forest **c)** represents their (coinciding) low-projection. Observe that in spite of being evaluated in two low-equal memories and only manipulating visible values, the evaluation of $\mathsf{move}_{\lightning}(div_0, \text{“}\mathit{DIV}\text{”}, 3)$ yields two different values.

The key insight for securing the new information flows introduced by the $\mathsf{move}_{\lightning}$ primitive is that this primitive allows an attacker to operate on the nodes with the same tag in the same tree as if they were siblings. Hence, it is necessary to adjust the notion of a node's position in order to take into account this new way of traversing the DOM forest. Let the *live index* of a node be its position in the list of nodes obtained by searching its corresponding tree for the node with

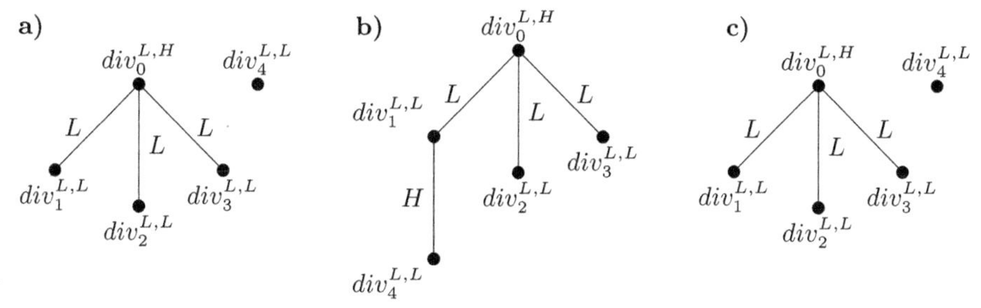

its tag in document order. The position of a node is now understood as the triple consisting of its parent, its index, and its live index. Hence, changing the position of a node in a tree causes the positions of the nodes with the same tag in the same tree with higher live indexes to change. In order to deal with this kind of flow, the proposed enforcement mechanism guarantees that the execution of a live move only goes through if, for every tag name m and node n, the position levels of the nodes with tag m in the tree rooted at n monotonically increase in document order. For instance, in the figure above, the final forest **b)** obtained when $h = 1$ does not comply with this requirement because the position level of div_4 is not lower than or equal to the position level of div_2, while the live index of div_4 is lower than the live index of div_2.

4.3 Revised Attacker Model and Enforcement Mechanism

At the formal level, the introduction of the new live primitives poses two separate problems. First, the low-equality definition must be restated so as to correctly capture the observational power of an attacker disposing of these new primitives. Second, the monitor must be extended in such a way that it remains noninterferent. We modify the definition of low-projection so that an attacker at level σ can additionally see: (1) the live indexes of the nodes whose position levels are $\sqsubseteq \sigma$ and (2) the number of descendants of visible nodes with a given tag m such that $\sigma_m \sqsubseteq \sigma$. Formally:

$$
\begin{aligned}
f \restriction_{\lightning}^{\Sigma,\sigma} = f \restriction^{\Sigma,\sigma} &\cup \{(r, m, i, r') \mid f \vdash r \rightsquigarrow_m \omega \ \wedge\ \omega(i) = r' \ \wedge\ \Sigma(r').\mathsf{pos} \sqsubseteq \sigma\} \\
&\cup \{(r, m, n) \mid f \vdash r \rightsquigarrow_m \omega \ \wedge\ |\omega| = n \ \wedge\ \sigma_m \sqcup \Sigma(r).\mathsf{node} \sqsubseteq \sigma\}
\end{aligned}
$$

As expected, two labeled forests are low-equal at a given level σ, written $f_0, \Sigma_0 \sim_{\sigma}^{\lightning} f_1, \Sigma_1$, if they coincide in their respective low-projections.

We do not modify the previous monitor so that the new low-equality is preserved by monitored executions. Instead, we establish a predicate – $\mathcal{WL}(f, \Sigma)$ – for labeled forests, such that any two labeled forests verifying this predicate and related by the first low-equality are also related by the new low-equality. This is formally stated as follows:

Theorem 2 (Low-Equality Strengthening). *Given two forests f_0 and f_1 respectively labeled by Σ_0 and Σ_1 and a security level σ such that $\mathcal{WL}(f_0, \Sigma_0)$ and $\mathcal{WL}(f_1, \Sigma_1)$ and $f_0, \Sigma_0 \sim_\sigma f_1, \Sigma_1$, it holds that: $f_0, \Sigma_0 \sim_{\sigma}^{\lightning} f_1, \Sigma_1$.*

LIVE MOVE

$$\frac{\sigma' = \sigma_0 \sqcup \sigma_1 \sqcup \sigma_2 \sqcup \Sigma(r).\mathsf{pos} \qquad \mathcal{WL}(f, \Sigma)}{\langle \Gamma, \Sigma, o, \zeta :: \sigma_0 :: \sigma_1 :: \sigma_2 \rangle \overset{\lightning(f,r)}{\rightarrow} \langle \Gamma, \Sigma, o, \zeta :: \sigma' \rangle}$$

LIVE LENGTH

$$\frac{\sigma' = \sigma_0 \sqcup \sigma_1 \sqcup \sigma_m \sqcup \Sigma(r).\mathsf{node} \qquad \mathcal{WL}(f, \Sigma)}{\langle \Gamma, \Sigma, o, \zeta :: \sigma_0 :: \sigma_1 \rangle \overset{\mathsf{len}_{\lightning}(f,r,m)}{\rightarrow} \langle \Gamma, \Sigma, o, \zeta :: \sigma' \rangle}$$

Fig. 6. Extension of the Monitor to Live Primitives

Informally, $\mathcal{WL}(f, \Sigma)$ holds if and only if: (1) the position levels of all the nodes in f are lower than or equal to the respective global position levels, (2) the position levels of the nodes with the same tag monotonically increase in document order, and (3) the position level of every node is higher than or equal to the position levels of all its descendants (meaning that if the position of a node is secret, the positions of all its descendants are also secret). The predicate $\mathcal{WL}(f, \Sigma)$ is defined with the help of a predicate $\mathcal{WL}_{f,\Sigma} \vdash^r \phi_{\lightning} \rightsquigarrow \phi'_{\lightning}$, defined below, that holds if the tree rooted at r is well-labeled. The function $\phi_{\lightning}$ maps each tag name to the position level of the last node with that tag name preceding the node pointed to by r in f in document order. The function $\phi'_{\lightning}$ maps each tag name to the position level of the last node with that tag name in the tree rooted at r (if no such node exists, $\phi'_{\lightning}$ coincides with $\phi_{\lightning}$). Formally, the predicate $\mathcal{WL}(f, \Sigma)$ holds if and only if for all orphan nodes pointed to by a reference r there are two functions $\phi_{\lightning}$ and $\phi'_{\lightning}$ such that $\mathcal{WL}_{f,\Sigma} \vdash^r \phi_{\lightning} \rightsquigarrow \phi'_{\lightning}$.

ORPHAN NODE

$$\frac{\begin{array}{c} f(r).\mathsf{tag} = m \\ |f(r).\mathsf{children}| = 0 \\ \phi_{\lightning}(m) \sqsubseteq \Sigma(r).\mathsf{pos} \sqsubseteq \sigma_m \\ \phi'_{\lightning} = \phi_{\lightning}\,[m \mapsto \Sigma(r).\mathsf{pos}] \end{array}}{\mathcal{WL}_{f,\Sigma} \vdash^r \phi_{\lightning} \rightsquigarrow \phi'_{\lightning}}$$

NON-ORPHAN NODE

$$\frac{\begin{array}{c} f(r).\mathsf{tag} = m \qquad \phi_{\lightning}(m) \sqsubseteq \Sigma(r).\mathsf{pos} \sqsubseteq \sigma_m \\ |f(r).\mathsf{children}| = n > 0 \qquad \phi^0_{\lightning} = \phi_{\lightning}\,[m \mapsto \Sigma(r).\mathsf{pos}] \\ \forall_{0 \le i < n}\ \Sigma(r).\mathsf{pos} \sqsubseteq \Sigma(f(r).\mathsf{children}(i)).\mathsf{pos} \\ \forall_{0 \le i < n}\ \mathcal{WL}_{f,\Sigma} \vdash^{f(r).\mathsf{children}(i)} \phi^i_{\lightning} \rightsquigarrow \phi^{i+1}_{\lightning} \end{array}}{\mathcal{WL}_{f,\Sigma} \vdash^r \phi_{\lightning} \rightsquigarrow \phi^n_{\lightning}}$$

Finally, the extension of the security monitor to the new live primitives is given in Figure 6. The evaluation of these primitives only goes through if the corresponding forest is well-labeled.

5 Related Work and Conclusions

The increasing popularity of scripting languages has motivated further research on runtime mechanisms for securing information flow, such as *monitors*. In contrast to *purely dynamic monitors* [3–5] that do not rely on any kind of static analysis, *hybrid monitors* [8,15,16] use static analysis to reason about the implicit flows that arise due to untaken execution paths. Given the dynamic nature of tree operations, designing such a static analysis for Core DOM is far from trivial. Hence, we have chosen to present a purely dynamic monitor and we leave the design of its hybrid version for future work.

Russo et al. [13] were the first to study the problem of securing information flow in DOM-like dynamic tree structures. They present a monitor for a WHILE language with primitives for manipulating DOM-like trees and prove it sound.

However, references are not modeled in this language; instead, program configurations include the current working node of the program. This is, as the authors point out, the main difference with respect to JavaScript DOM operations, since in JavaScript tree nodes are treated as first-class values. In particular, in [13] it is not possible to change the position of a node in the DOM forest without deleting and re-creating it – its position remains the same during its whole "lifetime". Consequently, the *position level* of a node coincides with its *node level*. By treating nodes as first-class values we were able to give separate treatment to position leaks, which cannot be directly expressed in the language of [13].

Hedin et al. [9] implemented the first information flow monitor for fully-fledged JavaScript together with "statefull information-flow models" for the standard API, as well as several APIs that are present in a browser environment such as the DOM API. The presentation includes an informal explanation on how the problem of live collections returned by the method `getElementsByName` is dealt with. Their approach for dealing with live leaks coincides with the technique we employ to the particular case of the $\mathsf{len}_{\not\iota}$ primitive.

Gardner et al. [7] propose a compositional and concise formal specification of the DOM called Minimal DOM. The authors show that their semantics has no redundancy and that it is sufficient to describe the structural kernel of DOM Core Level 1. Additionally, they apply local reasoning based on Separation Logic and prove invariant properties of simple JavaScript programs that interact with the DOM. Given that our aim is to track information flow in the DOM, we use a simplified semantics that allows us to label DOM resources in a natural way. Like Minimal DOM, Core DOM is also compositional. Furthermore, all the primitives of Minimal DOM can be easily translated to Core DOM. Hence, we expect the authors' sufficiency claim to be applicable to Core DOM.

This paper contributes to the challenge of enforcing secure information flow in client-side Web applications by presenting a provably sound flow-sensitive security monitor that enforces noninterference over Core DOM, an expressive representative subset of the DOM API. The proposed solution tackles open issues in IF security such as references and live collections in dynamic tree structures. By including references and live collections, Core DOM offers the expressive power of the DOM in the form of a simple language that is well tailored for automatic program analysis. We thus believe that it could be re-used in future research on security aspects of the DOM API.

Acknowledgments. This work was partially supported by the Portuguese Government via the PhD grant SFRH/BD/71471/2010.

References

1. The 5th edition of ECMA 262 June 2011: ECMAScript Language Specification. Technical report, ECMA (2011)
2. Almeida Matos, A., Fragoso Santos, J., Rezk, T.: An IF monitor for a core of DOM. http://web.ist.utl.pt/~ana.matos/14-AFR-if+monitor+coredom-full.pdf

3. Austin, T.H., Flanagan, C.: Efficient purely-dynamic information flow analysis. In: PLAS (2009)
4. Austin, T.H., Flanagan, C.: Permissive dynamic information flow analysis. In: PLAS (2010)
5. Austin, T.H., Flanagan, C.: Multiple facets for dynamic information flow. In: POPL (2012)
6. Banerjee, A., Naumann, D.A.: Secure information flow and pointer confinement in a Java-like language. In: CSFW (2002)
7. Gardner, P., Smith, Wheelhouse, M.J., Zarfaty, U.: DOM: Towards a formal specification. In: PLAN-X (2008)
8. Le Guernic, G.: Confidentiality Enforcement Using Dynamic Information Flow Analyses. PhD thesis, Kansas State University (2007)
9. Hedin, D., Birgisson, B., Bello, L., Sabelfeld, A.: Jsflow: Tracking information flow in JavaScript and its APIs. In: SAC (2014)
10. Hedin, D., Sabelfeld, A.: Information-flow security for a core of JavaScript. In: CSF (2012)
11. W3C Recommendation. DOM: Document Object Model (DOM). Technical report, W3C (2005)
12. Russo, A., Sabelfeld, A.: Dynamic vs. static flow-sensitive security analysis. In: CSF (2010)
13. Russo, A., Sabelfeld, A., Chudnov, A.: Tracking Information Flow in Dynamic Tree Structures. In: Backes, M., Ning, P. (eds.) ESORICS 2009. LNCS, vol. 5789, pp. 86–103. Springer, Heidelberg (2009)
14. Sabelfeld, A., Russo, A.: From Dynamic to Static and Back: Riding the Roller Coaster of Information-Flow Control Research. In: Pnueli, A., Virbitskaite, I., Voronkov, A. (eds.) PSI 2009. LNCS, vol. 5947, pp. 352–365. Springer, Heidelberg (2010)
15. Shroff, P., Smith, S.F., Thober, M.: Dynamic dependency monitoring to secure information flow. In: CSF (2007)
16. Venkatakrishnan, V.N., Xu, W., DuVarney, D.C., Sekar, R.: Provably Correct Runtime Enforcement of Non-interference Properties. In: Ning, P., Qing, S., Li, N. (eds.) ICICS 2006. LNCS, vol. 4307, pp. 332–351. Springer, Heidelberg (2006)

Finding a Forest in a Tree

The Matching Problem for Wide Reactive Systems

Giorgio Bacci[1(✉)], Marino Miculan[2], and Romeo Rizzi[3]

[1] Department of Computer Science, Aalborg University, Aalborg, Denmark
grbacci@cs.aau.dk

[2] Department of Mathematics and Computer Science, University of Udine, Udine, Italy
marino.miculan@uniud.it

[3] Department of Computer Science, University of Verona, Verona, Italy
romeo.rizzi@univr.it

Abstract. *Wide reactive systems* are rewriting systems specified by *wide* reaction rules, where redex and reactum are lists of terms (*forests*), i.e. rules of the form $\langle l_1(\boldsymbol{x}_1), \ldots, l_n(\boldsymbol{x}_n)\rangle \Rightarrow \langle r_1(\boldsymbol{y}_1), \ldots, r_n(\boldsymbol{y}_n)\rangle$ such that $\cup_i \boldsymbol{y}_i \subseteq \cup_i \boldsymbol{x}_i$. Wide reaction rules are particularly useful for process calculi for mobile and global computations, because they allow one to connect processes which can be *at different places* in the system, possibly crossing boundaries and firewalls. For instances, *remote procedure calls* can be modeled as a process in place i activating a reaction in a different place j; *code mobility* can be modeled by instantiating variables in $\boldsymbol{y}_i$ with terms using variables from $\boldsymbol{x}_j$, for a different j; etc.

In order to apply a wide reaction rule, we have to find a matching of the rule redex within the global state. This problem can be restated as follows: how to match a given forest (the redex) inside an unordered tree (the system), possibly finding the subtrees to be grafted at the forest's leaves (i.e., instantiating the variables)? We show that, although the problem is NP-complete in general, the exponential explosion depends only on the number n of roots of the forest (the *width* of the redex), and not on the size of the global tree (the system state). In most practical cases, the width is constant and small (i.e., ≤ 3), hence our results show that the wide reaction systems can be actually used for process calculi.

1 Introduction

It is common to present the dynamics of agents of process calculi by means of a *reduction semantics*, that is a relation of the form $a \rightarrowtriangle a'$, where a and a' are agents. This relation is usually defined by means of a set $\mathcal{R}$ of *(parametric) reaction (or reduction) rules* of the form $l(x_1, \ldots, x_n) \Rightarrow r(x_1, \ldots, x_n)$ where x_i are (agent) variables, and $l(\boldsymbol{x})$, $r(\boldsymbol{x})$ are terms called *redex* and *reactum*, respectively. Reaction rules induce reactions relations according the usual (non-deterministic) term rewriting: rule $l(\boldsymbol{x}) \Rightarrow r(\boldsymbol{x})$ can be applied to an agent (i.e., a closed term) a if $l(\boldsymbol{x})$ *matches* some subterm of a, that is, if $a = C[l(\boldsymbol{x})\sigma]$ for some context

This work is partially supported by MIUR PRIN project 2010LHT4KM, *CINA*.

M. Maffei and E. Tuosto (Eds.): TGC 2014, LNCS 8902, pp. 17–33, 2014.
DOI: 10.1007/978-3-662-45917-1_2

$C[\_]$ (indicating the position of the rewriting) and substitution σ. The result term of this rule application is then $a' = C[r(\boldsymbol{x})\sigma]$. Many general frameworks with efficient implementations have been developed around this concept, such as *term rewriting systems* [2] and *rewriting logics* [20].

However, the approach presented above considers just one subterm replacement at once (or, at most, parallel execution of independent reductions). In fact, we can easily generalize reactive systems to consider *wide* reaction rules, as in Milner's *reactive systems* [19]. A wide rule has the form $\boldsymbol{l}(\boldsymbol{x}) \Rightarrow \boldsymbol{r}(\boldsymbol{y})$, where $\boldsymbol{l}(\boldsymbol{x}) = \langle l_1(\boldsymbol{x}_1), \ldots, l_n(\boldsymbol{x}_n)\rangle$ and $\boldsymbol{r}(\boldsymbol{y}) = \langle r_1(\boldsymbol{y}_1), \ldots, r_n(\boldsymbol{y}_n)\rangle$ are lists of terms, i.e., *forests*; n is called their *width*. The variables in the reactum must be a subset of those in the redex (i.e., $\cup_i \boldsymbol{y}_i \subseteq \cup_i \boldsymbol{x}_i$). Applying such a rule to an agent a means 1) finding a context with n holes $C[X_1, \ldots, X_n]$ and a substitution σ for the variables $\boldsymbol{x}$ such that $a = C[\boldsymbol{l}(\boldsymbol{x})\sigma]$; 2) replace each $l_i(\boldsymbol{d}_i)$ with the corresponding $r_i(\boldsymbol{y}_i)[\sigma]$. This can be summarized in the following rule:

$$\frac{\boldsymbol{l}(\boldsymbol{x}) \Rightarrow \boldsymbol{r}(\boldsymbol{y}) \in \mathcal{R} \qquad a = C[\boldsymbol{l}(\boldsymbol{x})\sigma] \qquad a' = C[\boldsymbol{r}(\boldsymbol{y})\sigma]}{a \rightarrowtriangle a'} \tag{1}$$

Notice that subtrees $l_i(\boldsymbol{d})$ can occur in any order in the agent a, but not one under another. Traditional reactive systems are the particular case when $n = 1$.

Although not very widespread in practice, wide rules and wide reactive systems are quite useful and expressive, especially for process calculi for mobile and global computations. The key aspect is that in a wide rule we can deal with processes which can be *everywhere* in the system, not only "in the same place". For example, a *remote procedure call* can be modeled as a process in a place (i-th tree of the forest) activating a reaction in a different position (i.e., a rewriting of the j-th tree); *code mobility* can be modeled by instantiating some variables in $\boldsymbol{y}_i$ in place i with terms using variables from $\boldsymbol{x}_j$, for a different j; etc. This kind of reductions can be represented also using non-wide reaction rules, but at the expense of a more cumbersome and less natural reduction semantics.

As an example, let us consider CaSPiS [5], a session-centered calculus developed within the SENSORIA project as a core language for Service Oriented Computing programming. CaSPiS allows processes to synchronize even if they are far apart (as long as they share a channel). To define this behaviour using a standard reduction semantics, we would need an infinite set of rules of the form

$$C[s.P, \bar{s}.Q] \Rightarrow C[s.P|r \rhd P, r \rhd Q] \qquad (r \text{ fresh}) \qquad \text{(ServiceSync)}$$

one for each suitable context $C[\_{1}, \_{2}]$ with two holes. Actually, the same semantics can be readily defined using a single wide reaction rule:

$$\langle s.x_1, \bar{s}.x_2\rangle \Rightarrow \langle s.x_1|r \rhd x_1, r \rhd x_2\rangle \qquad (r \text{ fresh}) \qquad \text{(WideServiceSync)}$$

whilst $C[\_{1}, \_{2}]$ is the context where the redex $\langle s.x_1, \bar{s}.x_2\rangle$ is found and P, Q are the parameters the redex is instantiated to. In fact, the redex and the reactum are forests of two trees each, and the rule is rendered graphically as in Figure 1(a).

However, this added expressivity comes at a price: the problem of matching a wide redex within an agent is not as easy as the usual term matching.

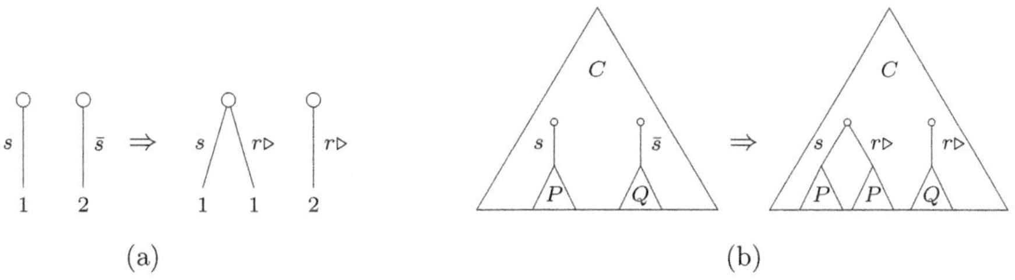

Fig. 1. A parametric rule (a), and its application as forest pattern matching (b).

In this paper, we address precisely this problem, which we call the *forest pattern matching*: given a forest $\boldsymbol{l(x)}$ (the *pattern*) and an unordered tree a (the *target*), how to match each of the trees of the pattern within the target (with no overlaps), singling out the subtrees $\boldsymbol{d}$ that instantiate the parameters for the pattern?

As one may expect, forest pattern matching is NP-complete, as we will prove by means of a reduction from 3-SAT. However, this reduction points out the real source of time-complexity: the requirement that pattern trees are not overlapping in the target. The good news is that this combinatorial explosion does not depend on the size of the target tree, but only on the pattern width! As a consequence, once we fix a reactive system the exponential part becomes a constant factor, and the cost of each reduction step is polynomial on the size of the agent. Moreover, in most cases, rule width is small: e.g., for Ambients, CaSPiS, etc, it is ≤ 3. Therefore, our results prove that wide reaction rules are feasible for many calculi and models for global computation, and the implementation of general abstract machines for calculi for distributed systems, like [16], is viable.

The rest of this paper is structured as follows. In Section 2 we define formally the forest matching problem, which we show to be NP-complete in Section 3. In Section 4 we address this issue using Downey and Fellows' parameterized complexity theory [10] and indeed in Section 5 we provide an algorithm for it. As a side result, we introduce the new *rainbow antichain* problem, which is NP-complete but fixed-parameter tractable. Final remarks are in Section 6.

2 Labeled Trees, Forest Patterns, and Matches

In this section we define the forest pattern matching problem with no overlaps. As a first step, we define edge-labeled unordered trees, adopting the syntax of ambient calculus without actions [6], and extending it to (linear) context trees.

Let m, n range over an enumerable set Λ of labels, and x, y, z over an enumerable set Ξ of variables. Finite sets of variables are ranged over by X, Y, Z. The set of terms is the set of labeled context trees, finitely branching and of finite depth, where variables are interpreted as leaves where other trees can be grafted. We denote by $T(X), S(X)$ trees whose variables are in X. The syntax of these trees is defined by the following grammar.

Syntax of context trees

$T(X) ::=$	$\mathbf{0}$	empty tree
	x	leaf, $x \in X$
	$m[\,T(X)\,]$	labeled tree
	$T(Y) \mid T'(Z)$	siblings, where $X = Y \uplus Z$

We often abbreviate $m[\,\mathbf{0}\,]$ as $m[\ ]$, and $T(X)$ as T. We assume that "|" associates to the right, i.e. $T \mid T' \mid T''$ is read $T \mid (T' \mid T'')$. Let $lab(T) \subset \Lambda$ be the set of node labels in T, and $vars(T) \subset \Xi$ be the set of the variables occurring in T (obviously, $vars(T(X)) \subseteq X$). We say that a term T is *ground* when $vars(T) = \emptyset$.

The intuitive interpretation of terms T as *unordered* trees induces an equivalence $T \equiv T'$ which is the minimal congruence that includes the commutative monoidal laws for $\mid$ and $\mathbf{0}$. This relation, similar to ambient calculus congruence, can be axiomatized as follows.

Structural congruence on context trees

$$\frac{}{T \equiv T}\ (\mathsf{refl}) \qquad \frac{T \equiv T'}{T' \equiv T}\ (\mathsf{symm}) \qquad \frac{T \equiv T' \quad T' \equiv T''}{T \equiv T''}\ (\mathsf{trans})$$

$$\frac{T \equiv T'}{T \mid T'' \equiv T' \mid T''}\ (\mathsf{sibl}) \qquad \frac{T \equiv T'}{m[\,T\,] \equiv m[\,T'\,]}\ (\mathsf{rooting})$$

$$\frac{}{T \mid T' \equiv T' \mid T}\ (\mathsf{comm}) \qquad \frac{}{T \mid (T' \mid T'') \equiv (T \mid T') \mid T''}\ (\mathsf{assoc}) \qquad \frac{}{T \mid \mathbf{0} \equiv T}\ (\mathsf{nil})$$

The axiomatization of structural congruence is adequate with respect to the semantic for unordered trees: $T \equiv T'$ iff T and T' represent the same tree structure (obviously, where siblings are not ordered). Moreover, if $T \equiv T'$ then $lab(T) = lab(T')$ and $vars(T) = vars(T')$.

Given two tree terms $T(X)$, $S(Y)$ with X, Y disjoint, we define term substitution, written $T\{S/x\}$, as usual: the occurrence x in T is replaced by the term S. For $x \in vars(T)$, $vars(T\{S/x\}) = (vars(T) \setminus \{x\}) \cup vars(S)$. Simultaneous substitution $T\{S_1/x_1, \ldots, S_k/x_k\}$ is defined by the substitution composition $T\{S_1/x_1\} \cdots \{S_k/x_k\}$, where $x_1, \ldots, x_n$ are supposed to be pairwise distinct; we denote it by $T\{\boldsymbol{S}/\boldsymbol{x}\}$.

Lemma 1. *If $S_i \equiv S_i'$ for $i \in \{1, \ldots, k\}$, then $T\{\boldsymbol{S}/\boldsymbol{x}\} \equiv T\{\boldsymbol{S'}/\boldsymbol{x}\}$.*

Intuitively, given a tree list $S = S_1, \ldots, S_n$, called a "pattern", searching for a (sub-)match of S in a tree T means to find an occurrence of each $S_1, \ldots, S_n$ within T, without overlaps and possibly by instantiating variables in S_i. This means that we have to decompose T in a subtree C where all S_i can be grafted, and a list of subtrees to be grafted to the leaves of S_i. Formally:

Definition 1. *A* forest matching instance, *denoted by $T \succeq \boldsymbol{S}$, is given by a tree T (*target*), and a list of trees $\boldsymbol{S}(X) = S_1(X_1), \ldots, S_n(X_n)$ (*pattern*) where X_i*

are all disjoint and $X = \cup_{i=1}^{n} X_i$. *We say that* $\boldsymbol{S}(X)$ matches in $T(Y)$ *if for some* context $C(Z)$ *and* parameters $\boldsymbol{D} = D_1, \ldots, D_m$,

$$T \equiv \big(C\{\boldsymbol{S}/\boldsymbol{z}\}\big)\{\boldsymbol{D}/\boldsymbol{x}\}, \qquad \textit{where } z_1, \ldots, z_n \in Z \textit{ and } x_1, \ldots, x_m \in X\,.$$

A match for $T \succeq \boldsymbol{S}$ *is denoted by* $C, \boldsymbol{D} \models T \succeq \boldsymbol{S}$, *and we write* $\models T \succeq \boldsymbol{S}$ *if* $C, \boldsymbol{D} \models T \succeq \boldsymbol{S}$ *for some* C, $\boldsymbol{D}$.

Proposition 1. *If* $\models T \succeq \boldsymbol{S}$ *and* $\models S_i \succeq \boldsymbol{Q}$, *for some* $1 \leq i \leq n$ *and* $n = |\boldsymbol{S}|$, *then* $\models T \succeq \boldsymbol{Q}$; *and in particular* $\models T \succeq S_1, \ldots, S_{i-1}, \boldsymbol{Q}, S_{i+1}, \ldots, S_n$.

Proof. We have to prove that if $\models T \succeq \boldsymbol{S}$ and $\models S_i \succeq \boldsymbol{Q}$, for some $1 \leq i \leq n$ and $n = |\boldsymbol{S}|$, then $\models T \succeq S_1, \ldots, S_{i-1}, \boldsymbol{Q}, S_{i+1}, \ldots, S_n$.

Since $\models T \succeq \boldsymbol{S}$ and $\models S_i \succeq \boldsymbol{Q}$ there exist contexts C, C' and parameters $\boldsymbol{D}$, and $\boldsymbol{D'}$ such that

$$\begin{aligned} T &\equiv (C\{S_1/z_1, \ldots, S_n/z_n\})\{\boldsymbol{D}/\boldsymbol{x}\} && \text{for some } z_1, \ldots, z_n \in \mathit{vars}(C) \\ S_i &\equiv (C'\{\boldsymbol{Q}/\boldsymbol{z'}\})\{\boldsymbol{D'}/\boldsymbol{x'}\} && \text{for some } z'_1, \ldots, z'_m \in \mathit{vars}(C') \end{aligned}$$

Without loss of generality, suppose $\{z_1, \ldots, z_n\}$ disjoint from $\{z'_1, \ldots, z'_m\}$, otherwise a variable renaming can be applied. Now, by an easy replacement of S_i and some rearrangements on the context and parameters, we obtain

$$\begin{aligned} T &\equiv (C\{S_1/z_1, \ldots, S_i/z_i, \ldots, S_n/z_n\})\{\boldsymbol{D}/\boldsymbol{x}\} \\ &\equiv (C\{S_1/z_1, \ldots, (C'\{\boldsymbol{Q}/\boldsymbol{z'}\})\{\boldsymbol{D'}/\boldsymbol{x'}\}/z_i, \ldots, S_n/z_n\})\{\boldsymbol{D}/\boldsymbol{z}\} \\ &\equiv ((C\{C'/z_i\})\{S_1/z_1, \ldots, \boldsymbol{Q}/\boldsymbol{z'}, \ldots, S_n/z_n\})\{\boldsymbol{D}, \boldsymbol{D'}/\boldsymbol{x}, \boldsymbol{x'}\}\,. \end{aligned}$$

This means that $(C\{C'/z_i\}, (\boldsymbol{D}, \boldsymbol{D'}))$ is a match for $S_1, \ldots, S_{i-1}, \boldsymbol{Q}, S_{i+1}, \ldots, S_n$ in T, that is, $\models T \succeq S_1, \ldots, S_{i-1}, \boldsymbol{Q}, S_{i+1}, \ldots, S_n$.

Similarly, we can prove that $(C\{S_i/z_1, \ldots, C'/z_i, \ldots, S_n/z_n\}, \boldsymbol{D'})$ is a match for $\boldsymbol{Q}$ in T, hence $\models T \succeq \boldsymbol{Q}$ holds too. □

Many tree term patterns give rise to trivial or redundant forest matchings. For example, the empty tree matches any target T as $T \equiv (T \mid x)\{\mathbf{0}/x\}$. Another example of trivial matching instance is when the tree pattern is a variable. Indeed, a variable x can be matched in any tree T (in fact, x has as many matches as the number of sub-terms in T). A typical situation of redundant matching instances occurs when the pattern has "unguarded" variables at the top level, e.g. it is of the form $x \mid R$. Intuitively, this pattern matches an occurrence of R "beside anything, possibly nothing". As an example, let $T = m[\mathbf{0}] \mid n[k[\mathbf{0}]]$ be the target and $S = x \mid m[\mathbf{0}]$ be the pattern. Then, we have three different matches, namely $(y, n[k[\mathbf{0}]])$, $(n[y], k[\mathbf{0}])$, and $(n[k[\mathbf{0}]], \mathbf{0})$), despite $m[\mathbf{0}]$ occurs only once in T. A similar situation happens also when sibling variables $x \mid y$ occurs in the pattern (note that they can replaced by a single variable z, because $(x \mid y)\{D_1/x, D_2/y\} = (z)\{D_1 \mid D_2/z\}$).

Interestingly, redundant matches can be avoided by restricting our attention to a particular class of patterns, which we call *solid* after [15].

Definition 2. *A pattern* $\boldsymbol{S}(X) = S_1(X_1), \ldots, S_n(X_n)$ *is* solid *if for* $1 \leq i \leq n$*:* $S_i \not\equiv \mathbf{0}$*, for no* $x \in X$ *and* S' *it is* $S_i \equiv x \mid S'$*, and no two variables* $x, y \in X_i$ *are siblings, that is,* $x \mid y$ *cannot occur in* S_i *(up to* $\equiv$*).*

We can prove that any matching instance can be reduced to a matching instance whose pattern is solid. To this end let we define the function *solid* over forest patterns (i.e., tree lists), which drops empty trees and unguarded variables, and collapses sibling variables in one:

Transformation into solid patterns

$$solid(\epsilon) = \epsilon \qquad solid(T, \boldsymbol{S}) = \begin{cases} solid(\boldsymbol{S}) & \text{if } T \equiv \mathbf{0} \\ solid(Q, \boldsymbol{S}) & \text{if } T \equiv x \mid Q \\ solid(sld(T), \boldsymbol{S}) & \text{otherwise} \end{cases}$$

$$\begin{aligned} sld(\mathbf{0}) &= \mathbf{0} & del(\mathbf{0}) &= \mathbf{0} \\ sld(x \mid T) &= x \mid del(T) & del(x \mid T) &= del(T) \\ sld(m[T] \mid S) &= m[sld(T)] \mid sld(S) & del(m[T] \mid S) &= m[sld(T)] \mid del(S) \end{aligned}$$

Solid patterns enjoy the following properties.

Proposition 2. *The following statements hold:*

(a) ***no empty trees:*** $\models T \succeq \mathbf{0}, \boldsymbol{S} \iff \models T \succeq \boldsymbol{S}$;
(b) ***no sibling variables:*** $\models T \succeq x \mid y \iff \models T \succeq x$;
(c) ***no unguarded variables:*** $\models T \succeq x \mid S \iff \models T \succeq S$.

Due to the above, solid patterns suffice for checking match existence.

Lemma 2. $\models T \succeq solid(T)$ *if and only if* $\models solid(T) \succeq T$.

Proof. It is an easy application of Proposition 2 and Proposition 1. In fact, Proposition 1 ensures that it suffices to check $\models \boldsymbol{T} \succeq \boldsymbol{T}' \iff \models \boldsymbol{T}' \succeq \boldsymbol{T}$ for each equation $\boldsymbol{T} = \boldsymbol{T}'$ defining *solid*. This is just a straightforward application of (a), (b), (c) of Proposition 2. □

Theorem 1. $\models T \succeq solid(\boldsymbol{S})$ *if and only if* $\models T \succeq \boldsymbol{S}$.

Proof. It follows directly from Lemma 2 and Proposition 1. □

Actually, all matches against a pattern $\boldsymbol{S}$ can be obtained from matches against $solid(\boldsymbol{S})$.

3 NP-Completeness of Forest Pattern Matching

The main result of this section is that the problem of finding a pattern matching of a list of patterns $\boldsymbol{S} = S_1, \ldots, S_n$ in a target tree T is NP-complete. We show this by a reduction from 3-SAT [7]. Although the reduction can be done directly, we do it in two steps by introducing an intermediate problem, called RAINBOWANTICHAIN, that points out the actual source of time-complexity hardness.

An instance of RAINBOWANTICHAIN is a tree $\mathcal{T}(\mathcal{V}, \mathcal{E})$ with nodes $\mathcal{V}$ and edges $\mathcal{E}$, and a finite set $\mathcal{P}$ of colors, said *palette*. Some of the nodes in $\mathcal{T}$ have been colored with colors taken from the palette $\mathcal{P}$. Note that, the same color can be associated with different nodes, and each node can be associated with more than one color. RAINBOWANTICHAIN asks whether there exists a *rainbow antichain* $\mathcal{R} \subseteq \mathcal{V}$ in $\mathcal{T}$, i.e., a subset of nodes such that for no pair $u, v \in \mathcal{R}$ of distinct nodes u is an ancestor of v (hence, an *antichain*) and where each color $c \in \mathcal{P}$ has exactly one representative in $\mathcal{R}$ (hence, *colorful* w.r.t. $\mathcal{P}$).

Theorem 2. RAINBOWANTICHAIN *is NP-complete.*

Proof. RAINBOWANTICHAIN is in NP, since, given a set of nodes $\mathcal{R}$, checking whether $\mathcal{R}$ is a rainbow antichain for $\mathcal{T}$ can be done in polynomial time by a breadth-first visit of $\mathcal{T}$, and for each $v \in \mathcal{R}$ found, first increase the node counter nc, then the color counter $p[i]$ $(1 \leq i \leq |\mathcal{P}|)$ if v has color $c_i \in \mathcal{P}$. The check fails whether $nc > |\mathcal{P}|$ or $p[j] = 0$ for some $1 \leq j \leq |\mathcal{P}|$; it succeeds otherwise.

Let $C = \{c_1, \ldots, c_m\}$ be an instance of 3-SAT on variables $\{x_1, \ldots, x_n\}$. From C we define a colored tree $\mathcal{T}$ as follows. Let r be the root node which is left uncolored. For each variable x_i let x_i and $\overline{x}_i$ be child nodes of r, and color them with a fresh color c_{x_i}, distinct for each variable. For each clause $c_j \in C$, let c_j^1, c_j^2, c_j^3 be children nodes of l_i in T if c_j contains l_i as negated, and assign to each of them a fresh color c_{c_j}, distinct for each clause. An example of construction for $c_1 = (\overline{x}_1 \vee x_2 \vee \overline{x}_3)$, $c_2 = (x_1 \vee x_2 \vee x_3)$ is shown below.

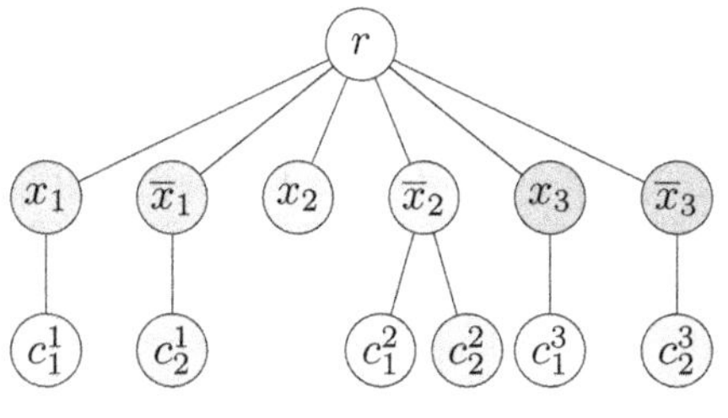

Let φ be a truth assignment satisfying the formula C. By construction, selecting only literal nodes l_i which are satisfied by φ, we obtain a rainbow antichain $\mathcal{R}'$ in $\mathcal{T}$ for the palette $\{c_{x_i} : 1 \leq i \leq n\}$. Now, we extend $\mathcal{R}'$ to $\mathcal{R}$ adding all clause nodes which are not children of a element in $\mathcal{R}'$. Such $\mathcal{R}$ is clearly an antichain for $\mathcal{T}$, but we must ensure that is colorful and no more than one representative per color is taken. To do this, it suffices to prove that $\mathcal{R}$ is colorful, indeed if a color occurs more than once in $\mathcal{R}$ we remove the others. By hypothesis, each clause c_j is satisfied by φ, hence c_j has at least one literal l_i such that $\varphi(l_i) = \mathbf{T}$. By construction of $\mathcal{T}$, there exist a node c_j^k $(1 \leq k \leq 3)$ child of $\overline{l_i}$, hence already in $\mathcal{R}$. This holds for all clauses c_j, hence $\mathcal{R}$ is colorful.

Conversely, let $\mathcal{R}$ be a rainbow antichain for $\mathcal{T}$. Let $\varphi\colon \{x_1, \ldots, x_n\} \to \mathit{Bool}$ be defined by $\varphi(x_i) = \mathbf{T}$ if x_i is a node in $\mathcal{R}$, and $\varphi(x_i) = \mathbf{F}$ if x_i is a node not in $\mathcal{R}$. Since $\mathcal{R}$ has exactly one representative per color, no opposite literals are in $\mathcal{R}$, hence φ is a truth assignment for C. By colorfulness of $\mathcal{R}$, for all colors c_{c_j} $(1 \leq j \leq m)$ there exists a node $c_j^k \in \mathcal{R}$ $(1 \leq k \leq 3)$ such that c_j^k has color c_{c_j}. By construction of $\mathcal{T}$, each $c_j^k \in \mathcal{R}$ is a children of a literal node $l_i \notin \mathcal{R}$, and moreover the clause c_j contains $\overline{l_i}$. Since $l_i \notin \mathcal{R}$, by definition $\varphi(\overline{l_i}) = \mathbf{T}$, hence $\varphi(c_j) = \mathbf{T}$. This holds for all $1 \leq j \leq m$, hence φ satisfies C. □

It is easy to see that an instance $\mathcal{T}, \mathcal{P} = \{c_1, \ldots, c_n\}$ of RAINBOWANTICHAIN can be reduced to a forest pattern matching problem, namely, the one that solves $\models T \succeq (c_1[x_1], \ldots, c_n[x_n])$, for a suitable tree term T defined upon $\mathcal{T}$. Thus:

Theorem 3. *The forest pattern matching problem is NP-complete.*

Theorem 2 states that the complexity hardness is merely due to finding a rainbow antichain in the given target, which corresponds to locate the list of trees of the pattern so that they are not in overlap in the target tree.

4 Tree Representation of Forest Pattern Matching

Despite the NP-completeness result from Theorem 3, in the next section we give a tractability result for the forest pattern matching problem, when the number of trees in the matching pattern is bounded by a (relatively small) constant h and their roots have at most k children, for some (relatively small) constant k. We propose a parameterized algorithm whose running time is $f(h,k) + O(n_s \cdot n_t^{3/2})$, for n_t and n_s the number of nodes in the target and pattern, respectively. This proves that the forest pattern matching is a fixed-parameter tractable problem (FPT) (we refer to [10] for the formal definition of this complexity class).

In presenting the algorithm we switch from edge-labeled tree terms to a more convenient node-labeled tree representations of them. This translation eases the description of the proposed algorithm and provides a closer connection between the concept of (labeled) subtree isomorphism and tree pattern matching.

Formally, a (rooted) node-labeled tree $\mathcal{T}(\mathcal{V}, \mathcal{E}, \mathit{label})$ is a triple, where $\mathcal{V}$ is the node set, $\mathcal{E} \subseteq \mathcal{V} \times \mathcal{V}$ the set of (oriented) edges, and $\mathit{label}\colon \mathcal{V} \to \Lambda^+ \times \{\mathit{op}, \mathit{cl}\}$ is a function associating with each node a label $m \in \Lambda^+ = \Lambda \uplus \{*\}$, and a flag *op* or *cl*. In the following we often abbreviate $\mathcal{T}(\mathcal{V}, \mathcal{E}, \mathit{label})$ with $\mathcal{T}$ and if $\mathit{label}(v) = (m, t)$ we say that v is m-labeled and *open* (resp. *closed*) if $t = \mathit{op}$ (resp. $t = \mathit{cl}$); $\mathit{root}(\mathcal{T})$ denotes the root node; $Ch(v)$ denotes the set of children of v; and $\mathcal{T}\lceil v$ denotes the subtree of $\mathcal{T}$ rooted at a node $v \in \mathcal{V}$. In the following, when $\mathcal{T}$ is the empty tree (i.e., $\mathcal{V} = \emptyset$), we assume $Ch(\mathit{root}(\mathcal{T})) = \emptyset$.

Definition 3. *A node-labeled tree $\mathcal{T}(\mathcal{V}, \mathcal{E}, \mathit{label})$ is said the* graphical representation *of an edge-labeled tree term $T \equiv m_1[T_1] \mid \cdots \mid m_n[T_n] \mid x_1 \mid \cdots \mid x_k$, for $n, k \geq 0$, if the following conditions hold:*

1. *if $n = 0$, then $\mathcal{T}$ is the empty tree ;*
2. *if $n > 0$, then*
   (a) $\mathcal{V} = \{r, v_1, \ldots, v_n\} \cup \mathcal{V}'$, where $\{r, v_1, \ldots, v_n\} \cap \mathcal{V}' = \emptyset$;
   (b) $\mathcal{E} = \bigcup_i(\{(r, v_i)\} \cup \{(v_i, w) \mid w \in Ch(\mathit{root}(\mathcal{T}_i))\}) \cup \mathcal{E}'$;

(c) label: $\mathcal{V} \to \Lambda^+ \times \{op, cl\}$ *is such that, for all* $v \in \mathcal{V}$

$$label(v) = \begin{cases} (*, op) & \text{if } v = r \text{ and } k = 0 \\ (*, cl) & \text{if } v = r \text{ and } k > 0 \\ (m_i, t) & \text{if } v = v_i \text{ and } label(root(\mathcal{T}_i)) = (m, t) \\ label_i(v) & \text{if } v \in \mathcal{V}_i \end{cases}$$

where $\mathcal{T}_i(\mathcal{V}_i, \mathcal{E}_i, label_i)$ *are the graphical tree representation of* T_i $(1 \leq i \leq n)$ *with pairwise disjoint node sets,* $\mathcal{V}' = \bigcup_i(\mathcal{V}_i \setminus \{root(\mathcal{T}_i)\})$, *and* $\mathcal{E}' = (\mathcal{V}' \times \mathcal{V}') \cap \bigcup_i \mathcal{E}_i$.

The graphical representation of a tree term is always rooted at a $*$-labeled node and converts m-labeled edges into m-labeled nodes, discarding variables. Note, however, that nodes in $\mathcal{T}$ are open iff they have a variable as a child in its tree term representation. In Figure 2 it is shown an example of translation into the graphical representation.

The following proposition relates the subtree isomorphism to the notion of tree pattern matching on terms, when the pattern is supposed to be solid.

Proposition 3. *For a term* T *and a solid one* T', *where* $\mathcal{T}(\mathcal{V}, \mathcal{E}, label)$ *and* $\mathcal{T}'(\mathcal{V}', \mathcal{E}', label')$ *are their tree representations, respectively, then* $\models T \succeq T'$ *if and only if there exists* $\mathcal{V}'' \subseteq \mathcal{V}$, *where* $|\mathcal{V}'| = |\mathcal{V}''|$, *and* $\rho\colon \mathcal{V}' \to \mathcal{V}''$ *a one-to-one function such that*

1. $(u, v) \in \mathcal{E}'$ *iff* $(\rho(u), \rho(v)) \in \mathcal{E}$;
2. *if* v *is* m*-labeled then* $\rho(v)$ *is* m*-labeled, for* $m \in \Lambda$;
3. *if* $v \in \mathcal{V}' \setminus \{root(\mathcal{T}')\}$ *is closed then* $\rho(v)$ *is closed and* $|Ch(v)| = |Ch(\rho(v))|$.

Conditions (1–2) in Proposition 3 correspond to the subtree isomorphism of $\mathcal{T}'$ in $\mathcal{T}$ with respect to Λ^+-labeled nodes (note that $*$ acts as a wildcard label). Condition (3) is required in situations like the one that follows. Let $T = m[\,n[\,\mathbf{0}\,]\,]$ and $T' = m[\,\mathbf{0}\,]$, then T' has no match in T even though, considering their graphical tree representations, there exists ρ satisfying conditions (1) and (2).

Proposition 3 induces the definition of the following relation: $\rho \models \mathcal{T} \succeq \mathcal{T}'$ iff there exists ρ satisfying conditions (1–3). Obviously $\models T \succeq T'$ iff $\rho \models \mathcal{T} \succeq \mathcal{T}'$ and $\mathcal{T}$, $\mathcal{T}'$ are graphical representations for T, T', respectively.

Now, let us consider the forest pattern matching problem, that is, when the pattern is a list of arbitrary length $h \geq 0$.

Proposition 4. *Given a term* T *and a solid (forest) pattern* $\boldsymbol{S} = S_1, \ldots, S_h$, *where* $\mathcal{T}$ *and* $\boldsymbol{\mathcal{S}} = \mathcal{S}_1, \ldots, \mathcal{S}_h$ *are their tree representations (with disjoint node sets), then* $\models T \succeq \boldsymbol{S}$ *if and only if*

1. $\rho_i \models \mathcal{T} \succeq \mathcal{S}_i$, *for* $1 \leq i \leq h$;
2. $\mathcal{R} = \{\rho_i(v) \mid v \in Ch(root(\mathcal{S}_i)), 1 \leq i \leq h\}$ *is an antichain in* $\mathcal{T}$.

Condition (1) is obvious, and follows by Proposition 3. Condition (2) states that the children of each $\mathcal{S}_i$-root must be mapped by ρ_i to form an antichain in $\mathcal{T}$. This ensures that the mapping of trees in the pattern are not overlapping in $\mathcal{T}$. Note that, different roots of the pattern can be mapped to the same target node, and that the antichain condition must be satisfied by the roots' children nodes only (see Figure 2 for an example).

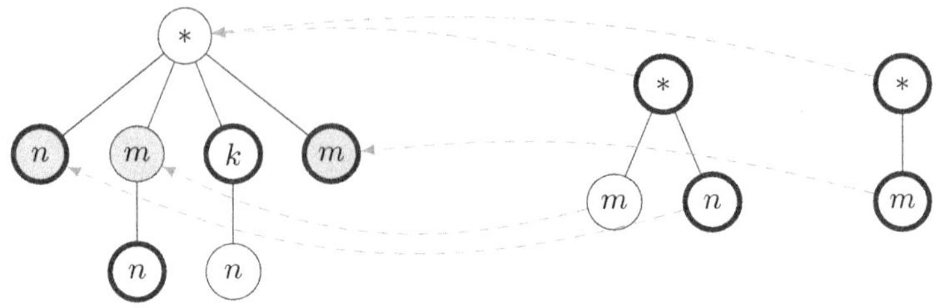

$T = n[\mathbf{0}] \mid m[y_1 \mid n[\mathbf{0}]] \mid k[n[y_2]] \mid m[\mathbf{0}] \mid y_3$ $\quad S_1 = m[x] \mid n[\mathbf{0}]$ $\quad S_2 = m[\mathbf{0}]$

Fig. 2. The forest pattern $\boldsymbol{S} = S_1, S_2$ has a match in T: for $C = z_1 \mid k[n[y_2]] \mid z_2 \mid y_3$ and $D = y_1 \mid n[\mathbf{0}]$, $T \equiv (C\{S_1/z_1, S_2/z_2\})\{D/x\}$. Bold-circled nodes are closed.

5 A Parameterized Algorithm

In this section, we provide a parameterized algorithm to solve the forest pattern matching problem. Let T be a term, $\boldsymbol{S} = S_1, \ldots, S_h$ a solid (forest) pattern, and $\mathcal{T} = (\mathcal{V}, \mathcal{E}, label)$, $\mathcal{S}_i = (\mathcal{V}_i, \mathcal{E}_i, label_i)$ be their respective tree representations, for $1 \leq i \leq h$, with pairwise disjoint node sets; according to the alternative characterization of Proposition 4, our algorithm will solve $\models \mathcal{T} \succeq \boldsymbol{\mathcal{S}}$, where the chosen parameters are $h = |\boldsymbol{\mathcal{S}}|$ and $k = \max_i |Ch(root(\mathcal{S}_i))|$.

The key idea is to find all possible matches of each $\mathcal{S}_i$ separately, identifying them by coloring the nodes in $\mathcal{T}$, and finally to search for a rainbow antichain. The proposed algorithm uses the so called *reduction to kernel size* technique [10] and works in three steps:

1. for each $\mathcal{S}_i$ in the pattern, we identify all possible mappings ρ_i satisfying $\rho_i \models \mathcal{T} \succeq \mathcal{S}_i$. These mappings correspond to tree matches and we identify them by coloring the nodes in $\mathcal{T}$: each $\mathcal{S}_i$ is associated with a color $f \in \mathcal{F}$, and nodes in $Ch(root(\mathcal{S}_i))$ with colors from the palette $\mathcal{P}_i$ (a color for each node). Palettes are supposed to be disjoint.
2. we reduce the size of the colored target tree $\mathcal{T}$, yielding a *reduced kernel* of size depending only on the parameters h and k.
3. we perform an exhaustive search for a rainbow antichain on palette $\bigcup_i \mathcal{P}_i$.

Coloring the target tree: By Proposition 3 we know that this corresponds to solving the subtree isomorphism problem for each $\mathcal{S}_i$ in the pattern and ensuring that the closedness property holds (i.e., condition (3) in Proposition 3). It is not hard to see that the Matula's algorithm [17] for the subtree isomorphism can be adapted to our aims. Let M be a Boolean matrix of size $n_s \times n_t$, where n_t and n_s are respectively the number of nodes of the target tree and of the pattern (the summation of each node set of the whole tree list). By dynamic programming on $\mathcal{T}$ and $\boldsymbol{\mathcal{S}}$ we can fill M as follows: for each node u in $\boldsymbol{\mathcal{S}}$ and node v in $\mathcal{T}$, $M[u, v] = \mathbf{T}$ if there exists an embedding (respecting node labeling and the closedness property) of $\boldsymbol{\mathcal{S}}\lceil u$ in $\mathcal{T}$ rooted at v, otherwise $M[u, v] = \mathbf{F}$ (see Matula [17] for details on how the matrix M is obtained).

From the matrix M we define the coloring functions for $\mathcal{T}$. Let $\mathcal{F}$ and $\mathcal{P}_i$, for $1 \leq i \leq h$, be disjoint palettes such that $|\mathcal{F}| = h$ and $|\mathcal{P}_i| = |Ch(root(\mathcal{S}_i))| \leq k$, and $\alpha\colon \{\mathcal{S}_1, \ldots, \mathcal{S}_h\} \to \mathcal{F}$ and $\beta_i\colon Ch(root(\mathcal{S}_i)) \to \mathcal{P}_i$ be bijections associating a color $f \in \mathcal{F}$ with each $\mathcal{S}_i$ in the pattern, and a color $p \in \mathcal{P}_i$ with each children of $root(\mathcal{S}_i)$. For each $v \in \mathcal{V}$, we define the sets $color_R(v) \subseteq \mathcal{F}$ and $color_i(v) \subseteq \mathcal{P}_i$, for $1 \leq i \leq h$ as follows:

$$\alpha(\mathcal{S}_i) \in color_R(v) \iff M[root(\mathcal{S}_i), v] \qquad\qquad \beta_i(u) \in color_i(v) \iff M[u, v]$$

Note that nodes may take color from different palettes, indeed a subtree of the target may have a match with more than one tree in the pattern.

Proposition 5. *If* $\alpha(\mathcal{S}_i) \in color_R(v)$ *then* $\bigcup_{u \in Ch(v)} color_i(u) = \mathcal{P}_i$.

The above implies that, if a node v in $\mathcal{T}$ is $\alpha(\mathcal{S}_i)$-colored, i.e., $\mathcal{S}_i$ has a match rooted at v, then there must exist $C \subseteq Ch(v)$ such that $|C| = |Ch(root(\mathcal{S}_i))|$ and, for all $u \in Ch(root(\mathcal{S}_i))$, $\mathcal{S}_i\restriction u$ has a match rooted at a node in C.

Reduction to kernel size: The reduction of $\mathcal{T}$ to kernel size consists in a decoloring procedure that aims at leaving as much nodes as possible completely uncolored in order to remove them from $\mathcal{T}$. Indeed, uncolored nodes have no influence in the detection of a possible rainbow antichain in $\mathcal{T}$.

Before starting with the description of the reduction, we need some technical definitions and notations. We say that a node is c-decolored if we remove c from all its color sets (note that $color_R$ and $color_i$ are disjoint, hence the set deletion of c influences only the corresponding color palette). By $\mathcal{T} \setminus v$ we denote the tree obtained from $\mathcal{T}$ removing the node v and such that the children of u are adopted by its parent (if u is the root node we just decolor it).

Definition 4. *Let $\mathcal{T}$ be a tree and u a node. We denote by* $\mathsf{fout}(u)$ *the* fan-out *of u, defined as* $\mathsf{fout}(u) = \sum_{v \in an(u)} |Ch(v)| - 1$, *where $an(v)$ is the set of all ancestors of v; and by* $\mathsf{fout}(\mathcal{T}) = \max_{v \in \mathcal{V}} \mathsf{fout}(v)$ *the maximal fan-out in $\mathcal{T}$.*

Intuitively, $\mathsf{fout}(u)$ is the out-degree of the whole path from u to the root of $\mathcal{T}$.

Lemma 3. *If v is uncolored and $\mathcal{T}$ admits a $\mathcal{P}$-rainbow antichain, then also $\mathcal{T} \setminus v$ has $\mathcal{P}$-rainbow antichain.*

Lemma 4. *If $\mathcal{T}$ has a $\mathcal{P}$-rainbow antichain, then it has one also when u is c-decolored, for color $c \in \mathcal{P}$, if one of the following conditions hold:*

(a) u is a (strict) ancestor of v, and both u, v are c-colored;
(b) $\mathcal{T}$ has only c-colored leaves and u is a leaf such that $\mathsf{fout}(u) \geq |\mathcal{P}|$.

Proof. (a) Let $\mathcal{R}$ be a rainbow antichain for $\mathcal{T}$ such that $u \in \mathcal{R}$. Since u belongs to $\mathcal{R}$, for some color $c_{\mathcal{R}} \in \mathcal{P}$ assigned to u, $\mathcal{R}$ must be rainbow on the palette $\mathcal{P}$. If we decolor u by c, there are two cases. If $c \neq c_{\mathcal{R}}$, $\mathcal{R}$ continues to be a rainbow antichain for $\mathcal{T}$, conversely, if $c = c_{\mathcal{R}}$, $\mathcal{R}$ is no more colorful on $\mathcal{P}$, since one of the representative of $\mathcal{P}$ lacks (i.e., c). By hypothesis, u has a c-colored descendant v. It is easy to see that $\mathcal{R}' = (\mathcal{R} \setminus \{u\}) \cup \{v\}$ is still an antichain and moreover it is colorful for $\mathcal{P}$.

(b) Let $\mathcal{T}$ be a colored tree on palette $\mathcal{P}$ such that, all its leaves are colored by $c \in \mathcal{P}$, and v is a leaf in $\mathcal{T}$ for which $\mathsf{fout}(v) \geq |\mathcal{P}|$. We want to prove that if $\mathcal{T}$ has a rainbow antichain, it continues to have one also if we c-decolor v. Let P be the path from the leaf v to the root of $\mathcal{T}$. To each outer-neighbour n_i $(1 \leq i \leq \mathsf{fout}(v))$ of P corresponds a subtree $\mathcal{T}\lceil n_i$ with all leaves colored by c, since $\mathcal{T}$ has only c-colored leaves. It is worth noting that all $\mathcal{T}\lceil n_i$ are not overlapping with each other, since $\bigcup_i \{n_i\}$ is an antichain for $\mathcal{T}$.

Suppose $\mathcal{R}$ be a rainbow antichain for $\mathcal{T}$ such that $v \in \mathcal{R}$. Since $v \in \mathcal{R}$, for some color $c_{\mathcal{R}} \in \mathcal{P}$ assigned to v, $\mathcal{R}$ must be rainbow on the palette $\mathcal{P}$. If we c-decolor v, there are two cases. If $c \neq c_{\mathcal{R}}$, $\mathcal{R}$ continues to be a rainbow antichain for $\mathcal{T}$, conversely, if $c = c_{\mathcal{R}}$, $\mathcal{R}$ is no more rainbow on $\mathcal{P}$, since one of the representative of $\mathcal{P}$ lacks. Note that $\mathcal{R}$, apart v, must reside in $\bigcup_i \mathcal{T}\lceil n_i$. Since $\mathsf{fout}(v) \geq |\mathcal{P}|$, there are more than $|\mathcal{P}|$ subtrees $\mathcal{T}\lceil n_i$ $(1 \leq i \leq \mathsf{fout}(v))$, hence there is no way to choose $|\mathcal{P}|$ distinct nodes from $\bigcup_i \mathcal{T}\lceil n_i$ such that each $\mathcal{T}\lceil n_i$ as at lest one of these nodes. Therefore, since each $\mathcal{T}\lceil n_i$ contains at least one node colored by c (all leaves are c-colored!), we can substitute the node $v \in R$ with one of the leaf node in the "untouched" $\mathcal{T}\lceil n_i$, thus obtaining a new antichain where v is not choosen (hence v can be safely decolored). □

Applying (a) we c-decolor all nodes that have a c-colored descendant, and by Lemma 3 we remove all the nodes that are left uncolored. Note that, this procedure can be applied both on palette $\mathcal{F}$ and on palette $\mathcal{P}_i$, for $1 \leq i \leq h$. This reduction returns a tree where all paths do not have color repetitions, hence, by Proposition 5 its height is at most $2h$. Condition (b) induces another decoloring procedure. In fact, once the previous reduction is applied, nodes with the same color must form an antichain and, in particular for each $f \in \mathcal{F}$ we can apply (b) just ignoring paths from a leaf up to a f-colored node. Note that this time we do not apply the reduction on palettes $\mathcal{P}_i$'s.

Proposition 6. *If* $\mathsf{fout}(\mathcal{T}) \leq m$, *then* $\mathcal{T}$ *has at most* 2^m *leaves.*

Proof. The proof is by induction on $m \geq 0$. If $m = 0$, then $\mathsf{fout}(\mathcal{T}) = 0$, hence $\mathcal{T}$ must be a single path, hence it has exactly one leaf. Let $m > 0$, and $\mathcal{T}$ be a tree with $t > 0$ children under its root (the case when $t = 0$ is trivial). By inductive hypothesis, each subtree rooted at a child of the root have at most 2^{k-t+1} leaves, since their fan-out is at most $k - (t - 1)$. Since there are t of those subtrees, the number of the leaves in $\mathcal{T}$ is at most $t \cdot 2^{k-t+1}$. We have $t \cdot 2^{k-t+1} = 2 \cdot \frac{t}{2^t} \cdot 2^k \leq 2^k$, since, for all $t > 0$, $\frac{t}{2^t} \leq \frac{1}{2}$. □

By Proposition 6, the reduced target tree have at most $2^{|\mathcal{F}|}$ (hence, 2^h) f-colored nodes, for each $f \in \mathcal{F}$. Note, however, that we do not have a bound on the total number of nodes in the reduced tree, indeed the reduction induced by Lemma 4 (b) is not applied on c-colored nodes, for $c \in \bigcup_i \mathcal{P}_i$. This problem is overcome just checking that for each color $f \in \mathcal{F}$, all f-colored nodes have no more than $|\bigcup_i \mathcal{P}_i|$ c-colored children, for $c \in \bigcup_i \mathcal{P}_i$. Since $|\bigcup_i \mathcal{P}_i| \leq h \cdot k$, we obtain a reduced tree $\mathcal{T}_{red}$ with at most $h\,(k+1) \cdot 2^h$ nodes.

Looking for rainbow antichains: What we actually need is the following for each node v in the reduced target tree: for each $X \subseteq \mathcal{F}$, determine whether the pattern trees corresponding to color in X can be mapped *simultaneously* in the subtree $\mathcal{T}_{red}\lceil v$. To compute this, we determine all the possible tuples $t = (c_1, \ldots, c_{|Ch(v)|})$ of colors associated to each child of v, then we check that for each $\alpha(S_i) \in X$, the tuple t contains $\mathcal{P}_i$. Since both $Ch(v)$ and $\bigcup_i \mathcal{P}_i$ have at most $h \cdot k$ elements, for each node v and subset X we need to check at most $(h \cdot k)^2$ tuples at a cost of $h \cdot k$ per tuple. We denote this by the predicate $N(v, X)$.

In order to determine whether there exists a rainbow antichain in the reduced target tree $\mathcal{T}$, we need to check that $A(\mathcal{T}_{red}, \mathcal{F})$ hold, where the predicate $A(\mathcal{T}, X)$, for $\mathcal{T}$, subtree of $\mathcal{T}_{red}$, and $X \subseteq \mathcal{F}$, is defined as follows:

$$A(\mathcal{T}, X) = N(v, X) \vee \bigvee_{Y \subseteq X} \Big(A(\mathcal{T}', Y) \wedge A(\mathcal{T}'', Y \setminus X) \Big),$$

where, $v = root(\mathcal{T})$, $\mathcal{T}' = \mathcal{T}\lceil u_1$ and $\mathcal{T}''$ is the tree obtained by collecting all $\mathcal{T}\lceil u_j$ under a fresh copy of the node v, for $Ch(v) = \{u_1, \ldots, u_m\}$ and $2 \leq j \leq m$.

Now, $A(\mathcal{T}, X)$ holds if and only if $\mathcal{T}$ admits a rainbow antichain $\mathcal{R}$ for the palette $\bigcup_{\alpha(S_i) \in X} \mathcal{P}_i$. Indeed, the antichain is either a subset of the immediate children of root (in this case $N(root(\mathcal{T}), X)$ holds), or it is split in the subtrees of $\mathcal{T}$ (in this case the right part of the formula holds). A formal argument for this fact can be provided by a straightforward induction on the height of $\mathcal{T}$.

In order to calculate $A(\mathcal{T}, X)$ we must solve a *subset convolution* problem for each node in the reduced target tree. Each subset convolution can be calculated in time $O(h^2 \cdot 2^h)$, by means of the fast subset convolution algorithm of [3], hence we can check $A(\mathcal{T}_{red}, \mathcal{F})$ in time $O(h \cdot k)^3 + O(h^3(k+1) \cdot 2^{2h})$ using a dynamic programming algorithm working bottom-up on the structure of $\mathcal{T}_{red}$.

Complexity analysis of the algorithm: The coloring phase costs $O(n_s \cdot n_t^{3/2})$ where n_t and n_s are the number of nodes in the target and pattern, respectively, [17]. Note that while coloring the nodes from leaves up to the root, it can be easily performed the first decoloring step, just do not coloring nodes by colors already assigned to some descendant.

The second decoloring phase must be performed after the previous decoloring. This is both necessary for the correctness of the reduction, and useful to increase the node fan-outs. The decoloring, for each $f \in \mathcal{F}$, first calculates the fan-out of each f-colored node just performing a simple depth-first visit of the tree, then it decolors the nodes by other h depth-first visits, one for each color in $\mathcal{F}$. The overall cost of the reduction is linear in n_t.

The cost for checking the existence of rainbow antichains in $\mathcal{T}_{red}$ has been already shown to be in $O(h \cdot k)^3 + O(h^3(k+1) \cdot 2^{2h})$.

Concluding, the overall cost of the algorithm is $O(h^3(k+1) \cdot 2^{2h}) + O(n_s \cdot n_t^{3/2})$.

Notice that the proposed algorithm proves also that the forest pattern matching problem is fixed-parameter tractable even if we choose as parameter simply $K = |\bigcup_i Ch(S_i)|$; indeed, in this case the upper bound would be $O(K^3 \cdot 2^{2K}) + O(n_s \cdot n_t^{3/2})$. We have preferred to consider the two parameters h, k, instead of the single K, because this yields a lower and more precise upper-bound.

6 Conclusions

In this paper we have considered the problem of matching a forest within an unordered tree, with no overlaps. This problem arises in many situations dealing with hierarchical structures; in particular, it covers the problem of matching the redex of wide reaction rules within processes. This case is particularly interesting in the definition and the implementation of the semantics of calculi for distributed and global computation.

We have shown that, although the problem is NP-complete in general, the combinatorial explosion depends only on the forest width. This parameter is usually fixed once we have chosen the reduction system (i.e., reaction rules do not change) and it is small (≤ 3), thus the exponential explosion is actually bounded and the problem is feasible. In fact, we have provided an algorithm that solves this problem, respecting these complexity bounds. Therefore, our results prove that wide reaction rules are feasible for many calculi for global computation.

As a side result of our proof techniques, we have singled out the new *rainbow antichain* problem, which is NP-complete but fixed-parameter tractable; we think that this problem can be useful also for the analysis and reductions of other problems about trees and forests.

Related work. Wide reaction systems can be seen as a particular case of *graph rewriting systems*. It is well-known that in general graph rewriting is NP-complete [9], as each step requires to solve a subgraph isomorphism problem. In this paper we have improved this situation in the case of wide reaction systems, by showing that subgraph isomorphism can be avoided in favour of the rainbow antichain problem—thus yielding a polynomial algorithm where the exponential part becomes a constant factor once we have fixed the set of reaction rules.

The problem of forest matching arises also in the case of *Bigraphical Reactive Systems*, i.e. wide reaction systems whose states are *bigraphs* [14,19]. This case is quite interesting because BRSs are intended to be a general meta-model for global computations. Several algorithms for bigraph matching have been proposed [8,18,21], but these solutions do not take advantage from the fact that combinatorial explosion depends only on redex widths, as we have shown here.

Future work. First, we plan to apply the results and algorithm presented in this paper to real calculi and frameworks. The cases of Bigraphical Reactive Systems, BioBigraphs [1] and Synchronized Hyperedge Replacement [11] are of particular interest. In these cases, we have to integrate forest pattern matching with sub(hyper)graph isomorphisms (needed to match e.g. the link part of bigraphs). We hope that the tractability results given in this paper will help to tame the complexity of subgraph isomorphism.

In [20], equational rewriting logics have been proposed as a framework for operational semantics. Comparing our algorithm with tools implementing rewriting logic (e.g., Maude) is not immediate, since rewriting logics do not directly support wide rewritings. A possible workaround is to encode wide reaction rules into standard ones by extending the syntax with a suitable "tensor product";

however, we expect our direct approach to outperform this indirect one. On the other hand, our results about wide reaction rules could be incorporated into tools like Maude, leading to a new and more expressive *wide rewriting logics.*

An interesting question is whether there are other possible reductions to be applied in the target tree in order to yield a smaller kernel instance. A positive result in this direction would provide a significant improvement of both time and space complexity upper bounds. At the moment, we know only that our problem does not fulfill the criteria in [4] that would imply the nonexistence of a polynomial-bounded kernel, so there is still hope.

Another interesting situation is that of wide reaction systems with *reaction rates*, like Stochastic Bigraphs [15]. These cases are of great interest in quantitative models of networks, biological systems, etc. Here, we are interested to pick out a single match among many possible matches of different rules, but still respecting rates and stochastic distributions. We think that it should be possible to derive a suitable *counting* algorithm from the one presented in this paper.

A Proofs of Technical Results

Proof (of Proposition 2). We prove each point separately.

(a, $\Longrightarrow$) Since $\models T \succeq \mathbf{0}, \boldsymbol{S}$, there exist a context C and parameters $\boldsymbol{D}$ such that $T \equiv (C\{\mathbf{0}/z, \boldsymbol{S}/\boldsymbol{z}\})\{\boldsymbol{D}/\boldsymbol{x}\}$ for some $\boldsymbol{z} = (z_1, \dots, z_n)$ and z in $vars(C)$. It is simple to prove that $C\{\mathbf{0}/z, \boldsymbol{S}/\boldsymbol{z}\} \equiv C\{\mathbf{0}/z\}\{\boldsymbol{S}/\boldsymbol{z}\}$, hence, by associativity of substitution composition, $T \equiv ((C\{\mathbf{0}/z\})\{\boldsymbol{S}/\boldsymbol{z}\})\{\boldsymbol{D}/\boldsymbol{x}\}$, that is, $\models T \succeq \boldsymbol{S}$.
(a, $\Longleftarrow$) Since $\models T \succeq \boldsymbol{S}$, there exist a context C and parameters $\boldsymbol{D}$ such that $T \equiv (C\{\boldsymbol{S}/\boldsymbol{z}\})\{\boldsymbol{D}/\boldsymbol{x}\}$ for some $\boldsymbol{z} = (z_1, \dots, z_n)$ in $vars(C)$. Observe that $C \equiv C \mid \mathbf{0} \equiv (C \mid z)\{\mathbf{0}/z\}$ for some $z \notin \{z_1, \dots, z_n\}$. From this we have that $T \equiv ((C \mid z)\{z/\mathbf{0}, \boldsymbol{S}/\boldsymbol{z}\})\{\boldsymbol{D}/\boldsymbol{x}\}$, that is, $\models T \succeq \mathbf{0}, \boldsymbol{S}$.
(b, $\Longrightarrow$) Since $\models T \succeq x \mid y$, there exist a context C and parameters $\boldsymbol{D}$ such that $T \equiv (C\{x \mid y/z\})\{\boldsymbol{D}/\boldsymbol{x}\}$ for some $z \in vars(C)$. Since $C\{x \mid y/z\} \equiv C\{y \mid w/z\}\{w/x\}$ (for w fresh), by associativity of substitution composition, we get $T \equiv ((C\{y \mid w/z\})\{x/w\})\{\boldsymbol{D}/\boldsymbol{x}\}$, that is, $\models T \succeq x$.
(b, $\Longleftarrow$) Since $\models T \succeq x$, there exist a context C and parameters $\boldsymbol{D}$ such that $T \equiv (C\{x/z\})\{\boldsymbol{D}/\boldsymbol{x}\}$ for some $z \in vars(C)$. It is easy to prove that $C\{x/z\} \equiv C\{x \mid \mathbf{0}/z\} \equiv C\{x \mid y/z\}\{\mathbf{0}/y\}$ for y fresh. Now by associativity and from the freshness of y, we obtain $T \equiv (C\{x \mid y/z\})\{\mathbf{0}/y, \boldsymbol{D}/\boldsymbol{x}\}$, that is, $\models T \succeq x \mid y$.
(c) has the same proof of (b), just replace x in (b) with S. □

Proof (of Theorem 3). Given a match $(C, \boldsymbol{D})$ for $T \succeq \boldsymbol{S}$, checking that $T \equiv (C\{\boldsymbol{S}/\boldsymbol{z}\})\{\boldsymbol{D}/\boldsymbol{x}\}$ corresponds to a tree isomorphism test, which is in P [12,13].

Let a colored tree $\mathcal{T}$ and a palette $\mathcal{P} = \{c_1, \dots, c_n\}$ be and instance of RainbowAntichain. Let us transform $\mathcal{T}$ into a tree term T as follows. If $\mathcal{T}$ is a single node v (a leaf) T is $m[\mathbf{0}]$, where $m = c$ if v has color c, otherwise $m = *$, a fresh name not in $\mathcal{P}$ denoting an uncolored node. If $\mathcal{T}$ has root r and $\mathcal{T}_1, \dots, \mathcal{T}_k$ are the (children) subtrees of r, T is $m[T_1 \mid \cdots \mid T_k]$, where m is as above for r, and $T_1, \dots, T_k$ are transformed trees of $\mathcal{T}_1, \dots, \mathcal{T}_k$.

Suppose $(C, \boldsymbol{D})$ be a match for $T \succeq (c_1[x_1], \ldots, c_k[x_n])$. In C, each $c_i[x_i]$ is grafted into a variable $z_i \in vars(C)$. Since variables can appear in terms only as leaves, in the transformation $\mathcal{T}$ of T, we have found a rainbow antichain for $\mathcal{P}$, since the matching pattern has all the colors in $\mathcal{P}$ exacty once.

Assume that $\mathcal{T}$ has a rainbow antichain $\mathcal{R}$. In order to recover context C and parameters $\boldsymbol{D}$, which are a match for $T \succeq (c_1[x_1], \ldots, c_k[x_n])$, it suffices to apply the construction explained above with some adjustments: we obtain C applying the transformation from the root of T, but if a node in $\mathcal{R}$ is reached it is transformed by a fresh variable z_i ($1 \leq i \leq n$) one for each element in $\mathcal{R}$; D_j's are recovered applying the original transformation starting from the subtrees rooted at the children of nodes in $\mathcal{R}$. It is straightforward to prove that $T \equiv (C\{c_1[x_1]/z_1, \ldots, c_k[x_n]/z_n\})\{\boldsymbol{D}/\boldsymbol{x}\}$, for $\boldsymbol{x} = x_1, \ldots, x_n$. □

References

1. Bacci, G., Grohmann, D., Miculan, M.: Bigraphical models for protein and membrane interactions. In: Ciobanu, G. (ed.) Proc. MeCBIC. Electronic Proceedings in Theoretical Computer Science, vol. 11, pp. 3–18 (2009)
2. Bezem, M., Klop, J.W., de Vrijer, R.: Term rewriting systems. CUP (2003)
3. Björklund, A., Husfeldt, T., Kaski, P., Koivisto, M.: Fourier meets Möbius: fast subset convolution. In: Proc. STOC 2007, pp. 67–74. ACM (2007)
4. Bodlaender, H.L., Downey, R.G., Fellows, M.R., Hermelin, D.: On Problems without Polynomial Kernels (Extended Abstract). In: Aceto, L., Damgård, I., Goldberg, L.A., Halldórsson, M.M., Ingólfsdóttir, A., Walukiewicz, I. (eds.) ICALP 2008, Part I. LNCS, vol. 5125, pp. 563–574. Springer, Heidelberg (2008)
5. Boreale, M., Bruni, R., De Nicola, R., Loreti, M.: Sessions and Pipelines for Structured Service Programming. In: Barthe, G., de Boer, F.S. (eds.) FMOODS 2008. LNCS, vol. 5051, pp. 19–38. Springer, Heidelberg (2008)
6. Cardelli, L., Gordon, A.D.: Mobile Ambients. In: Nivat, M. (ed.) FOSSACS 1998. LNCS, vol. 1378, pp. 140–155. Springer, Heidelberg (1998)
7. Cook, S.A.: The complexity of theorem-proving procedures. In: Proc. STOC 1971, pp. 151–158. ACM (1971)
8. Damgaard, T.C., Glenstrup, A.J., Birkedal, L., Milner, R.: An inductive characterization of matching in binding bigraphs. Formal Aspects of Computing **25**(2), 257–288 (2013)
9. Dörr, H.: Efficient graph rewriting and its implementation, vol. 922. LNCS. Springer (1995)
10. Downey, R.G., Fellows, M.R.: Fixed-parameter tractability and completeness I: Basic results. SIAM J. Comput. **24**(4), 873–921 (1995)
11. Ferrari, G.-L., Hirsch, D., Lanese, I., Montanari, U., Tuosto, E.: Synchronised Hyperedge Replacement as a Model for Service Oriented Computing. In: de Boer, F.S., Bonsangue, M.M., Graf, S., de Roever, W.-P. (eds.) FMCO 2005. LNCS, vol. 4111, pp. 22–43. Springer, Heidelberg (2006)
12. Hopcroft, J.E., Tarjan, R.E.: A v^2 algorithm for determining isomorphism of planar graphs. Inf. Process. Lett. **1**(1), 32–34 (1971)
13. Hopcroft, J.E., Wong, J.K.: Linear time algorithm for isomorphism of planar graphs (preliminary report). In: Proc. STOC 1974, pp. 172–184. ACM (1974)

14. Jensen, O.H., Milner, R.: Bigraphs and transitions. In: Proc. POPL, pp. 38–49. ACM (2003)
15. Krivine, J., Milner, R., Troina, A.: Stochastic bigraphs. In: Proc. MFPS. Electronic Notes in Theoretical Computer Science, vol. 218, pp. 73–96 (2008)
16. Mansutti, A., Miculan, M., Peressotti, M.: Towards distributed bigraphical reactive systems. In: Echahed, R., Habel, A., Mosbah, M. (eds.) Proc. GCM 2014, p. 45 (2014)
17. Matula, D.W.: Subtree isomorphism in $O(n^{5/2})$. Annals of Discrete Mathematics **2**, 91–106 (1978)
18. Miculan, M., Peressotti, M.: A CSP implementation of the bigraph embedding problem. In: Proc. 1st International Workshop on Meta Models for Process Languages (MeMo) (2014)
19. Milner, R.: The Space and Motion of Communicating Agents. CUP (2009)
20. Serbanuta, T.-F., Rosu, G., Meseguer, J.: A rewriting logic approach to operational semantics. Inf. Comput. **207**(2), 305–340 (2009)
21. Sevegnani, M., Unsworth, C., Calder, M.: A SAT based algorithm for the matching problem in bigraphs with sharing. Technical Report TR-2010-311, Department of Computer Science, University of Glasgow (2010)

Automata for Analysing Service Contracts

Davide Basile(✉), Pierpaolo Degano, and Gian Luigi Ferrari

Dipartimento di Informatica, Università di Pisa, Pisa, Italy
{basile,degano,giangi}@di.unipi.it

Abstract. A novel approach to the formal description of service contracts is presented in terms of automata. We focus on the basic property of guaranteeing that in the multi-party composition of principals each individual gets his requests satisfied, so that the overall composition reaches its goal. Depending on whether requests are satisfied synchronously or asynchronously, we construct an orchestrator that at static time either yields composed services enjoying the required properties or detects the individuals responsible for possible violations. To do that in the asynchronous case we resort to techniques from Operational Research.

1 Introduction

Service composition is the fundamental part of the service-oriented approach. Often, the computational capabilities offered by a coarse-grained service are implemented taking advantage of multiple, finer-grained and loosely-coupled services. APIs for service composition (orchestration and choreography) are an integral part of service-based systems. Different languages have been proposed for orchestrating Web Services, the most popular among which is BPEL [21]. However, several crucial issues naturally arise, e.g. the usage of resources, the guarantees on the results provided, the correctness of the whole business process in a variety of different operational environments.

Service orchestrations rely on the notion of *service contract* which specifies what a service is going to offer and what in turn it requires. In order to serve its client, the orchestrator defines the duties and responsibilities for each of the different services he calls. This *contract agreement* is obviously based on the contracts of the involved services, and ensures that all the duties are properly kept. The orchestrator can then proceed to organise the overall service composition and to propose the resulting contract to its own clients. This process is called *contract composition.* Contract composition assumes that none of the involved service violates its contract, i.e. that contract agreement is fulfilled, in which case so does the orchestration. Furthermore, a failing service contract can cause the orchestrator to breach the contract with its clients. Thus reaching the agreement among the services is the essential ingredient in designing orchestrations.

The main question addressed by our research is twofold. First, we aim at developing techniques capable of determining a correct contract composition by

This work has been partially supported by the MIUR project *Security Horizons* and IST-FP7-FET open-IP project *ASCENS.*

M. Maffei and E. Tuosto (Eds.): TGC 2014, LNCS 8902, pp. 34–50, 2014.
DOI: 10.1007/978-3-662-45917-1_3

considering the individual service contracts and their overall satisfaction within an orchestration. Second, we propose a rigorous formal technique, suitable to be automated, to compose contracts. Previous work have tackled similar issues. We only mention a few that use the λ-calculus [4,5,8], process calculi [1,14,15], non-classical logics [7].

Here, we introduce an automata-based model for contracts called *contract automata* (CA), that are a special kind of finite state automata endowed with two composition operators, involving many parties and reflecting two different orchestration policies. One operation joins a service to an existing orchestration with no reconfiguration; the second requires a global adaptive re-orchestration of all the services involved. We also define properties of CA that guarantee a group of contracts to agree under all circumstances. The first one is called *agreement* and considers the case when all the requests made are synchronously matched in pair by the offers, and thus satisfied; we also synthesise a suitable orchestrator to enforce contract composition to adhere to this behaviour. The second property, *weak agreement*, is more liberal, in that requests can be asynchronously matched, and an offer can be delivered even before a corresponding request.

We also establish conditions ensuring that a group of contracts agree in some specific cases (they *admit* agreement or weak agreement). We develop static techniques to detect which individual in a contract is *liable*, i.e. the responsibles for leading a contract composition into a failing state; as a matter of fact, our notion slightly differs form other versions of liability [6], mainly because we do not admit the possibility of redeem from culpability. While finding the individuals liable for a violation of agreement is not hard (inspecting the automaton plus a little calculation suffice), things become much more intricate when we consider weak agreement, that has a clear interpretation as a context-sensitive language. For the synchronous case, we offer a method for composing contract and detecting liability, that is inspired by so-called controllers of the Control Theory [12]. Instead, we check weak agreement and detect liability in an original manner by resorting to optimization techniques borrowed from Operational Research. In particular, we show that these notions are naturally handled in terms of optimization of network flows. The intuitive idea is that the problem of service composition is rendered as a flow itinerary in the networks, that is automatically constructed from the contract automata resulting from service composition.

Because of space limitation, all the proofs of our results are omitted and can be found in [9].

2 The Model

This section formally introduces the notion of contract automata. We start with some notation and preliminary definitions. Let $\Sigma = \mathbb{R} \cup \mathbb{O} \cup \{\square\}$ be the alphabet of *actions* partitioned in *requests* $\mathbb{R} = \{a, b, c, \ldots\}$ and *offers* $\mathbb{O} = \{\overline{a}, \overline{b}, \overline{c}, \ldots\}$ where $\mathbb{R} \cap \mathbb{O} = \emptyset$, and $\square \notin \mathbb{R} \cup \mathbb{O}$ is a distinguished element representing the *idle* action. We define the involution $co(\bullet) : \Sigma \mapsto \Sigma$ such that $co(\mathbb{R}) = \mathbb{O}$, $co(\mathbb{O}) = \mathbb{R}$, $co(\square) = \square$.

Let $\vec{v} = (v_1, ..., v_n)$ be a vector of *rank* $n = r_v \geq 1$, then $\vec{v}_i$ denotes the i-th element. We write $\vec{v}^1 \vec{v}^2 \dots \vec{v}^m$ for the concatenation of m vectors $\vec{v}^i$. The alphabet of a CA consists of vectors, each element of which records the activity of a single participant in the contract. In a vector there is either a single offer or a single request, or there is a pair of complementary request-offer that match; all the other elements of the vector contain the symbol $\square$, meaning that the corresponding individuals stay idle. In the following let $\square^m$ denote a vector of rank m, all components of which are $\square$.

Definition 1 (Actions). *Given a vector* $\vec{a} \in \Sigma^n$, *if*

- $\vec{a} = \square^{n_1} \alpha \square^{n_2}, n_1, n_2 \geq 0$, *then* $\vec{a}$ *is a* request *if* $\alpha \in \mathbb{R}$, *and is an* offer *if* $\alpha \in \mathbb{O}$
- $\vec{a} = \square^{n_1} \alpha \square^{n_2} co(\alpha) \square^{n_3}, n_1, n_2, n_3 \geq 0$, *then* $\vec{a}$ *is a* match, *where* $\alpha \in \mathbb{R} \cup \mathbb{O}$.

We define $\vec{a} \bowtie \vec{b}$ *iff* $\vec{a}$ *is an offer and* $\vec{b}$ *is a request or vice versa with* $\vec{a}_i = co(\vec{b}_j) \neq \square$ *and* $r_a = r_b$, *for two indexes* $i, j \leq r_a$.

Definition 2 (Observable). *Let* $w = \vec{a_1} \dots \vec{a_n}$ *be a sequence of vectors, and let* ε *be the empty one, then its observable is given by the partial function* $Obs(w) \in \mathbb{R} \cup \mathbb{O} \cup \{\tau\}$ *where:*

$$Obs(\varepsilon) = \varepsilon \qquad Obs(\vec{a}\, w') = \begin{cases} \vec{a}_i\, Obs(w') \text{ if } \forall j \neq i. \vec{a}_j = \square, (\vec{a} \text{ is a offer/request}) \\ \tau\, Obs(w') \ \ (\vec{a} \text{ is a match}) \end{cases}$$

From now onwards we will only consider strings w such that $Obs(w)$ is defined.

Definition 3 (Contract Automata). *Assume as given a finite set of states* $\mathfrak{Q} = \{q_1, q_2, \dots\}$. *Then a* contract automaton *(CA)* $\mathcal{A}$ *of rank* n *is a tuple* $\langle Q, \vec{q_0}, A^r, A^o, T, F \rangle$, *where*

- $Q = Q_1 \times \dots \times Q_n \subseteq \mathfrak{Q}^n$
- $\vec{q_0} \in Q$ *is the initial state*
- $A^r \subseteq \mathbb{R}, A^o \subseteq \mathbb{O}$ *are finite sets of actions*
- $F \subseteq Q$ *is the set of final states*
- $T \subseteq Q \times A \times Q$ *is the set of transitions, where* $A \subseteq (A^r \cup A^o \cup \{\square\})^n$ *and if* $(\vec{q}, \vec{a}, \vec{q'}) \in T$ *then:* $\begin{cases} \vec{a} \text{ is either a request or an offer or a match;} \\ \text{if } \vec{a}_i = \square \text{ then it must be } \vec{q}_i = \vec{q'}_i \end{cases}$

A principal *is a contract automaton of rank 1 such that* $A^r \cap co(A^o) = \emptyset$.
A step $(w, \vec{q}) \rightarrow (w', \vec{q'})$ *occurs iff* $w = \vec{a}w', w' \in A^*$ *and* $(\vec{q}, \vec{a}, \vec{q'}) \in T$.
The language of $\mathcal{A}$ *is* $\mathscr{L}(\mathcal{A}) = \{w \mid (w, \vec{q_0}) \rightarrow^* (\varepsilon, \vec{q}), \vec{q} \in F\}$ *where* $\rightarrow^*$ *is the reflexive, transitive closure of* $\rightarrow$.

Example 1. Figure 1 shows three CAs. The automa $\mathcal{A}_1$ may be understood as producing a certain number of resources through one or more offers $\overline{res}$ and it terminates with the request *sig*. The contract $\mathcal{A}_2$ starts by sending the signal $\overline{sig}$ and then collects resources produced by $\mathcal{A}_1$. The contract $\mathcal{A}_3$ represents the CA where $\mathcal{A}_1$ and $\mathcal{A}_2$ interact. We have that $\mathcal{A}_1, \mathcal{A}_2$ are of rank 1 while $\mathcal{A}_3$ is of rank 2.

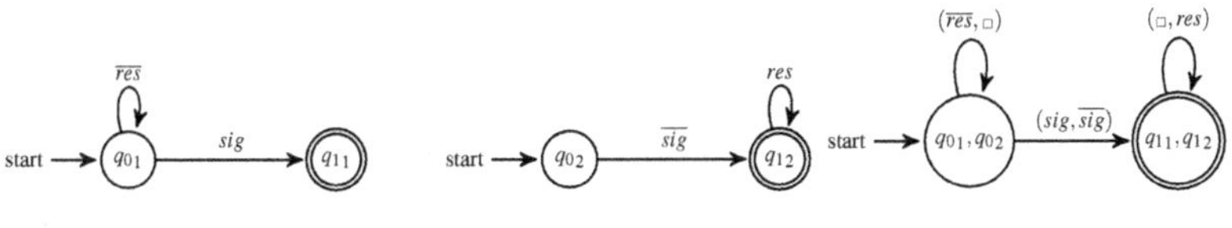

Fig. 1. Three contract automata: from left $\mathcal{A}_1, \mathcal{A}_2$, and $\mathcal{A}_3$

Contract automata can be composed, by making the cartesian product of their states and of the labels of the joined transitions, with the additional possibility of labels recording matching request-offer, as it happens for $\mathcal{A}_3$ in Figure 1.

We introduce two different operators for composing contract automata. Both products interleave all the transitions of their operands. We only force a synchronization to happen when two contract automata are ready on their respective request/offer action. These operators represent two different policies of orchestration. The first operator, $\otimes$, considers the case when a service S joins a group of services already clustered as a single orchestrated service S'. In this case S can only accept the still available offers (requests, respectively) of S' and vice versa. In other words, S cannot interact with the individual components of the orchestration S', but only with S' as a whole. This is not the case with the second operation of composition, $\boxtimes$, that puts instead all the components of S at the same level of those of S'. Any matching request-offer of either contract can be split, and the offers and requests, that become available again, can be re-combined with complementary actions. This second operation of composition turns out to satisfactorily model business processes in dynamically changing environments.

Definition 4 (Product). *Let $\mathcal{A}_i = \langle Q_i, \vec{q_0}^{\,i}, A_i^r, A_i^o, T_i, F_i\rangle, i \in 1\ldots n$ be CA of rank r_i. The product $\bigotimes_{i\in 1\ldots n} \mathcal{A}_i$ is the CA $\langle Q, \vec{q_0}, A^r, A^o, T, F\rangle$ of rank $m = \sum_{i\in 1\ldots n} r_i$, where:*

- $Q = Q_1 \times \ldots \times Q_n$, *where* $\vec{q_0} = \vec{q_0}^{1} \ldots \vec{q_0}^{n}$
- $A^r = \bigcup_{i\in 1\cdots n} A_i^r, \quad A^o = \bigcup_{i\in 1\cdots n} A_i^o$
- $F = \{\vec{q}^{\,1} \ldots \vec{q}^{\,n} \mid \vec{q}^{\,1} \ldots \vec{q}^{\,n} \in Q, \vec{q_i} \in F_i, i \in 1\ldots n\}$
- *T is the least subset of $Q \times A \times Q$ s.t. $(\vec{q}, \vec{c}, \vec{q}\,') \in T$ iff, letting $\vec{q} = \vec{q}_1 \ldots \vec{q}_n \in Q$,*
  - *either there are $1 \leq i < j \leq n$ s.t. $(\vec{q}_i, \vec{a}_i, \vec{q}_i\,') \in T_i$, $(\vec{q}_j, \vec{a}_j, \vec{q}_j\,') \in T_j$, $\vec{a}_i \bowtie \vec{a}_j$ and*
  $$\begin{cases} \vec{c} = \Box^u \vec{a}_i \Box^v \vec{a}_j \Box^z \text{ with } u = r_1 + \ldots + r_{i-1},\ v = r_{i+1} + \ldots + r_{j-1}, |\vec{c}| = m \\ \text{and} \\ \vec{q}\,' = \vec{q}_1 \ldots \vec{q}_{i-1}\ \vec{q}_i\,'\ \vec{q}_{i+1} \ldots\ \vec{q}_{j-1}\ \vec{q}_j\,'\ \vec{q}_{j+1} \ldots \vec{q}_n \end{cases}$$
  - *or $\vec{c} = \Box^u \vec{a}_i \Box^v$ with $u = r_1 + \ldots + r_{i-1}$, $v = r_{i+1} + \ldots + r_n$, and $\vec{q}\,' = \vec{q}_1 \ldots \vec{q}_{i-1}\ \vec{q}_i\,'\ \vec{q}_{i+1} \ldots \vec{q}_n$ when $(\vec{q}_i, \vec{a}_i, \vec{q}_i\,') \in T_i$ and for all $j \neq i$ and $(\vec{q}_j, \vec{a}_j, \vec{q}_j\,') \in T_j$ it does not hold that $\vec{a}_i \bowtie \vec{a}_j$.*

There is an obvious way of retrieving the principals involved in a composition.

Definition 5 (Projection). *Let* $\mathcal{A} = \langle Q, \vec{q_0}, A^r, A^o, T, F\rangle$ *be a contract automaton of rank* n*, then* $\prod^i(\mathcal{A}) = \langle \prod^i(Q), \vec{q}_{i0}, \prod^i(A^r), \prod^i(A^o), \prod^i(T), \prod^i(F)\rangle$ *where:*

$$\prod^i(Q) = \{\vec{q}_i \mid \vec{q} \in Q\} \quad \prod^i(F) = \{\vec{q}_i \mid \vec{q} \in F\} \quad \prod^i(A^r) = \{a \mid a \in A^r, (q, a, q') \in \prod^i(T)\}$$

$$\prod^i(T) = \{(\vec{q}_i, \vec{a}_i, \vec{q'}_i) \mid (\vec{q}, \vec{a}, \vec{q'}) \in T \wedge \vec{a}_i \neq \Box\} \quad \prod^i(A^o) = \{\overline{a} \mid \overline{a} \in A^o, (q, \overline{a}, q') \in \prod^i(T)\}$$

Consider the CAs of Figure 1, we have $\mathcal{A}_1 = \prod^1(\mathcal{A}_3)$ and $\mathcal{A}_2 = \prod^2(\mathcal{A}_3)$.

Property 1 (Product Decomposition). Let $\mathcal{A}_1, \ldots, \mathcal{A}_n$ be a set of principal contract automata, then $\prod^i(\bigotimes_{j \in 1 \ldots n} \mathcal{A}_j) = \mathcal{A}_i$.

Definition 6 (A-Product). *Let* $\mathcal{A}_1, \mathcal{A}_2$ *be two contract automata of rank* n *and* m*, and let* $I = \{\prod^i(\mathcal{A}_1) \mid 0 < i \leq n\} \cup \{\prod^j(\mathcal{A}_2) \mid 0 < j \leq m\}$. *The a-product of* $\mathcal{A}_1$ *and* $\mathcal{A}_2$ *is* $\mathcal{A}_1 \boxtimes \mathcal{A}_2 = \bigotimes_{\mathcal{A}_i \in I} \mathcal{A}_i$

From now on we assume that every contract automaton $\mathcal{A}$ of rank $r_{\mathcal{A}} > 1$ is composed by principal contract automata using the operations of product and a-product.

Note that if $\mathcal{A}, \mathcal{A}'$ are principal contract automata, then $\mathcal{A} \otimes \mathcal{A}' = \mathcal{A} \boxtimes \mathcal{A}'$. E.g. in Figure 1, we have that $\mathcal{A}_3 = \mathcal{A}_1 \otimes \mathcal{A}_2 = \mathcal{A}_1 \boxtimes \mathcal{A}_2$.

Both compositions are commutative, up to suitable rearrangement of the vectors of actions, and $\boxtimes$ is associative, while $\otimes$ is not.

Proposition 1. *The following properties hold:*
- $\exists \mathcal{A}_1, \mathcal{A}_2, \mathcal{A}_3.(\mathcal{A}_1 \otimes \mathcal{A}_2) \otimes \mathcal{A}_3 \neq \mathcal{A}_1 \otimes (\mathcal{A}_2 \otimes \mathcal{A}_3)$
- $\forall \mathcal{A}_1, \mathcal{A}_2, \mathcal{A}_3.(\mathcal{A}_1 \boxtimes \mathcal{A}_2) \boxtimes \mathcal{A}_3 = \mathcal{A}_1 \boxtimes (\mathcal{A}_2 \boxtimes \mathcal{A}_3)$

Example 2. In Figure 2 Alice offers a toy while Bob and Eve perform the same request for the toy of Alice. In the product $(Alice \otimes Bob) \otimes Eve$ the toy is assigned to Bob who first enters in the composition with Alice, no matter if Eve performs the same move. Equally, in the product $(Alice \otimes Eve) \otimes Bob$ the toy is assigned to Eve. In the last row we have the a-product $\mathcal{A}_1 \boxtimes (\mathcal{A}_2 \boxtimes \mathcal{A}_3) = (\mathcal{A}_1 \boxtimes \mathcal{A}_2) \boxtimes \mathcal{A}_3$ which represents a dynamic orchestration: no matter if Eve or Bob enters first the composition with Alice, the toy will be assigned to the first participant who makes the move.

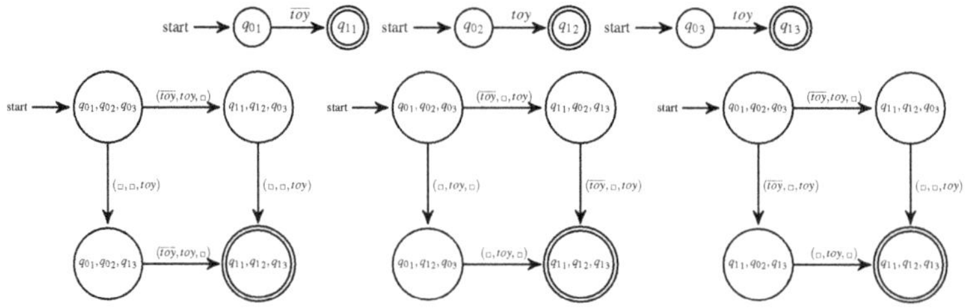

Fig. 2. From left to right and top-down: the contract automata of Alice, Bob and Eve, the contract automata $(Alice \otimes Bob) \otimes Eve$, $(Alice \otimes Eve) \otimes Bob$ and $Alice \boxtimes Bob \boxtimes Eve$.

3 Enforcing Agreement

An *agreement* between different contracts exists only when the final states of the product are reachable from the initial state by strings only made of match and offer actions. Our agreement resembles the notion of *compliance* of [14,15]. Since we use vectors of actions as labels, it is easy to track every action performed by each participant, and to find who is liable in a bad interaction. Our goal is to enforce the behaviour of participants so that they only follow the traces of the automaton which lead to agreement.

We now introduce the notion of *agreement* as a property of the language recognised by a CA; an auxiliary definition helps.

Definition 7 (Agreement). *A word accepted by a CA is in* agreement *if it belongs to the set*

$$\mathfrak{A} = \{w \in (\Sigma^n)^* \mid Obs(w) \in (\mathbb{O} \cup \{\tau\})^*, n > 1\}$$

Example 3. The automa $\mathcal{A}_3$ in Figure 1 has a word in agreement: $Obs((\overline{res}, \square)(sig, \overline{sig})) = \overline{res}\,\tau \in \mathfrak{A}$, and one not: $Obs((sig, \overline{sig})(\square, res)) = \tau\, res \notin \mathfrak{A}$.

Note that the set $\mathfrak{A}$ can be seen as a safety property, where the set of bad prefixes of $\mathfrak{A}$ contains those strings ending with a trailing request, i.e. $\{w\vec{a} \mid w \in \mathfrak{A}, Obs(\vec{a}) \in \mathbb{R}\}$.

Definition 8 (Safety). *A contract automaton $\mathcal{A}$ is* safe *if $\mathscr{L}(\mathcal{A}) \subseteq \mathfrak{A}$, otherwise it is* unsafe. *Additionally, if $\mathscr{L}(\mathcal{A}) \cap \mathfrak{A} \neq \emptyset$ then $\mathcal{A}$* admits agreement.

Example 4. The contract automaton $\mathcal{A}_3$ of Figure 1 is unsafe, but it admits agreement since $\mathscr{L}(\mathcal{A}_3) \cap \mathfrak{A} = (\overline{res}, \square)^*(sig, \overline{sig})$. The contract automaton $Alice \otimes Bob$ of Figure 2 is safe since $\mathscr{L}(Alice \otimes Bob) = (\overline{toy}, toy) \subset \mathfrak{A}$.

We now introduce a technique for driving a safe composition of contracts, in the style of the Supervisory Control for Discrete Event Systems [12]. These are automata, where accepting states represent successful termination of a task, while *forbidden states* are those that should not be traversed in "good" computations. Generally, the purpose is then to synthesize a controller that enforces this property. Here, we devise a way of synthesising an orchestration that leads to safely composed contracts. Also we assume that all the actions are controllable and observable, so the theory guarantees that a most permissive controller exists that never blocks a good computation. Furthermore we assume that a request leads to a forbidden state. Finally, the behaviours that we want to enforce upon $\mathcal{A}$ are exactly those words belonging to $\mathfrak{A} \cap \mathscr{L}(\mathcal{A})$. In order to effectively build such a controller, we introduce below the notion of hanged state, i.e. a state from which no final state can be reached.

Definition 9 (Controller). *Let $\mathcal{A}$ and $\mathcal{K}$ be contract automata, we call $\mathcal{K}$* controller *of $\mathcal{A}$ iff $\mathscr{L}(\mathcal{K}) \subseteq \mathfrak{A} \cap \mathscr{L}(\mathcal{A})$.*
$\mathcal{K}$ is a most permissive controller (mpc) *iff $\forall \mathcal{K}'$ controller of $\mathcal{A}$ it is $\mathscr{L}(\mathcal{K}') \subseteq \mathscr{L}(\mathcal{K})$.*

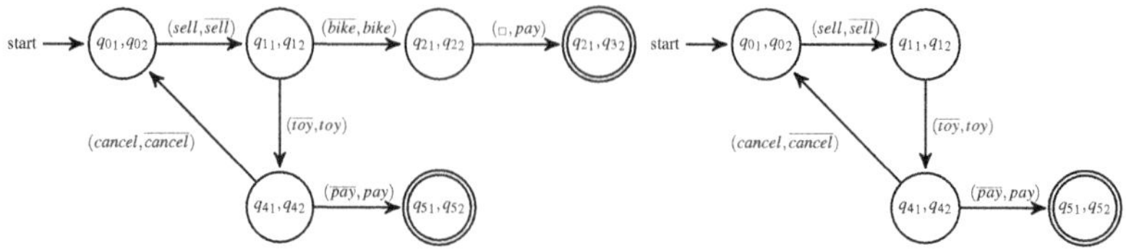

Fig. 3. In the left part the CA $\mathcal{A}$; in the right one its most permissive controller $K_{\mathcal{A}}$

Proposition 2. *Let $\mathcal{K}$ be a mpc of the CA $\mathcal{A}$, then $\mathscr{L}(\mathcal{K}) = \mathfrak{A} \cap \mathscr{L}(\mathcal{A})$.*

Definition 10 (Hanged state). *Let $\mathcal{A} = \langle Q, \vec{q_0}, A^r, A^o, T, F\rangle$ be a CA, then $\vec{q} \in Q$ is* hanged, *and belongs to the set $Hanged(\mathcal{A})$, if given $\vec{q_f} \in F, \nexists w.(w, \vec{q}) \rightarrow^* (\varepsilon, \vec{q_f})$.*

Definition 11 (Building the mpc)
Let $\mathcal{A} = \langle Q, \vec{q_0}, A^r, A^o, T, F\rangle$ be a CA, $\mathcal{K}_1 = \langle Q, \vec{q_0}, A^r, A^o, T \setminus (\{t \in T \mid t$ is a request transition $\}, F\rangle$ and define

$$\mathcal{K}_{\mathcal{A}} = \langle Q \setminus Hanged(\mathcal{K}_1), \vec{q_0}, A^r, A^o, T_{\mathcal{K}_1} \setminus \{(\vec{q}, a, \vec{q'}) \mid \{\vec{q}, \vec{q'}\} \cap Hanged(\mathcal{K}_1) \neq \emptyset\}, F\rangle$$

Proposition 3 (MPC). *The controller $\mathcal{K}_{\mathcal{A}}$ of Definition 11 is the mpc of the CA $\mathcal{A}$.*

Example 5. In Figure 3 we have a simple selling scenario involving two parties Alice and Bob, who is willing to pay the toy, only. We first compute the auxiliary set $\mathcal{K}_1$ that does not contain the transition $((q_{21}, q_{22}), (\Box, pay), (q_{21}, q_{32}))$ because it represents a request of the second participant which is not fulfilled. As a consequence, some states become hanged: $Hanged(\mathcal{K}_1) = \{(q_{21}, q_{22}), (q_{21}, q_{32})\}$. By removing them, we eventually obtain the mpc controller of $\mathcal{A}$. Indeed this transition represents a request of the second participant which is not fulfilled. Once the request is removed, some hanged states are generated, in particular we have $Hanged(\mathcal{K}_1) = \{(q_{21}, q_{22}), (q_{21}, q_{32})\}$. By removing the hanged states and corresponding transition the mpc $K_{\mathcal{A}}$ is obtained.

Property 2. Let $\mathcal{A}$ be a contract automaton and let $\mathcal{K}_{\mathcal{A}}$ be its mpc. If $\mathscr{L}(\mathcal{K}_{\mathcal{A}}) = \mathscr{L}(\mathcal{A})$ then $\mathcal{A}$ is safe, otherwise if $\mathscr{L}(\mathcal{K}_{\mathcal{A}}) \subset \mathscr{L}(\mathcal{A})$ then $\mathcal{A}$ is unsafe. Additionally, if $\mathscr{L}(\mathcal{K}_{\mathcal{A}}) \neq \emptyset$, then $\mathcal{A}$ admits agreement.

We introduce now a novel notion of *liability*, that characterises those participants potentially responsible of the divergence from the expected behaviour. The liable participants are those who perform the first transition in a run, that is not possible in the most permissive controller. As noticed above, after this step is done, a successful state cannot be reached any longer, and so the participants who performed it will be blamed. (Note in passing that hanged states play a crucial role here: just removing the request transitions from $\mathcal{A}$ would result in a CA language equivalent to the mpc, but detecting liable participants would be much more intricate).

Definition 12 (Liability). *Let $\mathcal{A}$ be a CA and $\mathcal{K}_{\mathcal{A}}$ be the mpc of Definition 11; let $\rightarrow_{\mathcal{A}}$ and $\rightarrow_{\mathcal{K}_{\mathcal{A}}}$ be steps performed by $\mathcal{A}$ and $\mathcal{K}_{\mathcal{A}}$, resp.; let $(v\vec{a}w, \vec{q_0}) \rightarrow^*_{\mathcal{K}_{\mathcal{A}}} (\vec{a}w, \vec{q})$ be a run such that $(\vec{a}w, \vec{q}) \rightarrow_{\mathcal{A}} (w, \vec{q'})$ and $(\vec{a}w, \vec{q}) \not\rightarrow_{K_{\mathcal{A}}} (w, \vec{q'})$. The participants $\Pi^i(\mathcal{A})$ such that $\vec{a}_i \neq \Box, i \in 1 \ldots r_{\mathcal{A}}$ are* liable for *$v\vec{a}$ and belong to $Liable(\mathcal{A}, v\vec{a})$.*

The set of liable *participants in $\mathcal{A}$ is $Liable(\mathcal{A}) = \{i \mid \exists w. i \in Liable(\mathcal{A}, w)\}$.*

Example 6. In Figure 3 we have $Liable(\mathcal{A}) = \{1, 2\}$, hence both Alice and Bob are possibly liable, because the match transition with label $(\overline{bike}, bike)$ can be performed, that leads to a violation of the agreement.

Proposition 4. *A CA $\mathcal{A}$ is safe iff $Liable(\mathcal{A}) = \emptyset$.*

Note that the set $Liable(\mathcal{A})$ is easily computable as follows.

Lemma 1. *Let $\mathcal{A}$ be a CA and $\mathcal{K}_{\mathcal{A}}$ be its mpc as in Definition 11, then*

$$Liable(\mathcal{A}) = \{i \mid (\vec{q}, \vec{a}, \vec{q'}) \in T_{\mathcal{A}}, \vec{a}_i \neq \Box, \vec{q} \in Q_{K_{\mathcal{A}}}, \vec{q'} \notin Q_{K_{\mathcal{A}}}\}$$

Some properties of $\otimes$ and $\boxtimes$ follow, that enable us to predict under which conditions a composition is safe without actually computing it.

We first introduce the notions of collaborative and competitive contracts. Intuitively, two contracts are *collaborative* if some requests of one meet the offers of the other, and are *competitive* if both can satisfy the same request.

Definition 13 (Competitive, Collaborative)
The pair of CA $\mathcal{A}_1 = \langle Q_1, q_{01}, A^r_1, A^o_1, T_1, F_1\rangle$ and $\mathcal{A}_2 = \langle Q_2, q_{02}, A^r_2, A^o_2, T_2, F_2\rangle$ are

- competitive *if $A^o_1 \cap A^o_2 \cap co(A^r_1 \cup A^r_2) \neq \emptyset$*
- collaborative *if $(A^o_1 \cap co(A^r_2)) \cup (co(A^r_1) \cap A^o_2) \neq \emptyset$.*

The offers shared by $\mathcal{A}_1$ and $\mathcal{A}_2$ are $A^o_1 \cap A^o_2$, while all their requests are $A^r_1 \cup A^r_2$. If there is an offer provided by both participants that is matched by a request of one of the two CAs, that is $A^o_1 \cap A^o_2 \cap co(A^r_1 \cup A^r_2) \neq \emptyset$, then the CAs are *competitive.* Note that *competitive* and *collaborative* are not mutually exclusive, as formally proved below. Moreover if two contract automata are *non-competitive* then all their match actions are preserved in the composition, indeed we have $\mathcal{A}_1 \boxtimes \mathcal{A}_2 = \mathcal{A}_1 \otimes \mathcal{A}_2$.

Example 7. The CAs *Alice*, *Bob*$\otimes$*Eve* in Figure 2 are collaborative and not competitive, indeed there is a match on the toy action but no participant interferes in this match. In Example 8 the pair $\mathcal{A}_1, \mathcal{A}_2$ is competitive since $\mathcal{A}_2$ interferes with $\mathcal{A}_1$ on the toy offer.

The next theorem says that the composition of safe non-competitive contracts prevents all participants from harmful interactions, unlike the case of safe competitive contracts. In other words, when $\mathcal{A}_1$ and $\mathcal{A}_2$ are safe, no participants will be found liable in $\mathcal{A}_1 \otimes \mathcal{A}_2$ (i.e. $Liable(\mathcal{A}_1 \otimes \mathcal{A}_2) = \emptyset$), and the same happens for $\mathcal{A}_1 \boxtimes \mathcal{A}_2$ if the two are also non-competitive (i.e. $Liable(\mathcal{A}_1 \boxtimes \mathcal{A}_2) = \emptyset$).

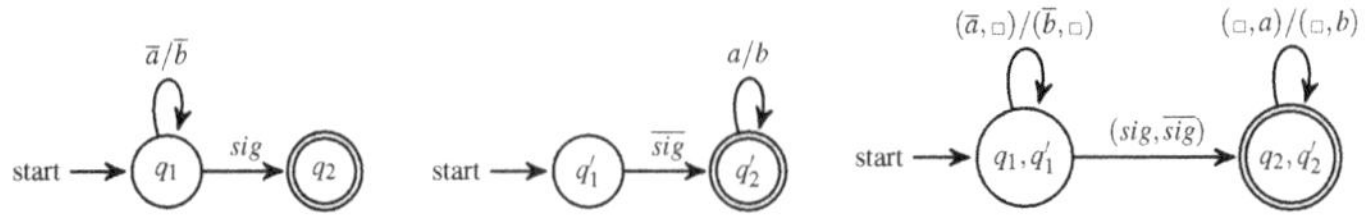

Fig. 4. From left to right: $\mathcal{A}_4, \mathcal{A}_5$, and $\mathcal{A}_4 \otimes \mathcal{A}_5$

Theorem 1. *If two CA $\mathcal{A}_1$ and $\mathcal{A}_2$ are*

1. *competitive then they are collaborative,*
2. *safe then $\mathcal{A}_1 \otimes \mathcal{A}_2$ is safe, $\mathcal{A}_1 \boxtimes \mathcal{A}_2$ admits agreement,*
3. *non-collaborative, and one or both unsafe, then $\mathcal{A}_1 \otimes \mathcal{A}_2, \mathcal{A}_1 \boxtimes \mathcal{A}_2$ are unsafe,*
4. *safe and non-competitive, then $\mathcal{A}_1 \boxtimes \mathcal{A}_2$ is safe.*

Example 8. We feel free to present contract automata through a sort of extended regular expressions. So, let $\mathcal{A}_1 = \overline{toy} + bike \otimes toy + \overline{bike}$ and $\mathcal{A}_2 = \overline{toy}$. Both contracts are safe, but competitive, and $\mathcal{A}_1 \boxtimes \mathcal{A}_2$ is unsafe because $(\Box, toy, \overline{toy})(bike, \Box, \Box) \in \mathscr{L}(\mathcal{A})$.

4 Weak Agreement

The literature considers many different types of agreement, including one where actions are taken on credit if in the future the obligations will be honoured. This last notion is introduced for accepting as good those compositions of contracts where all the requests are matched by offers, but an agreement is not reached due to lack of synchronous match actions. This is a common scenario in contract composition, where each participant requires its requests to be satisfied before providing the corresponding offers. This kind of agreement has been faced using a variety of formal techniques as Process Algebras, Petri Nets, non classical Logics, Event Structures [2,3,6,7]. A simple example follows.

Example 9. Suppose Alice and Bob want to share a bike and a toy, but neither trusts the other. Before providing their offer they first ask for the complementary request. As regular expressions: $Alice = toy.\overline{bike}$ and $Bob = bike.\overline{toy}$. Their composition is: $Alice \otimes Bob = (toy, \Box)(\overline{bike}, bike)(\Box, \overline{toy}) + (\Box, bike)(toy, \overline{toy})(\overline{bike}, \Box)$. In both possible runs the contracts fail on exchanging the bike or the toy, hence $\mathscr{L}(Alice \otimes Bob) \cap \mathfrak{A} = \emptyset$ and the composition does not admit agreement.

The circularity in the requests/offers is solved by weakening the notion of agreement, allowing a request to be performed on credit if in the future a complementary offer will occur. We will say that a contract automaton admits *weak agreement* if there exists a run in which every request can be paired with the corresponding offer, allowing asynchronous matches between requests and offers. Of course, agreement is a proper subset of weak agreement. As for agreement, we have an auxiliary definition.

Definition 14 (Weak Agreement). *A word accepted by a CA of rank* $n > 1$ *is in* weak agreement *if it belongs to* $\mathfrak{W} = \{w \in (\Sigma^n)^* \mid |w| = m, \exists$ *a function* $f : [1..m] \to [1..m]$ *total and injective on the requests of* w*, and such that* $f(i) = j$ *only if* $\vec{a}^i \bowtie \vec{a}^j\}$.

Example 10. Consider $\mathcal{A}_3$ in Figure 1, whose run $(\overline{res}, \square)(sig, \overline{sig})(\square, res)$ is in $\mathfrak{W}$ but not in $\mathfrak{A}$, while $(\overline{res}, \square)(sig, \overline{sig})(\square, res)(\square, res) \notin \mathfrak{W}$.

Definition 15 (Weak Safety). *A contract automaton* $\mathcal{A}$ *is* weakly safe *if* $\mathscr{L}(\mathcal{A}) \subseteq \mathfrak{W}$*, otherwise is weakly unsafe. If* $\mathscr{L}(\mathcal{A}) \cap \mathfrak{W} \neq \emptyset$ *then* $\mathcal{A}$ admits weak agreement.

Example 11. In Example 9 we have $\mathscr{L}(Alice \otimes Bob) \subset \mathfrak{W}$, hence the composition of *Alice* and *Bob* is weakly safe.

The following is an analogous of Theorem 1.

Theorem 2. *Let* $\mathcal{A}_1, \mathcal{A}_2$ *be two CA, then if* $\mathcal{A}_1, \mathcal{A}_2$ *are*

1. *weakly safe then* $\mathcal{A}_1 \otimes \mathcal{A}_2$ *is weakly safe,* $\mathcal{A}_1 \boxtimes \mathcal{A}_2$ *admits weak agreement*
2. *non-collaborative and one or both unsafe, then* $\mathcal{A}_1 \otimes \mathcal{A}_2, \mathcal{A}_1 \boxtimes \mathcal{A}_2$ *are weakly unsafe*
3. *safe and non-competitive, then* $\mathcal{A}_1 \boxtimes \mathcal{A}_2$ *is weakly safe.*

The example below shows that weak agreement is not a context-free notion, in language theoretical sense; rather it is context-sensitive. Therefore, we cannot define a controller for weak agreement in terms of CA.

Example 12. Let $\mathcal{A}_4$, $\mathcal{A}_5$ and $\mathcal{A}_4 \otimes \mathcal{A}_5$ be the automata in Figure 4, then we have that $L = \mathfrak{W} \cap \mathscr{L}(\mathcal{A}_4 \otimes \mathcal{A}_5) \neq \emptyset$ is not context-free. Consider the following regular language $L' = \{(\overline{a}, \square)^*(\overline{b}, \square)^*(sig, \overline{sig})(\square, a)^*(\square, b)^*\}$. We have that $L \cap L'$ is not context-free (by pumping lemma), and since L' is regular L is not context-free.

Theorem 3. $\mathfrak{W}$ *is a context-sensitive language, but not context-free.*

The language $\mathfrak{W}$ is *mildly* context-sensitive, and checking membership can be done through *two way deterministic pushdown automata* (2DPDA) in $O(n^2 log(n))$ time and $O(n)$ space [17]. A 2DPDA is a push-down automaton with a read-only input tape readable backward and forward. To check whether $w \in \mathfrak{W}$ we scroll the input tape twice for each action: the first time all the requests of the selected action are pushed and then, the second time we scroll the tape, when an offer of the same action is encountered we pop a request from the stack. At the end if the stack is empty the string w is in $\mathfrak{W}$.

In general, it is undecidable deciding whether a regular language L is included in a context-sensitive one, as well as checking emptiness of the intersection of a regular language with a context-sensitive one. In our case, however, these problems are decidable and so we can check whether a contract automaton $\mathcal{A}$ is weakly safe, or whether it admits weak agreement.

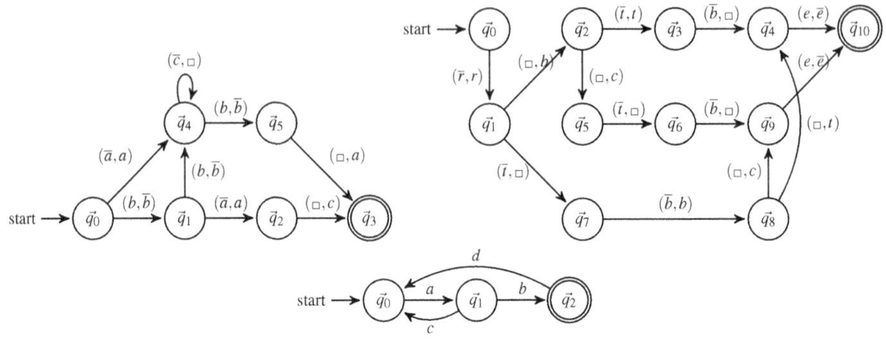

Fig. 5. Top left: a product of two CA; top right a booking service; bottom: a principal CA.

The technique we propose amounts to find optimal solutions of network flow problems [18]. We first fix some useful notation. Assume as given a CA $\mathcal{A}$, with a single final state $\vec{q_f} \neq \vec{q_0}$ (this condition can easily be met, by slightly manipulating a CA with many final states); assume the requests and the transitions of $\mathcal{A}$ be enumerated, i.e. $A^r = \{a^i \mid i \in I_l = \{1, 2, \ldots, l\}\}$ and $T = \{t_1, \ldots, t_n\}$; let $FS(\vec{q}) = \{(\vec{q}, \vec{a}, \vec{q'}) \mid (\vec{q}, \vec{a}, \vec{q'}) \in T\}$ be the *forward star* of a node $\vec{q}$, and let $BS(\vec{q}) = \{(\vec{q'}, \vec{a}, \vec{q}) \mid (\vec{q'}, \vec{a}, \vec{q}) \in T\}$ be its *backward star*. For each transition t_i we introduce the flow variables $x_{t_i} \in \mathbb{N}$, and $z_{t_i}^{\vec{q}} \in \mathbb{R}$ where $\vec{q} \in Q, \vec{q} \neq \vec{q_0}$. Now we define the following set $F_{\vec{s},\vec{d}}$ of *flow constraints*, an element of which $\vec{x} = (x_{t_1}, \ldots, x_{t_n}) \in F_{\vec{s},\vec{d}}$ defines runs from the source state $\vec{s}$ to the target state $\vec{d}$; as an abbreviation, we will write F_x for $F_{\vec{q_0},\vec{q_f}}$. The intuition is that each variable x_{t_i} represents how many times the transition t_i is traversed in the runs defined by $\vec{x}$. A simple example follows; hereafter we identify a transition by its source and target states.

Example 13. Figure 5 (right) shows a simple service of booking. The contract of the client requires to book a room (r), including breakfast (b) and a transport service, by car (c) or taxi (t); finally it sends a signal of termination ($\overline{e}$); briefly $C = r.b.(c + t).\overline{e}$. The hotel offers a room, breakfast and taxi: $H = \overline{r}.\overline{t}.\overline{b}.e$. The composition $C \otimes H$ has four complete traces: $w_1 = (\overline{r}, r)(\square, b)(\overline{t}, t)(\overline{b}, \square)(e, \overline{e})$, $w_2 = (\overline{r}, r)(\square, b)(\square, c)(\overline{t}, \square)(\overline{b}, \square)(e, \overline{e})$, $w_3 = (\overline{r}, r)(\overline{t}, \square)(\overline{b}, b)(\square, t)(e, \overline{e})$, $w_4 = (\overline{r}, r)(\overline{t}, \square)\ (\overline{b}, b)(\square, c)(e, \overline{e})$. We now detail the flows associated with each trace giving the set of variables with value 1, all the others having value 0, because there are no loops. For w_1: $\{x_{\vec{q_0},\vec{q_1}}, x_{\vec{q_1},\vec{q_2}}, x_{\vec{q_2},\vec{q_3}}, x_{\vec{q_3},\vec{q_4}}, x_{\vec{q_4},\vec{q_{10}}},\}$ for w_2: $\{x_{\vec{q_0},\vec{q_1}}, x_{\vec{q_1},\vec{q_2}}, x_{\vec{q_2},\vec{q_5}}, x_{\vec{q_5},\vec{q_6}}, x_{\vec{q_6},\vec{q_9}}, x_{\vec{q_9},\vec{q_{10}}}\}$; for w_3: $\{x_{\vec{q_0},\vec{q_1}}, x_{\vec{q_1},\vec{q_7}}, x_{\vec{q_7},\vec{q_8}}, x_{\vec{q_8},\vec{q_4}}, x_{\vec{q_4},\vec{q_{10}}}\}$; and for w_4: $\{x_{\vec{q_0},\vec{q_1}}, x_{\vec{q_1},\vec{q_7}}, x_{\vec{q_7},\vec{q_8}}, x_{\vec{q_8},\vec{q_9}}, x_{\vec{q_9},\vec{q_{10}}}\}$.

As a matter of fact, a flow $\vec{x}$ may represent many runs that have the same balance of requests/offers for each action occurring therein. As an example, consider the CA at the bottom of Figure 5 and the flow $x_{\vec{q_0},\vec{q_1}} = 3, x_{\vec{q_1},\vec{q_2}} = 2, x_{\vec{q_2},\vec{q_0}} = x_{\vec{q_1},\vec{q_0}} = 1$ that represents both $w_1 = acabdab$ and $w_2 = abdacab$.

The definition of $F_{\vec{s},\vec{d}}$ follows. The auxiliary variables $z^{\vec{q}}_{t_i}$ occurring there represent $|Q|-1$ auxiliary flows and make sure that $\vec{x}$ represent valid runs, i.e. there are no disconnected cycles with positive flow; a more detailed discussion on them is in Example 14 below. Note also that the values of $z^{\vec{q}}_{t_i}$ are *not* integers, and so we are defining Mixed Integer Linear Programming problems that have efficient solutions [18].

$$F_{\vec{s},\vec{d}} = \{(x_{t_1},\ldots,x_{t_n}) \mid \forall \vec{q} : (\sum_{t_i \in BS(\vec{q})} x_{t_i} - \sum_{t_i \in FS(\vec{q})} x_{t_i}) = \begin{cases} -1 \text{ if } \vec{q} = \vec{s} \\ 0 \quad \text{if } \vec{q} \neq \vec{s}, \vec{d} \\ 1 \quad \text{if } \vec{q} = \vec{d} \end{cases}$$

$$\forall \vec{q} \neq \vec{s}, t_i. \quad 0 \leq z^{\vec{q}}_{t_i} \leq x_{t_i},$$

$$\forall \vec{q} \neq \vec{s}, \forall \vec{q'} : (\sum_{t_i \in BS(\vec{q'})} z^{\vec{q}}_{t_i} - \sum_{t_i \in FS(\vec{q'})} z^{\vec{q}}_{t_i}) = \begin{cases} -p^{\vec{q}} \text{ if } \vec{q'} = \vec{s} \\ 0 \quad \text{if } \vec{q'} \neq \vec{s}, \vec{q} \\ p^{\vec{q}} \quad \text{if } \vec{q'} = \vec{q} \end{cases} \quad \text{where}$$

$$p^{\vec{q}} = \begin{cases} 1 \text{ if } \sum_{t_i \in FS(\vec{q})} x_{t_i} > 0 \\ 0 \; otherwise \end{cases} \qquad \}$$

We eventually define a set of variables $a^i_{t_j}$ for each action and each transition, that take the value -1 for requests, 1 for offers, and 0 otherwise; they help counting the difference between offers and requests of an action in a flow.

$$\forall t_j = (\vec{q}, \vec{a}, \vec{q'}) \in T, \forall i \in I_l : \quad a^i_{t_j} = \begin{cases} 1 \quad \text{if } Obs(\vec{a}) = \overline{a^i} \\ -1 \text{ if } Obs(\vec{a}) = a^i \\ 0 \quad otherwise \end{cases}$$

Example 14. Figure 5 (left) depicts the contract $A \otimes B$, where $A = \overline{a}.\overline{c}^*.b + b.(b.\overline{c}^*.b + \overline{a})$ and $B = a.\overline{b}.a + \overline{b}.(\overline{b}.\overline{b}.a + a.c)$. To check whether there exists a run recognizing a trace w with less or equal requests than the offers (for each action) we solve $\sum_{t_j} a^i_{t_j} x_{t_j} \geq 0$, for $\vec{x} \in F_x$.

We now discuss the role of the auxiliary variables $z^{\vec{q}}_{t_i}$. As said, they are used to ensure that the solutions considered represent valid runs. Consider the following assignment to $\vec{x}$: $x_{\vec{q_0},\vec{q_1}} = x_{\vec{q_1},\vec{q_2}} = x_{\vec{q_2},\vec{q_3}} = 1, x_{\vec{q_4},\vec{q_4}} \geq 1$, and null everywhere else. It does not represent valid runs, because the transition $(\vec{q_4}, (\overline{c}, \square), \vec{q_4})$ cannot be fired in a run that only takes transitions with non-null value in $\vec{x}$. Note that the constraints on $\vec{x}$ are satisfied (e.g. we have $\sum_{t_j \in FS(\vec{q_4})} x_{t_j} = \sum_{t_j \in BS(\vec{q_4})} x_{t_j}$). Indeed, the constraints on the auxiliary $z^{\vec{q}}_{t_i}$ are introduced for checking if a node is reachable from the initial state on a run defined by the flow $\vec{x}$; note that their value being not integer is immaterial for checking that. The assignment above is not valid since for $z^{\vec{q_4}}$ we have $0 \leq z^{\vec{q_4}}_{(\vec{q_0},\vec{q_4})} \leq x_{(\vec{q_0},\vec{q_4})} = 0, 0 \leq z^{\vec{q_4}}_{(\vec{q_1},\vec{q_4})} \leq x_{(\vec{q_1},\vec{q_4})} = 0, 0 \leq z^{\vec{q_4}}_{(\vec{q_4},\vec{q_5})} \leq x_{(\vec{q_4},\vec{q_5})} = 0$, hence $\sum_{t_j \in BS(\vec{q_4})} z^{\vec{q_4}}_{t_j} = z^{\vec{q_4}}_{(\vec{q_4},\vec{q_4})}, \sum_{t_j \in FS(\vec{q_4})} z^{\vec{q_4}}_{t_j} = z^{\vec{q_4}}_{(\vec{q_4},\vec{q_4})}$ and we have $\sum_{t_j \in BS(\vec{q_4})} z^{\vec{q_4}}_{t_j} - \sum_{t_j \in FS(\vec{q_4})} z^{\vec{q_4}}_{t_j} = 0 \neq 1$.

Finally, note in passing that there are no valid flows $\vec{x} \in F_x$ for this problem.

Our main results follow.

Theorem 4. *Let $\vec{v}$ be a binary vector. Then a CA $\mathcal{A}$ is* weakly safe *iff min* $\gamma \geq 0$ *where:*

$$\sum_{i \in I_l} v_i \sum_{t_j \in T} a^i_{t_j} x_{t_j} \leq \gamma \quad \sum_{i \in I_l} v_i = 1 \quad \forall i \in I_l . v_i \in \{0,1\} \quad (x_{t_1} \dots x_{t_n}) \in F_x \quad \gamma \in \mathbb{R}$$

The minimum value of γ selects the trace and the action a for which the difference between the number of offers and requests is the minimal achievable from $\mathcal{A}$. If this difference is non negative, there will always be enough offers matching the requests, and so $\mathcal{A}$ will never generate a trace not in $\mathfrak{W}$: $\mathcal{A}$ is *weakly safe*, otherwise it is not.

Example 15. Consider again Example 13 and let $a^1 = r$, $a^2 = b$, $a^3 = t$, $a^4 = c$, $a^5 = e$.

If $v_1 = 1$, for each flow $\vec{x} \in F_x$, we have that $\sum_{t_j} a^1_{t_j} x_{t_j} = 0$ (for $i \neq 1$, we have $v_i = 0$). This means that the request of a room is always satisfied. Similarly for breakfast and the termination signal e. If $v_3 = 1$, for the flow representing the traces w_1, w_3 we have $\sum_{t_j} a^3_{t_j} x_{t_j} = 0$, while for the flow representing the traces w_2, w_4 the result is 1. Also in this case the requests are satisfied. Instead, when $v_4 = 1$, for the flow representing the traces w_1, w_4 we have $\sum_{t_j} a^4_{t_j} x_{t_j} = 0$, but for the flow representing w_2, w_3, the result is -1. Hence $\min \gamma = -1$, and the CA $H \otimes C$ is not *weak safe*, indeed we have $w_2, w_3 \notin \mathfrak{W}$.

Theorem 5. *The CA $\mathcal{A}$ admits weak agreement iff :*

$$max\ \gamma \geq 0 \quad and \quad \forall i \in I_l . \sum_{t_j \in T} a^i_{t_j}\ x_{t_j} \geq \gamma \quad (x_{t_1} \dots x_{t_n}) \in F_x \quad \gamma \in \mathbb{R}$$

The maximum value of γ in Theorem 5 selects the trace w that maximizes the least difference between offers and requests of an action in w. If this value is non negative, then there exists a trace w such that for all the actions in it, the offers are more or as many the requests. In this case, $\mathcal{A}$ admits weak agreement; otherwise it does not.

Example 16. In Example 13, $\max \gamma = -1$ for the flows representing the traces w_2, w_3 and $\max \gamma = 0$ for those of the traces w_1, w_4, that will be part of the solution and are indeed in weak agreement. Consequently, $H \otimes C$ admits *weak agreement.*

We define now the *weakly liable* participants: those who perform the first transition t of a run such that after t it is not possible any more to obtain a trace in $\mathfrak{W}$, i.e. leading to traces $w \in \mathscr{L}(\mathcal{A}) \setminus \mathfrak{W}$ that can not be extended to $ww' \in \mathscr{L}(\mathcal{A}) \cap \mathfrak{W}$.

Definition 16. *Let $\mathcal{A}$ be a CA and let $w = w_1 \vec{a} w_2$ such that $w \in \mathscr{L}(\mathcal{A}) \setminus \mathfrak{W}, \forall w'. ww' \notin \mathscr{L}(\mathcal{A}) \cap \mathfrak{W}, \forall w_3 . w_1 \vec{a} w_3 \notin \mathscr{L}(\mathcal{A}) \cap \mathfrak{W}$ and $\exists w_4 . w_1 w_4 \in \mathscr{L}(\mathcal{A}) \cap \mathfrak{W}$. The participants $\Pi^i(\mathcal{A})$ such that $\vec{a}_i \neq \square$ are* weakly liable *and are denoted with $i \in WLiable(\mathcal{A}, w_1 \vec{a})$.*

Let $WLiable(\mathcal{A}) = \{i \mid \exists w$ such that $i \in WLiable(\mathcal{A}, w)\}$ be the set of all potentially weakly liable *participants in $\mathcal{A}$.*

For computing the set $WLiable(\mathcal{A})$ we optimize a network flow problem for a transition $\bar{t}$ to check if there exists a trace w in which $\bar{t}$ reveals some weakly liable participants. By solving this problem for all transitions we obtain the set $WLiable(\mathcal{A})$.

Theorem 6. *The participant $\Pi^i(\mathcal{A})$ of a CA $\mathcal{A}$ is* weakly liable *if and only if there exists a transition $\bar{t} = (\vec{q_s}, \vec{a}, \vec{q_t})$, $\vec{a}_i \neq \Box$, and $\gamma_{\bar{t}} < 0$, where*

$$\gamma_{\bar{t}} = \mathsf{min}\ \{f(\vec{x}) \mid \vec{x} \in F_{\vec{q_0},\vec{q_s}},\ \vec{y} \in F_{\vec{q_s},\vec{q_f}},\ \forall i \in I_l.\ \sum_{t_j \in T} a^i_{t_j}(x_{t_j} + y_{t_j}) \geq 0\}$$

$$f(\vec{x}) = \mathsf{max}\ \{\gamma \mid \vec{u} \in F_{\vec{q_t},\vec{q_f}},\ \forall i \in I_l.\ \sum_{t_j \in T} a^i_{t_j}(x_{t_j} + u_{t_j}) + a^i_{\bar{t}} \geq \gamma, \gamma \in \mathbb{R}\}$$

Intuitively, the flow defined above is split into three parts: the flow $\vec{x}$ goes from $\vec{q_0}$ to $\vec{q_s}$, the flow $\vec{y}$ goes from $\vec{q_s}$ to $\vec{q_f}$, and the flow $\vec{u}$ goes from $\vec{q_t}$ to $\vec{q_f}$.

The function f takes in input the flow $\vec{x}$ and selects a flow $\vec{u}$ such that by concatenating $\vec{x}$ and $\vec{u}$ through $\bar{t}$ we obtain a trace w, where the least difference between offers and requests is maximized for an action in w. Using the same argument of Theorem 5, if the value computed is negative, then there not exists a flow $\vec{u}$ that composed with $\vec{x}$ selects traces in weak agreement.

Finally $\gamma_{\bar{t}}$ yields the minimal result of $f(\vec{x})$, provided that there exists a flow $\vec{y}$, that combined with $\vec{x}$ represents only traces in weak agreement. If $\gamma_{\bar{t}} < 0$ then the transition $\bar{t}$ identifies some *weakly liable* participants. Indeed the flow $\vec{x}$ represents the traces w such that (1) $\exists w_1$, represented by $\vec{y}$, with $ww_1 \in \mathscr{L}(\mathcal{A}) \cap \mathfrak{W}$ and (2) $\forall w_2$, represented by $\vec{u}$, with $w\vec{a}w_2 \in \mathscr{L}(\mathcal{A}) \setminus \mathfrak{W}$. Note that if a flow $\vec{x}$ reveals some weakly liable participants, the minimization carried on by $\gamma_{\bar{t}}$ guarantees that the relevant transition $\bar{t}$ is found.

Example 17. In Figure 5 (right), the transitions $(\vec{q_2}, (\Box, c), \vec{q_5}), (\vec{q_8}, (\Box, c), \vec{q_9})$ reveal the participant 2 *weakly liable.* Indeed from $\vec{q_2}$ the trace $(\bar{r}, r)(\Box, b)$ can be extended to one in weak agreement, while $(\bar{r}, r)(\Box, b)(\Box, c)$ cannot. Also the trace $(\bar{r}, r)(\bar{t}, \Box)(\bar{b}, b)$ can be extended to one in weak agreement while $(\bar{r}, r)(\bar{t}, \Box)(\bar{b}, b)(\Box, c)$ cannot.

For the transition $(\vec{q_2}, (\Box, c), \vec{q_5})$ we have the trace $(\bar{r}, r)(\Box, b)$ for the flow $\vec{x}$ and $(\bar{t}, t)(\bar{b}, \Box)(e, \bar{e})$ for the flow $\vec{y}$, and we have $\forall i \in I_l. \sum_{t \in T} a^i_t(x_t + y_t) \geq 0$. Note that if we select as flow $\vec{y}$ the trace $(\Box, c)(\bar{t}, \Box)(\bar{b}, \Box)(e, \bar{e})$ then the constraints $\forall i \in I_l. \sum_{t_j \in T} a^i_{t_j}(x_{t_j} + y_{t_j}) \geq 0$ are not satisfied for the action $a^4 = c$. For the flow $\vec{u}$ the only possible trace is $(\bar{t}, \Box)(\bar{b}, \Box)(e, \bar{e})$, and $\mathsf{max}\ \gamma = -1 = \gamma_{(\vec{q_2},(\Box,c),\vec{q_5})}$ since $\sum_{t_j \in T} a^4_{t_j}(x_{t_j} + u_{t_j}) + (-1) = -1$.

For the transition $(\vec{q_8}, (\Box, c), \vec{q_9})$ the flow $\vec{x}$ selects the trace $(\bar{r}, r)(\bar{t}, \Box)(\bar{b}, b)$, the flow $\vec{y}$ selects the trace $(\Box, t)(e, \bar{e})$, since the other possible trace, that is $(\Box, c)(e, \bar{e})$, does not respect the constraints for the action a^4. Finally, for the flow $\vec{u}$ we have the trace $(e, \bar{e})$, and as the previous case $\mathsf{max}\ \gamma = -1 = \gamma_{(\vec{q_8},(\Box,c),\vec{q_9})}$.

5 Conclusions and Related Work

We have introduced an original approach to contract composition for services. In our proposal contract composition is handled formally by taking advantage of the novel class of Contract Automata and of their compositional operators. The algebra of Contract Automata allows one to compose services according to two different notions of orchestrations: one when a participant joins an existing orchestration without a global reconfiguration, and the other when a global adaptive re-orchestration is required. We have defined notions that illustrate when a composition of contracts enjoys interesting properties, namely agreement and safety, both in the case when requests are satisfied by offers synchronously and asynchronously. Furthermore, a notion of liability has been put forward. A liable participant is the service leading the contract composition into a failing state. Key results of the paper prove the correctness of our approach by taking advantage of optimization techniques borrowed from Operational Research. Using them, we efficiently find the optimal solutions of the flow in the network automatically derived from contract automata. An interesting topic to investigate concerns whether and how our results and techniques can be used to define choreographies of services and their properties, in particular liability.

A main advantage of our framework is that it supports development of automatic verification tools for checking and verifying properties of contract composition. The formal treatment of contract composition in terms of optimal solutions of network flows paves the way of exploiting efficient optimization algorithms. We plan to develop such verification tools.

Related Work. The problem of formalizing contracts for service oriented computing, specifying and verifying the properties of a good composition received a lot of attention. In [1,14] behavioural contracts are expressed via suitable process algebras, where the interactions between services are modelled via I/O actions. Two different choice operators, namely internal and external, describe how two services interact. The internal choice requires the other party to be able to synchronize with all the possible branches. This approach is extended to a multi party version by exploiting the π-calculus in [15]. The above papers focus on formalising the notion of progress of interactions. In our model, the internal choice is represented as a branching of requests. Also, we consider stronger properties than theirs: with agreement/weak agreement we require that all the requests of the contracts are satisfied, while for the property of progress it suffices that a subset of contracts meets their requests.

An extension of Intuitionistic Logic called Propositional Contract Logic (PCL) [7] has been proposed for modelling contracts with circular offers/requests. A new operator called *contractual implication* is introduced for dealing with actions taken on credit, if in the future the obligations will be honoured. Our notion of *weak agreement* is quite similar, and we also have a decision procedure to check if a contract automaton admits weak agreement.

Processes and contracts are two separate entities in [6], unlike ours. A process can fulfil its duty by obeying its contract or it behaves dishonestly and becomes *culpable* — and become honest again by performing later on the prescribed actions. We also do not assume participants to be honest, and our notion of *liability* is slightly different. It is inspired by Control Theory [12] and expressed in language-theoretic terms.

Session types are studied, among others, in [13,19] where *global types* represent a formal specification of a choreography of services in terms of their interactions. The projection of a safe global type to its components yields a safe *local type*, which is a term of a process algebra similar to [14]. From given safe local types, a choreography is synthesized, as a safe global type in [20]. In [16] local types are proved to correspond to communicating machines (CM) [11], that are finite state automata similar to ours. The main difference between the two is that CM interact through FIFO buffers, hence a participant can receive an input only if it was previously enqueued, while CA can offer/request on credit. However, under mild conditions, CA and CM can be proved equivalent [10], so establishing a first bridge between orchestration and choreography.

Acknowledgments. We are indebted with Giancarlo Bigi and Emilio Tuosto for many enlightening discussions.

References

1. Acciai, L., Boreale, M., Zavattaro, G.: Behavioural contracts with request-response operations. Sci. Comput. Program. **78**(2), 248–267 (2013)
2. Bartoletti, M., Cimoli, T., Pinna, G.M.: Lending Petri nets and contracts. In: Arbab, F., Sirjani, M. (eds.) FSEN 2013. LNCS, vol. 8161, pp. 66–82. Springer, Heidelberg (2013)
3. Bartoletti, M., Cimoli, T., Zunino, R.: A theory of agreements and protection. In: Basin, D., Mitchell, J.C. (eds.) POST 2013. LNCS, vol. 7796, pp. 186–205. Springer, Heidelberg (2013)
4. Bartoletti, M., Degano, P., Ferrari, G.L.: Planning and verifying service composition. Journal of Computer Security **17**(5), 799–837 (2009)
5. Bartoletti, M., Degano, P., Ferrari, G.L., Zunino, R.: Call-by-contract for service discovery, orchestration and recovery. In: Wirsing, M., Hölzl, M. (eds.) SENSORIA Project. LNCS, vol. 6582, pp. 232–261. Springer, Heidelberg (2011)
6. Bartoletti, M., Tuosto, E., Zunino, R.: Contract-oriented computing in co2. Sci. Ann. Comp. Sci. **22**(1), 5–60 (2012)
7. Bartoletti, M., Zunino, R.: A logic for contracts. In: Cherubini, A., Coppo, M., Persiano, G. (eds.) ICTCS, pp. 34–37 (2009)
8. Basile, D., Degano, P., Ferrari, G.-L.: Secure and unfailing services. In: Malyshkin, V. (ed.) PaCT 2013. LNCS, vol. 7979, pp. 167–181. Springer, Heidelberg (2013)
9. Basile, D., Degano, P., Ferrari, G.L., Tuosto, E.: Automata for analysing service contracts. Extended version: http://www.di.unipi.it/~basile/TGC14.pdf
10. Basile, D., Degano, P., Ferrari, G.L., Tuosto, E.: From orchestration to choreography through Contract Automata. In: ICE (to appear, 2014)
11. Brand, D., Zafiropulo, P.: On communicating finite-state machines. J. ACM **30**(2), 323–342 (1983)
12. Cassandras, C.G., Lafortune, S.: Introduction to Discrete Event Systems. Springer-Verlag New York Inc., Secaucus (2006)

13. Castagna, G., Dezani-Ciancaglini, M., Padovani, L.: On global types and multiparty session. Logical Methods in Computer Science **8**(1) (2012)
14. Castagna, G., Gesbert, N., Padovani, L.: A theory of contracts for web services. ACM Trans. Program. Lang. Syst. **31**(5) (2009)
15. Castagna, G., Padovani, L.: Contracts for mobile processes. In: Bravetti, M., Zavattaro, G. (eds.) CONCUR 2009. LNCS, vol. 5710, pp. 211–228. Springer, Heidelberg (2009)
16. Deniélou, P.-M., Yoshida, N.: Multiparty compatibility in communicating automata: Characterisation and synthesis of global session types. In: Fomin, F.V., Freivalds, R., Kwiatkowska, M., Peleg, D. (eds.) ICALP 2013, Part II. LNCS, vol. 7966, pp. 174–186. Springer, Heidelberg (2013)
17. Gray, J., Harrison, M.A., Ibarra, O.H.: Two-way pushdown automata. Information and Control **11**(1/2), 30–70 (1967)
18. Hemmecke, R., Koppe, M., Lee, J., Weismantel, R.: Nonlinear integer programming. In: Junger, M., Liebling, T.M., Naddef, D., Nemhauser, G.L., Pulleyblank, W.R., Reinelt, G., Rinaldi, G., Wolsey, L.A. (eds.) 50 Years of Integer Programming 1958–2008, pp. 561–618. Springer, Heidelberg (2010)
19. Honda, K., Yoshida, N., Carbone, M.: Multiparty asynchronous session types. In: Necula, G.C., Wadler, P. (eds.) POPL, pp. 273–284. ACM (2008)
20. Lange, J., Tuosto, E.: Synthesising choreographies from local session types. In: Koutny, M., Ulidowski, I. (eds.) CONCUR 2012. LNCS, vol. 7454, pp. 225–239. Springer, Heidelberg (2012)
21. OASIS-Technical-Committee: OASIS WSBPEL TC, Web services business process execution language version 2.0 (2007), technical Report, OASIS. http://docs.oasis-open.org/wsbpel/2.0/OS/wsbpel-v2.0-OS.html

On Duality Relations for Session Types

Giovanni Bernardi[1](✉), Ornela Dardha[2], Simon J. Gay[2], and Dimitrios Kouzapas[2,3]

[1] IMDEA Software Institute, Madrid, Spain
bernargi@tcd.ie
[2] School of Computing Science, University of Glasgow, Glasgow, UK
{Ornela.Dardha,Simon.Gay,Dimitrios.Kouzapas}@glasgow.ac.uk
[3] Department of Computing, Imperial College London, London, UK

Abstract. Session types are a type formalism used to describe communication protocols over private session channels. Each participant in a binary session owns one endpoint of a session channel. A key notion is that of *duality*: the endpoints of a session channel should have dual session types in order to guarantee communication safety. Duality relations have been independently defined in different ways and different works, without considering their effect on the type system. In this paper we systematically study the existing duality relations and some new ones, and compare them in order to understand their expressiveness. The outcome is that those relations are split into two groups, one related to the naïve inductive duality, and the other related to a notion of mutual compliance, which we borrow from the literature on contracts for web-services.

1 Introduction

A *session* is a private connection between a finite number of participants, and a *binary* session involves exactly two participants. A binary session can be thought of as a private communication channel, say a, with two *endpoints*, respectively a^+ and a^-. Each participant in a binary session owns one of the session endpoints and uses it to communicate with the other participant.

Session types are type-theoretic specifications of communication protocols. They can be incorporated into a programming language type system so that the correctness of the communication operations in a program can be verified by static type checking. In this paper we focus on types for binary sessions, that is binary session types [12].

A typical formalism to study binary sessions is the π-calculus, where session channels are identified by private names $a, b, c, \ldots$, and their endpoints are distinguished syntactically, $a^+, a^-, \ldots$. For instance, consider two agents A and B which communicate over a session c according to the following protocol: A sends an integer to B and then receives a boolean value from B. In the π-calculus with session types this is written as

$$(\nu c\colon S)\left(c^+![4].c^+?[v\colon \mathsf{bool}].\mathbf{0} \mid c^-?[n\colon \mathsf{int}].c^-![\mathsf{false}].\mathbf{0}\right)$$

where the protocol for A is described by the session type $S = ![\,\mathsf{int}\,].?[\,\mathsf{bool}\,].\text{END}$. This type describes only half of the overall protocol, namely what takes place

M. Maffei and E. Tuosto (Eds.): TGC 2014, LNCS 8902, pp. 51–66, 2014.
DOI: 10.1007/978-3-662-45917-1_4

in c^+. The other half of the protocol takes place in c^-, and is described by the session type $T = ?[\mathsf{int}].![\mathsf{bool}].\text{END}$ which models the protocol for agent B.

In the syntax of types, output is denoted by !, input is denoted by ?, and END denotes the type of the successfully terminated session. The "." models the continuation of the session type. Moreover, it is possible to define types with a branching structure in which one agent selects from a set of possibilities offered by the other agent.

A session type system checks that *i)* the communication operations in A match the type S; *ii)* the communication operations in B match the type T; and *iii)* S and T are related by an appropriate *duality* relation: $S \mathcal{D} T$, which intuitively describes opposite behaviours between two communicating agents. The above three steps ensure that communications within sessions are error-free.

The duality relation is a distinctive feature of session type systems, with no clear analogue in, for example, λ-calculus type systems. Recently Bernardi and Hennessy [2] have shown that duality relations have a non-trivial impact on the type systems, therefore should be carefully defined. This is the case in particular in the presence of non-tail recursive session types, like $\mu X.![X].\text{END}$. The following example exhibits a safe process that uses the aforementioned non-tail recursive session type.

Example 1. Consider the following processes,

$$P = (\nu t\colon \sharp T_b)\,(\nu u\colon \sharp S)\,(\,(\nu b\colon T_b)\,(\,t![b^+].u![b^-].\mathbf{0}\,)\mid !R\,)$$
$$R = t?[x\colon T_x].u?[y\colon T_y].(\nu a\colon T_a)\,(\,x![a^+].\mathbf{0}\mid y?[z\colon T_z].t![z].u![a^-].\mathbf{0}\,)$$

where $!R$ denotes the replication of R.

Intuitively, process P is safe because its reductions never lead to communication errors. By following the type system presented in the next section, the type derivation tree for P requires the type T_a to be $\mu X.![X].\text{END}$, which is non-tail recursive (see [2, Section 5.2]). □

Beyond the obvious point that duality should reverse the direction of messages, existing papers on session types do not give explicit justification for the exact way in which they define duality, and different authors follow different intuitions.

The aim of this paper is to study the existing duality relations in a systematic way; we contrast and compare a number of these relations as follows.

First, we compare the duality relations in a set-theoretic way, and we show that they can be classified in two groups, one related to a symmetric notion of testing, called "peer compliance", and the other related to the standard inductive duality defined by Honda *et al.* [12].

Second, we show that the type system of Gay and Hole [10] is robust with respect to the dualities in the peer compliance group, in the sense that its typing relation is the same for all *syntactic* duality relations in that group. This means that type-checkers implementing the type system can use the smallest duality in the peer compliance group.

Structure of the paper: In Section 2 we define the π-calculus with sessions based on [10]. It presents the statics and the dynamics of the calculus. We then consider several syntax-oriented definitions of duality in the presence of recursive types. In Section 3 we recall the behavioural theory of session types defined in [2]. In Section 4 we make a set-theoretic comparison of all the duality relations, establish a hierarchy with respect to inclusion, and consider the duality relation as a parameter of the type system. We discuss related work in Section 5, and conclude the paper in Section 6.

2 The π-Calculus with Sessions

In this section we introduce the π-calculus with session types: the syntax of types and terms, the operational semantics and the typing discipline which enjoys type preservation and type safety [10], thus guaranteeing error-free communications.

2.1 Session Types

Let I, J, K range over $\mathcal{I} = \{\, X \subseteq \mathbb{N} \mid X \text{ finite, non-empty } \}$, and let L_{SType} be the language of terms defined by the grammar (a):

$$(a)\ S, T \ ::= \text{END} \mid X \mid ?[T].S \mid ![T].S \mid \&\langle l_i : S_i\rangle_{i\in I} \mid \oplus \langle l_i : S_i\rangle_{i\in I} \mid \mu X.S$$

$$(b)\ M, N ::= S \mid \sharp M \mid X \mid \mu X.M$$

where the labels l_i in terms are pairwise distinct. Let *SType* be the set of session type terms which are *closed* (they contain no free type variables) and *guarded* (they contain a non-recursive type constructor between every type variable and its μ binder). We refer to the terms in *SType* as *session types* [2, Appendix A].

Type END is the type of a terminated session channel; $?[T].S$ and $![T].S$ indicate respectively the types for receiving and sending a message of type T and continuation of type S. Branch and select, $\&\langle l_i : S_i\rangle_{i\in I}$ and $\oplus\langle l_i : S_i\rangle_{i\in I}$ are sets of labelled session types indicating, respectively, external and internal choice. X and $\mu X.S$ model recursive session types.

The language of type terms is given by the grammar (b) above.We refer to the set of closed and guarded type terms as *types.* A type can be a session type, a standard shared channel type, a type variable or a recursive type.

In the present paper session types are higher-order, and their messages do not contain shared channel types. We use the pure higher-order session types approach to respect the semantic model defined in later Section 3.

Usually, the typing discipline of session types includes a duality *function* which constructs a specific dual type for any given session type. The following is the definition of inductive duality [12].

Definition 1 (Inductive Duality). *The inductive duality function is defined as:*

$$\overline{X} = X \quad \overline{?[T].S} = ![T].\overline{S} \quad \overline{\&\langle l_i : S_i\rangle_{i\in I}} = \oplus\langle l_i : \overline{S_i}\rangle_{i\in I} \quad \overline{\mu X.S} = \mu X.\overline{S}$$

$$\overline{\text{END}} = \text{END} \quad \overline{![T].S} = ?[T].\overline{S} \quad \overline{\oplus\langle l_i : S_i\rangle_{i\in I}} = \&\langle l_i : \overline{S_i}\rangle_{i\in I}$$

□

Although standard and broadly used, in [2,3] it was observed that inductive duality is not adequate in the presence of recursive session types, as it does not commute with the unfolding of non-tail-recursive types such as $\mu X.![X].\text{END}$, which in general are necessary (see Example 1 in the Introduction).

In order to overcome this inadequacy, Bono and Padovani [3], and Bernardi and Hennessy [2] independently defined an alternative function, called by the latter authors *complement*, and here denoted as cplt. In the following we give the definition of the complement function on session type terms, by adapting the corresponding one in [2].

Definition 2 (Complement Function). *The function* cplt : $L_{SType} \longrightarrow L_{SType}$ *is defined as:*

$$\begin{array}{llll}
\mathsf{cplt}(?[T].S) = ![T].\mathsf{cplt}(S) & \mathsf{cplt}(X) = X \\
\mathsf{cplt}(![T].S) = ?[T].\mathsf{cplt}(S) & \mathsf{cplt}(\text{END}) = \text{END} \\
\mathsf{cplt}(\&\langle l_i : S_i \rangle_{i\in I}) = \oplus\langle l_i : \mathsf{cplt}(S_i)\rangle_{i\in I} & \mathsf{cplt}(\mu X.S) = \mu X.\mathsf{cplt}(S\lfloor^{\mu X.S}/_{X}\rfloor) \\
\mathsf{cplt}(\oplus\langle l_i : S_i \rangle_{i\in I}) = \&\langle l_i : \mathsf{cplt}(S_i)\rangle_{i\in I}
\end{array}$$

□

The complement relies on a syntactic substitution $\lfloor^{-}/_{-}\rfloor$, which acts only on the carried types. The details are in [2, Section 5] and the formal definition is as follows,

$$\begin{array}{llll}
?[T].S'\lfloor^{S}/_{X}\rfloor = ?[T\{^{S}/_{X}\}].(S'\lfloor^{S}/_{X}\rfloor) & Y\lfloor^{S}/_{X}\rfloor = Y \\
![T].S'\lfloor^{S}/_{X}\rfloor = ![T\{^{S}/_{X}\}].(S'\lfloor^{S}/_{X}\rfloor) & \text{END}\lfloor^{S}/_{X}\rfloor = \text{END} \\
\&\langle l_i : S_i\rangle_{i\in I}\lfloor^{S}/_{X}\rfloor = \&\langle l_i : S_i\lfloor^{S}/_{X}\rfloor\rangle_{i\in I} & (\mu Y.S')\lfloor^{S}/_{X}\rfloor = \mu Y.(S'\lfloor^{S}/_{X}\rfloor) \text{ if } Y \neq X \\
\oplus\langle l_i : S_i\rangle_{i\in I}\lfloor^{S}/_{X}\rfloor = \oplus\langle l_i : S_i\lfloor^{S}/_{X}\rfloor\rangle_{i\in I} & (\mu X.S')\lfloor^{S}/_{X}\rfloor = \mu X.S'
\end{array}$$

In the presence of recursive types and their unfoldings, another standard approach is to define duality to be a *relation* rather than a function. For instance, $\mu X.?[\mathsf{int}].X$ and $![\mathsf{int}].\mu X.![\mathsf{int}].X$ model dual behaviours and should be considered dual types. However, this duality is not captured by the complement function. For this reason we define in the following the *co-inductive duality* relation [10]. In order to define co-inductive duality, we first have to define unfolding of terms and the subtyping relation.

The unfolding function UNF unfolds a recursive type until the first type constructor different from $\mu X.-$ is reached. Formally, UNF is defined on syntactic terms as the smallest relation that satisfies the following inference rules:

$$\frac{S\{^{\mu X.S}/_{X}\} \text{ UNF } S'}{\mu X.S \text{ UNF } S'} \qquad\qquad \frac{}{S \text{ UNF } S}\; S \neq \mu X.S'$$

The relation UNF is by definition a partial function on terms of the language L_{SType}, and it is defined on every closed and guarded term [2, Lemma A.8].

Definition 3 (Subtyping). *Let* $\mathcal{F} : \mathcal{P}(SType^2) \longrightarrow \mathcal{P}(SType^2)$ *be the functional defined so that* $(T, S) \in \mathcal{F}(\mathcal{R})$ *whenever all the following conditions hold:*

(i) if $\text{UNF}(T) = \text{END}$ *then* $\text{UNF}(S) = \text{END}$
(ii) if $\text{UNF}(T) = ![T_m].T'$ *then* $\text{UNF}(S) = ![S_m].S'$ *and* $S_m \,\mathcal{R}\, T_m$ *and* $T' \,\mathcal{R}\, S'$

(iii) *if* $\text{UNF}(T) = ?[T_m].T'$ *then* $\text{UNF}(S) = ?[S_m].S'$ *and* $T_m \mathcal{R} S_m$ *and* $T' \mathcal{R} S'$
(iv) *if* $\text{UNF}(T) = \oplus\langle l_i : T_i \rangle_{i\in I}$ *then* $\text{UNF}(S) = \oplus\langle l_j : S_j \rangle_{j\in J}$, $J \subseteq I$, $T_j \mathcal{R} S_j$ *for all* $j \in J$
(v) *if* $\text{UNF}(T) = \&\langle l_i : T_i \rangle_{i\in I}$ *then* $\text{UNF}(S) = \&\langle l_j : S_j \rangle_{j\in J}$, $I \subseteq J$, $T_i \mathcal{R} S_i$ *for all* $i \in I$

If $\mathcal{R} \subseteq \mathcal{F}(\mathcal{R})$, *then we say that* $\mathcal{R}$ *is a* type simulation. *Standard arguments ensure that there exists the greatest solution of the equation* $X = \mathcal{F}(X)$. *Let* $\preccurlyeq_{\mathsf{sbt}} = \nu X.\mathcal{F}(X)$, *and let* $=_{\mathsf{sbt}}$ *be the equivalence generated by* $\preccurlyeq_{\mathsf{sbt}}$. *We call* $\preccurlyeq_{\mathsf{sbt}}$ *the* subtyping relation. □

Observe that the relation $\preccurlyeq_{\mathsf{sbt}}$ defined above is less general than the original one in [10], in that it is not defined on channel types, and less general than the one in [2] in that here we do not have base types. Both are insignificant restrictions since subtyping on standard channel types and base types can be easily integrated into our framework.

Definition 4 (Co-inductive Duality, Syntactic Compliance). *Let* $\mathcal{G} : \mathcal{P}(SType^2) \times \mathcal{P}(SType^2) \times \mathcal{P}(\mathcal{I}^2) \longrightarrow \mathcal{P}(SType^2)$ *be the functional defined so that* $(T, S) \in \mathcal{G}(\mathcal{R}, \mathcal{B}, \mathcal{C})$ *whenever all the following conditions hold:*

(i) *If* $\text{UNF}(T) = \text{END}$ *then* $\text{UNF}(S) = \text{END}$
(ii) *If* $\text{UNF}(T) = ?[T_m].T'$ *then* $\text{UNF}(S) = ![S_m].S'$, $T' \mathcal{R} S'$, *and* $T_m \mathcal{B} S_m$
(iii) *If* $\text{UNF}(T) = ![T_m].T'$ *then* $\text{UNF}(S) = ?[S_m].S'$, $T' \mathcal{R} S'$, *and* $T_m \mathcal{B} S_m$
(iv) *If* $\text{UNF}(T) = \oplus\langle l_i : T_i \rangle_{i\in I}$ *then* $\text{UNF}(S) = \&\langle l_j : S_j \rangle_{j\in J}, I\ \mathcal{C}\ J$, $T_i \mathcal{R} S_i$ *for all* $i \in I$
(v) *If* $\text{UNF}(T) = \&\langle l_i : T_i \rangle_{i\in I}$ *then* $\text{UNF}(S) = \oplus\langle l_j : S_j \rangle_{j\in J}, J\ \mathcal{C}\ I$, $S_j \mathcal{R} T_j$ *for all* $j \in J$

Standard techniques ensure that for every $\mathcal{B}$ *and* $\mathcal{C}$ *there exists the greatest solution of the equation* $X = \mathcal{G}(X, \mathcal{B}, \mathcal{C})$. *We let* $\perp_{\mathsf{c}} = \nu X.\mathcal{G}(X, =_{\mathsf{sbt}}, =)$, *and let* $\boldsymbol{dual}^{sbt} = \nu X.\mathcal{G}(X, \preccurlyeq_{\mathsf{sbt}}, \subseteq)$. *We call* $\perp_{\mathsf{c}}$ coinductive duality *and* $\boldsymbol{dual}^{sbt}$ syntactic compliance. □

In Definition 3 and Definition 4 we treat recursion explicitly, because we do not take the widespread approach whereby $(\star)$ "a type can be freely replaced by its unfolding". In general assuming $(\star)$ is inconsistent, as shown in the following example.

Example 2. Here we prove a false equality by assuming $(\star)$ and using the function $\#\text{–}\mathsf{height}(T)$ of [13], which counts the number of top-most recursive constructors in T. For instance, the equalities (a) $\#\text{–}\mathsf{height}(\mu X.\text{END}) = 1$, (b) $\#\text{–}\mathsf{height}(\text{END}) = 0$ and (c) $\#\text{–}\mathsf{height}(\mu X.\text{END}) = \#\text{–}\mathsf{height}(\mu X.\text{END})$ are true. Thanks to $(\star)$, in the right-hand side of (c) we replace $\mu X.\text{END}$ with END, thereby obtaining $\#\text{–}\mathsf{height}(\mu X.\text{END}) = \#\text{–}\mathsf{height}(\text{END})$. Now (a) and (b) imply the equality $1 = 0$, which is false. □

$$x^p\,?[y{:}S];P \mid x^{\bar p}\,![z^q];Q \xrightarrow{x,-} P\{^{z^q}/_y\} \mid Q \quad \text{R-Com}$$

$$\frac{P \xrightarrow{\alpha,l} P'}{P \mid Q \xrightarrow{\alpha,l} P' \mid Q}\ \text{R-Par}$$

$$\frac{p \text{ is either } + \text{ or } - \qquad j \in I}{x^p \triangleright \{l_i : P_i\}_{i\in I} \mid x^{\bar p} \triangleleft l_j.Q \xrightarrow{x,l_j} P_j \mid Q}\ \text{R-Select}$$

$$\frac{P' \equiv P \quad P \xrightarrow{\alpha,l} Q \quad Q \equiv Q'}{P' \xrightarrow{\alpha,l} Q'}\ \text{R-Cong}$$

$$\frac{P \xrightarrow{\alpha,l} P' \qquad \alpha \neq x \qquad M \text{ not session type}}{(\nu x : M)P \xrightarrow{\alpha,l} (\nu x : M)P'}\ \text{R-New}$$

$$\frac{P \xrightarrow{x,l} P'}{(\nu x : S)P \xrightarrow{\tau,-} (\nu x : tail(S,l))P'}\ \text{R-NewS}$$

Fig. 1. The reduction relation

2.2 Session Processes

Our language is the π-calculus with session types, defined in [10]. We do not allow standard channels as messages, but this restriction is enforced by the syntax of types, not by modifications to the language. We also restrict messages to be monadic, for notational convenience and to match the semantic model of session types in Section 3. The syntax of session processes is defined by the following grammar:

$$P, Q ::= \mathbf{0} \mid (P|Q) \mid !P \mid x^p?[y\colon M].P \mid x^p![y^p].P \mid (\nu x\colon M)\,P \mid x\triangleright\{l_i : P_i\}_{i\in I} \mid x\triangleleft l.P$$

Let $x, y, z \ldots$ range over names, and $l_1, l_2, \ldots$ over labels. Names may be *polarised* in order to distinguish between the endpoints of a channel, occurring as x^+ or x^- or simply as x. We write x^p for a general polarised name, where p is $+$, $-$, or empty. Duality on polarities, written $\overline{p}$, exchanges $+$ and $-$. Process $(\nu x{:}T)P$ binds x in P and process $x^p\,?\,[y{:}T]; P$ binds y in P. In $(\nu x{:}T)P$, both x^+ and x^- may occur in P, and both are bound. In $x^p\,?\,[y{:}T]; P$, only y (unpolarised) may occur in P. If a name is not bound in P then it is free in P. $\textsc{fn}(P)$ denotes the set of free names in P. For simplicity, binding occurrences of names are annotated with types. We work up to α-equivalence and we assume the convention that all bound names are distinct from each other and from all free names. A process P can be a terminated process $\mathbf{0}$; a parallel composition of processes $P \mid Q$; a replicated process $!P$; an input $x^p?[y\colon M].P$ or an output $x^p![y^p].P$ on a polarised channel x^p with continuation P; a restriction $(\nu x\colon M)\,P$, where name x can be either a session channel or a standard channel and finally a branching $x \triangleright \{l_i : P_i\}_{i\in I}$ or selection $x\triangleleft l.P$, modelling respectively, the external and internal choice.

The operational semantics of processes is given in terms of a reduction relation and structural congruence [10] and is presented in Figure 1. The explanation of the fairly standard rules can be found in [10]. The substitution of polarised names for unpolarised variables in rule R-Com is an adaptation of Stoughton's general approach [14], and rule R-NewS uses the auxiliary *tail* function defined as follows,

$$tail(?[T].S, \_) = S \quad tail(\&\langle l_i\colon S_i\rangle_{i\in I}, l_j) = S_j$$
$$tail(![T].S, \_) = S \quad tail(\oplus\langle l_i\colon S_i\rangle_{i\in I}, l_j) = S_j \quad tail(\mu X.S, l) = tail(S\{^{\mu X.S}/_X\}, l)$$

$$\frac{\Gamma \text{ completed}}{\Gamma \vdash \mathbf{0}}\ \text{T-NIL} \qquad \frac{\Gamma_1 \vdash P \quad \Gamma_2 \vdash Q}{\Gamma_1 + \Gamma_2 \vdash P \mid Q}\ \text{T-PAR} \qquad \frac{\Gamma \vdash P \quad \Gamma \text{ unlimited}}{\Gamma \vdash\ !P}\ \text{T-REP}$$

$$\frac{\Gamma, x{:}M \vdash P \quad M \text{ is not a session type}}{\Gamma \vdash (\nu x{:}M)P}\ \text{T-NEW} \qquad \frac{\Gamma, x^+{:}S, x^-{:}S' \vdash P \quad S \perp_{\mathsf{c}} S'}{\Gamma \vdash (\nu x{:}S)P}\ \text{T-NEWS}$$

$$\frac{\Gamma, x^p{:}S, y{:}T \vdash P}{\Gamma, x^p{:}\,?[T].S \vdash x^p\,?\,[y{:}T];P}\ \text{T-INS} \qquad \frac{\Gamma, x^p{:}S \vdash P}{(\Gamma, x^p{:}\,![T].S) + y^q{:}T \vdash x^p\,!\,[y^q];P}\ \text{T-OUTS}$$

$$\frac{\Gamma, x{:}\sharp\, S, y{:}S \vdash P}{\Gamma, x{:}\sharp\, S \vdash x\,?\,[y{:}S];P}\ \text{T-IN} \qquad \frac{\Gamma, x{:}\sharp\, S \vdash P}{(\Gamma, x{:}\sharp\, S) + y^q{:}S \vdash x\,!\,[y^q];P}\ \text{T-OUT}$$

$$\frac{\forall i \in I \quad (\Gamma, x^p{:}S_i \vdash P_i)}{\Gamma, x^p{:}\&\langle l_i : S_i\rangle_{i\in I} \vdash x^p \triangleright \{l_i : P_i\}_{i\in I}}\ \text{T-OFFER} \qquad \frac{\Gamma, x^p{:}S \vdash P}{\Gamma, x^p{:}\oplus\langle l : S\rangle \vdash x^p \triangleleft l.P}\ \text{T-CHOOSE}$$

$$\frac{\Gamma, x^p : S \vdash P \quad T \preccurlyeq_{\mathsf{sbt}} S}{\Gamma, x^p : T \vdash P}\ \text{T-SUBSS}$$

Fig. 2. Typing rules

Reductions are annotated with labels of the form α, l, which indicate the channel name and branching / selection label, if any, being involved in each reduction.

2.3 Type System

In this section we present the typing discipline for the π-calculus with sessions. An environment Γ is a partial function from optionally polarised names to types. We adopt the standard convention that $\Gamma, x^p : M$ is defined if $x^p \notin dom(\Gamma)$. Moreover, the "," operator on environments is defined in a way that respects the polarity of names [10]. An environment Γ is *unlimited* if it contains no session types; *completed* if every session type in Γ is END; and $\mathcal{D}$-*balanced*, for some duality relation $\mathcal{D}$, if whenever $x^+ : S \in \Gamma$ and $x^- : S' \in \Gamma$ then $S\ \mathcal{D}\ S'$. Typing judgements are of the form $\Gamma \vdash P$, meaning "process P is well-typed in the environment Γ". The type system is given in Figure 2. It uses the $+$ operator on environments which combines two type environments without duplication of polarised session channels. The type system differs from the original one in [10] in that subtyping relation is removed from the typing rules and is instead included in the subsumption rule, T-SUBSS for session types. Rule T-NIL states that the terminated process $\mathbf{0}$ is well-typed in any completed environment Γ. Rule T-PAR is standard and uses the $+$ operator to combine two environments. Rule T-REP states that process $!P$ is well-typed if process P is well-typed in the same unlimited environment Γ. Rules T-NEW and T-NEWS type the restriction process where the new name x is a shared channel and a session channel, respectively. In the latter, the premise of the rule ensures that the opposite endpoints of the session channel x have dual types according to $\bot_{\mathsf{c}}$. Typing rules for input and output processes are duplicated in order to distinguish between actions on session channels and shared channels. Rule T-INS typechecks an input process that receives messages of a session type T on a session channel x^p of type $?[T].S$. Rule T-IN typechecks an input process that receives messages of type S on a shared channel x of type $\sharp\ S$. Rules T-OUTS and T-OUT typecheck the output process sending messages on session channel x^p and shared channel x, respectively and follow the same line as the typing rules for input processes. Rule T-OFFER typechecks branching $x^p \triangleright \{l_i : P_i\}_{i \in I}$ under the assumption that x^p has type $\&\langle l_i : S_i\rangle_{i \in I}$. Rule T-CHOOSE typechecks selection $x^p \triangleleft l.P$ under the assumption that x^p has type $\oplus\langle l : S\rangle$. Notice that the types of the session channel x^p in the previous two rules are exactly what is required for the processes to be well-typed. However, by using subtyping and rule SUBSS it is possible to obtain subtypes in breadth and in depth for branch and select types.

The type system enjoys the properties of type preservation and type safety. The proofs can be found in the online version of the paper [1].

Theorem 1 (Type Preservation).

1. *If $\Gamma \vdash P$ and $P \xrightarrow{\tau,-} Q$ then $\Gamma \vdash Q$.*
2. *If $\Gamma, x^+{:}S, x^-{:}S' \vdash P$, $S \perp_c S'$, and $P \xrightarrow{x,l} Q$ then $\Gamma, x^+{:}tail(S,l), x^-{:}tail(S',l) \vdash Q$.*
3. *If $\Gamma, x{:}T \vdash P$ and $P \xrightarrow{x,-} Q$ then $\Gamma, x{:}T \vdash Q$.*

To state the type safety result, we first define safe processes. Given a type environment Γ, we say that a process P is *Γ-safe* whenever:

1. If $P \equiv (\nu\widetilde{u}{:}\widetilde{T})(x\,?\,[y{:}V]; P_1 \mid x\,!\,[z^q]; P_2 \mid Q)$ then among $\Gamma, \widetilde{u}{:}\widetilde{T}$ we have $x{:}\sharp\ U$ and $z^q{:}W$ with $W \preccurlyeq_{\mathsf{sbt}} U \preccurlyeq_{\mathsf{sbt}} V$.
2. If $P \equiv (\nu\widetilde{u}{:}\widetilde{T})(x^p\,?\,[y{:}V]; P_1 \mid x^{\overline{p}}\,!\,[z^q]; P_2 \mid Q)$ with $p = {}^+$ or $p = {}^-$ then $x^+, x^- \notin \text{FN}(Q)$ and among $\Gamma, \widetilde{u}{:}\widetilde{T}$ we have $x^p{:}\,?[U].S$ and $x^{\overline{p}}{:}\,![U'].S'$ with $U =_{\mathsf{sbt}} U'$ and $z^q{:}W$ with $W \preccurlyeq_{\mathsf{sbt}} U \preccurlyeq_{\mathsf{sbt}} V$.
3. If $P \equiv (\nu\widetilde{u}{:}\widetilde{T})(x^p \triangleright \{l_i : P_i\}_{i \in I} \mid x^{\overline{p}} \triangleleft l_j.Q \mid R)$ then $j \in I$ and $x^+, x^- \notin \text{FN}(R)$.

Intuitively a process is Γ-safe whenever it contains no data mismatches between the data expected in the inputs, and the data sent by the outputs. Type safety follows from Proposition 3 and a more general result, Theorem 4, which are given in Section 4.

Corollary 1. *For every process P and $\perp_{\mathsf{c}}$-balanced Γ, if $\Gamma \vdash P$ then P is Γ-safe.*

3 A Behavioural Theory for Session Types

Bernardi and Hennessy [2] developed a behavioural theory for session types, in terms of session *contracts*, which gives an extensional meaning to subtyping (Theorem 2 in [2]).

In this section we recall some of their definitions and results, which are needed to give our contribution in the next section. We also consider the traces performed by session contracts, and show that complementation of a contract corresponds to exchanging inputs and outputs in its traces (Lemma 1).

The grammar for the language L_{SCts} of session contract terms is

$$\rho, \sigma ::= 1 \mid !(\sigma).\sigma \mid ?(\sigma).\sigma \mid x \mid \mu x.\sigma \mid \sum_{i \in I} ?l_i.\sigma_i \mid \bigoplus_{i \in I} !l_i.\sigma_i$$

where we assume the labels l_i to be pairwise distinct. We use SCts to denote the set of contract terms which are guarded and closed. We refer to these terms as *session contracts*, or just *contracts*.

In order to define the operational meaning of contracts we define the set of visible actions, Act, ranged over by λ, as the union of two sets, namely $\{\, ?l, \, !l \mid l \in L \,\}$, and $\{\, ?(\sigma), \, !(\sigma) \mid \sigma \in \mathsf{SCts} \,\}$. We use Act_τ to denote the set $\mathsf{Act} \cup \{\, \tau \,\}$. We define judgements of the form $\sigma_1 \xrightarrow{\mu} \sigma_2$, where $\mu \in \mathsf{Act}_\tau$ and $\sigma_1, \sigma_2 \in \mathsf{SCts}$, by using standard axioms.

$$\frac{}{\sum_{i \in I} ?l_i.\sigma_i \xrightarrow{?l_i} \sigma_i} \qquad \frac{}{\mu x.\sigma \xrightarrow{\tau} \sigma \{ {}^{\mu x.\sigma}/_{x} \}} \qquad \frac{}{\lambda.\sigma \xrightarrow{\lambda} \sigma}$$

$$\frac{}{\bigoplus_{i \in I} !l_i.\sigma_i \xrightarrow{\tau} !l_i.\sigma_i} \; |I| > 1 \qquad \frac{}{\bigoplus_{i \in I} !l_i.\sigma_i \xrightarrow{!l_i} \sigma_i} \; |I| = 1$$

We also have the predicate $1 \xrightarrow{\checkmark}$, which intuitively means that 1 is the *satisfied* contract.

In order to define the *peer compliance* relation [2] between contracts ρ, σ, we need to define when these contracts can interact. This is accounted for by judgements of the form $\rho \mid\mid \sigma \xrightarrow{\tau}_{\mathcal{B}} \rho' \mid\mid \sigma'$ which are inferred using the following rules.

$$\frac{\rho \xrightarrow{\tau} \rho'}{\rho \mid\mid \sigma \xrightarrow{\tau}_{\mathcal{B}} \rho' \mid\mid \sigma} \qquad \frac{\sigma \xrightarrow{\tau} \sigma'}{\rho \mid\mid \sigma \xrightarrow{\tau}_{\mathcal{B}} \rho \mid\mid \sigma'} \qquad \frac{\rho \xrightarrow{\lambda_1} \rho' \quad \sigma \xrightarrow{\lambda_2} \sigma'}{\rho \mid\mid \sigma \xrightarrow{\tau}_{\mathcal{B}} \rho' \mid\mid \sigma'} \; \lambda_1 \bowtie_{\mathcal{B}} \lambda_2$$

The rules are standard, except for the interaction relation $\bowtie_{\mathcal{B}}$, which in turn is parameterised by a relation $\sigma_1 \; \mathcal{B} \; \sigma_2$ between contracts. Intuitively, $\mathcal{B}$ determines when the contract σ_1 can be accepted when σ_2 is required, and we use $\bowtie_{\mathcal{B}}$ to account for higher-order interactions. The relation $\bowtie_{\mathcal{B}}$ is defined as the union of the sets $\{\, (?l, \, !l), \, (!l, \, ?l), \mid l \in L \,\}$, and $\{\, (?(\sigma_2), \, !(\sigma_1)), \, (!(\sigma_1), \, ?(\sigma_2)) \mid \sigma_1 \; \mathcal{B} \; \sigma_2 \,\}$.

Definition 5 ($\mathcal{B}$-Peer Compliance). *Let $\mathcal{C}^{\text{P2P}} : \mathcal{P}(\mathsf{SCts}^2) \times \mathcal{P}(\mathsf{SCts}^2) \longrightarrow \mathcal{P}(\mathsf{SCts}^2)$ be the rule functional defined so that $(\rho, \sigma) \in \mathcal{C}^{\text{P2P}}(\mathcal{R}, \mathcal{B})$ whenever (i) if $\rho \mid\mid \sigma \not\xrightarrow{\tau}_{\mathcal{B}}$ then $\rho \xrightarrow{\checkmark}$, and $\sigma \xrightarrow{\checkmark}$; and (ii) if $\rho \mid\mid \sigma \xrightarrow{\tau}_{\mathcal{B}} \rho' \mid\mid \sigma'$ then $\rho' \; \mathcal{R} \; \sigma'$.*

*Fix a $\mathcal{B}$. If $\mathcal{R} \subseteq \mathcal{C}^{\text{P2P}}(\mathcal{R}, \mathcal{B})$, then we say that $\mathcal{R}$ is a $\mathcal{B}$-*coinductive peer compliance*. Standard arguments ensure that there exists the greatest solution of the equation $X = \mathcal{C}^{\text{P2P}}(X, \mathcal{B})$; we call this solution the $\mathcal{B}$-*peer compliance*, and we denote it $\dashv^{\mathcal{B}}_{\text{P2P}}$.* □

Definition 6 (Peer Subcontract Preorder). *For every $\mathcal{B}$, we write $\sigma_1 \sqsubseteq^{\mathcal{B}} \sigma_2$ whenever $\rho \dashv^{\mathcal{B}}_{\text{P2P}} \sigma_1$ implies $\rho \dashv^{\mathcal{B}}_{\text{P2P}} \sigma_2$ for every ρ. We also let $\mathcal{P}re$ denote the collection of preorders over the set* SCts, *and let $\mathcal{F}^{\text{P2P}} : \mathcal{P}re \longrightarrow \mathcal{P}re$ be the function defined by $\mathcal{F}^{\text{P2P}}(\mathcal{B}) = \sqsubseteq^{\mathcal{B}}$. We let $\precsim$ be $\nu X.\mathcal{F}^{\text{P2P}}(X)$, and we refer to $\precsim$ as the* peer subcontract preorder. □

The full abstraction result depends on a bijection $\mathcal{M}$ between session types and session contracts, which maps END to 1, branch types $\&\langle - \rangle$ to external sums $\sum$, choice types $\oplus\langle - \rangle$ to internal sums $\bigoplus$, and leaves the variables and recursion $\mu - .-$ essentially unchanged (see [1, Appendix B]).

Theorem 2 (Full Abstraction [2]). *For every $T, S \in SType$, $S \preccurlyeq_{\mathsf{sbt}} T$ if and only if $\mathcal{M}(S) \precsim \mathcal{M}(T)$.*

In view of Theorem 2, $S \preccurlyeq_{\mathsf{sbt}} T$ means that the contracts ρ in $\precsim$-peer compliance with $\mathcal{M}(S)$ are in $\precsim$-peer compliance also with $\mathcal{M}(T)$. In other words, the contract $\mathcal{M}(T)$ satisfies all the contracts satisfied by $\mathcal{M}(S)$, if the higher-order interactions among contracts are prescribed by $\precsim$.

The proof of Theorem 2 relies on the complement function $\mathsf{comp} = \mathcal{M} \cdot \mathsf{cplt}$. We will need the property that the contract $\mathsf{comp}(\sigma)$ performs the traces of σ, but with inputs and outputs exchanged. To prove this, let $\overset{s}{\Longrightarrow}$ denote the least relation that satisfies the following conditions, (i) $\sigma \overset{\varepsilon}{\Longrightarrow} \sigma$ for every σ, (ii) $\sigma \overset{\lambda s}{\Longrightarrow} \sigma'$ if $\sigma \overset{\lambda}{\longrightarrow} \sigma''$ and $\sigma'' \overset{s}{\Longrightarrow} \sigma'$, and (iii) $\sigma \overset{s}{\Longrightarrow} \sigma'$ if $\sigma \overset{\tau}{\longrightarrow} \sigma''$ and $\sigma'' \overset{s}{\Longrightarrow} \sigma'$. We write $\sigma \overset{s}{\Longrightarrow}$ when $\sigma \overset{s}{\Longrightarrow} \sigma'$ for some contract σ'.

Given a visible action λ, we flip it to $\overline{\lambda}$ by exchanging ! and ?. To exchange inputs and outputs along finite traces we extend $\bar{\cdot}$ inductively to $\mathsf{flip} : \mathsf{Act}^{\star} \longrightarrow \mathsf{Act}^{\star}$.

Lemma 1. *For every $\rho \in$ SCts and $s \in \mathsf{Act}^{\star}$, $\rho \overset{s}{\Longrightarrow}$ if and only $\mathsf{comp}(\rho) \overset{\mathsf{flip}(s)}{\Longrightarrow}$.*

4 Dualities for Session Types

In this section we present the set-theoretical comparison of various duality relations defined so far in the literature. These relations are divided into two groups: the first group contains the dualities related to the $\mathcal{B}$-peer compliance obtained by instantiating the parameter $\mathcal{B}$ with the peer preorder $\precsim$; the second group contains the dualities defined using the inductive duality. We call the first group "peer compliance hierarchy" and the second group "naïve recursion dualities".

4.1 Peer Compliance Hierarchy

We use the peer subcontract preorder to single out one $\mathcal{B}$-peer compliance relation.

Definition 7 (Peer Compliance). *Let $\dashv\!\vdash_{\text{P2P}} = \dashv^{A}_{\text{P2P}}$ where $A = \precsim$, and call $\dashv\!\vdash_{\text{P2P}}$ the* peer compliance *relation.* □

The next result gives a syntactic characterisation of peer compliance which also accounts for the mapping between contracts and session types.

Lemma 2 (Syntactic Characterisation of Compliance). *For all session types* S, T, $S\,\mathtt{dual}^{sbt} T$ *if and only if* $\mathcal{M}(S) \dashv\vdash_{\text{P2P}} \mathcal{M}(T)$.

The characterisation given by the previous lemma eases the comparison between the peer compliance and the other dualities for session types. Now we proceed with the formal comparison.

Co-inductive duality is contained in syntactic compliance. This follows mainly from the set inclusion $=_{\mathsf{sbt}} \subseteq \preccurlyeq_{\mathsf{sbt}}$ and from Definition 4.

Corollary 2. $\perp_{\mathsf{c}} \subseteq \mathtt{dual}^{sbt}$.

The converse inclusion does not hold. The reason is that $\perp_{\mathsf{c}}$ requires branch or select to have the same set of labels, whereas $\mathtt{dual}^{sbt}$ relates also choice types whose sets of labels are in a set inclusion relation.

Example 3. Here we exhibit two types such that $S\mathtt{dual}^{sbt}T$ and $S \not\perp_{\mathsf{c}} T$. Let $S = \&\langle \mathtt{moka}\colon \text{END} \rangle$ and $T = \&\langle \mathtt{moka}\colon \text{END}, \mathtt{tea}\colon \text{END} \rangle$. To prove that $S\mathtt{dual}^{sbt}T$ it suffices to observe that $\mathcal{R} \subseteq \mathcal{G}(\mathcal{R}, \preccurlyeq_{\mathsf{sbt}}, \subseteq)$, where $\mathcal{R} = \{\, (S, T), (\text{END}, \text{END}) \,\}$.

The reason why $S \not\perp_{\mathsf{c}} T$ is that by definition $\perp_{\mathsf{c}}$ requires the sets of labels in S and T to be equal and this is false, because $\{\,\mathtt{moka}\,\} \neq \{\,\mathtt{moka},\ \mathtt{tea}\,\}$. □

Next we consider a duality relation based on the *finite* traces performed by session contracts. Let $\mathsf{fTr}(\sigma) = \{\, s \in \mathsf{Act}^{\star} \mid \sigma \stackrel{s}{\Longrightarrow} \,\}$.

Definition 8 (Trace-Oriented Duality). *Write* $\rho \;\Phi\; \sigma$ *whenever* $\mathit{fTr}(\rho) = \mathsf{flip}(\mathit{fTr}(\sigma))$. *If* $\rho \,\Phi\, \sigma$ *we say that* ρ *and* σ have dual finite traces. □

Note that the definition of *multiparty compatibility* in [8] is more general than Definition 8, in that it also accounts for the participants of sessions. However, in the setting of binary session types, our relation Φ and multiparty compatibility coincide up-to minor syntactic annotations.

The co-inductive duality $\perp_{\mathsf{c}}$ — modulo $\mathcal{M}$ — is strictly larger than the trace-based duality. This is true because the traces of a contract ρ and of its unfolding, $\text{UNF}(\rho)$, are the same, as shown in the following.

Lemma 3. *For every session contract* ρ, $\mathit{fTr}(\rho) = \mathit{fTr}(\text{UNF}(\rho))$.

Proposition 1. *For every session types* S, T, *if* $\mathcal{M}(S) \;\Phi\; \mathcal{M}(T)$ *then* $S \perp_{\mathsf{c}} T$.

The converse inclusion is false: the coinductive duality $\perp_{\mathsf{c}}$ - modulo $\mathcal{M}$ - is not contained in the relation Φ. As we show in the next example, the reason is that trace equality does not compare contracts modulo unfolding.

Example 4. We show two types T_1 and T_2 such that $T_1 \perp_{\mathsf{c}} T_2$ and $\mathcal{M}(T_1)\ \Phi\ \mathcal{M}(T_2)$ is false. Let S_1 be $?[\,\text{END}\,].S_2$ where $S_2 = \mu X.\, ?[\,\text{END}\,].X$, and let $T_1 = \,![\,S_1\,].\text{END}$, and $T_2 = ?[\,T_2\,].\text{END}$.

$$\begin{array}{ccc} \mathsf{comp} \subsetneq \Phi \subsetneq_{\mathcal{M}} \perp_{\mathsf{c}} \subsetneq & \mathtt{dual}^{\mathsf{sbt}} & =_{\mathcal{M}} \dashv\!\vdash_{\mathsf{P2P}} \\ & = & \\ & \mathsf{cplt} \cdot \preccurlyeq_{\mathsf{sbt}} = & \preccurlyeq_{\mathsf{sbt}} \cdot \mathsf{cplt} \end{array}$$

Fig. 3. Hierarchy of duality relations

First we prove that $T_1 \perp_{\mathsf{c}} T_2$. Definition 4 requires us to exhibit a suitable co-inductive duality, namely $\mathcal{R} = \{ (T_1, T_2), (\text{END}, \text{END}) \}$, and a suitable co-inductive subtyping, namely $\mathcal{S} \cup \mathcal{S}^{-1}$, where $\mathcal{S} = \{ (S_1, S_2), (S_2, S_2), (\text{END}, \text{END}) \}$.

Now we show that $\mathcal{M}(T_1) \; \Phi \; \mathcal{M}(T_2)$ is false. It suffices to exhibit a trace $s \in \mathsf{fTr}(\mathcal{M}(T_1))$ such that $s \notin \mathsf{flip}(\mathsf{fTr}(\mathcal{M}(T_2)))$. Notice that $\mathcal{M}(T_1) \stackrel{!(\sigma_1)}{\Longrightarrow}$ with $\sigma_1 = \mathcal{M}(S_1)$, so $!(\sigma_1) \in \mathsf{fTr}(\mathcal{M}(T_1))$, and that $\mathsf{fTr}(\mathcal{M}(T_2)) = \{ \varepsilon, ?(\sigma_2) \}$ and $\sigma_2 = \mathcal{M}(S_2) \neq \mathcal{M}(S_1) = \sigma_1$, so $?(\sigma_1) \notin \mathsf{flip}(\mathsf{fTr}(\mathcal{M}(T_2)))$. □

The trace-oriented duality is strictly larger than the complement function. This is true for two reasons, one is that the complementary contracts have flipped traces (see Lemma 1); the other is that the trace-oriented duality relates contracts with their unfoldings, whereas the complement function does not (see Example 5).

Corollary 3. *For all* $\rho \in \mathsf{SCts}$, $\rho \; \Phi \; \mathsf{comp}(\rho)$.

Example 5. We exhibit two contracts ρ and σ such that $\rho \; \Phi \; \sigma$ and $(\rho, \sigma) \notin \mathsf{comp}$. Let $\rho = \mu x.?(1).x$ and $\sigma = !(1).\mu x.!(1).x$. Plainly ρ and σ have the same finite traces up-to an application of $\mathsf{flip}(\cdot)$, thus $\mu x.?(1).x \; \Phi ?(\text{END})x.\mu x.?(1).x$. However, $\mathsf{comp}(\mu x.?(1).x) = \mu x.!(1).x \neq !(1).\mu x.!(1).x$, so $(\rho, \sigma) \notin \mathsf{comp}$. □

Finally, we relate complement, subtyping and syntactic compliance.

Proposition 2. $\mathit{dual}^{sbt} = \mathsf{cplt} \cdot \preccurlyeq_{\mathsf{sbt}} = \preccurlyeq_{\mathsf{sbt}} \cdot \mathsf{cplt}$.

Figure 3 summarises the results of this section, where the symbols $=_{\mathcal{M}}$, and $\subseteq_{\mathcal{M}}$ stand for set equality and set inclusion up-to encoding via $\mathcal{M}$, respectively.

4.2 Naïve Recursion Dualities

The duality functions $\overline{(\cdot)}$ and cplt do not relate types modulo unfolding, for instance in general $\mathsf{cplt}(T) \neq \mathsf{cplt}(\text{UNF}(T))$. To overcome this limitation, Vallecillo *et al.* [16] defined a *compatibility* relation by composing inductive duality with subtyping. Gay and Vasconcelos [11] took a similar approach, but defined compatibility differently.

Definition 9 (Compatibility [11,16]).
Let $\bowtie = \{(T, S) \mid T \preccurlyeq_{\mathsf{sbt}} \overline{S}\}$, *and* $\asymp = \{(T, S) \mid \overline{T} \preccurlyeq_{\mathsf{sbt}} S\}$. □

As far as we know, the relations $\bowtie$ and $\asymp$ were intended to coincide and to be symmetric. However, by considering the type $\mu X.![X].\text{END}$ and its inductive dual, we find that $\bowtie$ and $\asymp$ are different, and that neither relation is symmetric:

$$\mu X.![X].\text{END} \asymp ?[\mu X.?[X].\text{END}].\text{END} \qquad ?[\mu X.?[X].\text{END}].\text{END} \not\asymp \mu X.![X].\text{END}$$
$$\mu X.![X].\text{END} \not\bowtie ?[\mu X.?[X].\text{END}].\text{END} \qquad ?[\mu X.?[X].\text{END}].\text{END} \bowtie \mu X.![X].\text{END}$$

The lack of symmetry contradicts Proposition 3.3 in [16] and Proposition 3 in [11].

Proposition 2 ensures that if one defines compatibility in terms of complement instead of in terms of inductive duality then the resulting relations are equivalent, and coincide with the relation $\mathtt{dual}^{sbt}$, which is symmetric. Lemma 2 and the inclusion $\dashv\vdash_{\text{P2P}} \cdot \precsim \subseteq \dashv\vdash_{\text{P2P}}$ suggest that the peer compliance $\dashv\vdash_{\text{P2P}}$ captures the intuition behind the compatibility relations.

4.3 The Typing Relation as a Function of Duality

In order to show the impact that different dualities have on the typing relation $\vdash$, we parameterise its definition by a binary relation $\mathcal{D}$ on session types. Let $\vdash_{\mathcal{D}}$ be the relation defined by the rules in Fig. 2, where rule T-NEWS is replaced by the following rule,

$$\frac{\Gamma, x^+ : S, x^- : S' \vdash_{\mathcal{D}} P \qquad S\ \mathcal{D}\ S'}{\Gamma \vdash_{\mathcal{D}} (\boldsymbol{\nu} x : S)P}\ \text{T-NEWS'}$$

The relation $\vdash_{\mathcal{D}}$ is a function of $\mathcal{D}$ and it is monotone.

Proposition 3. *For every $\mathcal{D} \subseteq \mathcal{D}' \subseteq SType^2$, $\vdash_{\mathcal{D}} \subseteq \vdash_{\mathcal{D}'}$.*

Considering the hierarchy in Figure 3, from $\mathsf{comp} \subsetneq_{\mathcal{M}} \perp_{\mathsf{c}}$ and the definitions of cplt and $\mathcal{M}$ we have $\mathsf{cplt} \subsetneq \perp_{\mathsf{c}}$; also $\perp_{\mathsf{c}} \subsetneq \mathtt{dual}^{sbt}$. Proposition 3 then yields:

Corollary 4. *For every Γ and P, $\Gamma \vdash_{\mathsf{cplt}} P$ implies $\Gamma \vdash_{\perp_{\mathsf{c}}} P$, and $\Gamma \vdash_{\perp_{\mathsf{c}}} P$ implies $\Gamma \vdash_{\mathtt{dual}^{sbt}} P$.*

The difference between cplt and $\perp_{\mathsf{c}}$ is that $\perp_{\mathsf{c}}$ includes arbitrary unfolding, and the difference between $\perp_{\mathsf{c}}$ and $\mathtt{dual}^{sbt}$ is that $\mathtt{dual}^{sbt}$ includes subtyping. Since the rule T-SUBSS allows the use of subtyping relation in the derivation trees, also the converse of Corollary 4 is true:

Theorem 3. *$\Gamma \vdash_{\mathsf{cplt}} P$ if and only if $\Gamma \vdash_{\perp_{\mathsf{c}}} P$ if and only if $\Gamma \vdash_{\mathtt{dual}^{sbt}} P$.*

Example 6. Here we show that Theorem 3 is false if in T-SUBSS we replace $\preccurlyeq_{\mathsf{sbt}}$ with the equivalence $=_{\mathsf{sbt}}$. Let $T = \oplus\langle a{:}\text{END}\rangle$, $S = \&\langle a{:}\text{END}, b{:}\text{END}\rangle$, $P = (\nu x{:}S)(x^+ \triangleright \{a{:}\mathbf{0}, b{:}\mathbf{0}\} \mid x^- \triangleleft a.\mathbf{0})$, and let the symbol $\vdash'_{\mathcal{D}}$ denote the type relation given by the rules in Figure 2, where T-NEWS' is used in place of T-NEWS. The derivation of $\vdash'_{\mathtt{dual}^{sbt}} P$ exists, because $S \mathtt{dual}^{sbt} T$, while a derivation of $\vdash'_{\perp_{\mathsf{c}}} P$ does not exist, because $S \perp_{\mathsf{c}} T$ is false. □

Type safety is true also for the dualities cplt and $\mathtt{dual}^{sbt}$.

Theorem 4. *For every process P, if $\Gamma \vdash_{\mathbf{dual}^{sbt}} P$ and Γ is $\mathbf{dual}^{sbt}$-balanced, then P is Γ-safe*

Two immediate consequences are Corollary 1, previously stated, and the analogous result for cplt. The proof that cplt is a safe duality is essential, and was not given in [2].

5 Related Work

Session types: The concept of a session type originated in the work of Honda *et al.* [12,15]. There is now a substantial literature, which has been surveyed by Dezani and de'Liguoro [9]. Subtyping for recursive session types was proposed in [10], and full abstraction for that subtyping was achieved in [2]. Another semantic theory of session types is defined in [5], and it is independent of the theory of [10].

Subtyping: Recent work by Chen *et al.* [6] has considered *preciseness* of subtyping, meaning the combination of soundness and completeness. A subtyping relation is complete if it is the largest safe subtyping relation for a given type system. Given the connections between subtyping and duality (e.g. Proposition 2), the results about preciseness are likely to be relevant for finding the largest safe duality. On the other hand, if one removes subtyping from the type system, then the choice of duality relation becomes relevant and impacts the resulting typing relation. We leave the investigation of the relation between subtyping and duality for future work.

Complement and inductive duality: The only difference between the complement function and the inductive duality lies in the treatment of recursive terms. Although apparently small, this difference leads to noticeable differences in the typing relations (see [2, Section 5]). In turn, the different treatment of recursion boils down to the use of the substitution $\lfloor \cdot / . \rfloor$. This substitution was first proposed in [3], where it is called *inner substitution*. The reason why [2,3] use this substitution is to inductively construct the duals of types like $\mu X.![X].\text{END}$. This is borne out in [3, Proposition 3.1 (2)] and [2, Theorem 5.10]. The duality of [3] is syntactically defined, whereas the $\mathcal{B}$-mutual compliances are operationally defined. As a consequence the proof of Proposition 3.1 (2) is simpler than the proof of [2, Theorem 5.10]. Also, while [3] uses the fact that complement and unfold commute, the authors of [2] prove this result.

Further dualities: One extensional duality which we have not considered in this comparison is the one of [5, Definition 2.5]. The reason for this omission is that the framework of that paper is significantly different from ours. However, we leave the comparison with the dualities we studied here and the one of [5] for future work.

Two other approaches to defining duality emerged from the connection between session types and propositions [4,17]. In the intuitionistic setting of Caires and Pfenning [4], duality boils down to the cut-rule, according to which the dual of requiring a behaviour A (on the left of a judgement) is an offer of A (on the right of a judgment). This implicit duality is in contrast with the situation in the classical setting studied by Wadler [17], where duality of session types amounts to duality on propositions: every proposition A has an inductively defined explicit dual $A^{\perp}$.

Finally, an interesting aspect of duality on session types is its relation to the opposite input / output channel capabilities in the standard π-calculus. In [7] the authors study an encoding of binary session types into linear channel π-types. Due to the *continuation-passing style* of the encoding, the duality on session types reduces to merely opposite input / output linear channel capabilities, but only in the outermost level of the type, with the carried types being (syntactically) equal.

6 Conclusion and Future Work

The duality relation is an essential and distinctive feature of session type systems. However, the questions of how to define duality, and of the effect of duality on the typing relation, have not received careful attention; different authors have used different definitions for various reasons of convenience without considering the consequences. Particular care is needed in the presence of recursive types, and the informal convention of working "up to unfolding" is problematic. In the present paper, we have begun a systematic study of duality relations, and we have made the following contributions.

First, we have emphasised the problems of treating session types "up to unfolding", and we have carefully defined a session type system without this assumption.

Second, we have explicitly considered a range of duality relations and established their relationships. We have included several existing relations defined on the syntax of session types, and some new relations derived from a semantic model of session types.

Third, we have considered the duality relation as a parameter of the session type system, and studied the typing relations resulting from different choices of duality relation. The result is that the type system is robust, in the sense that the choice of duality relation among the syntax-based relations does not matter.

Future Work. The model of session types developed in [2] does not account for standard channel types. This is a severe limitation, because in settings based on that model, standard channels cannot be sent over session channels. This limitation applies to the present paper. We plan to investigate how to extend the model of [2] to channel types.

If a duality $\mathbb{D}$ allows unsafe processes to be typed, then there is no point in using it, so the obvious basis for judging a duality relation $\mathbb{D}$ is the definition of safe process. In turn, once we fix the set of safe processes $\mathcal{S}$, an obvious question is: what is the greatest duality $\mathbb{D}$ such that $\vdash_{\mathbb{D}} P$ implies $P \in \mathcal{S}$? To the best of our knowledge this problem has never been investigated. Once such a greatest $\mathbb{D}$ is found, a similar problem is to find the *smallest* duality d such that $\vdash_d = \vdash_{\mathbb{D}}$. An answer to this problem might have worthwhile practical consequences: for example, an algorithm to decide d may be more efficient than one to decide $\mathbb{D}$. Identifying $\mathbb{D}$ and d would also answer the open question of what should be the *canonical* definition of duality for session types.

Acknowledgments. Bernardi was supported by the Portuguese FCT project PTDC/EIA-CCO/122547/2010. Dardha, Gay and Kouzapas are supported by the UK EPSRC project *From Data Types to Session Types: A Basis for Concurrency and Distribution (ABCD)* (EP/K034413/1). Kouzapas is also supported by an EPSRC Doctoral Prize Fellowship. The research reported in this paper was made possible by a Short-Term Scientific Mission grant to Bernardi from COST Action IC1201: Behavioural Types for Reliable Large-Scale Software Systems (BETTY).

References

1. Bernardi, G., Dardha, O., Gay, S.J., Kouzapas, D.: On duality relations for session types (2014). http://www.dcs.gla.ac.uk/~ornela/my_papers/BDGK14-Extended.pdf
2. Bernardi, G., Hennessy, M.: Using higher-order contracts to model session types. CoRR, abs/1310.6176 (2013)
3. Bono, V., Padovani, L.: Typing copyless message passing. Logical Methods in Computer Science **8**(1) (2012)
4. Caires, L., Pfenning, F.: Session types as intuitionistic linear propositions. In: Gastin, P., Laroussinie, F. (eds.) CONCUR 2010. LNCS, vol. 6269, pp. 222–236. Springer, Heidelberg (2010)
5. Castagna, G., Dezani-Ciancaglini, M., Giachino, E., Padovani, L.: Foundations of session types. In: Porto, A., López-Fraguas, F.J. (eds.) PPDP, pp. 219–230. ACM (2009)
6. Chen, T., Dezani-Ciancaglini, M., Yoshida, N.: On the preciseness of subtyping in session types. In: Proceedings of the 16th International Symposium on Principles and Practice of Declarative Programming (PPDP) (2014)
7. Dardha, O., Giachino, E., Sangiorgi, D.: Session types revisited. In: PPDP, pp. 139–150. ACM (2012)
8. Deniélou, P.-M., Yoshida, N.: Multiparty compatibility in communicating automata: Characterisation and synthesis of global session types. In: Fomin, F.V., Freivalds, R., Kwiatkowska, M., Peleg, D. (eds.) ICALP 2013, Part II. LNCS, vol. 7966, pp. 174–186. Springer, Heidelberg (2013)
9. Dezani-Ciancaglini, M., de'Liguoro, U.: Sessions and session types: An overview. In: Laneve, C., Su, J. (eds.) WS-FM 2009. LNCS, vol. 6194, pp. 1–28. Springer, Heidelberg (2010)
10. Gay, S.J., Hole, M.: Subtyping for session types in the pi calculus. Acta Inf. **42**(2–3), 191–225 (2005)
11. Gay, S.J., Vasconcelos, V.T.: Linear type theory for asynchronous session types. J. Funct. Program. **20**(1), 19–50 (2010)
12. Honda, K., Vasconcelos, V.T., Kubo, M.: Language primitives and type discipline for structured communication-based programming. In: Hankin, C. (ed.) ESOP 1998. LNCS, vol. 1381, pp. 122–138. Springer, Heidelberg (1998)
13. Pierce, B.C.: Types and Programming Languages. MIT Press (2002)
14. Stoughton, A.: Substitution revisited. Theor. Comput. Sci. **59**, 317–325 (1988)
15. Takeuchi, K., Honda, K., Kubo, M.: An interaction-based language and its typing system. In: Halatsis, C., Philokyprou, G., Maritsas, D., Theodoridis, S. (eds.) PARLE 1994. LNCS, vol. 817, pp. 398–413. Springer, Heidelberg (1994)
16. Vallecillo, A., Vasconcelos, V.T., Ravara, A.: Typing the behavior of software components using session types. Fundam. Inform. **73**(4), 583–598 (2006)
17. Wadler, P.: Propositions as sessions. In: ICFP, pp. 273–286 (2012)

Characterising Testing Preorders for Broadcasting Distributed Systems

Andrea Cerone[1](✉) and Matthew Hennessy[2]

[1] IMDEA Software Institute, Madrid, Spain
Andrea.Cerone@imdea.org
[2] Trinity College Dublin, Dublin, Ireland
Matthew.Hennessy@scss.tcd.ie

Abstract. We present a process calculus for both specifying the desired behaviour of distributed systems and for describing their actual implementation; the calculus is aimed at the internet layer of the TCP/IP reference model. This allows us to define behavioural preorders in the style of DeNicola and Hennessy, relating specifications and implementations for distributed systems at this level of abstraction. The main result of the paper is a complete characterisation of these preorders, for a large class of systems, in terms of traces of extensional actions. This result underpins a sound and complete proof methodology which is demonstrated by the verification of the correct behaviour of a virtual shared memory protocol.

1 Introduction

Different approaches have been made to the problem of verifying the behaviour of distributed systems. This includes model checking [6,12,15] and process calculi [8,10,13,17,18]. In the latter a language, or calculus, is designed for both specifying desired behaviour, for example of a distributed system, and describing the proposed implementation. Verification then consists of formally proving that the two descriptions are *behaviourally equivalent*. The success of this approach is dependent not only on having a robust notion of *behavioural equivalence*, but also a high-level characterisation of the equivalence which can be used for verification purposes.

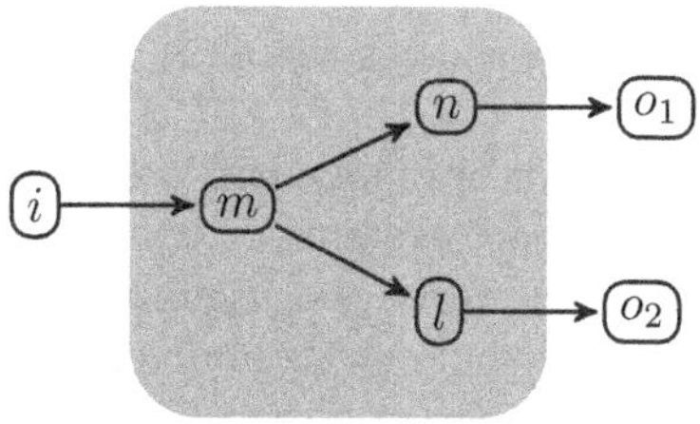

We define a process calculus for modelling (distributed) systems at a high level of abstraction, roughly at the level of the *Internet Layer* of the *TCP/IP* reference model [20]. We assume non-blocking broadcast communication between independent computational entities, although the introduction of point-to-point communication would not invalidate our results. A typical system may be seen to the left. It consists of a number of nodes or stations at

Supported by SFI project SFI 06 IN.1 1898.
Andrea Cerone: Supported by SFI project SFI 06 IN.1 1898.

M. Maffei and E. Tuosto (Eds.): TGC 2014, LNCS 8902, pp. 67–81, 2014.
DOI: 10.1007/978-3-662-45917-1_5

which code is executed by independent processes, with an *accessibility* relation between the nodes. So in this example only stations n and l are in the range of broadcasts from station m while o_2 is the only station which can pick up messages broadcast from station l. Thus in general communication is *multicast*, in that messages can be received by multiple entities simultaneously; for example messages transmitted from m can be picked up at both n and l simultaneously. However either of the nodes n, l, or indeed both, can choose to ignore messages, or more generally may be in a state where broadcasts cannot currently be received. Thus broadcasts are *non-blocking* in that messages can be transmitted from m regardless of whether or not anybody is currently listening at n or l.

There are two kinds of nodes. The first, the internal nodes, are those at which code is executing, broadcasting and receiving messages; in our example these are m, n and l. Here, and throughout the rest of the paper, we use shadowing to represent these internal nodes. The second are *interface nodes*, such as i, o_1 and o_2, which are not executing any code; however they can be used either to test the internal behaviour of the system by placing test code there, or more generally combining smaller systems to construct larger ones.

More formally, a system $\mathcal{M}$ is a pair of the form $\Gamma \triangleright M$, where Γ is a directed graph describing the *accessibility relation* between nodes, or the system topology, and M is a system term from a process calculus which describes the code running at the internal nodes. In this paper we focus on a sub-calculus of that of [2,3] in which the station code is non-probabilistic. From these papers we also borrow the (non-trivial) partial operator $\mathcal{M} \not\Vdash\!\!> \mathcal{N}$ for composing systems to form larger ones. For our purposes, we focus on a relevant, large class of *composable* systems, which do not allow connections between interface nodes. It can be shown that all composable systems can be generated by *atomic systems*, which contain only one node, using the operator $\not\Vdash\!\!>$. As explained in [2,3], the composite system $\mathcal{M} \not\Vdash\!\!> \mathcal{N}$ may be viewed as $\mathcal{N}$ extending $\mathcal{M}$ by adding new stations and adding code to execute at the interface nodes of $\mathcal{M}$; it may also be viewed as $\mathcal{N}$ *blackbox testing* the system $\mathcal{M}$ by placing probing code at its interface.

This compositional view of systems leads in a natural way to an adaptation of the standard testing based preorders [7] which we denote by $\mathcal{M} \sqsubseteq_{\mathrm{may}} \mathcal{N}$ and $\mathcal{M} \sqsubseteq_{\mathrm{must}} \mathcal{N}$. Intuitively the former means that if the application of any *blackbox* test $\mathcal{T}$, represented by the composite system $\mathcal{M} \not\Vdash\!\!> \mathcal{T}$, can lead to a success, then so can the application to $\mathcal{N}$; the latter, $\mathcal{M} \sqsubseteq_{\mathrm{must}} \mathcal{N}$, on the other hand is determined by the tested processes $\mathcal{M}$, $\mathcal{N}$ guaranteeing success when probed by any testing system $\mathcal{T}$.

Testing preorders can be used to capture the concept of refinement; a system $\mathcal{M}$ corresponds to an implementation of a more abstract system $\mathcal{N}$, known as the specification, if $\mathcal{M} \sqsubseteq_{\mathrm{may}} \mathcal{N}$ and $\mathcal{M} \sqsubseteq_{\mathrm{must}} \mathcal{N}$. However the usefulness of this notion of refinement depends on our ability to reason about these preorders. This is the topic of this paper.

In standard process calculi, such as CCS and CSP, testing preorders can be characterised by the traces, that is sequences of actions, which processes can perform, together with so-called *acceptances* or *failures*. Here however the situation is much more complicated. For example messages are broadcast asynchronously; in this respect the approach in [8] is of help. But with distributed systems we also have the problem of whether a multicast, that is the simultaneous broadcast of a message to multiple nodes, can be distinguished from a series of individual broadcasts to each of the nodes in turn. More importantly the ability of tests to interrogate the behaviour of a system depends on the distribution of its nodes, the accessibility between them and the accessibility to these internal nodes from the interface.

In this paper we isolate a set of *extensional actions* for systems; their definition is independent of the distribution of the internal nodes in the system and depends only on their accessibility from the interface nodes. They also take into account the multicasts which systems can perform, represented by the set of interface nodes which can receive the broadcast of a value at any point in time.

Traces of such extensional actions provide a sound proof method for the preorder $\sqsubseteq_{\mathrm{may}}$.

Further, for those systems which do not exhibit non-terminating behaviour when considered in isolation, so-called *strongly-convergent systems*, it is sufficient to record deadlocks into traces to obtain a sound proof method for the preorder $\sqsubseteq_{\mathrm{must}}$. As a further contribution, we show that our proof methods are complete; specifically

(1) extensional traces are complete for $\sqsubseteq_{\mathrm{may}}$ for arbitrary systems
(2) deadlock extensional traces are complete for $\sqsubseteq_{\mathrm{must}}$ when restricted to strongly convergent systems which are in addition *finite spanning*, meaning they can reach a finite number of states by performing a transition.

In this extended abstract we concentrate on outlining the proof of (2) which relies on exhibiting characteristic tests for (deadlock) traces of extensional actions. The definition of such tests is non-trivial; one of the main challenges when defining the characteristic test of a trace is that of coordinating the independent activities of its nodes.

As a sample application of our proof techniques, we prove the correctness of a simple virtual shared memory implementation.

The remainder of the paper is organised as follows. The calculus is presented in §2. In §3 we recall the theory of composition for networks of [3], upon which we define the testing preorders $\sqsubseteq_{\mathrm{may}}$, $\sqsubseteq_{\mathrm{must}}$. In §4 we explain the extensional semantics, and define both the sets of traces and deadlock traces of systems. These are used to determine our characterisations for both testing preorders in §5, where we put an emphasis on the completeness result for $\sqsubseteq_{\mathrm{must}}$. An application of the resulting proof techniques is given in §6, in which we prove the correctness of a virtual shared memory. We end the paper with a brief comparison with related work, in §7.

Due to the lack of space, the technical details of §5 and §6 are covered in an extended version of the paper [4]. A thorough discussion of the topics treated in this paper is given in [2], to which the reader is referred for detailed proofs of the results and further applications of the proof methods to real world scenarios.

2 A Calculus for Distributed Systems

Syntax. A directed connectivity graph $\Gamma = \langle \Gamma_V, \Gamma_E \rangle$ consists of a set of vertices Γ_V, representing the set of nodes of a distributed system, and a relation $\Gamma_E \subseteq (\Gamma_V \times \Gamma_V)$ containing the connections between nodes. If $(m, n) \in \Gamma_E$ then node n can receive messages broadcast by m. Given $\Gamma = \langle \Gamma_V, \Gamma_E \rangle$, we use $\Gamma \vdash m$ for $m \in \Gamma_V$, $\Gamma \vdash m \rightarrow n$ for $(m, n) \in \Gamma_E$ and $\Gamma \vdash m \not\rightarrow n$ for its negation.

A distributed system is modelled as a tuple $\Gamma \triangleright M$, where Γ is a connectivity graph and M is a system term which associates processes to nodes, generated by the grammar below.

$$M, N ::= \mathbf{0} \mid n[\![P]\!] \mid (M \mid N)$$

A (system) term M is a collection of sub-terms of the form $m[\![P]\!]$, which binds process P to node m; the term $\mathbf{0}$ corresponds to the system term in which no nodes are executing processes. The code for processes will be presented shortly. We will often use the metavariables $\mathcal{M}, \mathcal{N}, \cdots$ when referring to a system $\Gamma \triangleright M$.

Let nodes(M) be the set of the node names appearing in M. We only consider the sublanguage of well-formed systems $\Gamma \triangleright M$ such that nodes$(M) \subseteq \Gamma_V$, and such that each node name occurs at most once in M. These constraints ensure that in systems, nodes running code are part of the system topology, and no node can be bound to multiple processes. It is possible for nodes appearing in Γ not to occur in M. At least intuitively, such nodes represent the external environment of a system and will be used to test its behaviour (§3). The set of the external nodes of a system $\Gamma \triangleright M$, formally defined as $\Gamma_V \setminus$ nodes(M), is called the interface of the system and denoted by $\mathsf{Intf}(\Gamma \triangleright M)$.

The syntax for processes, given below, is a straightforward instance of a standard process calculus, and their constructs should be self explanatory. Here we assume a (at most countable) set of process definitions of the form $A \Leftarrow P$.

$$P,\ Q ::= \mathbf{0} \mid c!\langle e \rangle .P \mid c?(x).P \mid \tau.P \mid \omega \mid P + Q \mid \mathsf{if}\ b\ \mathsf{then}\ P\ \mathsf{else}\ Q \mid A(\tilde{x})$$

For processes we assume some language for Boolean expressions, $b, b', \cdots$ which includes variables, $x, y, \cdots$ and the Boolean values, $\{\mathsf{true}, \mathsf{false}\}$. In the standard manner we assume an interpretation function $[\![\cdot]\!]$ which maps all closed Boolean expressions to some Boolean value. In a similar manner we assume another language of (value) expressions, $e, e', \cdots$, which again may contain variables, and values $v, w, \cdots$ from some *finite* value set; this language also comes equipped with an interpretation function, mapping each closed expression into one of the finite set of values.

We also assume a special clause ω which will be used for testing purposes in §3. Any system which has no occurrence of the special clause is called *proper*.

Intensional Semantics. We define a collection of *Structured Operational Semantics* rules, whose judgements take the form $(\Gamma \triangleright M) \xrightarrow{\mu} (\Gamma \triangleright N)$, to define the behaviour of systems. The action μ can have either the form **(a)** $m.c!v$, node m broadcasts value v along channel c, **(b)** $m.c?v$, the system receives a broadcast of

$$\text{(B-BROAD)}\ \frac{P \xrightarrow{c!v} Q}{\Gamma \rhd n[\![P]\!] \xrightarrow{n.c!v} \Gamma \rhd n[\![Q]\!]} \qquad \text{(B-REC)}\ \frac{P \xrightarrow{c?v} Q \qquad \Gamma \vdash m \rightarrow n}{\Gamma \rhd n[\![P]\!] \xrightarrow{m.c?v} \Gamma \rhd n[\![Q]\!]}$$

$$\text{(B-DEAF)}\ \frac{P \stackrel{c?v}{\not\longrightarrow}}{\Gamma \rhd n[\![P]\!] \xrightarrow{m.c?v} \Gamma \rhd n[\![P]\!]} \qquad \text{(B-DISC)}\ \frac{\Gamma \vdash m \not\rightarrow n}{\Gamma \rhd n[\![P]\!] \xrightarrow{m.c?v} \Gamma \rhd n[\![P]\!]}$$

$$\text{(B-0)}\ \frac{}{\Gamma \rhd \mathbf{0} \xrightarrow{m.c?v} \Gamma \rhd \mathbf{0}} \qquad \text{(B-}\tau\text{)}\ \frac{P \xrightarrow{\tau} Q}{\Gamma \rhd n[\![P]\!] \xrightarrow{\tau} \Gamma \rhd n[\![Q]\!]}$$

$$\text{(B-}\tau\text{.PROP-L)}\ \frac{\Gamma \rhd M \xrightarrow{\tau} \Gamma \rhd L}{\Gamma \rhd M \mid N \xrightarrow{\tau} \Gamma \rhd L \mid N} \qquad \text{(B-}\tau\text{.PROP-R)}\ \frac{\Gamma \rhd N \xrightarrow{\tau} \Gamma \rhd L}{\Gamma \rhd M \mid N \xrightarrow{\tau} \Gamma \rhd M \mid L}$$

$$\text{(B-SYNC)}\ \frac{\Gamma \rhd M \xrightarrow{\mu_1} \Gamma \rhd M' \quad \Gamma \rhd N \xrightarrow{\mu_2} \Gamma \rhd N'}{\Gamma \rhd M \mid N \xrightarrow{(\mu_1 \circ \mu_2)} \Gamma \rhd M' \mid N'}$$

$\mu_1 \circ \mu_2$	$m.c!v$	$m.c?v$
$m.c!v$		$m.c!v$
$m.c?v$	$m.c!v$	$m.c?v$

Fig. 1. Labelled Transition Semantics for (high level) systems

$$\text{(S-SND)}\ \frac{[\![e]\!] = v}{c!\langle e\rangle .P \xrightarrow{c!v} P} \qquad \text{(S-RCV)}\ \frac{}{c?(x).P \xrightarrow{c?v} \{v/x\}P}$$

$$\text{(S-}\tau\text{)}\ \frac{}{\tau.P \xrightarrow{\tau} P} \qquad \text{(S-SUM-L)}\ \frac{P \xrightarrow{\alpha} P'}{P + Q \xrightarrow{\alpha} P'}$$

$$\text{(S-THEN)}\ \frac{P \xrightarrow{\alpha} P' \qquad [\![b]\!] = \mathsf{true}}{\mathsf{if}\ b\ \mathsf{then}\ P\ \mathsf{else}\ Q \xrightarrow{\alpha} P'} \qquad \text{(S-PDEF)}\ \frac{A(\tilde{x}) \Leftarrow P \qquad \{\tilde{e}/\tilde{x}\}P \xrightarrow{\alpha} Q}{A\langle\tilde{e}\rangle \xrightarrow{\alpha} Q}$$

Fig. 2. Pre-semantics of processes

value v along channel c from the external node m, or **(c)** τ, some node performs an internal activity.

The rules of the labelled transition semantics are depicted in Figure 1. They are based on a pre-semantics for processes, whose rules are given in Figure 2 and should be self-explanatory. Some symmetric rules have been omitted.

Rule (B-BROAD) models a node which is willing to transmit a value v, while the next four rules deal with how stations react to such a broadcast. When a station is within the transmitter's range and is waiting to detect a value along channel c, it will receive it correctly (Rule (B-REC)). On the other hand, if either the station is not waiting to detect a value along channel c (Rule (B-DEAF)) or is not in the sender's transmission range (rule (B-DISC)), then the broadcast is ignored. In rule (B-DEAF), $P \stackrel{c?v}{\not\longrightarrow}$ means that $P \xrightarrow{c?v} Q$ for no process Q. Finally, the $\mathbf{0}$ system term ignores all transmissions (Rule (B-$\mathbf{0}$)).

Rule (B-SYNC) models how nodes interact. The action performed by a system $(\Gamma \rhd M \mid N)$ is determined by the individual actions performed by $\Gamma \rhd M$ and $\Gamma \rhd N$, according to a (partial) binary operator for actions $\circ$ defined at the right of Rule (B-SYNC) in Figure 1. Here it is important to note that the action induced by a transmission and a reception is again a transmission, thus implementing broadcast communication; see [18] for a detailed discussion. The remaining rules, modelling internal activity, are straightforward.

Example 1. Consider the system $\mathcal{M} = \Gamma \triangleright M$, where Γ is the directed graph depicted on page 67, M is $m[\![A]\!] \mid n[\![A]\!] \mid l[\![A]\!]$ and $A \Leftarrow c?(x).c!\langle x \rangle$. All the internal nodes m, n, l are waiting to receive a value via channel c in $\mathcal{M}$; once any of these nodes has received such a value, it will forward it along the same channel. One possible behaviour of $\mathcal{M}$ can be summarised as follows; first node m detects a broadcast of an arbitrary value v along channel c, performed by node i. Nodes n, l are not affected by this broadcast, since they are not in the range of transmission of i. Using Rules (B-REC), (B-DISC) and (B-SYNCH) we can infer the transition $\mathcal{M} \xrightarrow{i.c?v} \mathcal{M}_1$, where $\mathcal{M}_1 = \Gamma \triangleright m[\![P_v]\!] \mid n[\![A]\!] \mid l[\![A]\!]$ and $P_v = c!\langle v \rangle$.

Next node m forwards value v to both nodes n and l, which are in its range of transmission. This is formalised by the transition $\mathcal{M}_1 \xrightarrow{m.c!v} \mathcal{M}_2$, where $\mathcal{M}_2 = \Gamma \triangleright m[\![\mathbf{0}]\!] \mid n[\![P_v]\!] \mid l[\![P_v]\!]$, which is obtained using rules (B-BROAD), (B-REC) and (B-SYNCH). Finally, we have a broadcast fired by n followed by one fired by l. Let $\mathcal{M}_3 = \Gamma \triangleright m[\![\mathbf{0}]\!] \mid n[\![\mathbf{0}]\!] \mid l[\![P_v]\!]$ and $\mathcal{M}_4 = \Gamma \triangleright m[\![\mathbf{0}]\!] \mid n[\![\mathbf{0}]\!] \mid l[\![\mathbf{0}]\!]$; then we have $\mathcal{M}_2 \xrightarrow{n.c!v} \mathcal{M}_3 \xrightarrow{l.c!v} \mathcal{M}_4$. □

Reduction Semantics. In the following we will want to discuss the behaviour of systems when isolated from its interface; that is, when input actions of interface nodes are inhibited. To this end, we define a reduction relation $\twoheadrightarrow$ by letting $\mathcal{M} \twoheadrightarrow \mathcal{N}$ if either $\mathcal{M} \xrightarrow{m.c!v} \mathcal{N}$ or $\mathcal{M} \xrightarrow{\tau} \mathcal{N}$; any maximal sequence of reductions rooted in a system $\mathcal{M}$ is called a computation for $\mathcal{M}$. Note that reductions $\twoheadrightarrow$ can be defined directly via a reduction semantics; see [2], §2.2 and §2.4.

3 Testing Distributed Systems

Extension of Systems. Following the approach of [3] we focus on a specific class of systems and how they can be extended to obtain larger systems.

Definition 1 (Composable Systems). *A system* $\mathcal{M} = \Gamma \triangleright M$ *is* composable *if whenever* $\Gamma \vdash m \to n$ *then either* $m \in nodes(M)$ *or* $n \in nodes(M)$. □

Henceforth we will always assume that systems are composable. Such systems do not allow connections between nodes in their interface; from the point of view of a system, the only visible information about its external environment consists of the set of access points to the system. In our terminology its interface.

Focusing on composable systems is not restrictive, in that connections between external nodes do not affect the behaviour of systems, so that any system $\mathcal{M}$ can be reduced to a composable one $\mathcal{M}'$ without affecting the transitions it can perform. Below we define an extension operator which allows us to infer a larger system from a given one, in which nodes which were external in the latter may now be connected.

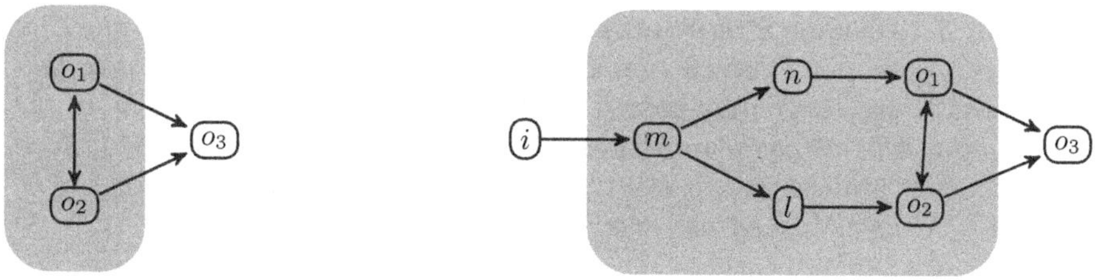

Fig. 3. Two systems $\mathcal{N}$ and $\mathcal{L} = (\mathcal{M} \Vdash \mathcal{N})$

Definition 2 (Systems Extension). *Let* $\mathcal{M} = (\Gamma_M \triangleright M), \mathcal{N} = (\Gamma_N \triangleright N)$ *be (composable) systems; the extension of* $\mathcal{M}$ *with* $\mathcal{N}$*,* $(\mathcal{M} \Vdash \mathcal{N})$*, is defined whenever* $nodes(M) \cap (\Gamma_N)_V = \emptyset$*, and it is equivalent to* $(\Gamma_M \cup \Gamma_N) \triangleright (M \mid N)$*, where* $\Gamma_M \cup \Gamma_N$ *is defined as the pointwise union of their sets of vertices and edges.* □

Intuitively, $\mathcal{M} \Vdash \mathcal{N}$ describes an extension of the system $\mathcal{M}$, where the information about its external environment is supplied by a second system $\mathcal{N}$; such system can contain the code run by interface nodes of $\mathcal{M}$, and the connections between its interface nodes. But it can also contain new nodes, which did not appear in $\mathcal{M}$. Also, in the composite system, the topological structure of $\mathcal{M}$ is left unchanged; this property is desirable, as we wish to use the operator $\Vdash$ to implement blackbox testing. In [3] we proved that $\Vdash$ is associative and closed with respect to the set of composable systems, and that it is the most expressive operator which can be used to implement blackbox testing.

Example 2. Let $\mathcal{M}$ be the system of Example 1; its interface $\mathsf{Intf}(\mathcal{M}) = \{i, o_1, o_2\}$ represents its external environment. By using the extension operator $\Vdash$ we can obtain a new system which contains $\mathcal{M}$, and which also gives new information about the connections of the nodes in the external environment of $\mathcal{M}$.

For example, consider the system $\mathcal{N} = \Gamma_N \triangleright o_1[\![A]\!] \mid o_2[\![A]\!]$, depicted on the left of Figure 3; here A is as defined in Example 1. This system specifies the code nodes o_1, o_2 are running, together with their connections; it also has a fresh node o_3 in its own interface. The composite system $\mathcal{L} = (\mathcal{M} \Vdash \mathcal{N})$ is well-defined, and it models the system obtained by extending $\mathcal{M}$ with the information regarding its external environment provided by $\mathcal{N}$. The system $\mathcal{L}$ is depicted to the right of Figure 3. Here the sub-system $\mathcal{N}$ could be viewed as a black box tester for the original system $\mathcal{M}$, placing probing code at two of $\mathcal{M}$'s interface nodes, and having another node o_3 where the results of this probing could be collected. □

Testing Preorders. We say that a system $\mathcal{M}$ is successful if the clause ω appears unguarded in the code of one of its nodes, while a computation of a system $\mathcal{M}$ is said to be successful if it contains a successful system. Given two systems $\mathcal{M}, \mathcal{T}$ we say that $\mathcal{M}$ **may-pass** $\mathcal{T}$ if $\mathcal{M} \Vdash \mathcal{T}$ has a successful computation, while $\mathcal{M}$ **must-pass** $\mathcal{T}$ if all its computations are successful.

Definition 3 (Testing Preorders). *Let $\mathcal{M}, \mathcal{N}$ be two systems; we say that $\mathcal{M} \sqsubseteq_{may} \mathcal{N}$ if for any $\mathcal{T}$ which can be used to extend both $\mathcal{M}, \mathcal{N}$ we have that $\mathcal{M}$* **may-pass** *$\mathcal{T}$ implies $\mathcal{N}$* **may-pass** *$\mathcal{T}$. Similarly, we define $\mathcal{M} \sqsubseteq_{must} \mathcal{N}$ in the same way, this time using the* **must-pass** *testing relation. We say that $\mathcal{M} \sqsubseteq \mathcal{N}$ if both $\mathcal{M} \sqsubseteq_{may} \mathcal{N}$ and $\mathcal{M} \sqsubseteq_{must} \mathcal{N}$ are true; finally, we use the notation $\mathcal{M} \simeq \mathcal{N}$ if both $\mathcal{M} \sqsubseteq \mathcal{N}$ and $\mathcal{N} \sqsubseteq \mathcal{M}$ are true.* □

Example 3 (Deadlocks). Let Γ represent the system topology containing two nodes m, e and having as its only connections $\Gamma \vdash m \rightarrow e, e \rightarrow m$. Let $\mathcal{M} = \Gamma \triangleright m[\![P]\!], \mathcal{N} = \Gamma \triangleright m[\![Q]\!]$, where $P = c!\langle v \rangle$, $Q = c?(x)\,.c!\langle v \rangle$. Both systems have the ability to broadcast value v along channel c; however, in $\mathcal{N}$ this broadcast is enabled only after a broadcast along channel c has been performed by node e. That is, $\mathcal{N} \not\rightarrow \mathcal{N}'$ for no $\mathcal{N}'$.

These two systems can be distinguished via the **must-pass** testing relation by the test $\mathcal{T} = \Gamma_e \triangleright e[\![c?(x)\,.\omega]\!]$; here Γ_e is the graph with the single node e. Note that $\mathcal{M}$ **must-pass** $\mathcal{T}$, while $\mathcal{N}$ **must-pass** $\mathcal{T}$ is not true. Therefore $\mathcal{M} \not\sqsubseteq_{\text{must}} \mathcal{N}$.

It is also possible to exhibit a test which $\mathcal{N}$ **must-pass**es, but $\mathcal{M}$ does not. To this end, let $\mathcal{T}' = \Gamma_e \triangleright e[\![c?(x)\,.\,\mathbf{0} + \tau.\omega]\!]$. It is easy to see that $\mathcal{M} \not\triangleright \mathcal{T}'$ has an unsuccessful computation; however, since $\mathcal{N}$ is deadlocked and cannot broadcast a value, the only possibility for $\mathcal{N} \not\triangleright \mathcal{T}'$ is that the testing component performs a τ action, thus entering a successful state. $\mathcal{N}$ **must-pass** $\mathcal{T}'$, hence $\mathcal{N} \not\sqsubseteq_{\text{must}} \mathcal{M}$.

What distinguishes $\mathcal{M}$ from $\mathcal{N}$ is that the latter cannot broadcast value v without first receiving a value from node e first, that is it is deadlocked. However suppose that we add the possibility to $\mathcal{N}$ to directly broadcast value v, leading to the system $\mathcal{N}' = \Gamma \triangleright m[\![Q']\!]$, where $Q' = Q + c!\langle v \rangle$; as we will see, it is impossible to distinguish $\mathcal{N}'$ from $\mathcal{M}$. Note that $\mathcal{N}'$ is not deadlocked.

Also, note that P, Q' are valid value-passing CCS processes, and that their sets of acceptances are different. In fact, in value-passing CCS, P **must-pass**es the test $c!\langle v \rangle + \tau.\omega$, but the same is not true for Q'; also, Q' **must-pass**es the test $c!\langle v \rangle\,.\omega$, but this is not true for P. This example gives an intuition that deadlocks, rather than acceptances, should be taken into account when giving a characterisation of the preorder $\sqsubseteq_{\text{must}}$. □

4 Extensional Semantics

The extensional semantics of systems is defined in Figure 4; its transitions $\mathcal{M} \xmapsto{\lambda} \mathcal{N}$ can be either **(a)** internal activities τ, **(b)** inputs $i.c?v$ performed by an input node i or **(c)** broadcast actions $c!v \triangleright \eta$, observable at a non-empty set of output nodes η. Note that any node name mentioned in the action of the transition occurs in the interface of the source configuration $\mathcal{M}$. The set of extensional actions is denoted by EAct_τ, while $\text{EAct} = \text{EAct}_\tau \setminus \{\tau\}$.

Rules (S-TAU) and (S-SHH) model unobservable activities. The first rule propagates internal activities of nodes to systems, while the second rule states that broadcasts which cannot be detected by any external node of a system cannot be observed. Rule (S-IN) propagates input actions to the extensional

$$(\text{S-TAU})\,\frac{\mathcal{M} \xrightarrow{m.\tau} \mathcal{N}}{\mathcal{M} \overset{\tau}{\longmapsto} \mathcal{N}} \qquad (\text{S-SHH})\,\frac{\mathcal{M} \xrightarrow{m.c!v} \mathcal{N} \qquad \{n \in \mathsf{Intf}(\mathcal{M}) \mid \mathcal{M} \vdash m \to n\} = \emptyset}{\mathcal{M} \overset{\tau}{\longmapsto} \mathcal{N}}$$

$$(\text{S-IN})\,\frac{\mathcal{M} \xrightarrow{i.c?v} \mathcal{N}}{\mathcal{M} \overset{i.c?v}{\longmapsto} \mathcal{N}} \qquad (\text{S-OUT})\,\frac{\mathcal{M} \xrightarrow{m.c!v} \mathcal{N} \qquad \eta := \{n \in \mathsf{Intf}(\mathcal{M}) \mid \mathcal{M} \vdash m \to n\} \neq \emptyset}{\mathcal{M} \overset{c!v \triangleright \eta}{\longmapsto} \mathcal{N}}$$

Fig. 4. Extensional Semantics

semantics; finally, Rule (S-OUT) models outputs which can be observed by a set of external nodes η.

The extensional semantics endows systems with the structure of a LTS [14], which we call the extensional LTS of systems. Most of the terminology used for LTSs in the literature can be then readapted to systems. However our definition of *weak* extensional actions, taken from [3] needs to be non-standard.

Definition 4 (Weak Extensional Actions). *For any systems $\mathcal{M}, \mathcal{N}$, we say that $\mathcal{M} \overset{\tau}{\models\!\!\Longrightarrow} \mathcal{N}$ if $\mathcal{M} \overset{\tau}{\longmapsto}^{*} \mathcal{N}$; here $\overset{\tau}{\longmapsto}^{*}$ is the reflexive, transitive closure of $\overset{\tau}{\longmapsto}$. Further, we say that $\mathcal{M} \overset{i.c?v}{\models\!\!\Longrightarrow} \mathcal{N}$ if $\mathcal{M} \overset{\tau}{\models\!\!\Longrightarrow}\overset{i.c?v}{\longmapsto}\overset{\tau}{\models\!\!\Longrightarrow} \mathcal{N}$. Finally, we say that $\mathcal{M} \overset{c!v \triangleright \eta}{\models\!\!\Longrightarrow} \mathcal{N}$ if either $\mathcal{M} \overset{\tau}{\models\!\!\Longrightarrow}\overset{c!v \triangleright \eta}{\longmapsto}\overset{\tau}{\models\!\!\Longrightarrow} \mathcal{N}$, or if there exist two non-empty sets of nodes η_1, η_2 such that $\eta_1 \cup \eta_2 = \eta, \eta_1 \cap \eta_2 = \emptyset$ and $\mathcal{M} \overset{c!v \triangleright \eta_1}{\models\!\!\Longrightarrow}\overset{c!v \triangleright \eta_2}{\models\!\!\Longrightarrow} \mathcal{N}$.*

These single weak transitions are extended to sequences $\mathcal{M} \overset{s}{\models\!\!\Longrightarrow} \mathcal{N}$, for $s \in EAct^{*}$, in the obvious manner. □

The complication in the definition of $\mathcal{M} \overset{c!v \triangleright \eta}{\models\!\!\Longrightarrow} \mathcal{N}$ is necessary in order to be able to simulate a multicast $c!v \triangleright \eta$, where the set η contains more than one node name, by a sequence of single broadcasts; this is shown in the Example below.

Example 4. Let $\mathcal{M} = \Gamma_M \triangleright m[\![c!v]\!]$, where $\Gamma_M \vdash m \to o_1, m \to o_2$. Also, let $\mathcal{N} = \Gamma_N \triangleright m[\![c!v]\!] \mid n[\![c!v]\!]$, where $\Gamma_N \vdash m \to o_1, n \to o_2$. Both systems are able to deliver value v, along channel c, to the interface nodes o_1, o_2. However, while $\mathcal{M}$ does it with a single broadcast, $\mathcal{N}$ uses two broadcasts which can be detected by nodes o_1, o_2 individually.

One could expect that there is a test that allows us to distinguish $\mathcal{M}$ from $\mathcal{N}$, in the sense of $\sqsubseteq_{\text{may}}$. However, at least intuitively, the broadcast of $\mathcal{M}$ can be simulated in system $\mathcal{N}$, by firing the two broadcasts in sequence. That is, the action $\mathcal{M} \overset{c!v \triangleright \{o_1, o_2\}}{\models\!\!\Longrightarrow}$ can be matched by another action $\mathcal{N} \overset{c!v \triangleright \{o_1, o_2\}}{\models\!\!\Longrightarrow}$, where the latter can be inferred from $\mathcal{N} \overset{c!v \triangleright \{o_1\}}{\models\!\!\Longrightarrow}\overset{c!v \triangleright \{o_2\}}{\models\!\!\Longrightarrow}$ using our non-standard definition of weak extensional actions.

If a test $\mathcal{T}$ is used to test the system $\mathcal{M}$, each configuration $\mathcal{T}'$ reached by the test $\mathcal{T}$ after $\mathcal{M}$ has broadcast value v, can be also obtained when $\mathcal{T}$ is used to test the system $\mathcal{N}$, by letting the latter fire its two broadcasts in sequence. That is, $\mathcal{M} \sqsubseteq_{\text{may}} \mathcal{N}$.

On the other hand, $\mathcal{N} \not\sqsubseteq_{\text{may}} \mathcal{M}$. To prove this, it is sufficient to provide a test $\mathcal{T}$ which $\mathcal{N}$ **may-passes**, but $\mathcal{M}$ does not. The reader can easily check that $\Gamma_T \triangleright o_1[\![c?(x).c!\langle w\rangle]\!] \mid o_2[\![c?(x).c?(y).\mathsf{if}\ (x = y)\ \mathsf{then}\ \mathbf{0}\ \mathsf{else}\ \omega]\!]$, where $\Gamma_T \vdash o_1 \rightarrow o_2$, is one such test.

A similar argument shows that $\mathcal{N} \sqsubseteq_{\text{must}} \mathcal{M}$, while $\mathcal{M} \not\sqsubseteq_{\text{must}} \mathcal{N}$. □

5 Characterisation of the Testing Preorders

Traces and Deadlock Traces. A system $\mathcal{M}$ is *finite spanning* if any $\mathcal{N}$ in the extensional LTS generated by $\mathcal{M}$ can reach a finite number of systems by performing a transition. It is *convergent* if it has no infinite computation, *strongly convergent* if every state in the extensional LTS it generates is convergent.

From Example 3 we know that must-testing preorder is sensitive to deadlocks; this is the essential ingredient to the following definition:

Definition 5 (Traces, Deadlock Traces). *Let $\delta \notin EAct$. For any $\mathcal{M}$ we let*

$$Traces(\mathcal{M}) = \{\, s \in EAct^* \mid \mathcal{M} \overset{s}{\models\!\!\Longrightarrow} \mathcal{N} \text{ for some } \mathcal{N} \,\}$$

$$Dtraces(\mathcal{M}) = \{\, s{::}\delta \mid \mathcal{M} \overset{s}{\models\!\!\Longrightarrow} \mathcal{N} \text{ for some } \mathcal{N}, s \in EAct^* \text{ such that } \mathcal{N} \not\models\!\triangleright \,\}$$

We use the symbol :: *to separate occurrences of elements in lists.* □

Example 5. Consider again the system $\mathcal{M}, \mathcal{N}$ of Example 3. We have already noted that $\mathcal{M} \not\sqsubseteq_{\text{must}} \mathcal{N}$, and $\mathcal{N} \not\sqsubseteq_{\text{must}} \mathcal{M}$. Also, we have that $\delta \in \text{Dtraces}(\mathcal{N})$ (note that $\mathcal{N} \not\models\!\triangleright$), while $\delta \notin \text{Dtraces}(\mathcal{M})$. Further, we have that $c!v \triangleright \{e\}{::}\delta \in \text{Dtraces}(\mathcal{M})$, but this trace is not in $\text{Dtraces}(\mathcal{N})$; in fact, in the latter system the broadcast of value v can happen only after a value has been received along channel c. That is, $c?w{::}c!v \triangleright \{e\}{::}\delta \in \text{Dtraces}(\mathcal{M})$ for an arbitrary value w.

Now consider the system $\mathcal{N}'$ of Example 3. Note that $c!v \triangleright \{e\}{::}\delta \in \text{Dtraces}(\mathcal{N}')$, and $\delta \notin \text{Dtraces}(\mathcal{N}')$. Even more, the two systems $\mathcal{M}$, $\mathcal{N}'$ share the same set of deadlock traces, the minimal fragment of which we are interested in being $\{c!\langle v\rangle {::}\delta, c?(w) {::}\delta \mid w \text{ arbitrary value}\,\}$. Theorem 1, coming up, implies that $\mathcal{M}$ and $\mathcal{N}'$ cannot be distinguished by the **must-pass** relation. □

Full Abstraction. We can now state the main result of the paper:

Theorem 1 (Characterisation of the testing preorders). *Let $\mathcal{M}, \mathcal{N}$, be two proper systems. Then*

(1) $\mathcal{M} \sqsubseteq_{may} \mathcal{N}$ if and only if $Traces(\mathcal{M}) \subseteq Traces(\mathcal{N})$,
(2) if $\mathcal{M}, \mathcal{N}$ are finite spanning and strongly convergent then $\mathcal{M} \sqsubseteq_{must} \mathcal{N}$ if and only if $Dtraces(\mathcal{M}) \supseteq Dtraces(\mathcal{N})$.

The restriction to proper systems is natural, as the special action ω should only appear in systems used for testing. The restriction to strongly convergent systems in part (2) is needed because in our definition of deadlock traces we did not take divergence into account. Doing so would be quite complicated as, due to the non-blocking nature of broadcasts, it is possible to define two divergent systems $\mathcal{M}, \mathcal{N}$ which are not must-testing related. This is in contrast with the standard theory of must-testing [7]. See [2], Remark 4.4.3, Page 88, for a detailed discussion. See also §4.4.3, Page 98, for a potential solution to this problem.

In this extended abstract we only have space to give an outline of Theorem 1(2). This is split into two parts, soundness and completeness.

Theorem 2 (Soundness for $\sqsubseteq_{\mathbf{must}}$). *If Dtraces($\mathcal{M}$) $\supseteq$ Dtraces($\mathcal{N}$) then $\mathcal{M}$ $\sqsubseteq_{must}$ $\mathcal{N}$, for proper, finite spanning, strongly convergent systems.*

Proof. It suffices to show that inclusion of deadlock traces is preserved when extending systems by adding a new node. That is, if Dtraces($\mathcal{M}$) $\supseteq$ Dtraces($\mathcal{N}$), and $\mathcal{T} = \Gamma_T \triangleright e[\![P]\!]$ is a system such that $\mathcal{M} \not\models \mathcal{T}$ and $\mathcal{N} \not\models \mathcal{T}$ are defined, then Dtraces($\mathcal{M} \not\models \mathcal{T}$) $\supseteq$ Dtraces($\mathcal{N} \not\models \mathcal{T}$). See [2], §4.3.1 and §4.4.1, for a proof. □

The standard approach to prove the converse to Theorem 2 is that of providing characteristic tests for deadlock traces.

Proposition 1 (Characteristic Tests). *Let $\mathcal{M}$ be a proper, finite spanning, strongly convergent system. Then for any set of nodes η such that* $\mathsf{Intf}(\mathcal{M}) \subseteq \eta$ *and trace t there exists a system $\mathcal{T}_t^\eta$ such that $t \notin$ Dtraces($\mathcal{M}$) if and only if* $\mathcal{M}$ **must-pass** $\mathcal{T}_t^\eta$. *We say that $\mathcal{T}_t^\eta$ is a* characteristic test *for t.*

Proof. See §4.3.2 and §4.4.2 of [2]. □

Characteristic tests are parameterised by a set of nodes η; in general the topology of a test depends on the interface of the system being tested. Here we only describe the informal behaviour of the characteristics tests $\mathcal{T}_t^\eta$, while formal definitions are given in [4], §A.

A characteristic test $\mathcal{T}_t^\eta$ contains all the nodes in η and a fresh node cn, called controller node. The controller node is connected (in both directions) with each of the nodes in η. The test $\mathcal{T}_t^\eta$ tests whether a system does not exhibit the deadlock trace t by testing sequentially for every action included in t (or for deadlock when testing for δ), then declaring success whenever it determines that the current action being tested cannot be performed by the tested system.

To achieve this, in $\mathcal{T}_t^\eta$ the nodes in η constantly report (via a fresh channel) the observed behaviour of the tested system to the controller node; these partial information are then used by the latter to infer whether the (extensional) action being tested has been performed by the tested system, in which case $\mathcal{T}_t^\eta$ proceeds by testing for the next action in t. In the process of inferring whether an extensional action has been performed by the tested system, the controller node also asks nodes in η to report the absence of observed behaviour. For example, detecting an action of the form $c!v \triangleright \eta'$ requires that no node in $\eta \setminus \eta'$ observed a broadcast. Or, when testing for deadlock, no node in η should detect a broadcast.

Below we give a detailed explanation of the protocol used by $\mathcal{T}_t^\eta$ to detect an extensional action, with a particular emphasis to an output action of the form $c!v \triangleright \eta'$; the protocol runs in three stages.

Detect: The controller node waits for a relevant subset of nodes in η, consisting of those nodes mentioned in the action being tested, to report to the controller node that their local contribution to the action being tested has been performed. In the case of an action of the form $c!v \triangleright \eta'$, node cn awaits a message from each of the nodes in cn. Each of such nodes broadcasts to the cn only if it detects a broadcast of value v along channel c.

Check: The controller node requests to all the nodes in η whether they observed any other additional activity from the tested system, and awaits a response from each of such nodes; in contrast, the latter do not answer to such a request if they observed some activity from the tested system. In the case of an action of the form $c!v \triangleright \eta'$, nodes in $\eta' \setminus \eta$ do not answer whether they detected a broadcast performed by the tested system.

Proceed: The controller node sends a request to all nodes in η that it is ready to detect the next action in the trace being tested. If nodes in η observe some activity performed by the testee, they deadlock, causing the execution of $\mathcal{T}^\eta$ to be eventually unable to proceed.

Failure: At any given point, the controller node can non-deterministically declare success, exception made for when it detects that the entire trace being tested has been performed by the testee. In this case $\mathcal{T}_t^\eta$ deadlocks, thus causing the test to fail.

Theorem 3 (Completeness for $\sqsubseteq_{\mathbf{must}}$). *$\mathcal{M} \sqsubseteq_{must} \mathcal{N}$ implies Dtraces($\mathcal{M}$) $\supseteq$ Dtraces($\mathcal{N}$), assuming both are finite spanning, strongly convergent, proper systems.*

Proof. Suppose $\mathcal{M} \sqsubseteq_{\text{must}} \mathcal{N}$ is true and $t \in$ Dtraces($\mathcal{N}$); we need to show that $t \in$ Dtraces($\mathcal{M}$). This will follow from the previous proposition if $\mathcal{M}$ **must-pass** $\mathcal{T}_t^\eta$ is not true, where we choose η to be $\mathsf{Intf}(\mathcal{M}) \cup \mathsf{Intf}(\mathcal{N})$.

But this follows form the assumption $\mathcal{M} \sqsubseteq_{\text{must}} \mathcal{N}$ because again the previous proposition gives that $\mathcal{N}$ **must-pass** $\mathcal{T}_t^\eta$ is false. □

6 Application: Virtual Shared Memory

To show the usefulness of our results, we prove the correctness of a *Virtual Shared Memory* (**VSM**) protocol without replicas. To keep the discussion simple, we consider the case in which the VSM is accessed by two users; however, our case study can be generalised to an arbitrary number of users. We only give an informal description of the specification and the implementation we provide for VSMs, while we defer all formal definitions to [4], §B.

The Specification. In a virtual shared memory protocol, a distributed system provides to two or more users the ability to write and read memory locations which are physically stored at different nodes, while giving them the illusion that the whole memory is stored at a single node.

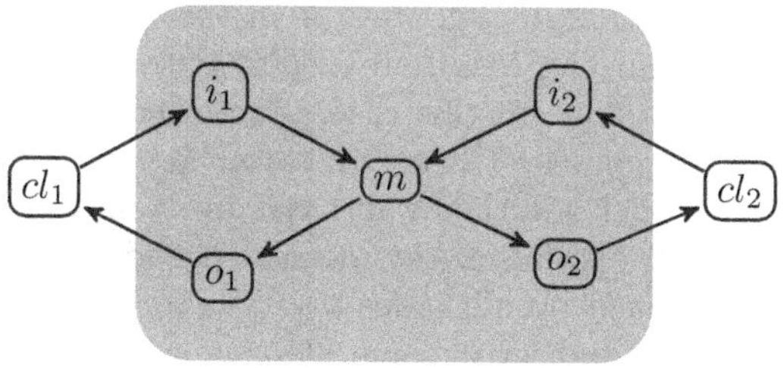

The system $\mathcal{V}$ specifying a VSM is depicted on the left. Nodes i_j, o_j, where $j = 1, 2$, regulate the flow of messages between a client cl_j and the site where the memory is actually stored, m. Node i_j discards any ill-formed request issued by client cl_j, while o_j ensures that the answer by m corresponds to a request originally performed by cl_j. More specifically, let $j = 1, 2$. Upon receiving a message of the form **read**(x), or **write**(x, n), node i_j will store it in a local queue. At any given point, it will dequeue the next element stored and will forward it through channel c_j. Node m is equipped with two queues, q_1 and q_2; upon receiving a request from node i_j, it will enqueue it in q_j. At any given point, node m can dequeue the next request from one of the queues q_k, $k = 1, 2$. If such a request has the form read x, then it will forward the value stored at its memory location x along channel d_k. If the request has the form write(x,n), node m will update the content of variable x to n, then it will broadcast the new value of x along channel d_k. Upon receiving a message along channel d_k, node o_k stores it in a local queue. At any given point, it non-deterministically dequeues the next stored element, and forwards it to client cl_k.

Since our proof methods are sound only for finite spanning systems, we can assume that the size of the memory stored at node m is finite, since the nodes cl_j, $j = 1, 2$ can only send a finite amount of requests to the system $\mathcal{V}$.

The Implementation. Next we turn our attention to a possible distributed implementation of our VSM. The idea is that of partitioning the memory stored at node m of the specification, among different nodes, $m_1, \cdots, m_k$.

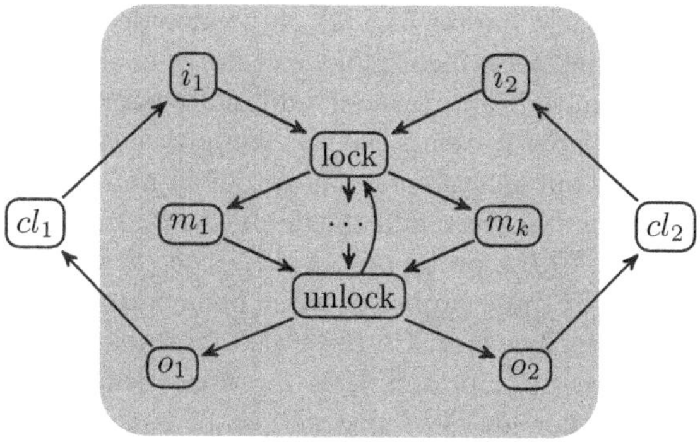

Each node contains only a subset of the locations stored in the total memory, and no memory location is stored in more than one node. To ensure that requests are processed in the same order in which they have been issued by a client, the access to nodes $m_1, \cdots, m_k$ is regulated by two nodes, called *lock* and *unlock*. These two nodes ensure that nodes $m_1, \cdots, m_k$ never handle two requests concurrently.

In the implementation $\mathcal{I}$, the behaviour of nodes cl_j, i_j and o_j, where $j = 1, 2$, is the same as in the specification $\mathcal{V}$. Therefore we concentrate on describing the behaviour of the other nodes. Node lock is equipped with two queues q_1, q_2. Upon receiving a request along channel c_j, $j = 1, 2$, it will store it in the queue q_j. Node lock is also equipped with a boolean flag l, initially set to true. At any given time, node lock checks if l is set to true; in this case, it sets the flag to false, then it selects a queue q_k, $k = 1, 2$, dequeues the next message stored in it, and broadcasts it along channel c_k. Node lock will then wait to receive a message along channel d_k, before resetting the flag l to false. Any message broadcast by node lock along channels d_k will be received by all nodes $m_1, \cdots, m_k$. Such a message contains either a request to read and write some memory location x, which is stored in exactly one of such nodes, say m_n. Node m_n will reply to this request, updating the contents of location x, if needed, by broadcasting a message along channel d_k, which will in turn received by node unlock. Upon receiving a message along channel d_k, node unlock immediately broadcasts it along the same channel, causing both the message to be delivered at node o_k, and node lock to set its internal flag to true.

In [4], §B, we give a formal description in our language of both the Specification, as the system $\mathcal{V}$, and the distributed Implementation, as the system term $\mathcal{I}$. The proof that the Implementation satisfies the Specification consists in establishing that $\mathcal{I} \simeq \mathcal{V}$. This is achieved by using the alternative characterisations of the preorders in terms of traces and Deadlock traces. A more detailed explanation of both the specification and implementation of our virtual shared memory can be found in [2], §5.5 at Page 124.

Theorem 4. *Dtraces*($\mathcal{I}$) = *Dtraces*($\mathcal{V}$) *and Traces*($\mathcal{I}$) = *Traces*($\mathcal{V}$). *In particular,* $\mathcal{I} \simeq \mathcal{V}$. □

7 Conclusions

The achievements of this paper have been more theoretical than practical, although we have also provided some evidence of applicability, via a case study. Many other applications can be found in Chapter 5 of [2]; these include connectionless and connection-oriented routing, for which implementations at different levels of the TCP/IP reference model have been provided, and multicast routing.

To the best of our knowledge, this paper presents the first completeness result for testing preorders applied to distributed systems. The proof is non-trivial, requiring the isolation of our *extensional actions*, and the detailed programming of the characteristic testing contexts. These probe systems via the *extensional actions* and then combine the results of these probes to elicit behavioural characteristics. The ability to define these characteristic tests also depends on the level of our abstraction of our system descriptions. It is far from clear if the completeness result remains true at other levels of abstraction, or if more general systems are considered. For example we already know from [3] that if we add probabilistic behaviour to nodes then the natural generalisation to probabilistic simulations no longer characterises the (probabilistic) testing preorders. Indeed it was this surprising phenomenon which prompted the research reported in the current paper. So it will be interesting to see what extra constructs can be added to our current non-probabilistic calculus without invalidating our characterisation results. Possibilities include introducing features which can be found in wireless networks, such as node mobility [9,16,19], or introducing time and/or collisions, as in [1,5,11,13,21].

References

1. Bugliesi, M., Gallina, L., Marin, A., Rossi, S., Hamadou, S.: Interference-sensitive preorders for manets. In: QEST, pp. 189–198 (2012)
2. Cerone, A.: Foundations of Ad Hoc Wireless Networks. PhD thesis, Trinity College Dublin (2012). http://software.imdea.org/~andrea.cerone/works/thesis.pdf
3. Cerone, A., Hennessy, M.: Modelling probabilistic wireless networks. LMCS 9(3) (2013)
4. Cerone, A., Hennessy, M.: Characterising testing preorders for broadcasting distributed systems (extended version) (2014). http://software.imdea.org/~andrea.cerone/works/TGC14extended.pdf
5. Cerone, A., Hennessy, M., Merro, M.: Modelling MAC-Layer Communications in Wireless Systems. In: De Nicola, R., Julien, C. (eds.) COORDINATION 2013. LNCS, vol. 7890, pp. 16–30. Springer, Heidelberg (2013)
6. Daws, C., Kwiatkowska, M.Z., Norman, G.: Automatic verification of the ieee-1394 root contention protocol with kronos and prism. Electr. Notes Theor. Comput. Sci. **66**(2), 104–119 (2002)
7. De Nicola, R., Hennessy, M.: Testing equivalences for processes. TCS **34**, 83–133 (1984)
8. Ene, C.F., Muntean, T.: Testing theories for broadcasting processes. Sci. Ann. Cuza Univ. **11**, 214–230 (2002)
9. Ghassemi, F., Fokkink, W., Movaghar, A.: Equational reasoning on mobile ad hoc networks. Fund. Inf. **105**(4), 375–415 (2010)
10. Hennessy, M., Rathke, J.: Bisimulations for a calculus of broadcasting systems. TCS, 200 (1998)
11. Lanese, I., Sangiorgi, D.: An operational semantics for a calculus for wireless systems. TCS **411**(19), 1928–1948 (2010)
12. Lerda, F., Sisto, R.: Distributed-Memory Model Checking with SPIN. In: Dams, D.R., Gerth, R., Leue, S., Massink, M. (eds.) SPIN 1999. LNCS, vol. 1680, pp. 22–39. Springer, Heidelberg (1999)
13. Merro, M., Ballardin, F., Sibilio, E.: A timed calculus for wireless systems. TCS **412**(47), 6585–6611 (2011)
14. Milner, R.: A calculus of communicating systems. LNCS, 92 (1980)
15. Musuvathi, M., Engler, D.R.: Model checking large network protocol implementations. In: NSDI, pp. 155–168 (2004)
16. Nanz, S., Hankin, C.: A framework for security analysis of mobile wireless networks. TCS, 367 (2006)
17. Nanz, S., Hankin, C.: Static analysis of routing protocols for ad-hoc networks (March 25, 2004)
18. Prasad, K.: A calculus of broadcasting systems. SCP, 25 (1995)
19. Singh, A., Ramakrishnan, C.R., Smolka, S.A.: A process calculus for mobile ad hoc networks. SCP **75**(6), 440–469 (2010)
20. Tanenbaum, A.S.: Computer Networks. 4th ed. Prentice Hall PTR (2002)
21. Wang, M., Lu, Y.: A timed calculus for mobile ad hoc networks. arXiv preprint arXiv:1301.0045 (2013)

Tests for Establishing Security Properties

Vincent Cheval[1,2], Stéphanie Delaune[3(✉)], and Mark Ryan[1]

[1] LORIA, CNRS and Inria Nancy - Grand Est, Paris, France
[2] School of Computer Science, University of Birmingham, Birmingham, UK
[3] LSV, CNRS and ENS Cachan, Paris, France
delaune@lsv.ens-cachan.fr

Abstract. Ensuring strong security properties in some cases requires participants to carry out tests during the execution of a protocol. A classical example is electronic voting: participants are required to verify the presence of their ballots on a bulletin board, and to verify the computation of the election outcome. The notion of *certificate transparency* is another example, in which participants in the protocol are required to perform tests to verify the integrity of a certificate log.

We present a framework for modelling systems with such 'testable properties', using the applied pi calculus. We model the tests that are made by participants in order to obtain the security properties. Underlying our work is an attacker model called "malicious but cautious", which lies in between the Dolev-Yao model and the "honest but curious" model. The malicious-but-cautious model is appropriate for cloud computing providers that are potentially malicious but are assumed to be cautious about launching attacks that might cause user tests to fail.

1 Introduction

Security protocols are short distributed programs designed to achieve a security goal, such as authentication or secure messaging. In an ideal situation, the security goal is guaranteed to participants provided they adhere to the protocol. Sometimes, however, it is not possible to devise a protocol which is certain to achieve the goal; instead, the protocol guarantees that, if the goal fails, then the participants have a means to discover that fact.

Electronic voting protocols are such an example. In voting protocols, the participants are voters, and it is assumed that the election authorities and the network and other infrastructure is controlled by the attacker. Under those assumptions, there is no protocol which guarantees that the authorities declare the correct election outcome. Therefore, protocols aim for a weaker property, namely, if the election authorities declare an incorrect outcome then the participants can discover the fact. More precisely, the protocol outputs certain data, and the participants have a set of tests they perform on the data, and if the tests return a positive result then the declared outcome is guaranteed to be correct [11], or correct with high probability [5]. One can apply this idea to the incoercibility property of voting systems: in *Caveat Coercitor*, voters can perform a test to determine if certain kinds of coercion have taken place [10]. Bitcoin [14]

M. Maffei and E. Tuosto (Eds.): TGC 2014, LNCS 8902, pp. 82–96, 2014.
DOI: 10.1007/978-3-662-45917-1_6

is also an example: a Bitcoin user being offered a bitcoin can be sure that it has not already been spent only by performing tests on the public log of spent bitcoins.

In this paper, we propose a model and a framework to analyse protocols where partipants run tests on output data in order to determine if the expected properties hold. We call such properties *testable properties*. We elaborate two case studies. The first one is about *certificate transparency*, which is a protocol designed to provide greater evidence about the trustworthiness of public-key certificates [12]. Certificate transparency relies on certificate authorities maintaining a public log, and on client browsers performing tests on the log. The desired security property is expected to hold if the tests are positive. The second case study is about the French electronic passport, which has been shown not to satisfy expected privacy properties in some circumstances [2]. Although the French passport user can't guarantee that her privacy is preserved, she can perform a test to detect if her privacy may have been violated. If the test is negative, then the desired privacy property holds.

Instead of thinking that the protocols we consider provide testable properties (that is, properties that hold conditionally on certain run-time tests), one may consider that the original properties hold, but in the context of a weaker attacker that is not willing to take actions that can be detected by the tests. This view corresponds to situations in which the "attacker" is actually a service provider; in voting, it is the election authority, and in certificate transparency, it is the network provider. Such service providers have an incentive to give good service, and therefore traditional Dolev-Yao attacker model is too strong for them. To cope with this issue, an alternative model of an attacker has been considered in the literature: *honest-but-curious*. Roughly, an honest-but-curious provider will follow the protocol but he will also try to derive some information from the messages he learned during the execution. However, this model is too weak for our examples; there is simply no reason to suppose that the service provider will not engage in active attacks if he can do so undetectably. We adopt the term "malicious-but-cautious"; the service provider is assumed to be malicious if he can get away with it, but cautious in not leaving any verifiable evidence of its misbehaviour. This attacker model is related to the *covert adversary* [3] and *active security adversary* [8] introduced in the setting of secure multiparty computation. Malicious-but-cautious attackers are weaker than the all-powerful Dolev-Yao attackers, but stronger than the honest-but-curious attackers that confine themselves to passive attacks.

Our Contributions. We develop a model and framework based on the applied pi calculus to analyse security protocols that rely on participants carrying out tests. Our model includes new primitives to allow participants to record information which will later be inputs to the tests. We specify a language for formulating the tests that are performed by participants. We illustrate our framework with two case studies. One of the case studies, called certificate transparency, is a new protocol which has not yet been studied by the academic community. We give a model and formalisation for the first time.

2 Model for Security Protocols

In this section, we introduce the cryptographic process calculus that we will use for describing protocols. This calculus is close to the applied pi calculus as defined in [1]. However, in order to model tests performed on logs after an execution, we add a special construct (namely rec) to allow participants of a protocol to record the information that will be used for that purpose.

2.1 Messages

A protocol consists of some agents communicating on a network. The messages sent by the agents are modelled using an abstract term algebra. For this, we assume an infinite set $\mathcal{N}$ of *names* which are used for representing keys, nonces, channels, and also public data like agent names. We also consider an infinite set $\mathcal{X}$ of *variables*, and a *signature* $\mathcal{F}$ consisting of a finite set of function symbols.

Terms are defined as names, variables, and function symbols applied to other terms. Let $N \subseteq \mathcal{N}$, $X \subseteq \mathcal{X}$ and $F \subseteq \mathcal{F}$. The set of terms built from N and X by applying function symbols from F is denoted $\mathcal{T}(F, X \cup N)$. We write $fv(u)$ (resp. $fn(u)$) for the set of variables (resp. names) occurring in a term u. A term is *closed* if it does not contain any variable.

To model algebraic properties of cryptographic primitives, we define an *equational theory* by a finite set E of equations $u = v$ with $u, v \in \mathcal{T}(\mathcal{F}, \mathcal{X})$, *i.e.*, u and v do not contain names. We define $=_\mathsf{E}$ to be the smallest equivalence relation on terms, that contains E and that is closed under application of function symbols and substitutions of terms for variables.

Example 1. A typical signature that can be used to model security protocols that rely on signature, asymmetric encryption, and list is $\mathcal{F}_\mathsf{sign}$ where:

$\mathcal{F}_\mathsf{sign} = \{\mathsf{sign},\ \mathsf{getmsg},\ \mathsf{vk},\ \mathsf{aenc},\ \mathsf{adec},\ \mathsf{pk},\ \langle\ \rangle,\ \mathsf{proj}_1,\ \mathsf{proj}_2,\ \mathsf{h},\ ::,\ \mathsf{head},\ \mathsf{tail},\ \perp\}$.

The function symbols sign, getmsg, and vk are used to represent signatures, whereas aenc, adec, and pk are used to model asymmetric encryption. We consider hashes (of arity 2), pairs and operators to manipulate lists. Then, we consider the equational theory E_sign, defined by the following equations ($i \in \{1, 2\}$):

$$\begin{array}{rcr} \mathsf{getmsg}(\mathsf{sign}(x,y),\mathsf{vk}(y)) = x & \mathsf{proj}_1(\langle x_1, x_2\rangle) = x_1 & \mathsf{head}(x::y) = x \\ \mathsf{adec}(\mathsf{aenc}(x,\mathsf{pk}(y)),y) = x & \mathsf{proj}_2(\langle x_1, x_2\rangle) = x_2 & \mathsf{tail}(x::y) = y \end{array}$$

Many interesting security properties, in particular privacy-type properties (*e.g.* in [2,4,9]) are formalised relying on the notion of *static equivalence* that compares frames. A frame is a sequence of the form $\nu\,\mathcal{E}.[w_1 \rhd u_1, \ldots, w_n \rhd u_n]$ where $\mathcal{E}$ is a finite set of restricted names (intuively the fresh ones), and the remaining part can be seen as a substitution with domain $\mathrm{dom}(\varphi) = \{w_1, \ldots, w_n\}$. The variables w_i enable us to refer to ground terms u_i. We denote by $=_\alpha$ the relation between frames that corresponds to α-renaming of bound names. Two frames are equivalent when the attacker cannot detect the difference between the two situations they represent, that is, his ability to distinguish whether two recipes M and N produce the same term does not depend on the frame.

Definition 1. *Let φ be a frame, and $M, N \in \mathcal{T}(\mathcal{F}, \mathcal{N} \cup \mathcal{X})$. We say that M and N are* equal in *the frame φ, and write $(M = N)\varphi$, if there exists $\mathcal{E}$ such that $\varphi =_\alpha \mathsf{new}\ \mathcal{E}.\sigma$, $(fn(M) \cup fn(N)) \cap \mathcal{E} = \emptyset$, and $M\sigma =_\mathsf{E} N\sigma$.*

We say that two frames φ and φ' are statically equivalent, *and write $\varphi \sim \varphi'$ when* $\mathrm{dom}(\varphi) = \mathrm{dom}(\varphi')$; *and for all $M, N \in \mathcal{T}(\mathcal{F}, \mathcal{N} \cup \mathcal{X})$, we have that:*

$$(M = N)\varphi \Leftrightarrow (M = N)\varphi'.$$

Example 2. Relying on the signature and equational theory introduced in Example 1, let $\varphi_v = \mathsf{new}\{sk\}.[w_1 \rhd \mathsf{aenc}(v, \mathsf{pk}(sk))]$. We have that $\varphi_{yes} \sim \varphi_{no}$. Intuitively, the equivalence holds since the attacker is not able to reconstruct the ciphertext or to open it. However, we have that $\varphi'_{yes} \not\sim \varphi'_{no}$ where:

$$\varphi'_v = \mathsf{new}\{sk\}.[w_1 \rhd \mathsf{aenc}(v, \mathsf{pk}(sk)),\ w_2 \rhd \mathsf{pk}(sk)].$$

2.2 Processes

Our *processes* are as in the applied pi calculus [1], except for the record message $\mathsf{rec}(x, v).P$ construct discussed below. Moreover, the applied pi calculus relies extensively on the renaming of bound variables and names. This is practical in presence of replication (! construct) but becomes a problem when one needs to refer to some particular variable and/or name after a protocol execution. In order to have a reliable way to talk about variables and names, we decorate each bang operator with an index, and we introduce the notion of *pattern*.

$$\begin{array}{rll} \overline{u} := & x[\mathsf{i}_1, \ldots, \mathsf{i}_k] & \text{variable pattern} \\ & \mid n[\mathsf{i}_1, \ldots, \mathsf{i}_k] & \text{name pattern} \\ & \mid \mathsf{f}(\overline{u_1}, \ldots, \overline{u_n}) & \text{function symbol application} \end{array}$$

where each i_j is either an index variable or an integer. The index variables will be instantiated each time the bang operator carrying this index will be unfolded. Using this notation, the set $\mathcal{N}$ of names (resp. $\mathcal{X}$ of variables) introduced in the previous section is made up of element of the form $n[i_1, \ldots, i_k]$ (resp. $x[i_1, \ldots, i_k]$) with $i_1, \ldots, i_k \in \mathbb{N}$. Note that a term is a pattern. We sometimes write $\overline{n}$ (resp. $\overline{x}$) instead of $n[\mathsf{i}_1, \ldots, \mathsf{i}_k]$ (resp. $x[\mathsf{i}_1, \ldots, \mathsf{i}_k]$). We also write n instead of $n[]$.

The grammar of our *processes* is as follows:

$$\begin{array}{rl} P, Q := 0 \mid (P \mid Q) \mid \mathsf{new}\,\overline{n}.P \mid !^{\mathsf{i} \geq j}\, P \mid \mathsf{if}\ \overline{u} = \overline{v}\ \mathsf{then}\ P\ \mathsf{else}\ Q \\ \mid \mathsf{in}(\overline{u}, \overline{x}).P \mid \mathsf{out}(\overline{u}, \overline{v}).P \mid \mathsf{rec}(\overline{z}, \overline{v}).P \end{array}$$

where i is an index variable, j an integer, $\overline{u}, \overline{v}$ are patterns, and $\overline{n}$ (resp. $\overline{x}$) is a name (resp. variable) pattern. For sake of clarity, we simply write $!^{\mathsf{i}_1}$ instead of $!^{\mathsf{i}_1 \geq 1}$, and we omit "$\mathsf{else}\ Q$" when $Q = 0$. We also use $\mathsf{let}\ x = u\ \mathsf{in}\ P$ as syntactic sugar for $P\{x \mapsto u\}$, *i.e.*, P in which occurrence of x has been replaced by u.

Example 3. The process $!\mathsf{new}\ n_1.!\mathsf{new}\ n_2.\mathsf{out}(c, \langle n_1, n_2 \rangle)$ in applied pi calculus becomes $!^{\mathsf{i}_1}\ \mathsf{new}\ n_1[\mathsf{i}_1].!^{\mathsf{i}_2}\ \mathsf{new}\ n_2[\mathsf{i}_1, \mathsf{i}_2].\mathsf{out}(c[], \langle n_1[\mathsf{i}_1], n_2[\mathsf{i}_1, \mathsf{i}_2] \rangle)$.

The applied pi calculus is very convenient to model memoryless protocols. However, in this calculus, it is very difficult to express protocols that rely on logs. To address this issue, we add the construction $\mathsf{rec}(z, v)$ to represent the record of the term v in the log through the variable z. The record message construct $\mathsf{rec}(z, v).P$ introduces the possibility to log special entries. Intuitively, this construct will be used to allow a participant to record some information which he may later use to perform some tests.

As usual, names and variables have scopes that are delimited by restrictions, inputs, and rec contructs. We respectively write $\overline{fv}(P), \overline{bv}(P), \overline{fn}(P)$ and $\overline{bn}(P)$ for the sets of *free variables pattern, bound variables pattern, free names pattern,* and *bound names pattern* of a process P. We assume that processes are *name pattern and variable pattern distinct, i.e.,*

- $\overline{bn}(P) \cap \overline{fn}(P) = \overline{bv}(P) \cap \overline{fv}(P) = \emptyset$, and
- any name pattern and variable pattern is at most bound once.

Moreover, a variable that is bound by a rec construct can only occur once in the process, and each bang operator is annotated with a distinct index variable.

Example 4. The process $P_{\mathsf{CA}} := \; !^{\mathsf{i}_1 \geq 1}\; \mathsf{in}(c, x[\mathsf{i}_1]).\ \mathsf{rec}(z_{\mathsf{log}}[\mathsf{i}_1], x[\mathsf{i}_1])$ models an agent, *e.g.*, a certificate authority, who logs all the messages that he receives on channel c. We have $\overline{fn}(P_{\mathsf{CA}}) = \{c\}$, $\overline{bv}(P_{\mathsf{CA}}) = \{x[\mathsf{i}_1], z_{\mathsf{log}}[\mathsf{i}_1]\}$, and $\overline{fv}(P_{\mathsf{CA}}) = \emptyset$.

2.3 Semantics

The semantics is given by a relation defined over *configurations*.

Definition 2. *A* configuration *is a tuple* $(\mathcal{E}; \mathcal{P}; \Phi_{\mathcal{A}}; \Phi_{log})$ *where:*

- $\mathcal{E}$ *is a set of names;*
- $\mathcal{P}$ *is a multiset of processes such that* $\overline{fv}(P) = \emptyset$ *for any* $P \in \mathcal{P}$*; and*
- $\Phi_{\mathcal{A}}$ *and* Φ_{log} *are sequences of the form* $[w_1 \rhd u_1, \ldots, w_n \rhd u_n]$ *where* $u_1, \ldots, u_n$ *are ground terms and* $w_1, \ldots, w_n$ *are variables.*

The set $\mathcal{E}$ represents the names that are unknown by the attacker; $\Phi_{\mathcal{A}}$ represents the messages that have been sent on some public channels, and that are known by the attacker; whereas Φ_{log} represents the messages that have been stored (*e.g.*, in a log file) by some participants during the execution of the protocol. Such a sequence Φ can be seen as a substitution and we denote $\mathrm{dom}(\Phi)$ its domain. Note that the two sequences of messages may have some messages in common. To model a message that is stored in the log and given to the attacker, we have to use both the rec and the out constructs in the process. Configurations are denoted A, B, *etc*, and we write $fn(A)$ (resp. $bn(A)$) the set of free (resp. bound) names of a configuration A. Given a process P, sometimes we simply write P instead of $(\emptyset; \{P\}; \emptyset; \emptyset)$.

We now define the relation $\xrightarrow{\ell}$ between configurations where ℓ is either an input, an output or a silent action (see below). Note that the sent messages are exclusively stored in the frame $\Phi_{\mathcal{A}}$ and not in the labels (the outputs are made by "reference"), whereas the messages stored in the logs (through the rec construct) are stored in Φ_{log} and are not visible by the attacker (silent action).

THEN
$$(\mathcal{E}; \{\mathsf{if}\ u = v\ \mathsf{then}\ P\ \mathsf{else}\ Q\} \uplus \mathcal{P}; \Phi_{\mathcal{A}}; \Phi_{log}) \xrightarrow{\tau} (\mathcal{E}; \{P\} \uplus \mathcal{P}; \Phi_{\mathcal{A}}; \Phi_{log}) \quad \text{if } u =_{\mathsf{E}} v$$
ELSE
$$(\mathcal{E}; \{\mathsf{if}\ u = v\ \mathsf{then}\ P\ \mathsf{else}\ Q\} \uplus \mathcal{P}; \Phi_{\mathcal{A}}; \Phi_{log}) \xrightarrow{\tau} (\mathcal{E}; \{Q\} \uplus \mathcal{P}; \Phi_{\mathcal{A}}; \Phi_{log}) \quad \text{if } u \neq_{\mathsf{E}} v$$
COMM
$$(\mathcal{E}; \{\mathsf{in}(u,x).P; \mathsf{out}(v,u').Q\} \uplus \mathcal{P}; \Phi_{\mathcal{A}}; \Phi_{log}) \xrightarrow{\tau} (\mathcal{E}; \{P\{^{u'}/_x\}; Q\} \uplus \mathcal{P}; \Phi_{\mathcal{A}}; \Phi_{log}) \quad \text{if } u =_{\mathsf{E}} v$$
OUT
$$(\mathcal{E}; \{\mathsf{out}(u,v).P\} \uplus \mathcal{P}; \Phi_{\mathcal{A}}; \Phi_{log}) \xrightarrow{\nu w.\mathsf{out}(M,w)} (\mathcal{E}; \{P\} \uplus \mathcal{P}; \Phi_{\mathcal{A}} \uplus [w \rhd v]; \Phi_{log})$$
$$\text{if } M\Phi_{\mathcal{A}} =_{\mathsf{E}} u,\ fn(M) \cap \mathcal{E} = \emptyset,\ fv(M) \subseteq \mathrm{dom}(\Phi_{\mathcal{A}}) \text{ and } w \text{ is a fresh variable}$$
INPUT
$$(\mathcal{E}; \{\mathsf{in}(u,x).P\} \uplus \mathcal{P}; \Phi_{\mathcal{A}}; \Phi_{log}) \xrightarrow{\mathsf{in}(M,N)} (\mathcal{E}; \{P\{^v/_x\}\} \uplus \mathcal{P}; \Phi_{\mathcal{A}}; \Phi_{log})$$
$$\text{if } M\Phi_{\mathcal{A}} =_{\mathsf{E}} u,\ fn(M) \cap \mathcal{E} = \emptyset,\ fv(M) \subseteq \mathrm{dom}(\Phi_{\mathcal{A}})$$
$$\text{if } N\Phi_{\mathcal{A}} =_{\mathsf{E}} v,\ fn(N) \cap \mathcal{E} = \emptyset,\ fv(N) \subseteq \mathrm{dom}(\Phi_{\mathcal{A}})$$
RECORD
$$(\mathcal{E}; \{\mathsf{rec}(z,u).P\} \uplus \mathcal{P}; \Phi_{\mathcal{A}}; \Phi_{log}) \xrightarrow{\tau} (\mathcal{E}; \{P\} \uplus \mathcal{P}; \Phi_{\mathcal{A}}; \Phi_{log} \uplus [z \rhd u])$$
REPL
$$(\mathcal{E}; \{!^{\mathsf{i} \geq j}\ P\} \uplus \mathcal{P}; \Phi_{\mathcal{A}}; \Phi_{log}) \xrightarrow{\tau} (\mathcal{E}; \{!^{\mathsf{i} \geq j+1}\ P; P\{^j/_{\mathsf{i}}\}\} \uplus \mathcal{P}; \Phi_{\mathcal{A}}; \Phi_{log})$$
NEW
$$(\mathcal{E}; \{\mathsf{new}\ n[i_1,...,i_k].P\} \uplus \mathcal{P}; \Phi_{\mathcal{A}}; \Phi_{log}) \xrightarrow{\tau} (\mathcal{E} \cup \{n[i_1,...,i_k]\}; \{P\} \uplus \mathcal{P}; \Phi_{\mathcal{A}}; \Phi_{log})$$
PAR
$$(\mathcal{E}; \{P \mid Q\} \uplus \mathcal{P}; \Phi_{\mathcal{A}}; \Phi_{log}) \xrightarrow{\tau} (\mathcal{E}; \{P; Q\} \uplus \mathcal{P}; \Phi_{\mathcal{A}}; \Phi_{log})$$

Then, the relation $\xrightarrow{\ell_1 \ldots \ell_n}$ between configurations is defined in the usual way. Given a sequence tr of observable actions tr, we write $A \stackrel{\mathsf{tr}}{\Rightarrow} B$ when there exists a sequence $\ell_1, \ldots, \ell_n$ such that $A \xrightarrow{\ell_1 \ldots \ell_n} B$ and tr is obtained from $\ell_1 \ldots \ell_n$ by erasing all occurrences of τ.

2.4 Tests Performed by Users

As previously mentioned, we consider that participants may store some messages in their own private log during the execution of the protocol, and can then verify some properties on their log. For sake of simplicity, we model one global log using Φ_{log}, and we assume that participants only access to the part of the log that is public, and to the values stored in their private log.

We consider formulas built upon elementary formulas, mainly equations and disequations between terms, of the form $M =^? N$ and $M \neq^? N$, and that use classical connectives (*e.g.*, $\wedge, \vee, \Rightarrow, \exists, \ldots$). In particular, we consider that indices can be existentially and universally quantified over $\mathbb{N}$. Given a log Φ_{log}, we write:

- $\Phi_{log} \models M =^? N$ when $fv(M,N) \subseteq \mathrm{dom}(\Phi_{log})$ and $M\Phi_{log} =_{\mathsf{E}} N\Phi_{log}$.
- $\Phi_{log} \models M \neq^? N$ when $fv(M,N) \subseteq \mathrm{dom}(\Phi_{log})$ and $M\Phi_{log} \neq_{\mathsf{E}} N\Phi_{log}$.

We consider that this grammar of logical formulas on the log Φ_{log} is powerful enough to express most of the properties that could be desired to be verified by participants of a protocol. One might still want to extend this grammar given the needs of specific protocols, but so far, we do not have examples of protocols that could not be expressed in our model.

Example 5. Consider $\phi = \forall i \in \mathbb{N}. \forall j \in \mathbb{N}. (z_{start}[i,j] =^? \mathsf{true} \Rightarrow z_{end}[i,j] \neq^? \mathsf{error})$. This formula expresses that for every pair of integers (i,j) that corresponds to a session that has been launched, *i.e.*, $z_{start}[i,j]$ is in the domain of the log and is equal to the constant true, then the session has ended without any error, *i.e.*, the variable $z_{end}[i,j]$ is in the domain too and is different from the constant error.

Given a configuration A and a formula ϕ, we define the set of traces of A that satisfy ϕ as follows:

$$\mathsf{trace}(A,\phi) = \{(\mathsf{tr}, \mathsf{new}\,\mathcal{E}.\Phi_{\mathcal{A}}) \mid A \overset{\mathsf{tr}}{\Rightarrow} (\mathcal{E}; \mathcal{P}; \Phi_{\mathcal{A}}; \Phi_{log}) \text{ and } \Phi_{log} \models \phi\}$$

This is in line with the definition of trace proposed in *e.g.*, [7] when $\phi = \mathsf{true}$.

3 Certificate Transparency Protocol

To ensure the authenticity of the public keys used in cryptographic protocols, the X.509 public key infrastructure (X.509-PKI) introduced the notion of certificate authorities. A public key is considered as authentic if a certificate authority is able to provide a valid certificate for such public key. However, recent attacks [15, 16] showed the weakness of this public key infrastructure.

Indeed, by blindly trusting certificate authorities, one allows a malicious certificate authority to provide fake certificates to any client.

The Certificate Transparency (CT) protocol, proposed by Laurie, Kasper and Langley [12], aims to remove the requirement to trust the certificate authorities by making certificate management transparent. The main idea behind the protocol is not to prevent a certificate authority to misbehave but to be able to detect when a certificate authority did misbehave. In this section, we first describe the protocol and the tests that are supposed to be satisfied by the logs in order to ensure the security properties that the protocol is supposed to achieve.

3.1 Description of the Protocol

The protocol relies on public append-only logs in which certificate authorities are compelled to write information that will allow a user or a monitor to verify that they behave properly. In particular, certificate authorities will be required to provide *proofs* to anyone who desires to verify the content of the log. For this extent, the CT protocol relies on Merkle trees [13] as structure for providing proofs. Intuitively, a Merkle tree is a binary tree whose nodes are labeled by the hash of the labels of his children, and where the leaves are labeled with the data of the logs, *i.e.*, certificates in this case. Merkle trees enable one to efficiently prove presence of data in the log, and to prove that the log is maintained append only. These proofs can also be done with a simpler data structure, namely, hash chains, although the proofs are less efficient in that case. Since Merkle trees and hash chains are equivalent from the point of view of the proofs (differing only in terms of efficiency), we choose, for sake of simplicity, to model *hash chains*.

Example 6. Consider certificates c_1, c_2, and c_3. A log file composed of c_1, then c_2, followed by c_3 will be accompanied with the hash chain $\mathsf{h}(c_3, \mathsf{h}(c_2, \mathsf{h}(c_1, \bot)))$.

Typically, this hash whose purpose is to represent the current state of a log will be displayed and given to any participant accessing the log. This will allow him to verify that a certificate is indeed in a log (called *proof of presence*), or that the current log is an extension of a previous one (called *proof of extension*).

Proof of Presence and Proof of Extension. The proof of presence of a certificate c inside a hash chain h_{log} can be done by giving the hash h_{inter} representing the state of the log before the certificate c was added together with the list $[c_1, \dots, c_n]$ of certificates corresponding to those that have been added in the log after the certificate c. With these elements, it is now easy to reconstruct h_{log} from h_{inter}. This ensures the presence of c (and also of each c_i) in the hash h_{log}. More formally, we consider a function symbol $\mathsf{checklog}$ that satisfies the following equations:

$$\mathsf{checklog}(z, z, \bot) = \mathsf{true} \quad \mathsf{checklog}(z, z', x{::}y) = \mathsf{checklog}(z, \mathsf{h}(x, z'), y)$$

Intuitively, $\mathsf{checklog}(h_{\mathsf{log}}, h_{\mathsf{inter}}, [c, c_1, \dots, c_n])$ is true when h_{log} can be derived from h_{inter} by adding c, c_1, …, c_n in this order.

In this setting, a proof of extension is similar to a proof of presence. Indeed, proving that h_{log} is an extension of h_{inter} can be done by giving the certificates that allow one to reconstruct h_{log} from h_{inter}.

The Request Protocol described below is used when Alice wants to obtain (through a certificate authority) the public key of Bob.

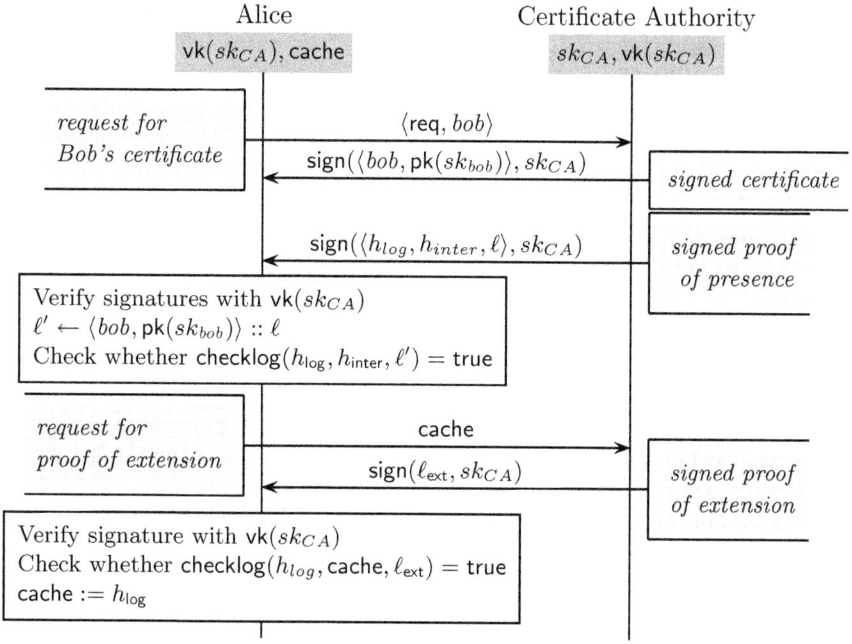

We assume that Alice has a *cell* denoted cache that allows her to store some information. In particular, this cell will be used to store the previous hash value she received from the certificate authority. Note that even though cells are not part of our calculus, it is possible to model them using private channels. However, for sake of clarity, we will keep the notation of cells.

Alice first sends a request to the certificate authority to ask for the public key of Bob. The certificate authority answers with the certificate of Bob, composed in fact with Bob's name and public key, signed with his own private signing key, *i.e.*, $\mathsf{sign}(\langle bob, \mathsf{pk}(sk_{bob})\rangle, sk_{CA})$. Moreover, the certificate authority sends several elements, signed with its private key, that will allow the participant to be sure that the certificate for Bob's public key is indeed in the hash chain h_{log} (proof of presence). After performing the checks, Alice will ask the certificate authority the elements to be sure that the current hash chain, *i.e.*, h_{log}, is indeed an extension of the previous hash that Alice has stored in cache (proof of extension). If so, she stores the updated value of the hash chain in her cell cache.

The Registering Protocol is used when Bob wants to register his public key to the certificate authority. Actually, this protocol is very similar to the previous protocol between Alice and the certificate authority. Bob will send first a request to register his public key by sending the message $\langle \mathsf{reg}, bob, \mathsf{pk}(sk_{bob})\rangle$, and then he will perform the tests as in the request protocol (messages 3, 4, and 5).

The Verification Process. The purpose of the public logs is to allow anyone to check the log and so to detect any possible misbehaviour of the certificate authority. In addition to the checks done by the users when requesting and registering a public key, some further checks have to be performed.

Check 1. To prevent a certificate authority of binding false public keys to a participant, each participant has to ensure that all the keys associated to him in the log are indeed public keys for which he asked a registration.

Check 2. It is important for the security of the protocol to consider that the users can obtain the current hash value of the log from a different source than the certificate authority itself. Otherwise, the authority could provide different values of the log to different users without them being able to detect anything. The goal here is to ensure that all users have the same (up to some extension) hash value of the public log. Google is exploring the possibility of implementing a gossip protocol to allow users to directly share information. One could also imagine the existence of servers mirroring the public logs as alternative sources for the hash value. In this paper, we abstract ourselves from the implementation and we simply propose an abstract test to ensure that users have the same hash value for the public log (up to some extension).

3.2 The Protocol in Our Calculus

The modelling of the protocol follows the informal description given in Section 3.1. We only present some elements in this section. Note that, in our model, the certificate authority is not assumed to be trustworthy, and thus we do not really need to model it. We simply have to model the fact that the authority has to write information on a public log. Thus, the process modelling the protocol CT is made of three components:

$$P_{\mathsf{CT}} = !^{\mathsf{r}}\, \mathsf{in}(c,x).\mathsf{rec}(zlog[r],x) \mid !^{\mathsf{i}}\, (!^{\mathsf{j}}\, \mathsf{new}\, sk_{agent}[\mathsf{i},\mathsf{j}].P_{\mathsf{Reg}}[\mathsf{i},\mathsf{j}] \mid !^{\mathsf{i}'}\, !^{\mathsf{k}}\, P_{\mathsf{Req}}[\mathsf{i},\mathsf{i}',\mathsf{k}])$$

The process $\mathsf{in}(c,x).\mathsf{rec}(zlog[r],x)$ corresponds to the authority writing on a public log represented by the variables $zlog[r]$. The process $P_{\mathsf{Reg}}[\mathsf{i},\mathsf{j}]$, partially described below, models a session during which the agent $agent[\mathsf{i}]$ registers a new public key $\mathsf{pk}(sk_{agent}[\mathsf{i},\mathsf{j}])$. Note that a given agent $agent[\mathsf{i}]$ may register several public keys. A variable pattern, denoted $zlog^{reg}_{agent}$, is used to store the hash chains of the public log that are sent by the certificate authority.

$$P_{\mathsf{Reg}}[\mathsf{i},\mathsf{j}] = \begin{cases} \mathsf{out}(c, \langle \mathsf{reg}, agent[i], \mathsf{pk}(sk_{agent}[\mathsf{i},\mathsf{j}])\rangle). & \textit{(* register and log} \\ \mathsf{rec}(pk_{agent}[\mathsf{i},\mathsf{j}], \mathsf{pk}(sk_{agent}[\mathsf{i},\mathsf{j}])). & \textit{his own public key *)} \\ \ldots & \\ \mathsf{rec}(zlog^{reg}_{agent}[\mathsf{i},\mathsf{j}], h_{log}). & \end{cases}$$

The process $P_{\mathsf{Req}}[\mathsf{i},\mathsf{i}',\mathsf{k}]$ models a session during which the agent $agent[\mathsf{i}]$ requests the public key of another agent $agent[\mathsf{i}']$. Such a request may happen several times. This is modeled using the parameter k. A variable pattern, denoted $zlog^{req}_{agent}$, is used to store the hash chains of the public log that is sent by the certificate authority. The last line is used to model that a fresh secret is sent on the public channel c using the Bob's public key (the one obtained through the certificate authority).

$$P_{\mathsf{Req}}[\mathsf{i},\mathsf{i}',\mathsf{k}] = \begin{cases} \mathsf{out}(c, \langle \mathsf{req}, agent[\mathsf{i}']\rangle). & \textit{(* request agent[i']'s certificate *)} \\ \ldots & \\ \mathsf{rec}(zlog^{req}_{agent}[\mathsf{i},\mathsf{i}',\mathsf{k}], h_{log}). & \\ \mathsf{new}\, s[\mathsf{i},\mathsf{i}',\mathsf{k}].\,\mathsf{out}(c, \mathsf{aenc}(s[\mathsf{i},\mathsf{i}',\mathsf{k}], pk_b)) & \end{cases}$$

We now detail the tests performed by users. First, each participant $agent[\mathsf{i}]$ has to check that any public keys bound to his name are indeed public keys for which he asked a registration. Intuitively, $\phi_{keys}(\mathsf{i})$ holds if each key pertaining to $agent[\mathsf{i}]$ in the CT log is indeed one of $agent[\mathsf{i}]$'s keys.

$$\phi_{keys}(\mathsf{i}) = \forall \mathsf{r} \in \mathbb{N}. \begin{cases} \mathsf{proj}_1(zlog[\mathsf{r}]) =^? agent[\mathsf{i}] \\ \qquad \Rightarrow (\exists \mathsf{j} \in \mathbb{N}.\, \mathsf{proj}_2(zlog[\mathsf{r}]) =^? \mathsf{pk}(sk_{agent}[\mathsf{i},\mathsf{j}])) \end{cases}$$

Next, participants must perform a test to ensure that they are tracking the same version of the public log as each other. We encode this test by specifying that the agent checks that each hash value it received during the registration and request protocols is indeed the value of some edition of the log (up to some extension). Thus, we define ϕ_{track} as follows:

$$\begin{aligned} \phi_{track}(\mathsf{i}) = {} & \forall \mathsf{j} \in \mathbb{N}.\, \exists \mathsf{r} \in \mathbb{N}. (zlog^{reg}_{agent}[\mathsf{i},\mathsf{j}] =^? \mathsf{h}(zlog[\mathsf{r}], \mathsf{h}(\ldots, \mathsf{h}(zlog[1], \bot))) \\ & \wedge \forall \mathsf{i}', \mathsf{k} \in \mathbb{N}.\, \exists \mathsf{r} \in \mathbb{N}. (zlog^{req}_{agent}[\mathsf{i},\mathsf{i}',\mathsf{k}] =^? \mathsf{h}(zlog[\mathsf{r}], \mathsf{h}(\ldots, \mathsf{h}(zlog[1], \bot))) \end{aligned}$$

For example, if both formulas $\phi_{track}(1)$ and $\phi_{track}(2)$ are true, then it means that the agents $agent[1]$ and $agent[2]$ share the same hash values for the public log (up to some extension).

3.3 Security Properties: Secrecy

The CT protocol was developed to improve the management of public keys. The main security property that this protocol is supposed to ensure is the secrecy of any message that a user could encrypt with the requested public key. This can be expressed as usual as the non-deducibility of the given term for any scenario. However, the usual secrecy property that one can find in the literature is in fact not satisfied by the protocol.

Consider for example that Alice wants to talk to Bob. When Alice asks the certificate for Bob's public key, the attacker can always adds a fake public key in the log associated to Bob and sends this public key to Alice. From the point of view of Alice, the protocol will succeed flawlessly. Hence, Alice will encrypt her secret message with the fake public key created by the certificate authority. The secrecy of the message will be broken. As previously mentioned, the CT protocol does not prevent such man-in-the-middle attack but it will leave some traces that this attack occurred. Thus, we have to adapt the definition of secrecy to include additional tests that the participants will apply afterwards.

Definition 3 (**ϕ-testable secrecy**). *The CT protocol satisfies ϕ-testable secrecy of $\overline{s}$ if for all $\mathsf{i}_0, \mathsf{i}'_0, \mathsf{j}_0 \in \mathbb{N}$, for all $(\mathsf{tr}, \mathsf{new}\, \mathcal{E}.\Phi) \in \mathsf{trace}(P_{\mathsf{CT}}, \phi(\mathsf{i}_0, \mathsf{i}'_0, \mathsf{j}_0))$, there is no M such that $fn(M) \cap \mathcal{E} = \emptyset$, $fv(M) \subseteq \mathrm{dom}(\Phi)$ and $M\Phi =_{\mathsf{E}} s[\mathsf{i}_0, \mathsf{j}_0, \mathsf{i}'_0]$.*

Intuitively, a protocol satisfies ϕ-testable secrecy as soon as the traces of the protocol under study that satisfy the formula ϕ do not reveal the secret s. All traces that do not satisfy ϕ are discarded. Note that when considering the formula $\phi_0 = \mathsf{true}$, the ϕ_0-testable secrecy is in fact the usual secrecy property of the literature (no trace is discarded). We have seen that the P_{CT} protocol does not satisfy the secrecy property in this case. We may consider a formula ϕ_1 which represents the fact that everyone apply their own tests:

$$\phi_1(\_, \_, \_) = \forall \mathsf{i} \in \mathbb{N}.\big(\phi_{keys}(\mathsf{i}) \wedge \phi_{track}(\mathsf{i})\big)$$

Note that the trace corresponding to the previous attack does not satisfy this test since Bob will see that the certificate authority added a fake certificate to his name. Thus, this trace is discarded when checking the ϕ_1-testable secrecy on the CT protocol. We can actually state a more general security property that requires only some checks by the participants who exchanged the secret. This is the purpose of the following formula ϕ_2:

$$\phi_2(\mathsf{i}_0, \mathsf{i}'_0, \_) = \phi_{track}(\mathsf{i}_0) \wedge \phi_{track}(\mathsf{i}'_0) \wedge \phi_{keys}(\mathsf{i}'_0).$$

$\phi_{track}(\mathsf{i}_0) \wedge \phi_{track}(\mathsf{i}'_0)$ models the fact that the participants $agent[\mathsf{i}_0]$ and $agent[\mathsf{i}'_0]$ have to be synchronised, and $\phi_{keys}(\mathsf{i}'_0)$ models the fact that $agent[\mathsf{i}'_0]$ has to check that only his keys are bound to his name in the public log. Thus the ϕ_2-testable secrecy ensures the secrecy of the secret sent by $agent[\mathsf{i}_0]$ to $agent[\mathsf{i}'_0]$ if the two participants have done their tests. It also means that even if others participants did not check their tests or even if the certificate authority misbehaved towards other participants, the secret between $agent[\mathsf{i}_0]$ and $agent[\mathsf{i}'_0]$ is still secure.

These examples show the usefulness of different kinds of test. It still remains to be formally demonstrated that the properties hold when the tests are true, but that requires some tool support.

4 The E-Passport Application

To illustrate the usefulness of our approach on the analysis of privacy-type properties, we consider the e-passport application, and we review the existing linkability attack that exists on the French version of the BAC protocol [2]. In particular, we will explain how the holder of such an e-passport who has some concerns with his privacy, can at least detect if he has been attacked.

4.1 Protocol Description

To describe and model this protocol, we consider the function symbols senc, sdec, $\langle\ \ \rangle$, proj_1, proj_2, mac, f_1, f_2, and the equations $\mathsf{sdec}(\mathsf{senc}(x,y),y) = x$, $\mathsf{proj}_1(\langle x_1, x_2\rangle) = x_1$, and $\mathsf{proj}_2(\langle x_1, x_2\rangle) = x_2$ to take into account the algebraic properties of these operators.

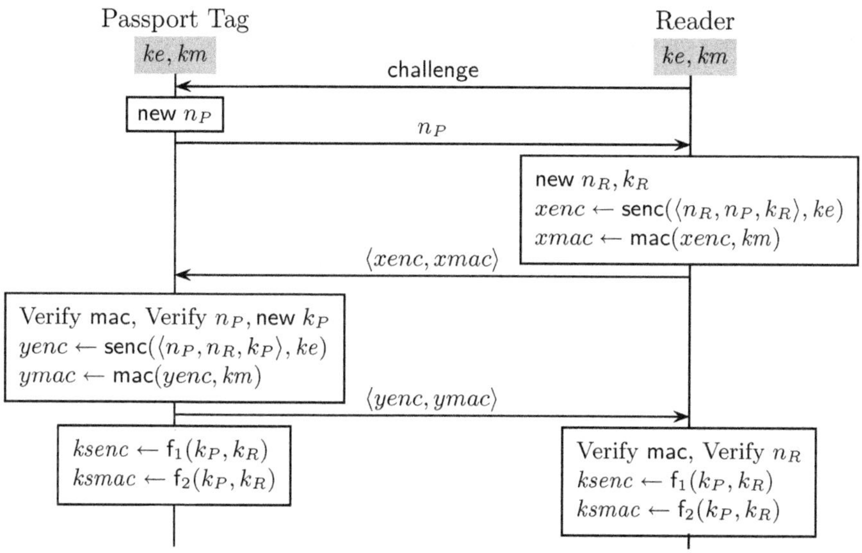

The reader first asks for a challenge, and the passport answers to this request by sending a fresh nonce n_P. The reader will then encrypt n_P together with a fresh nonce of his own (n_R) using the shared key ke, and mac everything with the key km. The keys ke and km are derived from some information printed on the passport, which has, in theory, been scanned before the wireless communication begins. At this point, the passport checks the mac, and then decrypts the ciphertext to verify whether his own nonce n_P is indeed inside. The keys $ksenc$ and $ksmac$ are then derived from the keys k_R and k_P that have been exchanged.

So far, this description holds for the English and the French version of this protocol. However, the ICAO does not specify what kind of error messages the passport should return when an operation fails. Actually, a French passport responds to an incorrect MAC with the error code 6300, which means no information given. If the MAC is correct, and the passport went on to find that the nonce did not match then it responds with an error code 6A80, meaning incorrect parameters. This actually leads to a real life attack on anyone carrying a French e-passport [2].

Description of the Attack. After listening to one session of the BAC protocol between the targeted passport and an honest reader, the attacker in presence of an unidentified passport, will be able to replay the message:

$$\langle xenc, \mathsf{mac}(xenc, km)\rangle \text{ where } xenc = \mathsf{senc}(\langle n_R, n_P, k_R\rangle, ke).$$

The unidentified passport will answer with an error message. This message will be either the error code 6300 or the error code 6A80. This code allows the attacker to know whether the passport in presence is the targeted passport.

4.2 Security Properties: Unlinkability

The purpose of the BAC protocol is to establish a fresh session that will be used to protect the personnal data before sending those information to the reader. A typical scenario can be modeled using the process:

$$P_{\mathsf{BAC}} = !^{\mathsf{i}}\, \mathsf{new}\ ke[\mathsf{i}].\mathsf{new}\ km[\mathsf{i}].!^{\mathsf{j}}\, (P_{\mathsf{Pass}}[\mathsf{i},\mathsf{j}] \mid P_{\mathsf{Reader}}[\mathsf{i},\mathsf{j}])$$

The two replications model several passports lauching possibly several instances of the protocol. Moreover, the process $P_{\mathsf{Reader}}[\mathsf{i},\mathsf{j}]$ is used to model the operations done by readers already sharing the private keys $ke[\mathsf{i}], km[\mathsf{i}]$ of the passport (*e.g.* through optical reading).

To formalize unlinkability, we annotate processes as it was done in [2]. In particular, we label the actions of our processes to know *e.g.*, whether two actions have been performed by the same passport, or in the same session. In our framework, this can be done by annotating each visible action with a distinct label parametrized with the index variables occurring in the replication above this action.

Example 7. For a process $!^{\mathsf{i}}\, \mathsf{out}(c, ok).!^{\mathsf{j}}\, \mathsf{in}(c, x[\mathsf{i},\mathsf{j}])$, the augmented process is $!^{\mathsf{i}}\, \mathsf{out}^{\ell[\mathsf{i}]}(c, u).!^{\mathsf{j}}\, \mathsf{in}^{\ell'[\mathsf{i},\mathsf{j}]}(c, x[i, j])$ where ℓ and ℓ' are two different labels, *i.e.*, constants, parametrized with i and i,j respectively.

The semantics of our processes would also display these annotations. Now, given such a sequence of annotated actions we can associate a sequence of actions and a sequence of annotations. Given an annotated trace tr, we denote by $\mathsf{act}(\mathsf{tr})$ the sequence of actions, and by $\mathsf{ann}(\mathsf{tr})$ the sequence of annotations. We will denote $\tilde{P}$ the augmented process obtained from P.

Relying on these annotations, we can now define the notion of ϕ-testable unlinkability.

Definition 4 (ϕ-testable unlinkability). *We say that P_{BAC} satisfies ϕ-testable unlinkability if for all $\mathsf{i}_0, \mathsf{j}_0, \mathsf{j}_0' \in \mathbb{N}$, for all $(\mathsf{tr}, \varphi) \in \mathit{trace}(\tilde{P}_{BAC}, \phi(\mathsf{i}_0, \mathsf{j}_0, \mathsf{j}_0'))$ with $\mathsf{ann}(\mathsf{tr}) = \ell_1[i_1, j_1].\dots.\ell_n[i_n, j_n]$, for all $k, r \in \{1, \dots, n\}$, if $i_k = i_r = \mathsf{i}_0$, $\mathsf{j}_0 = j_k$, $\mathsf{j}_0' = j_r$ and $j_k \neq j_r$ then there exists $(\mathsf{tr}', \varphi') \in \mathit{trace}(\tilde{P}_{BAC}, \phi(\mathsf{i}_0, \mathsf{j}_0, \mathsf{j}_0'))$ such that $\mathsf{ann}(\mathsf{tr}') = \ell_1'[i_1', j_1'].\dots.\ell_n'[i_n', j_n']$ with $\mathsf{act}(\mathsf{tr}) = \mathsf{act}(\mathsf{tr}')$, $i_k' \neq i_r'$, and $\varphi \sim \varphi'$.*

Assuming $\phi = \mathsf{true}$, this definition is in line with the original definition proposed in [2], and not satisfied by the French version of the passport. Intuitively, the previous definition indicates that for any trace of the protocol where passports can execute several sessions, if two actions are executed by the same passport during two different sessions then there exists an other equivalent trace where these two actions are executed by two different passports.

The main advantage of this definition is that it also allows us to state a weaker form of unlinkability. We can express the unlinkability of a set of French e-passports that do not emit the error Error6A80. For this, assuming the process modelling the role of the passport has been modified to store in its log when it starts and ends a session, and also the error code that it has emitted so far. In other words, we assume here that each owner of a passport has a private log on which he can write. One can assume for example the presence of a small device that listens messages sent by the passport and writes messages on logs.

We can thus consider the following test:

$$\phi_1(\_,\_,\_) = \forall \mathsf{i} \in \mathbb{N}.\forall \mathsf{j} \in \mathbb{N}.(z_{\mathsf{start}}[\mathsf{i},\mathsf{j}] =^? \mathsf{true} \Rightarrow z_{\mathsf{end}}[\mathsf{i},\mathsf{j}] \neq^? \mathsf{Error6A80}).$$

However, we may also be interested to state an unlinkability property w.r.t. to a given passport i_0 without saying anything on the other ones. This can be achieved by considering the following test:

$$\phi_2(\mathsf{i}_0,\_,\_) = \forall \mathsf{j} \in \mathbb{N}.(z_{\mathsf{start}}[\mathsf{i}_0,\mathsf{j}] =^? \mathsf{true} \Rightarrow z_{\mathsf{end}}[\mathsf{i}_0,\mathsf{j}] \neq^? \mathsf{Error6A80}).$$

Note that the ϕ_2-testable unlinkability ensures the non-tracability of a passport as long as this particular passport never emitted Error6A80. However, we may want to strengthen even more the security property. Indeed, requiring that a passport never emit Error6A80 during all its sessions is quite strong. Actually, we may say something about the unlinkability of two sessions of the same passport instead of all sessions. To do so, we consider the following test:

$$\phi_3(\mathsf{i}_0,\mathsf{j}_0,\mathsf{j}_0') = z_{\mathsf{end}}[\mathsf{i}_0,\mathsf{j}_0] \neq^? \mathsf{Error6A80} \wedge z_{\mathsf{end}}[\mathsf{i}_0,\mathsf{j}_0'] \neq^? \mathsf{Error6A80}.$$

The ϕ_3-testable unlinkability ensures that two sessions (here indexed by j_0 and j_0') of a given passport indexed i_0 cannot be linked if they both did not emit the error Error6A80. Amongst the other security properties, the ϕ_3-testable unlinkability is the strongest property that the French e-passport can satisfy.

5 Conclusion

Many kinds of cloud and online services involve providers which are not trustworthy, but also not fully malicious in the sense that they are willing to offer evidence of their correct behaviour. Such providers could cheat, but doing so would eventually be detected by their customers. We have presented a model and framework to analyse such services, in which users carry out tests on data that have been logged during the execution of the protocol. If these tests succeed, then security properties are assured. For that reason, we call them testable properties.

Currently, no software tool exists that can automatically verify testable properties. Nevertheless, it should be possible to adapt some existing tools to analyse these kind of properties. In particular, among the tools which can check trace equivalence for a bounded number of sessions, the APTE tool [6] can analyse protocols in presence of inequalities. Thus, this framework seems to be particularly well-suited to being generalised to testable properties.

Acknowledgments. The authors acknowledge partial support from the EPSRC projects *Trustworthy Voting Systems* and *Analysing Security and Privacy Properties*, and the project ProSecure ERC grant agreement n258865, as well as the project JCJC VIP ANR-11-JS02-006.

References

1. Abadi, M., Fournet, C.: Mobile values, new names, and secure communication. In: Proc. 28th ACM Symp. on Principles of Programming Lanes (POPL 2001) (2001)
2. Arapinis, M., Chothia, T., Ritter, E., Ryan, M.: Analysing unlinkability and anonymity using the applied pi calculus. In: Proc. 23rd IEEE Computer Security Foundations Symposium (CSF 2010) (2010)
3. Aumann, Y., Lindell, Y.: Security against covert adversaries: Efficient protocols for realistic adversaries. In: Vadhan, S.P. (ed.) TCC 2007. LNCS, vol. 4392, pp. 137–156. Springer, Heidelberg (2007)
4. Bruso, M., Chatzikokolakis, K., den Hartog, J.: Formal verification of privacy for RFID systems. In: Proc. 23rd IEEE Computer Security Foundations Symposium (CSF 2010). IEEE Computer Society Press (2010)
5. Bursuc, S., Grewal, G.S., Ryan, M.D.: Trivitas: Voters directly verifying votes. In: Kiayias, A., Lipmaa, H. (eds.) VoteID 2011. LNCS, vol. 7187, pp. 190–207. Springer, Heidelberg (2012)
6. Cheval, V.: APTE (Algorithm for Proving Trace Equivalence) (2013). http://projects.lsv.ens-cachan.fr/APTE/
7. Cheval, V., Comon-Lundh, H., Delaune, S.: Trace equivalence decision: Negative tests and non-determinism. In: Proc. 18th ACM Conference on Computer and Communications Security (CCS 2011) (2011)
8. Damgård, I., Keller, M., Larraia, E., Pastro, V., Scholl, P., Smart, N.P.: Practical covertly secure mpc for dishonest majority – or: Breaking the spdz limits. In: Crampton, J., Jajodia, S., Mayes, K. (eds.) ESORICS 2013. LNCS, vol. 8134, pp. 1–18. Springer, Heidelberg (2013)
9. Delaune, S., Kremer, S., Ryan, M.D.: Verifying privacy-type properties of electronic voting protocols. Journal of Computer Security **4**, 435–487 (2008)
10. Grewal, G.S., Ryan, M.D., Bursuc, S., Ryan, P.Y.A.: Caveat coercitor: Coercion-evidence in electronic voting. In: IEEE Symposium on Security and Privacy, pp. 367–381 (2013)
11. Kremer, S., Ryan, M., Smyth, B.: Election verifiability in electronic voting protocols. In: Gritzalis, D., Preneel, B., Theoharidou, M. (eds.) ESORICS 2010. LNCS, vol. 6345, pp. 389–404. Springer, Heidelberg (2010)
12. Laurie, B., Langley, A., Kasper, E.: Certificate Transparency. RFC 6962 (Experimental) (2013)
13. Merkle, R.C.: A digital signature based on a conventional encryption function. In: Pomerance, C. (ed.) CRYPTO 1987. LNCS, vol. 293, pp. 369–378. Springer, Heidelberg (1988)
14. Nakamoto, S.: Bitcoin: A peer-to-peer electronic cash system (2008)
15. Roberts, P.: Phony SSL certificates issued for Google. Skype, others, Yahoo (March 2011)
16. Sterling, T.: Second firm warns of concern after Dutch hack (September 2011)

A Class of Automata for the Verification of Infinite, Resource-Allocating Behaviours

Vincenzo Ciancia[1(✉)] and Matteo Sammartino[2(✉)]

[1] ISTI-CNR, Pisa, Italy
vincenzoml@gmail.com
[2] Dipartimento di Informatica, Università di Pisa, Pisa, Italy
sammarti@di.unipi.it

Abstract. Process calculi for service-oriented computing often feature generation of fresh resources. So-called nominal automata have been studied both as semantic models for such calculi, and as acceptors of languages of finite words over infinite alphabets. In this paper we investigate nominal automata that accept infinite words. These automata are a generalisation of deterministic Muller automata to the setting of nominal sets. We prove decidability of complement, union, intersection, emptiness and equivalence, and determinacy by ultimately periodic words. The key to obtain such results is to use finite representations of the (otherwise infinite-state) defined class of automata. The definition of such operations enables model checking of process calculi featuring infinite behaviours, and resource allocation, to be implemented using classical automata-theoretic methods.

1 Introduction

This paper aims at contributing to the theory of formal verification of *global computing* systems, by extending the theory of Muller automata to the case of infinite alphabets, while retaining decidability. In this way, it is possible to adapt the classical automata-theoretic approach to formal specification and verification [2] to systems with resource generation capabilities, where the number of possible resources is infinite, provided that these systems enjoy a *finite memory* property.

Transition structures, in the form of automata, are used to represent logic formalisms interpreted over finite and infinite words, dating back to [3,4]. The possibility of translating modal logic formulas to automata led to the development of *model checking*. Systems that feature resource allocation (e.g. [5]), typically in the form of *name allocation*, pose specific challenges. For instance, they have ad-hoc notions of bisimulation, which cannot be captured by standard set-theoretic models. Transition structures that correctly model name allocation have been proposed in various forms, including coalgebras over presheaf categories [6–10], history-dependent automata [11], and automata over nominal sets [12]. Equivalence of these models has been established both at the level of base

Research partially funded by projects EU ASCENS (nr. 257414), EU QUANTICOL (nr. 600708), IT MIUR CINA and PAR FAS 2007-2013 Regione Toscana TRACE-IT.
An extended version containing full proofs is available at [1]

M. Maffei and E. Tuosto (Eds.): TGC 2014, LNCS 8902, pp. 97–111, 2014.
DOI: 10.1007/978-3-662-45917-1_7

categories [13–15] and of coalgebras [16]. More recently, the field of *nominal automata* has essentially used the same structures, no longer as semantic models, but rather as acceptors of languages of finite words (see e.g., [12,17–19]). In particular, the obtained languages are based on infinite alphabets, but still enjoy finite memory (in fact, the well known *register automata* of Francez and Kaminski can be regarded as nominal automata, see [12]).

The case of infinite words over nominal alphabets is more problematic, as an infinite word over an infinite alphabet is generally not *finitely supported.*[1] Consider a machine that reads any symbol from an infinite, countable alphabet, and never stores it. Clearly, such a machine has finite (empty) memory. The set of its traces is simply described as the set of all infinite words over the alphabet. However, in the language we have various species of words. Some of them are finitely supported, e.g. words that consist of the infinite repetition of a finite word. Some others are not finitely supported, such as the word enumerating all the symbols of the alphabet. Such words lay inherently out of the realm of nominal sets. However, the existence of these words does not give infinite memory to the language. More precisely, words without finite support can not be "singled out" by a finite memory machine; if a machine accepts one of them, then it will accept infinitely many others, including finitely supported words.

This work aims at translating the above intuitions into precise mathematical terms, in order to define a class of languages made of infinite words over infinite alphabets, enjoying finite-memory properties. We extend automata over nominal sets to handle infinite words, by imposing a (Muller-style) acceptance condition over the *orbits* (not the states!) of automata. By doing so, it turns out that our languages not only are finite-memory, but they retain computational properties, such as closure under boolean operations and decidability of emptiness (thus, containment and equivalence), which we prove by providing finite representations, and effective constructions. As in the case of standard ω-automata, the shift to infinite words requires these results to be proved from scratch, as it is not possible to merely extend proofs from the finite words case. These results enable automata-theoretic model checking to be performed on systems with infinite resources, using traditional model-checking algorithms.

Furthermore, we prove that the defined languages are determined by their ultimately-periodic fragments. This theorem is fundamental for *learning* logical properties (see e.g., [20], or [21]) and has been used to provide a complete minimisation procedure for equivalent representations of Muller automata [22]. Establishing this theoretical result in the nominal case is an important step towards the application of such techniques to global computing scenarios.

2 Example: Peer-to-Peer System

In order to introduce the presented topic, in this section we discuss an application of nominal automata to distributed systems. Consider an idealized *peer-to-peer*

[1] The notion of finite support, coming from the theory of nominal sets, will be clarified later; roughly, finitely supported elements just use a finite set of names.

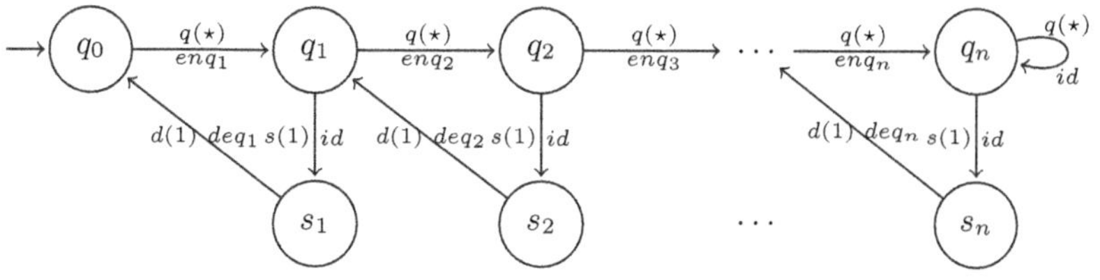

Fig. 1. Automaton for the FCFS policy

system where each peer receives queries from an arbitrary, unbounded number of other peers, represented by an infinite set of unique identifiers. Each peer buffers requests in a finite queue. Then one query is selected, among the buffered ones, and is served by establishing a temporary connection with the target. Peers are not normally supposed to terminate, thus their relevant properties ought to predicate on infinite words. On the other hand, actions executed by peers carry information about other peers, which are drawn from an infinite set, therefore the symbols constituting words are infinite. Finally, each peer has finite memory. This is the key to maintain decidability, and is mathematically modeled by the notion of *finite support* in nominal automata. Once established that our languages are made of infinite words over an infinite alphabet, but retain a finite memory property, we can use automata to characterize properties of local peers in a global environment. We assume three kinds of observable actions for peers: arrival of a new query from p, written $q(p)$; selection of a query to serve and connection to its sender p, written $s(p)$; disconnection from p, written $d(p)$.

Variants of a communication protocol in this setting may have very different behaviors. Policies characterizing desired ones, for instance fairness requirements, can be specified by automata. For decidability reasons, policies should be *deterministic*: they should always consider all possible actions from a given state, even if not all of them will be accepted, and each action should have a unique outcome. Our main example will be the specification of a "first come first serve" peer selection policy for queries, named *FCFS fair policy*; we shall also discuss a policy that takes into account a number of locally identified "friend peers" taking priority over the others, that we call *friend policy*.

FCFS fair policy. We model query selection by a *fair* FCFS discipline: queries from already buffered peers are discarded. We assume that the buffer has size n. The automaton is shown in Figure 1. Each state q_i, s_i is equipped with i registers, for $i = 1, \ldots, n$, and q_0 has no registers. Registers can store identifiers, and are local to states (we will discuss this aspect throughout the paper), thus each transition is equipped with a function expressing how registers in the target state take values from those of the source state. We have two such functions: $enq_i(x)$, mapping i to $\star$ and $x < i$ to x, and deq_i, mapping x to $x + 1$. The intuition is that transitions from q_i to q_{i+1} labeled with $\star$ correspond to buffering a "fresh" query, from a peer whose identiy is not already known, and thus it is stored in register $i + 1$. The loop on q_n discards new peers when the buffer is full. The transition from q_i to s_i picks the query p from register 1, that is always the oldest one, and establishes a connection to p; the transition from s_i to q_{i-1} removes p from the buffer, and shifts the registers' content so that register 1 contains the query that arrived right after the one of p. Our automaton should (1) be deterministic and (2) have a Muller-style accepting condition. For (1), we assume each state has all possible outgoing transitions: those not shown in Figure 1 are assumed to go to a sink state. For (2), we take all subsets of the states, excluding the sink one, as Muller sets; that is: behaviors that go through states and transitions depicted in Figure 1 are all accepted.

Friend queries. A *friend query* is a query coming from a "friend" peer, which should be served as soon as possible, that is: after the current query has been served. To model such scenarios, one can introduce an action $q_f(p)$ to model a friend query from p. An automaton that correctly handles such queries can be obtained from the one of Figure 1 as follows: we add a transition from q_i to q_{i+1}, for each $i = 0, \ldots, n-1$, labelled with $q_f(\star)$ and with the map top_i, sending 1 to $\star$ and $x > 1$ to $x - 1$; furthermore, a looping transition on q_n is added with label $q_f(\star)$ and map id, which discards friend queries when the buffer is full. Intuitively, top_i always stores the friend query in register 1, so that transitions $s(1)$ will always pick it, and shifts the priority of all the other peers.

3 Background

Notation. Throughout the paper: $f : X \to Y$ is a total function, $f : X \rightarrowtail Y$ is total and injective, $f : X \rightharpoonup Y$ is partial; $\mathrm{dom}(f)$ is the subset of X where f is defined, $Im(f)$ its image. Symbol ω denotes the set of natural numbers. For s a sequence, we let s_i or $s(i)$ denote its ith element. R^* is the symmetric, transitive, reflexive closure of binary relation R. We use $\circ$ for (partial) function composition and also for "relational" composition, as usual, by seeing functions as relations.

We shall now briefly introduce nominal sets; we refer the reader to [23] for more details on the subject. We assume a countable set of *names* $\mathcal{N}$, and we write $\mathbb{P}$ for the group of finite-kernel permutations of $\mathcal{N}$, namely those bijections $\pi : \mathcal{N} \to \mathcal{N}$ such that the set $\{a \mid \pi(a) \neq a\}$ is finite.

Definition 1. *A* nominal set *is a set X along with an action for $\mathbb{P}$, that is a function $\cdot : \mathbb{P} \times X \to X$ such that, for all $x \in X$ and $\pi, \pi' \in \mathbb{P}$, $id_{\mathcal{N}} \cdot x = x$ and $(\pi \circ \pi') \cdot x = \pi \cdot (\pi' \cdot x)$. Also, it is required that each $x \in X$ has* finite support, *meaning that there exists a finite $S \subseteq \mathcal{N}$ such that, for all $\pi \in \mathbb{P}$, $\pi|_S = id_S$ implies $\pi \cdot x = x$. We denote the least[2] such S with $supp(x)$. An* equivariant function *from nominal set X to nominal set Y is a function $f : X \to Y$ such that, for all π and x, $f(\pi \cdot x) = \pi \cdot f(x)$.*

Definition 2. *Given $x \in X$, the* orbit *of x, denoted by $orb(x)$, is the set $\{\pi \cdot x \mid \pi \in \mathbb{P}\} \subseteq X$. For $S \subseteq X$, we write $orb(S)$ for $\{orb(x) \mid x \in S\}$. We call X* orbit-finite *when $orb(X)$ is finite.*

Note that $orb(X)$ is a partition of X. The prototypical nominal set is $\mathcal{N}$ with $\pi \cdot a = \pi(a)$ for each $a \in \mathcal{N}$; we have $supp(a) = \{a\}$, and $orb(a) = \mathcal{N}$.

[2] It is a theorem that whenever there is a finite support, there is also a least support.

4 Nominal ω-Regular Languages

In the following, we extend *Muller automata* to the case of nominal alphabets. Traditionally, automata can be deterministic or non-deterministic. In the case of finite words, non-deterministic nominal automata are not closed under complementation, whereas the deterministic ones are; similar considerations apply to the infinite words case. Thus, we adopt the deterministic setting in order to retain complementation.

Definition 3. *A* nominal deterministic Muller automaton *(nDMA) is a tuple* $(Q, \longrightarrow, q_0, \mathcal{A})$ *where:*

- Q *is an orbit-finite nominal set of* states, *with* $q_0 \in Q$ *the* initial state*;*
- $\mathcal{A} \subseteq \mathcal{P}(orb(Q))$ *is a set of sets of orbits, intended to be used as an acceptance condition in the style of Muller automata.*
- $\longrightarrow$ *is the* transition relation, *made up of triples* $q_1 \xrightarrow{a} q_2$, *having* source q_1, target q_2, label $a \in \mathcal{N}$*;*
- *the transition relation is* deterministic, *that is, for each* $q \in Q$ *and* $a \in \mathcal{N}$ *there is exactly one transition with source* q *and label* a*;*
- *the transition relation is* equivariant, *that is, invariant under permutation: there is a transition* $q_1 \xrightarrow{a} q_2$ *if and only if, for all* π, *also the transition* $\pi \cdot q_1 \xrightarrow{\pi(a)} \pi \cdot q_2$ *is present.*

In nominal sets terminology, the transition relation is an *equivariant function* of type $Q \times \mathcal{N} \rightarrow Q$. Notice that nDMA are infinite state, infinitely branching machines, even if orbit finite. For effective constructions we employ equivalent finite structures (see Section 5). Definition 3 induces a simple definition of acceptance, very close to the classical one. In the following, fix a nDMA $A = (Q, \longrightarrow, q_0, \mathcal{A})$.

Definition 4. *An infinite* word $\alpha \in \mathcal{N}^\omega$ *is an infinite sequence of symbols in* $\mathcal{N}$. *Words have* point-wise *permutation action, namely* $(\pi \cdot \alpha)_i = \pi(\alpha_i)$, *making a word finitely supported if and only if it contains finitely many different symbols.*

Definition 5. *Given a word* $\alpha \in \mathcal{N}^\omega$, *a* run *of* α *from* $q \in Q$ *is a sequence of states* $r \in Q^\omega$, *such that* $r_0 = q$, *and for all* i *we have* $r_i \xrightarrow{\alpha_i} r_{i+1}$. *By determinism (see Definition 3), for each infinite word* α, *and each state* q, *there is exactly one run of* α *from* q, *that we call* $r^{\alpha,q}$, *or simply* r^α *when* $q = q_0$.

Definition 6. *For* $r \in Q^\omega$, *let* $Inf(r)$ *be the set of* orbits *that* r *traverses infinitely often, i.e.,* $orb(q) \in Inf(r)$ *iff. for all* i, *there is* $j > i$ *s.t.* $r_j \in orb(q)$.

Definition 7. *A word* α *is* accepted *by state* q *whenever* $Inf(r^{\alpha,q}) \in \mathcal{A}$. *We let* $\mathcal{L}_{A,q}$ *be the set of all accepted words by* q *in* A*; we omit* A *when clear from the context, and* q *when it is* q_0, *thus* $\mathcal{L}_A$ *is the language of the automaton* A. *We say that* $\mathcal{L} \subseteq \mathcal{N}^\omega$ *is a* nominal ω-regular language *if it is accepted by a nDMA.*

Remark 1. We use $\mathcal{N}$ as alphabet. One can chose any orbit-finite nominal set; the definitions of automata and acceptance are unchanged, and finite representations are similar. Using $\mathcal{N}$ simplifies the presentation, especially in Section 5.

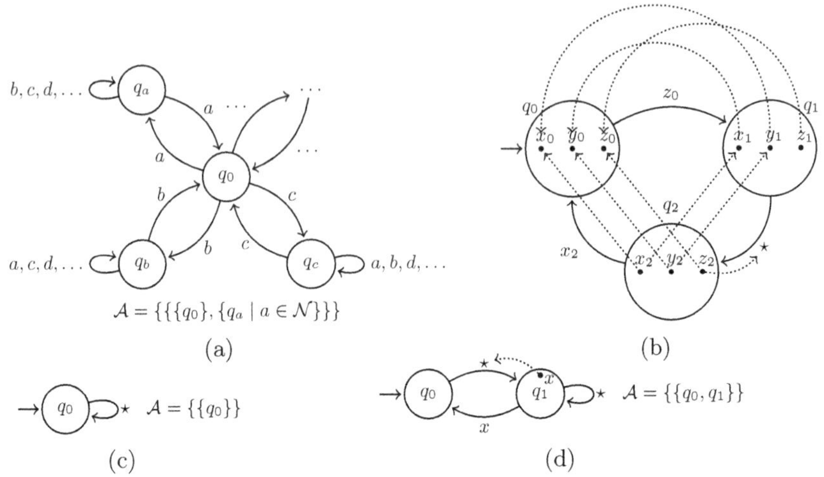

Fig. 2. Some automata, together with their accepting conditions

Example 1. Consider the nDMA in Figure 2(a). We have $Q = \{q_0\} \cup \{q_a \mid a \in \mathcal{N}\}$. For all π, we let $\pi \cdot q_0 = q_0$, $\pi \cdot q_a = q_{\pi(a)}$. We have $supp(q_0) = \emptyset$, and $supp(q_a) = \{a\}$. For all a, let $q_0 \xrightarrow{a} q_a$, $q_a \xrightarrow{a} q_0$, and for $b \neq a$, $q_a \xrightarrow{b} q_a$. Each of the infinite "legs" of the automaton rooted in q_0 remembers a different name, and returns to q_0 when the same name is encountered again. There are two orbits, namely $orb_0 = \{q_0\}$ and $orb_1 = \{q_a \mid a \in \mathcal{N}\}$. We let $\mathcal{A} = \{\{orb_0, orb_1\}\}$. For acceptance, a word needs to cross both orbits infinitely often. Thus, $\mathcal{L}_{q_0} = \{aua \mid a \in \mathcal{N}, u \in (\mathcal{N} \setminus \{a\})^*\}^\omega$. This is an idealized version of a service, where each in a number of potentially infinite users (represented by names) may access the service, reference other users, and later leave. Infinitely often, an arbitrary symbol occurs, representing an "access"; the next occurrence of the same symbol denotes a "leave". One could use an alphabet with two infinite orbits to distinguish the two kinds of action (see Remark 1), or reserve two distinguished names of $\mathcal{N}$ to be used as "brackets" before the different occurrences of other names, adding more states.

Accepted words may fail to be finitely supported. However, languages are. This adheres to the intuition that a machine running forever may read an unbounded amount of different pieces of data, but still have finite memory.

Theorem 1. *For $\mathcal{L}$ a language, and $\pi \in \mathbb{P}$, let $\pi \cdot \mathcal{L} = \{\pi \cdot \alpha \mid \alpha \in \mathcal{L}\}$. For each state q of an nDMA, $\mathcal{L}_q$ is finitely supported.*

5 Finite Automata

In this section, we introduce finite representations of nDMAs. These are similar to classical finite-state automata, but each state is equipped with local registers. There is a notion of assignment to registers, and it is possible to accept, and eventually store, *fresh* symbols. Technically, these structures extend *history-dependent automata* (see [24]), introducing acceptance of infinite words.

Definition 8. *A* history-dependent deterministic Muller automaton *(hDMA) is a tuple* $(Q, |-|, q_0, \rho_0, \longrightarrow, \mathcal{A})$ *where:*

- Q *is a finite set of* states*;*
- *for* $q \in Q$*,* $|q|$ *is a finite set of* local names *(or* registers*) of state* q*;*
- $q_0 \in Q$ *is the* initial state*;*
- $\rho_0 : |q_0| \rightarrowtail \mathcal{N}$ *is the* initial assignment*;*
- $\mathcal{A} \subseteq \mathcal{P}(Q)$ *is the* accepting condition*, in the style of* Muller automata*;*
- $\longrightarrow$ *is the* transition relation*, made up of quadruples* $q_1 \xrightarrow[\sigma]{l} q_2$*, having* source q_1, target q_2*, label* $l \in |q_1| \uplus \{\star\}$*, and* history $\sigma : |q_2| \rightarrowtail |q_1| \cup \{l\}$*;*
- *the transition relation is* deterministic *in the following sense: for each* $q_1 \in Q$*, there is exactly one transition with source* q_1 *and label* $\star$*, and exactly one transition with source* q_1 *and label* x *for each* $x \in |q_1|$*.*

Remark 2. To keep the notation lightweight, we do not use a *symmetry* attached to states of an hDMA. It is well known (see [11]) that symmetries are needed for existence of canonical representatives; we consider this aspect out of the scope of this work. Note that (classical) Muller automata do not have canonical representatives up-to language equivalence. To obtain those, one can use two-sorted structures as in [22]. Even though this idea could be applied to hDMAs, this is not straightforward, and requires further investigation.

In the following we fix an hDMA $A = (Q, |-|, q_0, \rho_0, \longrightarrow, \mathcal{A})$. We overload notation (e.g., for the inf-set of a word) from section 4, as it will be always clear from the context whether we are referring to an nDMA or to an hDMA. Acceptance of $\alpha \in \mathcal{N}^\omega$ is defined using the *configuration graph* of A.

Definition 9. *The set* $\mathcal{C}(A)$ *of* configurations *of* A *consists of the pairs* (q, ρ) *such that* $q \in Q$ *and* $\rho : |q| \rightarrowtail \mathcal{N}$ *is an injective* assignment *of names to registers.*

Definition 10. *The* configuration graph *of* A *is a graph with edges of the form* $(q_1, \rho_1) \xrightarrow{a} (q_2, \rho_2)$ *where the source and destination are configurations, and* $a \in \mathcal{N}$*. There is one such edge iff there is a transition* $q_1 \xrightarrow[\sigma]{l} q_2$ *in* A *and either* $l \in |q_1|$*,* $\rho_1(l) = a$*, and* $\rho_2 = \rho_1 \circ \sigma$*, or* $l = \star$*,* $a \notin Im(\rho_1)$*,* $\rho_2 = (\rho_1 \circ \sigma)[^a/_{\sigma^{-1}(\star)}]$*.*

The definition deserves some explanation. Fix a configuration (q_1, ρ_1). Say that name $a \in \mathcal{N}$ is *assigned to* the register $x \in |q_1|$ if $\rho_1(x) = a$. When a is not assigned to any register, it is *fresh* for a given configuration. Then the transition $q_1 \xrightarrow[\sigma]{l} q_2$, under the assignment ρ_1, consumes a symbol as follows: either $l \in |q_1|$ and a is the name assigned to register l, or l is $\star$ and a is fresh. The destination assignment ρ_2 is defined using σ as a binding between local registers of q_2 and local registers of q_1, therefore composing σ with ρ_1 and eventually adding a freshly received name, whenever $\star$ is in the image of σ. For readability, we assume that the functional update $[^a/_{\sigma^{-1}(\star)}]$ is void when $\star \notin Im(\sigma)$. The following lemma clarifies the notion of determinism that we use.

Lemma 1. *For each configuration* (q_1, ρ_1) *and symbol* $a \in \mathcal{N}$*, there is exactly one configuration* (q_2, ρ_2) *such that* $(q_1, \rho_1) \xrightarrow{a} (q_2, \rho_2)$*.*

We use the notation $(q_1, \rho_1) \overset{v}{\Longrightarrow} (q_2, \rho_2)$ to denote a path that spells v in the the configuration graph. Furthermore, we define runs of infinite words.

Definition 11. *A* run r *of an infinite word* $\alpha \in \mathcal{N}^\omega$ *from configuration* (q, ρ) *is a sequence* (q_i, ρ_i) *of configurations, indexed by* ω*, such that* $(q_0, \rho_0) = (q, \rho)$ *and for all* i*, in the configuration graph, we have* $(q_i, \rho_i) \xrightarrow{\alpha_i} (q_{i+1}, \rho_{i+1})$*.*

Finally, after a simple corollary of Lemma 1, we define acceptance of hDMAs.

Proposition 1. *Given* $(q_1, \rho_1) \in \mathcal{C}(A)$ *and* $v \in \mathcal{N}^\omega$*, there exists a unique path* $(q_1, \rho_1) \overset{v}{\Longrightarrow} (q_2, \rho_2)$ *in the configuration graph of* A*. Similarly, for each word* α *and configuration* (q, ρ)*, there is a unique run* $r^{\alpha, q, \rho}$ *from* (q, ρ)*. We omit* q *and* ρ *from the notation, when dealing with the* initial configuration (q_0, ρ_0).

Definition 12. *Consider the unique run* r *of an infinite word* α *from configuration* (q, ρ)*. Let* $Inf(r)$ *denote the set of states that appear infinitely often in the first component of* r*. By finiteness of* Q*,* $Inf(r)$ *is not empty. The automaton* A *accepts* α *whenever* $Inf(r) \in \mathcal{A}$*. In this case, we speak of the* language $\mathcal{L}_A$ *of words accepted by the automaton.*

As an example, the language $\mathcal{N}^\omega$ of all infinite words over $\mathcal{N}$ is recognised by the hDMA in Figure 2(c); the initial assignment ρ_0 is necessarily empty, and so is the history σ along the transition. Differently from nDMAs, hDMAs have finite states. Finite representations are useful for effective operations on languages, as we shall see later. The similarity between configuration graphs of hDMAs, and nDMAs, is deep and is the essence of the proof of Proposition 2 below. These are similar to the categorical equivalence results in [13,14]; however, notice that representing infinite branching systems using "allocating transitions" requires further machinery, similar to what is studied in [16].

Proposition 2. *For each (orbit-finite) nDMA there is a finite hDMA accepting the same language, and vice versa.*

Example 2. Consider the hDMA in Figure 2(d), where the labelled dot within q_1 represents its register, and the dashed line depicts the history from q_1 to q_0 (we omit empty histories). This automaton accepts the language of Example 1. In fact, q_0 is the only element in the orbit of the initial state of the nDMA, and q_1 canonically represents all q_a, $a \in \mathcal{N}$. This notation for hDMAs will be used throughout the paper.

6 Synchronized Product and Boolean Operations

The product of two finite automata uses the well-known *synchronized product* construction. In this section we define this operation on the underlying *transition structures* of hDMAs, i.e. on tuples $\mathcal{T} = (Q, |-|, q_0, \rho_0, \longrightarrow)$ (we want to be parametric w.r.t. the accepting condition). One should be careful in handling registers. When forming pairs of states, some of these registers could be constrained to have the same value. Thus, states have the form (q_1, q_2, R), where R is a relation linking registers of q_1 and q_2 that represent the same register in the synchronized product. This is implemented by quotienting registers w.r.t. the equivalence R^* induced by R; the construction is similar to the case of register automata, and to the construction of products in named sets given in [16].

Given two transition structures $\mathcal{T}_i = (Q_i, |-|_i, q_0^i, \rho_0^i, \longrightarrow_i)$, $i = 1, 2$, we define their synchronized product $\mathcal{T}_1 \otimes \mathcal{T}_2$. Given $q_1 \in Q_1, q_2 \in Q_2$, $Reg(q_1, q_2)$ is the set of relations that are allowed to appear in states of the form (q_1, q_2, R), namely those $R \subseteq |q_1|_1 \times |q_2|_2$ such that, for each $(x, y) \in R$, there is no other $(x', y') \in R$ with $x' = x$ or $y' = y$. This avoids inconsistent states where the individual assignment for q_1 or q_2 would not be injective. In the following we assume $[x]_{R^*}$ (the canonical representative of the equivalence class of x in R^*) to be $\{x\}$ when x does not appear in any pair of R.

Definition 13. *$\mathcal{T}_1 \otimes \mathcal{T}_2$ is the tuple $(Q_\otimes, |-|_\otimes, q_0^\otimes, \rho_0^\otimes, \longrightarrow_\otimes)$ where:*

- $Q_\otimes := \{(q_1, q_2, R) \mid q_1 \in Q_1, q_2 \in Q_2, R \in Reg(q_1, q_2)\}$;
- $|(q_1, q_2, R)|_\otimes := (|q_1|_1 \cup |q_2|_2)_{/R^*}$, *for* $(q_1, q_2, R) \in Q_\otimes$;
- $q_0^\otimes := (q_0^1, q_0^2, R_0)$, *where* $R_0 := \{(x_1, x_2) \in |q_0^1|_1 \times |q_0^2|_2 \mid \rho_0^1(x_1) = \rho_0^2(x_2)\}$;
- $\rho_0([x]_{R_0^*}) = \rho_0^i(x)$ *whenever* $x \in |q_0^i|_i$, $i \in \{1, 2\}$;
- *transitions are generated by the following rules*

(Reg)

$$\frac{q_1 \xrightarrow[\sigma_1]{l_1}_1 q_1' \qquad q_2 \xrightarrow[\sigma_2]{l_2}_2 q_2' \qquad \exists i \in \{1,2\} : l_i \in \mathcal{N} \wedge [l_i]_{R^*} = \{l_1, l_2\} \cap \mathcal{N}}{(q_1, q_2, R) \xrightarrow[\sigma_R]{[l_i]_{R^*}}_\otimes (q_1', q_2', S)}$$

(Alloc)

$$\frac{q_1 \xrightarrow[\sigma_1]{l_1}_1 q_1' \quad q_2 \xrightarrow[\sigma_2]{l_2}_2 q_2' \quad l_1, l_2 = \star}{(q_1, q_2, R) \xrightarrow[\sigma_A]{\star}_\otimes}$$

where $S := \sigma_2^{-1} \circ R \cup \{(l_1, l_2)\} \circ \sigma_1$ *and*

$$\sigma_\tau([x]_{S^*}) := \begin{cases} [\sigma_i(x)]_{R^*} & x \in |q_i'|_i \wedge \sigma_i(x) \neq \star \\ [l_{3-i}]_{R^*} & x \in |q_i'|_i \wedge \sigma_i(x) = \star \wedge \tau = R \\ \star & x \in |q_i'|_i \wedge \sigma_i(x) = \star \wedge \tau = A \end{cases}$$

Before explaining in detail the formal definition, we remark that the relation S is well defined, i.e. it belongs to $Reg(q_1', q_2')$: the addition of $\{(l_1, l_2)\}$ to R is harmless, as will be explained in the following, and σ_1 and σ_2^{-1} can never map the same value to two different values (as they are functions) or vice versa (as they are injective). The definition of $q_0^\otimes$ motivates the presence of relations in states: R_0-related registers are the ones that are assigned the same value by ρ_0^1 and ρ_0^2; these form the same register of $q_0^\otimes$, so $\rho_0^\otimes$ is well-defined. The synchronization mechanism is implemented by rules (Reg) and (Alloc): they compute transitions of $(q_1, q_2, R) \in Q_\otimes$ from those of q_1 and q_2 as follows.

Rule (Reg) handles two cases. First, if the transitions of q_1 and q_2 are both labelled by registers, say l_1 and l_2, and these registers correspond to the same one in (q_1, q_2, R) (condition $[l_i]_{R^*} = \{l_1, l_2\}$, recalling that $[l_i]_{R^*}$ cannot contain more labels due to injectivity of register maps), then (Reg) infers a transition labelled with $[l_i]_{R^*}$ (the specific i is not relevant). The target state of this transition is made of those of the transitions from q_1 and q_2, plus a relation S obtained by translating R-related registers to S-related registers via σ_1 and σ_2. In this case, adding the pair (l_1, l_2) to R in the definition of S has no effect, as it is already in R. The inferred history σ_R just combines σ_1 and σ_2, consistently with S^*.

The other case for (Reg) is when a fresh name is consumed from just one state, e.g. q_2. This name must coincide with the value assigned to the register l_1 labelling the transition of q_1. Therefore the inferred label is $[l_1]_{R^*}$. The target relation S changes slightly. Suppose there are $l_1' \in |q_1'|$ and $l_2' \in |q_2'|$ such that $\sigma_1(l_1') = l_1$ and $\sigma_2(l_2') = \star$; after q_1 and q_2 perform their transitions, both these registers are assigned the same value, so we require $(l_1', l_2') \in S$. This pair is forced to be in S by adding $(l_1, \star)$ to R when computing S. This does not harm well-definedness of S, because $[l_1]_{R^*}$ is a singleton (rule premise $[l_1]_{R^*} = \{l_1, \star\} \cap \mathcal{N} = \{l_1\}$), so no additional, inconsistent identifications are added to S^* due to transitivity. If either l_1 or $\star$ is not in the image of the corresponding history map, then augmenting R has no effect, as the relational composition discards $(l_1, \star)$. The history σ_R should map $[l_2']_{S^*}$ to $[l_1]_{R^*}$: this is treated by the second case of its definition; all the other values are mapped as before.

Transitions of q_1 and q_2 consuming a fresh name on both sides are turned by (Alloc) into a unique transition with freshness: S is computed by adding $(\star, \star)$ to R, thus the registers to which the fresh name is assigned (if any) form one register in the overall state; the inferred history σ_A gives the freshness status to this register, and acts as usual on other registers.

Remark 3. $\mathcal{T}_1 \otimes \mathcal{T}_2$ is finite-state and deterministic. In fact, every set in the definition of $Q_\otimes$ is finite. As for determinism, given $(q_1, q_2, R) \in Q_\otimes$, each $l \in |(q_1, q_2, R)|_\otimes \cup \{\star\}$ uniquely determines which labels l_1 and l_2 should appear in the rule premises (e.g. if $l = \{l_1\}$, with $l_1 \in |q_1|_1$, then $l_2 = \star$), and by determinism each q_i can do a unique transition labeled by l_i.

We shall now relate the configuration graphs of $\mathcal{T}_1 \otimes \mathcal{T}_2$, $\mathcal{T}_1$ and $\mathcal{T}_2$.

Definition 14. *Let $((q_1, q_2, R), \rho) \in \mathcal{C}(\mathcal{T}_1 \otimes \mathcal{T}_2)$. Its i-th projection, denoted π_i, is defined as $\pi_i((q_1, q_2, R), \rho) = (q_i, \rho_i)$ with $\rho_i := \lambda x \in |q_i|_i . \rho([x]_{R^*})$*

Projections always produce valid configurations in $\mathcal{C}(\mathcal{T}_1)$ and $\mathcal{C}(\mathcal{T}_2)$: injectivity of ρ_i follows from the definition of $Reg(q_1, q_2)$, ensuring that two different $x_1, x_2 \in |q_i|_i$ cannot belong to the same equivalence class of R^*, i.e. cannot have the same image through ρ_i. The correspondence between edges is formalized as follows.

Proposition 3. *Given $C \in \mathcal{C}(\mathcal{T}_1 \otimes \mathcal{T}_2)$: (i) if $C \xrightarrow{a} C'$ then $\pi_i(C) \xrightarrow{a} \pi_i(C')$, $i = 1, 2$; (ii) if $\pi_i(C) \xrightarrow{a}_i C_i$, $i = 1, 2$, then $\exists C' : C \xrightarrow{a} C'$ and $\pi_i(C) = C_i$.*

Corollary 1. *Let $C_0 = (q_0^\otimes, \rho_0)$. We have a path $C_0 \xrightarrow{a_0} \dots \xrightarrow{a_{n-1}} C_n$ in the configuration graph of $\mathcal{T}_1 \otimes \mathcal{T}_2$ if and only if we have paths $\pi_i(C_0) \xrightarrow{a_0} \dots \xrightarrow{a_{n-1}} \pi_i(C_n)$ in the configuration graphs of $\mathcal{T}_i$, for $i = 1, 2$. The correspondence clearly holds also for infinite paths, i.e. runs.*

This result allows us to relate the *Inf* of runs in the defined transition structures.

Theorem 2. *Given* $\alpha \in \mathcal{N}^\omega$, *let* r *be a run for* α *in the configuration graph of* $\mathcal{T}_1 \otimes \mathcal{T}_2$, *and let* r_1 *and* r_2 *be the corresponding runs for* $\mathcal{T}_1$ *and* $\mathcal{T}_2$, *according to Corollary 1. Then* $\pi_1(Inf(r)) = Inf(r_1)$ *and* $\pi_2(Inf(r)) = Inf(r_2)$.

Let $\mathcal{L}_1$ and $\mathcal{L}_2$ be ω-regular nominal languages, and let $A_1 = (\mathcal{T}_1, \mathcal{A}_1)$ and $A_2 = (\mathcal{T}_2, \mathcal{A}_2)$ be automata for these languages, where $\mathcal{T}_1$ and $\mathcal{T}_2$ are the underlying transition structures. By Theorem 2 above, we are now able to show that constructing the automaton for a boolean combination of $\mathcal{L}_1$ and $\mathcal{L}_2$ amounts to defining an appropriate accepting set for $\mathcal{T}_1 \otimes \mathcal{T}_2$.

Theorem 3. *Using the transition structure* $\mathcal{T}_1 \otimes \mathcal{T}_2$, *define the accepting conditions* $\mathcal{A}_\cap = \{S \subseteq Q_\otimes \mid \pi_1(S) \in \mathcal{A}_1 \wedge \pi_2(S) \in \mathcal{A}_2\}$, $\mathcal{A}_\cup = \{S \subseteq Q_\otimes \mid \pi_1(S) \in \mathcal{A}_1 \vee \pi_2(S) \in \mathcal{A}_2\}$ *and* $\mathcal{A}_{\overline{\mathcal{L}_1}} = \mathcal{P}(Q_1) \setminus \mathcal{A}_1$, *where* Q_1 *are the states of* A_1. *The obtained hDMAs accept, respectively,* $\mathcal{L}_1 \cap \mathcal{L}_2$, $\mathcal{L}_1 \cup \mathcal{L}_2$, *and* $\overline{\mathcal{L}_1}$.

Theorem 4. *Emptiness and, as a corollary, equality of* ω*-regular nominal languages are decidable.*

7 Ultimately-Periodic Words

An *ultimately periodic* word is a word of the form uv^ω, with u, v finite words. Given a language of infinite words $\mathcal{L}$, let $UP(\mathcal{L})$ be its *ultimately periodic fragment* $\{\alpha \in \mathcal{L} \mid \alpha = uv^\omega \wedge u, v \text{ are finite}\}$. It has been proven in [25,26] that, for every two ω-regular languages $\mathcal{L}_1$ and $\mathcal{L}_2$, $UP(\mathcal{L}_1) = UP(\mathcal{L}_2)$ implies $\mathcal{L}_1 = \mathcal{L}_2$, i.e. ω-regular languages are characterised by their ultimately periodic fragments. In this section we aim to extend this result to the nominal setting.

The preliminary result to establish, as in the classical case, is that every nonempty nominal ω-regular language $\mathcal{L}$ contains at least one ultimately periodic word. For ω-regular languages, this involves finding a loop through accepting states in the automaton and iterating it. For hDMAs, freshness constraints could forbid consuming the same name in consecutive traversals of the same transition. We first show that, given a loop in a hDMA, there always is a path induced by consecutive traversals of the loop, such that its initial and final configurations coincide. Thus, such path can be taken an arbitrary number of times.

Fix a loop $L := p_0 \xrightarrow[\sigma_0]{l_0} p_1 \xrightarrow[\sigma_1]{l_1} \dots \xrightarrow[\sigma_{n-1}]{l_{n-1}} p_0$ (the specific hDMA is not relevant). We write $\underline{i}$ for $i \mod n$. For all $i = 0, \dots, n-1$, let $\widehat{\sigma}_i \colon |p_{\underline{i+1}}| \rightharpoonup |p_i|$ be the partial maps telling the history of old registers and ignoring the new ones, formally $\widehat{\sigma}_i := \sigma_i \setminus \{(x, y) \in \sigma_i \mid y = \star\}$, and let $\widehat{\sigma} \colon |p_0| \rightharpoonup |p_0|$ be their composition $\widehat{\sigma}_0 \circ \widehat{\sigma}_1 \cdots \circ \widehat{\sigma}_{n-1}$. We define the set I as the greatest subset of $\mathrm{dom}(\widehat{\sigma})$ such that $\widehat{\sigma}(I) = I$, i.e. I are the registers of p_0 that "survive" along L. We denote by T all the other registers, namely $T := |p_0| \setminus I$. These are registers whose content is eventually discarded (not necessarily within a single loop traversal), as the following lemma states.

Lemma 2. *Given any $x \in T$, let $\{x_j\}_{j \in J_x}$ be the smallest sequence that satisfies the following conditions: $x_0 = x$ and $x_{j+1} = \sigma_{\underline{j}}^{-1}(x_j)$, where $j+1 \in J_x$ only if $\sigma_{\underline{j}}^{-1}(x_j)$ is defined. Then J_x has finite cardinality.*

Now, consider any assignment $\hat{\rho}_0 \colon |p_0| \to \mathcal{N}$. We give some lemmata about paths that start from $(p_0, \hat{\rho}_0)$ and are induced by consecutive traversals of L. The first one says that the assignment for I given by $\hat{\rho}_0$ is always recovered after a fixed number of traversals of L, regardless of which symbols are consumed. In the following, given a sequence of transitions P, we write $(q_1, \rho_1) \stackrel{v}{\Longrightarrow}_P (q_2, \rho_2)$ whenever $(q_1, \rho_1) \stackrel{v}{\Longrightarrow} (q_2, \rho_2)$ and such path is induced by P.

Lemma 3. *There is $\theta \geq 1$ such that, for all $v_0, \dots, v_{\theta-1}$ satisfying $(p_0, \hat{\rho}_0) \stackrel{v_0}{\Longrightarrow}_L (p_0, \hat{\rho}_1) \stackrel{v_1}{\Longrightarrow}_L \dots \stackrel{v_{\theta-1}}{\Longrightarrow}_L (p_0, \hat{\rho}_\theta)$ we have $\hat{\rho}_\theta|_I = \hat{\rho}_0|_I$.*

The second one says that, after a minimum number of traversals of L, a configuration can be reached where the initial values of T, namely those assigned by $\hat{\rho}_0$, cannot be found in any of the registers.

Lemma 4. *There is $\epsilon \geq 1$ s.t., for all $\gamma \geq \epsilon$,there are $v_0, \dots, v_{\gamma-1}$ satisfying $(p_0, \hat{\rho}_0) \stackrel{v_0}{\Longrightarrow}_L (p_0, \hat{\rho}_1) \stackrel{v_1}{\Longrightarrow}_L \dots \stackrel{v_{\gamma-1}}{\Longrightarrow}_L (p_0, \hat{\rho}_\gamma)$, with $Im(\hat{\rho}_\gamma) \cap \hat{\rho}_0(T) = \varnothing$.*

We give the dual of the previous lemma: if we start from a configuration where registers are not assigned values in $\hat{\rho}_0(T)$, then these values can be assigned back to T in a fixed number of traversals of L, regardless of the initial assignment.

Lemma 5. *There is $\zeta \geq 1$ such that, for any $\tilde{\rho}_0 \colon |p_0| \to \mathcal{N}$ with $Im(\tilde{\rho}_0) \cap \hat{\rho}_0(T) = \varnothing$, there are $v_0, \dots, v_{\zeta-1}$ satisfying $(p_0, \tilde{\rho}_0) \stackrel{v_0}{\Longrightarrow}_L (p_0, \tilde{\rho}_1) \stackrel{v_1}{\Longrightarrow}_L \dots \stackrel{v_{\zeta-1}}{\Longrightarrow}_L (p_0, \tilde{\rho}_\zeta)$, with $\tilde{\rho}_\zeta|_T = \hat{\rho}_0|_T$.*

Finally, we combine the above lemmata. We construct a path where: (1) the values assigned to T are forgotten and then recovered (2) the values assigned to I are swapped, but the initial assignment is periodically regained. Therefore, the length of such path should allow (1) and (2) to "synchronize", so that the final assignment is again $\hat{\rho}_0$.

Theorem 5. *For each loop L with initial state p_0, and assignment $\hat{\rho}_0 \colon |p_0| \to \mathcal{N}$, there are $v_0, \dots, v_n$ such that $(p_0, \hat{\rho}_0) \stackrel{v_0}{\Longrightarrow}_L (p_0, \hat{\rho}_1) \stackrel{v_1}{\Longrightarrow}_L \cdots \stackrel{v_n}{\Longrightarrow}_L (p_0, \hat{\rho}_0)$.*

Example 3. We justify the construction on the hDMA of Figure 2(b), with initial assignment $\rho_0(x_0) = a$,$\rho_0(y_0) = b$ and $\rho_0(z_0) = c$. Consider the loop L formed by all the depicted transitions. We have $I = \{x_0, y_0\}$ and $T = \{z_0\}$. Look at the path $(q_0, [{}^a/_{x_0}, {}^b/_{y_0}, {}^c/_{z_0}]) \xrightarrow{c} (q_1, [{}^b/_{x_1}, {}^a/_{y_1}, {}^c/_{z_1}]) \xrightarrow{d} (q_2, [{}^b/_{x_2}, {}^a/_{y_2}, {}^d/_{z_2}]) \xrightarrow{b} (q_0, [{}^b/_{x_0}, {}^a/_{y_0}, {}^d/_{z_0}])$ where $d \neq a, b, c$. The values of x_0 and y_0 are swapped according to the permutation $(a\ b)$, and d is assigned to z_0. Our aim is to recover ρ_0 again. According to Lemma 3, x_0 and y_0 get their assignment back in $\theta = 2$ traversals of L (in fact $(a\ b)^2 = (a\ b)$). As for z_0, its assignment is established in the second transition, but c should not have been assigned to any register of q_1 in order for it to be consumed during this transition. This is where Lemma 4 comes into play: it says that in at least $\epsilon = 1$ traversals of L the name c is discarded. This is exactly what happens in the path shown above. Then we can assign c to z_0 in another $\zeta = 1$ traversal of L, according to Lemma 5. Since $\epsilon + \zeta = \theta = 2$, traversing L twice is enough (e.g., consider the path $cdbdca$).

Finally we introduce the main results of this section.

Theorem 6. *When $\mathcal{L}$ is a non-empty nominal ω-regular language, $UP(\mathcal{L}) \neq \emptyset$.*

Theorem 7. *For $\mathcal{L}_1, \mathcal{L}_2$ nominal ω-regular, $UP(\mathcal{L}_1) = UP(\mathcal{L}_2) \implies \mathcal{L}_1 = \mathcal{L}_2$.*

Note that a similar result could not be achieved in the presence of so-called *global freshness* [17], e.g. the one-state automaton accepting only globally fresh symbols would have empty ultimately periodic fragment, just like the empty language. As a concluding remark, we note that, by Theorem 7, every ω-regular language is characterized by a sublanguage of finitely supported words (the support of uv^ω just contains the finitely many symbols in u and v). We find this result appealing, given the central role of the notion of support in the nominal setting.

8 Conclusions

This work is an attempt to provide a simple definition that merges the theories of nominal automata and ω-regular languages, retaining effective closure under boolean operations, and decidability of emptiness, and language equivalence. We sketch some possible future directions. A very relevant application of formal verification in the presence of fresh resources could be model-checking of nominal process calculi. However, the presented theory only accommodates the deterministic case; undecidability issues arise for non-deterministic systems. Future work will be directed to identify (fragments of) nominal calculi that retain decidability. For this, one needs to limit not only non-determinism, but also parallel composition (again, decidability may be an issue otherwise). A calculus that could be handled by the current theory is a deterministic, finite-control variant of the π-calculus; capturing analogous versions of more recent calculi, e.g., ψ-calculi [27], should be possible, as they are based on nominal structures with notions of permutation action, support, orbits. As mentioned in section 2, we argue that deterministic behavior is enough to specify meaningful policies. Furthermore, recall that automata correspond to logic formulae: hDMAs could be used to represent logic formulae with binders; it would also be interesting to investigate the relation with first-order logic on nominal sets [28]. There may be different logical interpretations of hDMAs, where causality or dependence [29,30] between events are made explicit. Finally, extending the two-sorted coalgebraic representation of Muller automata introduced in [22] to hDMAs would yield canonical representative of automata up to language equivalence.

Related work. Automata over infinite data words have been introduced to prove decidability of satisfiability for many kinds of logic: LTL with freeze quantifier [31]; safety fragment of LTL [32]; FO with two variables, successor, and equality and order predicates [33]; EMSO with two variables, successor and equality [34]; generic EMSO [35]; EMSO with two variables and LTL with additional operators for data words [36]. The main result for these papers is decidability of nonemptiness. These automata are ad-hoc, and often have complex acceptance conditions, while we aim to provide a simple and seamless nominal extension of a well-known class of automata. We can also cite variable finite automata (VFA) [37], that recognize patterns specified through ordinary finite automata, with variables on transitions. Their version for infinite words (VBA) relies on Büchi automata. VBA are not closed under complementation and determinism is not a syntactic property. For our automata, determinism is easily checked and we have closure under complementation. On the other hand, VBA can express "global" freshness, i.e. symbols that are different from all the others.

Acknowledgments. The authors thank Nikos Tzevelekos, Emilio Tuosto and Gianluca Mezzetti for several fruitful discussions related to nominal automata.

References

1. Ciancia, V., Sammartino, M.: A class of automata for the verification of infinite, resource-allocating behaviours - extended version. CoRR abs/1310.3945 (2014)
2. Clarke, E.M., Schlingloff, B.H.: Model checking. In: Handbook of Automated Reasoning, pp. 1635–1790. Elsevier (2001)
3. Büchi, J.R.: Weak second-order arithmetic and finite automata. Z. Math. Logik Grundl. Math. **6**, 66–92 (1960)
4. Elgot, C.C.: Decision problems of finite automata design and related arithmetics. Trans. Amer. Math. Soc. **98**, 21–51 (1961)
5. Milner, R., Parrow, J., Walker, D.: A calculus of mobile processes. I/II. Inf. Comput. **100**(1), 1–77 (1992)
6. Fiore, M.P., Turi, D.: Semantics of name and value passing. In: LICS 2001, pp. 93–104. IEEE Computer Society (2001)
7. Bonchi, F., Buscemi, M.G., Ciancia, V., Gadducci, F.: A presheaf environment for the explicit fusion calculus. J. Autom. Reasoning **49**(2), 161–183 (2012)
8. Miculan, M.: A categorical model of the fusion calculus. Electr. Not. Theor. Comp. Sci. **218**, 275–293 (2008)
9. Ghani, N., Yemane, K., Victor, B.: Relationally staged computations in calculi of mobile processes. Electr. Not. Theor. Comp. Sci. **106**, 105–120 (2004)
10. Montanari, U., Sammartino, M.: A network-conscious π-calculus and its coalgebraic semantics. Theor. Comput. Sci. **546**, 188–224 (2014)
11. Montanari, U., Pistore, M.: Structured coalgebras and minimal hd-automata for the π-calculus. Theor. Comput. Sci. **340**(3), 539–576 (2005)
12. Bojanczyk, M., Klin, B., Lasota, S.: Automata with group actions. In: LICS 2011, pp. 355–364. IEEE Computer Society (2011)
13. Gadducci, F., Miculan, M., Montanari, U.: About permutation algebras, (pre)sheaves and named sets. Higher-Ord. Symb. Comp. **19**(2–3), 283–304 (2006)
14. Fiore, M.P., Staton, S.: Comparing operational models of name-passing process calculi. Inf. Comput. **204**(4), 524–560 (2006)
15. Ciancia, V., Kurz, A., Montanari, U.: Families of symmetries as efficient models of resource binding. Electr. Not. Theor. Comp. Sci. **264**(2), 63–81 (2010)
16. Ciancia, V., Montanari, U.: Symmetries, local names and dynamic (de)-allocation of names. Inf. Comput. **208**(12), 1349–1367 (2010)
17. Tzevelekos, N.: Fresh-register automata. In: POPL 2011, pp. 295–306. ACM (2011)

18. Kurz, A., Suzuki, T., Tuosto, E.: On nominal regular languages with binders. In: Birkedal, L. (ed.) FOSSACS 2012. LNCS, vol. 7213, pp. 255–269. Springer, Heidelberg (2012)
19. Gabbay, M.J., Ciancia, V.: Freshness and name-restriction in sets of traces with names. In: Hofmann, M. (ed.) FOSSACS 2011. LNCS, vol. 6604, pp. 365–380. Springer, Heidelberg (2011)
20. Maler, O., Pnueli, A.: On the learnability of infinitary regular sets. Inf. Comput. **118**(2), 316–326 (1995)
21. Farzan, A., Chen, Y.-F., Clarke, E.M., Tsay, Y.-K., Wang, B.-Y.: Extending automated compositional verification to the full class of omega-regular languages. In: Ramakrishnan, C.R., Rehof, J. (eds.) TACAS 2008. LNCS, vol. 4963, pp. 2–17. Springer, Heidelberg (2008)
22. Ciancia, V., Venema, Y.: Stream automata are coalgebras. In: Pattinson, D., Schröder, L. (eds.) CMCS 2012. LNCS, vol. 7399, pp. 90–108. Springer, Heidelberg (2012)
23. Gabbay, M., Pitts, A.M.: A new approach to abstract syntax with variable binding. Formal Asp. Comput. **13**(3–5), 341–363 (2002)
24. Pistore, M.: History Dependent Automata. PhD thesis, University of Pisa (1999)
25. Calbrix, H., Nivat, M., Podelski, A.: Ultimately periodic words of rational w-languages. In: Main, M.G., Melton, A.C., Mislove, M.W., Schmidt, D., Brookes, S.D. (eds.) MFPS 1993. LNCS, vol. 802, pp. 554–556. Springer, Heidelberg (1994)
26. Büchi, J.R.: On a decision method in restricted second order arithmetic. In: 1960 International Congress on Logic, Methodology and Philosophy of Science, pp. 1–11. Stanford University Press (1962)
27. Bengtson, J., Johansson, M., Parrow, J., Victor, B.: Psi-calculi: a framework for mobile processes with nominal data and logic. LMCS **7**(1) (2011)
28. Bojańczyk, M.: Modelling infinite structures with atoms. In: Libkin, L., Kohlenbach, U., de Queiroz, R. (eds.) WoLLIC 2013. LNCS, vol. 8071, pp. 13–28. Springer, Heidelberg (2013)
29. Väänänen, J.A.: Dependence Logic - A New Approach to Independence Friendly Logic. London Mathematical Society student texts, vol. 70. Cambridge University Press (2007)
30. Galliani, P.: The Dynamics of Imperfect Information. PhD thesis, University of Amsterdam (September 2012)
31. Demri, S., Lazic, R.: LTL with the freeze quantifier and register automata. ACM Trans. Comput. Log. **10**(3) (2009)
32. Lazic, R.: Safety alternating automata on data words. ACM Trans. Comput. Log. **12**(2), 10 (2011)
33. Bojanczyk, M., David, C., Muscholl, A., Schwentick, T., Segoufin, L.: Two-variable logic on data words. ACM Trans. Comput. Log. **12**(4), 27 (2011)
34. Kara, A., Schwentick, T., Tan, T.: Feasible automata for two-variable logic with successor on data words. In: Dediu, A.-H., Martín-Vide, C. (eds.) LATA 2012. LNCS, vol. 7183, pp. 351–362. Springer, Heidelberg (2012)
35. Bollig, B.: An automaton over data words that captures emso logic. In: Katoen, J.-P., König, B. (eds.) CONCUR 2011. LNCS, vol. 6901, pp. 171–186. Springer, Heidelberg (2011)
36. Kara, A., Tan, T.: Extending Büchi automata with constraints on data values. CoRR abs/1012.5439 (2010)
37. Grumberg, O., Kupferman, O., Sheinvald, S.: Variable automata over infinite alphabets. In: Dediu, A.-H., Fernau, H., Martín-Vide, C. (eds.) LATA 2010. LNCS, vol. 6031, pp. 561–572. Springer, Heidelberg (2010)

Multiparty Session Nets

Luca Fossati[1], Raymond Hu[2], and Nobuko Yoshida[2(✉)]

[1] University of Cambridge, Cambridge, UK
[2] Imperial College London, London, UK
n.yoshida@imperial.ac.uk

Abstract. This paper introduces global session nets, an integration of multiparty session types (MPST) and Petri nets, for role-based choreographic specifications to verify distributed multiparty systems. The graphical representation of session nets enables more liberal combinations of branch, merge, fork and join patterns than the standard syntactic MPST. We use session net token dynamics to verify a flexible conformance between the graphical global net and syntactic endpoint types, and apply the conformance to ensure type-safety and progress of endpoint processes with channel mobility. We have implemented Java APIs for validating global session graph well-formedness and endpoint type conformance.

1 Introduction

Backgrounds and Motivations. In the early 2000s, there was an active debate on the ways in which various foundations could be applied to the description and verification of Web service standards, triggered by both researchers and developers working on Web services. Two of the major formalisms actively discussed are Petri nets and the π-calculus: the former can offer flexible graphical models of parallel workflows, while the latter can describe process interactions and mobility of channels in a textual format. A working group called Petri-and-Pi was led by Milner and van der Aalst in 2004 to seek meeting points. As a direction in a similar vein, this paper develops a new graphical formulation of multiparty session types (MPSTs) [12] based on Petri nets (PNs) that we call *session nets*. Our main motivations are (1) to offer graphical global specifications based on Petri nets that cannot be directly represented in MPST systems based on "linear" syntactic types [2,4,9,12]; and (2) to apply Petri net token dynamics to a *conformance validation* which can guarantee independent endpoint processes satisfy safety and progress. We believe the resulting graphical representation, similar to notations used in BPMN [3] and UML [17], and accompanying token model will help engineers to write and understand MPST global protocols.

Session Nets. An MPST framework starts with global descriptions of the message passing protocols by which the participants should interact. In session nets (Figure 1), global protocols are specified by a combination of multiparty role $(\mathtt{A}, \mathtt{B}, \mathtt{C}, \ldots)$ and message $(a, b, c, \ldots)$ information over a PN control flow structure. Global session execution is modelled by standard PN token dynamics: branches and merges at places correspond to internal and external choices in the protocol flow at the specified roles; unlabelled transitions correspond to internal

M. Maffei and E. Tuosto (Eds.): TGC 2014, LNCS 8902, pp. 112–127, 2014.
DOI: 10.1007/978-3-662-45917-1_8

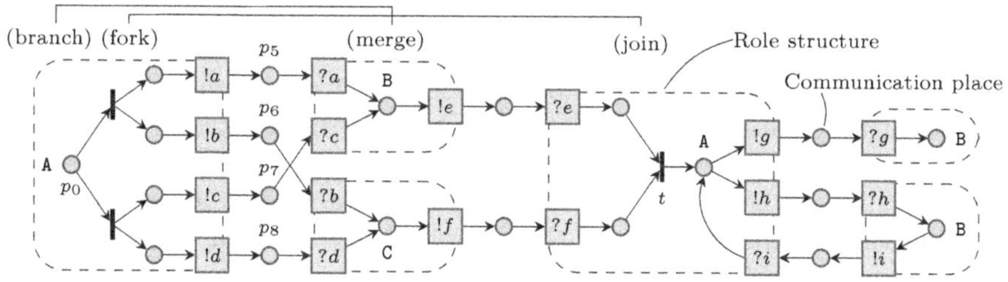

Fig. 1. Interleaved (i.e. non-nested) choice (branch-merge) and parallel (fork-join) structures with "criss-crossing" paths, leading to a recursive protocol segment

fork/join synchronisations; and labelled transitions to observable message I/O actions (e.g. $?a$ and $!a$). Decoupling I/O transitions gives a natural asynchronous model.

The session net in Figure 1 cannot be represented by the global type syntax of [2,4,9,12]. Firstly, because the "criss-crossing" of the middle two of the four paths from p_0 to t cannot be expressed in the tree structure of a linear syntax. Secondly, each of these paths flows from the initial branch through a fork, but then goes through a merge before the join. This interleaving of choice (branch-merge) and parallel (fork-join) structures is not supported by the nesting of choice and parallel constructors imposed by standard global type syntax. A technical report [19] includes session graphs of larger application protocols from [3].

Due to the flexibility of PN structures, a key design point in session nets is to characterise the nets that correspond to coherent protocols that are safely realisable as a system of distributed, asynchronous endpoints. In our framework, well-formed session graphs guarantee that net execution exhibits safety, in PN terminology (i.e. 1-boundedness), and an MPST-based form of progress. Safety states that no place is ever occupied by more than one token at a time. Progress means that every marking reachable from the initial marking enables a transition or is a terminal marking, in which tokens occupy only terminal places. § 2 defines session graphs, which are free-choice PNs by construction, their well-formedness conditions, and shows the above properties.

Conformance. Unlike the typical top-down projection from global to local types in previous MPST systems [2,4,9,12], we introduce a *conformance* relation between syntactic endpoint types and well-formed nets. § 3 shows our conformance allows each endpoint type to be validated against a net independently, while guaranteeing that their behaviour in composition respects the behaviour of the global net. Conformance between syntactic endpoints and global graphs is also motivated by practice: developers of Web services and other distributed applications often use expressive graphical patterns [3,7,24] for global specifications, but implement the endpoint programs using relatively primitive send/receive APIs, such as network socket or RPC interfaces. Our conformance accepts valid expansions of parallel specifications into a sequence of interleaved actions at the endpoint implementation level, and captures several session typing concepts, such as branch subtyping [8] and certain forms of asynchronous output permutations [6,15].

Conformance is validated as a bidirectional I/O simulation between the (localised) net execution of a session graph and the behaviour of an individual role given by its type. It works by checking that every output specified by a local output type is accepted by the session net (acting as an environment comprising the external roles), and that every message sent in the session net by another role to the local role is handled by a local input type. For example, T_1 and T_4 are different endpoint types that each conform to the session net in Figure 1 for the A role.

$$T_1 = !\{\mathtt{B}\langle a\rangle.!\mathtt{C}\langle b\rangle.T_2,\ \mathtt{C}\langle b\rangle.!\mathtt{B}\langle a\rangle.T_2,\ \mathtt{B}\langle c\rangle.!\mathtt{C}\langle d\rangle.T_2,\ \mathtt{C}\langle d\rangle.!\mathtt{B}\langle c\rangle.T_2\}$$
$$T_2 = ?\{\mathtt{B}\langle e\rangle.?\mathtt{C}\langle f\rangle.T_3,\ \mathtt{C}\langle f\rangle.?\mathtt{B}\langle e\rangle.T_3\}$$
$$T_3 = \mu\,\mathtt{t}.!\{\mathtt{B}\langle g\rangle.\mathtt{end},\ \mathtt{B}\langle h\rangle.?\{\mathtt{B}\langle i\rangle.\mathtt{t}\}\}$$
$$T_4 = !\{\mathtt{B}\langle a\rangle.!\mathtt{C}\langle b\rangle.T_5,\ \mathtt{B}\langle c\rangle.!\mathtt{C}\langle d\rangle.T_5\}$$
$$T_5 = ?\{\mathtt{B}\langle e\rangle.?\mathtt{C}\langle f\rangle.T_6,\ \mathtt{C}\langle f\rangle.?\mathtt{B}\langle e\rangle.T_6\}$$
$$T_6 = !\{\mathtt{B}\langle h\rangle.?\{\mathtt{B}\langle i\rangle.!\{\mathtt{B}\langle g\rangle.\mathtt{end}\}\}\}$$

The type $!\{\mathtt{B}\langle a\rangle.T, \mathtt{C}\langle b\rangle.T', \ldots\}$ denotes a choice between outputs $\mathtt{B}\langle a\rangle$ followed by T, $\mathtt{C}\langle b\rangle$ followed by T', etc.; dually $?\{...\}$ for input choice. For singleton choices, we can omit the curly braces, e.g. $!\mathtt{C}\langle b\rangle$. A recursive type is denoted by $\mu\mathtt{t}.T$. Type T_1 corresponds most "directly" to the structure relevant to A in the graph. The parallel forks after p_0 to B and C are expanded into the sequential interleaved outputs (a, b and c, d) in each branch. This is followed in T_2 by the interleaved inputs (e, f) in the next part joining at t. Conformance prioritizes parallel outputs over inputs to prevent deadlocks (§ 3). T_3 conforms to the final part (after t) with a recursive type containing the branch by A to either enact the loop (g) or end the protocol (h). T_4 differs from T_1 by safely under-specifying a subset of the interleaved outputs (analogously to MPST output subtyping) in the first part, and performing only one specific trace of the recursive branch; replacing T_6 with $!\{\mathtt{B}\langle g\rangle.\mathtt{end}\}$ would also be conformant. T_1 and T_4 are each guaranteed compatible with any independently conformant B and C endpoints.

In § 3, we use conformant endpoint types to type check endpoint session processes, including channel passing and session delegations [12]. We show that safety and progress of a well-formed session net are reflected in the MPST safety and progress of a system of conformant, well-typed endpoint processes. This approach gives a natural application for our novel notion of progress in PNs. We have implemented Java APIs for validating session graph well-formedness and endpoint type conformance to demonstrate the tractability of our framework, which are available from [18]. The technical report [19] contains use cases [3] and full proofs.

2 Session Net Graphs

2.1 Role Structures and Session Net Graphs

We first define the *labelled Petri net graphs* that we have adapted to represent message passing protocols in the manner of multiparty session types (MPST). We

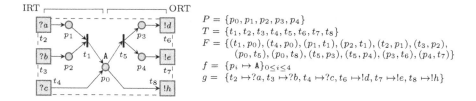

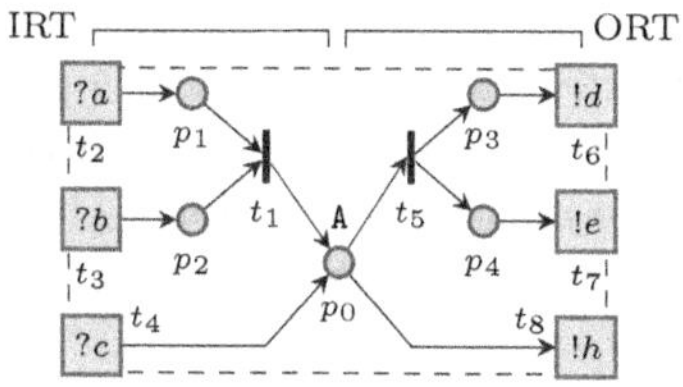

$$P = \{p_0, p_1, p_2, p_3, p_4\}$$
$$T = \{t_1, t_2, t_3, t_4, t_5, t_6, t_7, t_8\}$$
$$F = \{(t_1, p_0), (t_4, p_0), (p_1, t_1), (p_2, t_1), (t_2, p_1), (t_3, p_2), (p_0, t_5), (p_0, t_8), (t_5, p_3), (t_5, p_4), (p_3, t_6), (p_4, t_7)\}$$
$$f = \{p_i \mapsto \mathtt{A}\}_{0 \le i \le 4}$$
$$g = \{t_2 \mapsto ?a, t_3 \mapsto ?b, t_4 \mapsto ?c, t_6 \mapsto !d, t_7 \mapsto !e, t_8 \mapsto !h\}$$

Fig. 2. An example role structure

then introduce *role structures*, which are labelled Petri net graphs given by a few simple construction rules. Role structures are interconnected by asynchronous *communication places* to form a complete session net graph.

Petri Net Graphs. We extend standard Petri net graphs with functions f and g to specify MPST roles and message labels [12]. A *labelled Petri net graph* (henceforth, *Petri net graph*) is a tuple $\boldsymbol{P} = \langle P, T, F, f, g \rangle$, where: $P = \{p_0, \ldots, p_n\}$ is a finite set of *places*; $T = \{t_0, \ldots, t_m\}$ is a finite set of *transitions*; $F \subseteq (P \times T) \cup (T \times P)$ is a set of *arcs* (the *flow relation*); $f : P \rightharpoonup R$ is a partial function which associates places to *role names* from the set $R = \{\mathtt{A}, \mathtt{B}, \mathtt{C}, \ldots\}$; and $g : T \rightharpoonup L$ is a partial injective function which associates transitions to *message labels* from the set $L = \{\dagger_1 a,\ \dagger_2 b,\ \dagger_3 c, \ldots\}$ where $\dagger = ?\,|\,!$ is an *I/O decoration*. Places and transitions are required to be disjoint ($P \cap T = \emptyset$) and their union, denoted by X, is required to be non-empty ($X = P \cup T \neq \emptyset$). The elements $(x, y, \ldots)$ of X are called *nodes*. The *pre-set* of $x \in X$ is $\bullet x = \{y \in X \mid (y, x) \in F\}$ and its *post-set* is $x\bullet = \{y \in X \mid (x, y) \in F\}$.

We represent places as circles and arcs as arrows between places and transitions, as in the standard graphical representation. We call *observable* the transitions in the domain of g and represent them as boxes. The other transitions are called *internal* and represented as narrow rectangles, as in Figure 1. Observable transitions are annotated according to the g labelling function: ?-decorated observables are referred to as *inputs*, and !-decorated observables as *outputs*. Places can be annotated according to the f function.

Role Structures. An *inbound role tree* (IRT) is a Petri net graph $\boldsymbol{P} = \langle P, T, F, f, g \rangle$ with $\mathsf{dom}(f) = P$, which forms a directed tree rooted at a place, with set of nodes X and edges F, and such that: (1) every arc is directed towards the root (the root is reachable from every node); (2) every observable transition is an input; (3) if $|X| > 1$, the set of inputs contains all and only leaves. An *outbound role tree* (ORT) is defined dually, but permits observables in non-leaf positions: (1) every arc is directed away from the root; (2) every observable transition is an output; (3) if $|X| > 1$, every leaf is an output. An IRT or ORT with $|X| = 1$ is just a single root place.

Using common terminology [3,17], we refer to: a place in an IRT as a *merge*, and in an ORT as a *branch*; and a transition in an IRT as a *join*, and in an ORT as a *fork*. Intuitively, an IRT represents the internal synchronisations within a role after receiving control through the arrival of external messages (the input leaf nodes). An ORT represents the decisions leading to the transfer of control to other roles by dispatching external messages (the output leaf nodes). Their asymmetry reflects the I/O asymmetry of the conformance approach (see § 3).

A *role structure* consists of an IRT and an ORT, rooted at a shared place and disjoint elsewhere, for a single role. Figure 2 as a whole shows a RS for role A with core place p_0. We often annotate only the core place in each RS. Formally:

Definition 2.1 (Role structures). Let $\boldsymbol{P}_1 = \langle P_1, T_1, F_1, f_1, g_1\rangle$ be an IRT and $\boldsymbol{P}_2 = \langle P_2, T_2, F_2, f_2, g_2\rangle$ an ORT. Then $\boldsymbol{P} = \langle P_1 \cup P_2, T_1 \cup T_2, F_1 \cup F_2, f_1 \cup f_2, g_1 \cup g_2\rangle$ is a *role structure* (RS) iff: (1) $P_1 \cap P_2 = \{p\}$ and p, called the *core place*, is the root of P_1 and P_2; (2) $T_1 \cap T_2 = \emptyset$; (3) $f_1(p_1) = f_2(p_2) = \{\mathtt{A}\}$ for all $p_1 \in P_1, p_2 \in P_2$ and some $\mathtt{A} \in R$. We use $\boldsymbol{R}_1$, $\boldsymbol{R}_2$,... to denote role structures.

Session Net Graphs. We construct *session net graphs*, using *communication places* to compose role structures by connecting their input and output transitions.

Definition 2.2 (Session net graphs). A *session net graph* (*session graph* or SG for short) $\boldsymbol{G}$ is a Petri net graph generated by the following cases:

1. $\boldsymbol{G} = \boldsymbol{R}$ is a role structure;
2. $\boldsymbol{G} = \langle P_1 \cup P_2, T_1 \cup T_2, F_1 \cup F_2, f_1 \cup f_2, g_1 \cup g_2\rangle$ is the union of disjoint session graphs $\boldsymbol{G}_1 = \langle P_1, T_1, F_1, f_1, g_1\rangle$ and $\boldsymbol{G}_2 = \langle P_2, T_2, F_2, f_2, g_2\rangle$;
3. $\boldsymbol{G} = \langle P \cup \{p\}, T, F \cup \{(t_!, p), (p, t_?)\}, f, g\rangle$ where $\langle P, T, F, f, g\rangle$ is a session graph, $p \notin P$ is a *communication place*, $t_!$ is an output and $t_?$ is an input and: (1) $\exists_{a \in L}(g(t_!) = !a \wedge g(t_?) = ?a)$; (2) $\nexists_{p' \in P \setminus \mathsf{dom}(f)}((t_!, p') \in F \vee (p', t_?) \in F)$.

Communication places represent asynchronous message dependencies between the roles of the connected RSs. Condition 3 prevents connecting any observable transition to more than one communication place ($P \setminus \mathsf{dom}(f)$ gives the set of communication places). In Figure 1, communication places p_5 and p_7 connect the leftmost A and B RSs, while p_6 and p_8 connect the leftmost A and C RSs.

The behaviour of a role in an SG protocol is given by all the RSs for that role and the message causalities with other RSs. Each RS represents a control point in the protocol where an internal decision by the role is activated by incoming messages, leading to the dispatch of subsequent messages. This decision may then be handled as an external choice distributed over multiple RSs downstream. In Figure 1, A's internal choice to send g or h is handled by B over the two right-most B-RSs. Recursive protocols are also formed from the composition of RSs.

Free-choice graphs [10] are a well-known class of Petri net graphs, where complexity is limited by structurally preventing conflicts. A Petri net graph is *free-choice* if, for any arc from a place p to a transition t, either $\bullet t = \{p\}$ or $p\bullet = \{t\}$. The following states that every SG is *free-choice*.

Proposition 2.1. *If $\boldsymbol{G}$ is an SG, then $\boldsymbol{G}$ is a free-choice Petri net graph.*

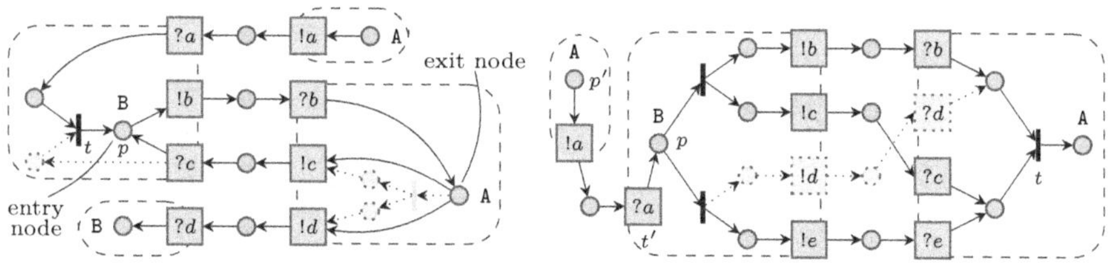

Fig. 3. Illustration of cycles and diamonds

2.2 Well-Formedness of Session Net Graphs

Paths, Cycles and Diamonds. Let $\boldsymbol{G} = \langle P, T, F, f, g\rangle$ and $X = P \cup T$. A node $x \in X$ is *initial* if $\bullet x = \emptyset$ and *terminal* if $x\bullet = \emptyset$. We write $Term(\boldsymbol{G})$ for the set of terminal nodes in $\boldsymbol{G}$. $F_{\text{-}x} = \{(x', x'') \mid x' \in X \setminus \{x\}, x'' \in X \setminus \{x\}, (x', x'') \in F\}$ denotes the restriction of F to $X \setminus \{x\}$. We extend this definition to a set of nodes in the natural way, where we omit set parenthesis, e.g. we write $F_{\text{-}x,y} = F_{\text{-}\{x,y\}}$. The reflexive and transitive closure of a relation $\Re$ is denoted $\Re^*$.

A *path* in $\boldsymbol{P}$ is a finite, non-empty sequence of nodes $x_0..x_n$ such that $(x_i, x_{i+1})_{0 \leq i \leq n-1} \in F$. We let $\sigma, \sigma', \ldots$ range over the set of paths augmented by the empty sequence ϵ; $\sigma\sigma'$ denotes the concatenation of σ and σ'. We sometimes treat σ as the set of nodes occurring in it, e.g. we write $\sigma \cup \sigma'$. We say σ is a *simple path* iff every $x \in \sigma$ occurs exactly once; σ *contains* a node x if $x \in \sigma$.

A *cycle* φ is a path $x\, x_1..x_n\, x$ where $x\, x_1..x_n$ is a simple path. A node x is: an *entry node of* φ iff there is a path σ from an initial node to x and $\sigma \cap \varphi = \{x\}$; an *exit node of* φ iff there is a path σ' from x to a terminal node and $\sigma' \cap \varphi = \{x\}$. Figure 3 (left) shows a cycle, along with its entry and exit nodes.

A *diamond* δ from *start* x to *end* y, $x \neq y$, is a pair of paths $\delta = \langle x\,\sigma_1\, y,\; x\,\sigma_2\, y\rangle$, where $\sigma_1 \cap \sigma_2 = \emptyset$, $\sigma_1 \cup \sigma_2 \neq \emptyset$ and $x, y \notin \sigma_1 \cup \sigma_2$. δ is *pre-cross-free* if for all $z' \in \sigma_1$ and $z'' \in \sigma_2$, $(z', z'') \notin F^*_{\text{-}x,y}$ or $(z'', z') \notin F^*_{\text{-}x,y}$. Informally, δ is pre-cross-free if it does not feature a pair of criss-crossing paths between its two sides. In Figure 3 (right), the diamond with start p and end t is pre-cross-free when the dotted part is ignored. Finally, δ is *cross-free* if it is pre-cross-free in the graph obtained by removing the nodes of a path, if any, from an initial node to each $z \in \bullet x$. That is, a cross-free diamond has an entry path via each $z \in \bullet x$ that does not overlap the diamond. The p–t diamond in Figure 3 (right) is cross-free due to the path from p' to t'.

The conditions for an SG to be well-formed are as follows.

Definition 2.3 (Well-formed session graph). An SG $\boldsymbol{G} = \langle P, T, F, f, g\rangle$ is *well-formed* if it is a connected graph that respects the following conditions:

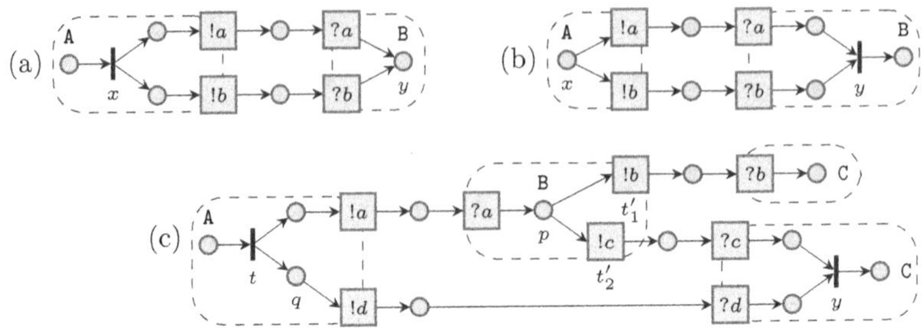

Fig. 4. Badly-formed session graphs illustrating conditions (D1)–(D3)

(Reachability) (R1) There is exactly one initial node: place $p_I \in P$

(R2) All terminal nodes are core places

(R3) $\forall_{x \in X} \, ((p_I, x) \in F^* \wedge \exists_{y \in Term(\mathbf{G})} \, ((x, y) \in F^*))$

(Labels) (L1) $\forall_{p \in P}, \forall_{t,t' \in p\bullet} \, (\{f(p') \mid (t, p') \in F^*\} = \{f(p') \mid (t', p') \in F^*\})$

(L2) $\forall_{t \in \mathsf{dom}(g)}, \exists_{p \in P \setminus \mathsf{dom}(f)} ((p, t) \in F \vee (t, p) \in F)$

(Cycles) (C1) If x is an entry node for some cycle φ, $x \in P$

(C2) If x is an exit node for some cycle φ, $x \in P$

(Diamonds) (D1) If $\langle x\sigma_1 y, x\sigma_2 y\rangle$ is a diamond, then $x \in T \Rightarrow y \in T$

(D2) If $\langle x\sigma_1 y, x\sigma_2 y\rangle$ is cross-free, then $x \in P \Rightarrow y \in P$

(D3) If $\langle t\sigma_1 y, t\sigma_2 y\rangle$ is cross-free, then for all $p \in \sigma_1$ and $t' \in p\bullet$, there is a σ'_1 such that $t' \in \sigma'_1 y$ and $\langle t\sigma'_1 y, t\sigma_2 y\rangle$ is cross-free

The first five conditions correspond to basic properties of MPST global types. (R1)–(R3) ensure that every node is reachable from the initial place and a terminal place is reachable from them. (L1) checks that the sets of roles involved in each case of a branch are equal (branch mergeability [4,9]). (L2) ensures that the SG construction has connected every input and output to a communication place.

The remaining conditions ensure safety and progress of token dynamics, by constraining the composition of branch-merge, fork-join and recursive structures to be a realisable MPST protocol. (C1) and (C2) state that an entry or exit node of any cycle is a place. (D1) requires a diamond starting at a transition to also end at a transition. (D2) imposes a dual condition only on cross-free diamonds. (D3) checks that branches along a cross-free transition-start diamond are re-merged before the diamond ends. Cross-free diamonds represent the "minimal" diamond structures for which these latter constraints need hold. Checking these conditions on cross-free diamonds only (i.e. not all diamonds) permits a larger set of well-formed SGs, e.g. the p_0–t diamond in Figure 1 is not checked for (D2).

We illustrate conditions (C1), (C2) and (D1)–(D3) by examples. In Figure 3 (left), if the dotted structure in the top-left RS for B is added, the transition t would be the entry node of a cycle, violating (C1): the net execution from the initial place would be immediately stuck. If instead the dotted structure in the bottom-right RS for A is added, the greyed-out internal transition would be an exit node, violating (C2): the net execution would be unsafe, allowing an unbounded number of tokens to accumulate within the cycle. Figure 4 (a)–(c) give badly-formed SGs that violate conditions (D1)–(D3), respectively. In (a), the diamond opened by a fork but closed by a place is unsafe (not 1-bounded). In (b), the (cross-free) diamond opened by a branch but closed by a transition will be stuck. Note that it is not necessary to apply this condition to non-cross-free diamonds, e.g. the p_0–t diamond in Figure 1. In (c), the branch at p along the upper side of the t–y diamond will prevent the net from terminating if t'_1 is chosen by B.

Proposition 2.2. *For any SG* $\mathbf{G}$*, well-formedness is decidable.*

Deciding well-formedness conditions (R1) to (C2) is straightforward from their definitions. For (D1) and (D2), we can show that if the properties hold for any SG diamond comprised of simple paths, they hold for all general diamonds that may be derived from the "simple diamond" by performing some number of cycles along its sides. The case of (D3) is similarly decided by checking only the diamonds restricted to simple paths from the start to p and from p to the end.

2.3 Session Nets

A *Petri net* $\langle \mathbf{P}, M\rangle$ is a Petri net graph $\mathbf{P} = \langle P, T, F, f, g\rangle$ with a *marking* $M : P \to \mathbb{N}_0$. The following is standard terminology. A place $p \in P$ contains n *tokens* in M, if $M(p) = n$. A transition $t \in T$ is *enabled* at M (written $\langle \mathbf{P}, M\rangle \xrightarrow{t}$) when $M(p) > 0$ for every $p \in \bullet t$. When t is enabled it may *fire*, yielding a new marking M' (written $\langle \mathbf{P}, M\rangle \xrightarrow{t} \langle \mathbf{P}, M'\rangle$) such that: $M'(p) = M(p) - 1$, for all $p \in (\bullet t \setminus t\bullet)$; $M'(p) = M(p) + 1$, for all $p \in (t\bullet \setminus \bullet t)$; $M'(p) = M(p)$, otherwise. We may omit $\mathbf{P}$ if it is clear from the context. A *firing sequence* $M_0 \xrightarrow{t_1} M_1 \ldots \xrightarrow{t_n} M_n$ can also be written $\phi : \langle \mathbf{P}, M_0\rangle \xrightarrow{s} \langle \mathbf{P}, M_n\rangle$, where $s = t_1 \ldots t_n$. A marking M' is *reachable* from M in $\mathbf{P}$ if there is a firing sequence ϕ from $\langle \mathbf{P}, M\rangle$ to $\langle \mathbf{P}, M'\rangle$.

Definition 2.4 (Session nets). *Let* $\mathbf{G} = \langle P, T, F, f, g\rangle$ *be a well-formed SG with initial place* $p_I \in P$. *A Petri net* $\mathbf{N} = \langle \mathbf{G}, M\rangle$ *is: 1) an* initial session net *and* M *is the* initial marking *for* $\mathbf{G}$ *iff* $M(p_I) = 1$, *and* $M(p) = 0$ *for all* $p \in P \setminus \{p_I\}$; *2) a* session net *iff* M *is reachable from the initial marking* M_0 *for* $\mathbf{G}$.

Session nets satisfy the standard safety of Petri nets [10,16], i.e. no place contains more than one token in any marking reachable from the initial marking. Formally: a Petri net $\langle \mathbf{P}, M\rangle$ is *safe* iff $M'(p) \leq 1$, for all p and M' reachable from M in $\mathbf{P}$.

Theorem 2.1 (Safety). *Every initial session net is safe.*

We want to ensure that sessions can always terminate successfully [2,12,20]. Standard Petri nets liveness [10,16] asks for continuous execution in a system such that no part ever becomes redundant, which is not practical for general sessions. Deadlock-freedom instead requires that every reachable marking enables some transition, which does not ensure the progress of all session participants.

Let $\langle \boldsymbol{G}, M\rangle$ be a session net for $\boldsymbol{G} = \langle P, T, F, f, g\rangle$. The marking M is *terminal* in $\boldsymbol{G}$ just when, for all $p \in P$, $M(p) > 0$ implies $p \in Term(\boldsymbol{G})$, i.e. only terminal places contain tokens. Progress asks for some terminal marking to be reachable:

Theorem 2.2 (Progress). *Let $\boldsymbol{N} = \langle \boldsymbol{G}, M\rangle$ be a session net. Then there is a terminal marking M' which is reachable from M in $\boldsymbol{G}$.*

The proofs of decidability of well-formedness (Proposition 2.2), safety (Theorem 2.1) and progress (Theorem 2.2) are based on a conspicuous set of basic properties of diamonds and cycles in well-formed SGs.

3 Endpoint Types and Conformance

Endpoint types represent the local view of a global protocol from the perspective of a role. This section defines *conformance* between well-formed SGs and syntactic endpoint types. Using the results of § 2, we show the key property of our framework: executing a system of independently conformant endpoints preserves conformance to the corresponding global net execution, thereby ensuring safety and progress.

Endpoint Multiparty Session Types. Syntactic endpoint types provide a more programmatic specification for implementation, to be verified by type checking (as shown in Theorem 3.2) or type inference (along the line of [23]). We define their syntax and LTS with message buffers for asynchronous FIFO communication.

Endpoint types are defined as follows:

$$T ::= \ ?\{\mathtt{r}_i\langle a_i\rangle.T_i\}_{i\in I} \ \mid \ !\{\mathtt{r}_i\langle a_i\rangle.T_i\}_{i\in I} \ \mid \ \mu\,\mathtt{t}.T \ \mid \ \mathtt{t} \ \mid \ \mathtt{end}$$

Input choice ($?\{\mathtt{r}_i\langle a_i\rangle.T_i\}_{i\in I}$) is an external choice, receiving one of the I-indexed messages labelled a_i from role $\mathtt{r}_i$ ($\mathtt{A}, \mathtt{B}, \ldots$). Dually, *output choice* ($!\{\mathtt{r}_i\langle a_i\rangle.T_i\}_{i\in I}$) internally chooses one of the a_i messages to send to $\mathtt{r}_i$. $\mathtt{t}$ is a recursion variable, $\mu\,\mathtt{t}.T$ is a recursive type that binds $\mathtt{t}$ in T, and $\mathtt{end}$ is the terminated type. We assume that all labels in types are distinct and recursive types are guarded, taking an equi-recursive view of types [2,12]. Let R be a set of roles, then:

$$C ::= (\vec{T}, \vec{w}) \qquad \vec{T} = (T_\mathtt{r})_{\mathtt{r}\in R} \qquad \vec{w} = (w_{\mathtt{r}\mathtt{r}'})_{\mathtt{r}\neq\mathtt{r}'\in R} \qquad w ::= \vec{a}$$

where C denotes *configurations* and w denotes *buffers*. Let m denote the *actions* $m ::= \mathtt{r}!\mathtt{r}'\langle a\rangle \mid \mathtt{r}?\mathtt{r}'\langle a\rangle$. We write $!m$ to stand for $\mathtt{r}!\mathtt{r}'\langle a\rangle$ for some $\mathtt{r}$, $\mathtt{r}'$ and a; similarly for $?m$. The relation $T \xrightarrow{m} T'$, on endpoint types for role $\mathtt{r}$, is given by:

$$!\{\mathtt{r}'_i\langle a_i\rangle.T_i\}_{i\in I} \xrightarrow{\mathtt{r}!\mathtt{r}'_i\langle a_i\rangle} T_i \qquad ?\{\mathtt{r}'_i\langle a_i\rangle.T_i\}_{i\in I} \xrightarrow{\mathtt{r}?\mathtt{r}'_i\langle a_i\rangle} T_i \qquad \frac{T[\mu\,\mathtt{t}.T/\mathtt{t}] \xrightarrow{m} T'}{\mu\,\mathtt{t}.T \xrightarrow{m} T'}$$

We write $T \xrightarrow{m}$ iff $T \xrightarrow{m} T'$ for some T'. Lastly, $(\vec{T}, \vec{w}) \xrightarrow{\mathtt{r}\dagger\mathtt{r}'\langle a\rangle} (\vec{T}', \vec{w}')$ iff:

$$\dagger = ! \implies (T_\mathtt{r} \xrightarrow{\mathtt{r}!\mathtt{r}'\langle a\rangle} T'_\mathtt{r} \wedge (i \neq \mathtt{r} \Rightarrow T'_i = T_i) \wedge w_{\mathtt{r}\mathtt{r}'} \cdot a = w'_{\mathtt{r}\mathtt{r}'} \wedge (ij \neq \mathtt{r}\mathtt{r}' \Rightarrow w_{ij} = w'_{ij}))$$

$$\dagger = ? \implies (T_\mathtt{r} \xrightarrow{\mathtt{r}?\mathtt{r}'\langle a\rangle} T'_\mathtt{r} \wedge (i \neq \mathtt{r} \Rightarrow T'_i = T_i) \wedge w_{\mathtt{r}'\mathtt{r}} = a \cdot w'_{\mathtt{r}'\mathtt{r}} \wedge (ij \neq \mathtt{r}'\mathtt{r} \Rightarrow w_{ij} = w'_{ij}))$$

Output by $\mathtt{r}$ to $\mathtt{r}'$ enqueues a message in the buffer. Input by $\mathtt{r}'$ consumes messages in the same order, checking that the label matches one of those expected.

Conformance. Conformance replaces the usual projection found in MPST systems [12]. Similarly to safe projections and session type subtyping [8], conformance relates the local protocol behaviour of a role to the global specification. Unlike projection, it uses the global behavioural model (i.e. net dynamics) to validate each local behaviour at endpoint level.

The functions $\texttt{local}(t)$ and $\texttt{remote}(t)$ lookup the *local* and the *remote role* of an observable transition t, respectively. Given $\boldsymbol{G} = \langle P, T, F, f, g\rangle$, let $t \in \mathsf{dom}(g)$. Then $\texttt{local}(t) = f(p)$, for $p \in \mathsf{dom}(f)$ such that $((p,t) \in F \vee (t,p) \in F)$. Similarly, $\texttt{remote}(t) = f(p)$, for $p \in \mathsf{dom}(f)$ such that there are $p' \notin \mathsf{dom}(f)$ and t', where either: $\{(p,t'),(t',p'),(p',t)\} \subseteq F$ if $g(t) = ?a$; or $\{(t,p'),(p',t'),(t',p)\} \subseteq F$ if $g(t) = !a$. We define the *projected LTS* on session nets for a role $\texttt{r}$ as follows:

1. $\langle \boldsymbol{G}, M\rangle \xrightarrow{\texttt{r}\dagger\texttt{r}'\langle a\rangle} \langle \boldsymbol{G}, M'\rangle$ if $M \xrightarrow{t} M'$, $g(t) = \dagger a$, $\texttt{local}(t) = \texttt{r}$ and $\texttt{remote}(t) = \texttt{r}'$
2. $\langle \boldsymbol{G}, M\rangle \xrightarrow{\tau_{\texttt{r}}} \langle \boldsymbol{G}, M'\rangle$ if $M \xrightarrow{t} M'$ and $\texttt{local}(t) \neq \texttt{r}$.
3. $\langle \boldsymbol{G}, M\rangle \xrightarrow{\tau} \langle \boldsymbol{G}, M'\rangle$ if $M \xrightarrow{t} M'$ and $t \notin \mathsf{dom}(g)$.

We write $\xrightarrow{\tau^*}$ for the reflexive and transitive closure of $\xrightarrow{\tau}$, and $\Rightarrow$ for the reflexive and transitive closure of $\xrightarrow{\tau} \cup \xrightarrow{\tau_{\texttt{r}}}$. Conformance is defined as follows.

Definition 3.1 (Conformance). An endpoint type $T_{\texttt{r}}$ *conforms to a session net* $\langle \boldsymbol{G}, M\rangle$, written $T_{\texttt{r}} \asymp \langle \boldsymbol{G}, M\rangle$, if the following conditions are satisfied:

1. (a) if $T_{\texttt{r}} \xrightarrow{\texttt{r!r}'\langle a\rangle} T'_{\texttt{r}}$, then $\langle \boldsymbol{G}, M\rangle \Rightarrow\xrightarrow{\texttt{r!r}'\langle a\rangle} \langle \boldsymbol{G}, M'\rangle$ and $T'_{\texttt{r}} \asymp \langle \boldsymbol{G}, M'\rangle$
   (b) if $T_{\texttt{r}} \xrightarrow{?m}$, then $\langle \boldsymbol{G}, M\rangle \Rightarrow\xrightarrow{?m'}$ for some $?m'$
2. (a) if $\langle \boldsymbol{G}, M\rangle \Rightarrow\xrightarrow{\texttt{r!r}'\langle a\rangle}$, then $T_{\texttt{r}} \xrightarrow{!m}$ for some m
   (b) if $\langle \boldsymbol{G}, M\rangle \Rightarrow\xrightarrow{\texttt{r?r}'\langle a\rangle} \langle \boldsymbol{G}, M'\rangle$, then:
   - $T_{\texttt{r}} \xrightarrow{\vec{m}}\xrightarrow{?m}$, for some $?m$ and sequence of output actions $\vec{m}$
   - if $T_{\texttt{r}} \xrightarrow{?m}$ for some $?m$, then $T_{\texttt{r}} \xrightarrow{\texttt{r?r}'\langle a\rangle} T'_{\texttt{r}}$ and $T'_{\texttt{r}} \asymp \langle \boldsymbol{G}, M'\rangle$
3. if $\langle \boldsymbol{G}, M\rangle \xrightarrow{\tau_{\texttt{r}}} \langle \boldsymbol{G}, M'\rangle$, then $T_{\texttt{r}} \asymp \langle \boldsymbol{G}, M'\rangle$

$T_{\texttt{r}} \asymp \boldsymbol{G}$ ($T_{\texttt{r}}$ *conforms to* $\boldsymbol{G}$) if $T_{\texttt{r}} \asymp \langle \boldsymbol{G}, M_0\rangle$ where M_0 is the initial marking.

The asymmetry between cases 1 and 2 is due to choice subtyping [8], and the omission of parallel endpoint types. In 1(a), every endpoint output must be simulated by the session net. In 2(a), an endpoint only has to perform *some* output when the net outputs. Thus endpoint outputs may safely underspecify the global model. Dually, endpoint inputs may be overspecified. In 2(b) and 1(b), the endpoint simulates every input by the net, but not vice versa. In 2(b), we allow the endpoint to output before simulating an input: this is sound because the net can do the same outputs without disabling the original input. Note that the subtyping [8] is included in the conformance: if $T_{\texttt{r}} \asymp \langle \boldsymbol{G}, M\rangle$ and $T'_{\texttt{r}} \leqslant T_{\texttt{r}}$ where $\leqslant$ is defined as in [8, Definition 8], then $T'_{\texttt{r}} \asymp \langle \boldsymbol{G}, M\rangle$ (see [19]).

Conformant endpoint types for the SG in Figure 1 were explained in § 1. Figure 5 shows a SG between roles $\texttt{A}$ and $\texttt{B}$, and endpoint types $T_{\texttt{A}}^{bad}$ and $T_{\texttt{B}}^{bad}$

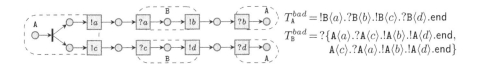

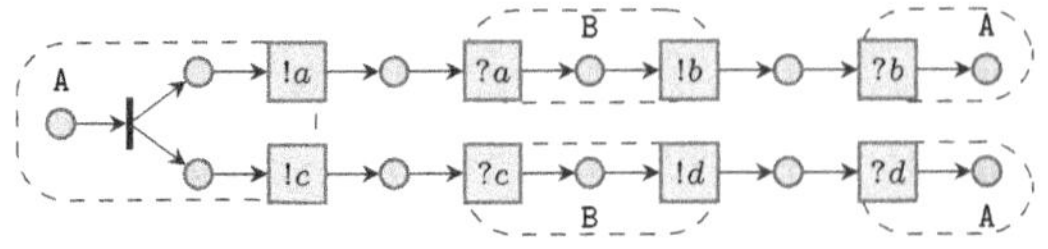

$T_{\mathtt{A}}^{bad} = \mathtt{!B}\langle a\rangle.\mathtt{?B}\langle b\rangle.\mathtt{!B}\langle c\rangle.\mathtt{?B}\langle d\rangle.\mathtt{end}$

$T_{\mathtt{B}}^{bad} = \mathtt{?}\{\mathtt{A}\langle a\rangle.\mathtt{?A}\langle c\rangle.\mathtt{!A}\langle b\rangle.\mathtt{!A}\langle d\rangle.\mathtt{end},\ \mathtt{A}\langle c\rangle.\mathtt{?A}\langle a\rangle.\mathtt{!A}\langle b\rangle.\mathtt{!A}\langle d\rangle.\mathtt{end}\}$

Fig. 5. Motivation for output priority in independent conformance to parallel SG flows

for A and B, respectively (using the abbreviated notation described in § 1). Note that these types do not independently conform to the SG: $T_{\mathtt{A}}^{bad}$ refines the global protocol by forcing a process to wait for an acknowledgement to a (message b), before sending c; similarly, $T_{\mathtt{B}}^{bad}$ mandates to wait for both a and c before doing any output. When composed together, they get stuck in a deadlock. Conformance is designed to prioritise outputs over inputs, thus ruling out incorrect protocols as $T_{\mathtt{A}}^{bad}$ and $T_{\mathtt{B}}^{bad}$. If output priority was to be relaxed, both $T_{\mathtt{A}}^{bad}$ and $T_{\mathtt{B}}^{bad}$ would be conformant and deadlocks would not be prevented.

Weak transition sequences of a net are finite; hence we have:

Proposition 3.1. *For any endpoint type $T_{\mathtt{r}}$ and SG $\boldsymbol{G}$, conformance is decidable.*

Theorem 3.1 (Soundness). *Let $\boldsymbol{G} = \langle P, T, F, f, g\rangle$ have initial marking M_0 and f have range R. Let $C_0 = (\vec{T}_0, \vec{\epsilon})$ be an* initial *configuration such that $T_{0\mathtt{r}} \asymp \langle \boldsymbol{G}, M_0\rangle$, for all $\mathtt{r} \in R$. Let also $C_0 \xrightarrow{m_1} C_1 \dots \xrightarrow{m_n} C_n$ be such that $C_i = (\vec{T}_i, \vec{w}_i)$, for all $i \in \{1, \dots, n\}$. Then $\langle \boldsymbol{G}, M_0\rangle \xrightarrow{\tau^*}\xrightarrow{m_1} \langle \boldsymbol{G}, M_1\rangle \dots \xrightarrow{\tau^*}\xrightarrow{m_n} \langle \boldsymbol{G}, M_n\rangle$, for some $M_1 \dots M_n$; such that $T_{i\mathtt{r}} \asymp \langle \boldsymbol{G}, M_i\rangle$, for all $i \in \{1, \dots, n\}$ and $\mathtt{r} \in R$.*

We now define the safety properties of a configuration C, following those in communicating automata [9, § 3]. We say C is terminal if $C = (\vec{\mathsf{end}}, \vec{\epsilon})$.

1. C is a *deadlock configuration* if $\vec{w} = \vec{\epsilon}$, while C is not terminal and no $T_{\mathtt{r}}$ is an output type, i.e. some types are blocked, waiting for messages.
2. C is an *orphan message configuration* if all $T_{\mathtt{r}} \in \vec{T}$ are end but $\vec{w} \neq \emptyset$, i.e. there is at least an orphan message in a buffer.
3. C is an *unspecified reception configuration* if there is $\mathtt{r} \in R$ such that $T_{\mathtt{r}}$ is an input and, for all $\mathtt{r}' \in R$ and a, $T_{\mathtt{r}} \xrightarrow{\mathtt{r?r'}\langle a\rangle} T'_{\mathtt{r}}$ implies that $|w_{\mathtt{r'r}}| > 0$ and $w_{\mathtt{r'r}} \neq a \cdot w$, i.e $T_{\mathtt{r}}$ is prevented from receiving any message from buffer $\mathtt{r'r}$.

We say C is *deadlock-free* (resp. *orphan message-free*, *reception error-free*) if no C' such that $C \xrightarrow{\vec{m}} C'$ is a deadlock (resp. orphan message, unspecified reception) configuration. C is *safe* if it is deadlock-free, orphan-free and reception error-free.

Theorem 3.2 (Safety and Progress). *Let $\boldsymbol{G} = \langle P, T, F, f, g\rangle$ be a well-formed SG, where the range of f is R. Let $C_0 = (\vec{T}_0, \vec{\epsilon})$ be an initial configuration such that $T_{0\mathtt{r}} \asymp \boldsymbol{G}$, for all $\mathtt{r} \in R$. Then (1) C_0 is safe; and (2) for all C such that $C_0 \xrightarrow{\vec{m}} C$, either C is terminal or $C \xrightarrow{m'} C'$, for some action m'.*

P ::=	$\overline{u}[\mathtt{r}_1, .., \mathtt{r}_n](c).P$	Request	h ::= $\epsilon \mid h \cdot l\langle v\rangle \mid h \cdot s[\mathtt{r}]$
$\mid$	$u[\mathtt{r}](c).P$	Accept	v ::= $a \mid s[\mathtt{r}] \mid x$ (values)
$\mid$	$c!\,\mathtt{r} : l\langle v\rangle; P$	Select	u ::= $a \mid x$ (identifiers)
$\mid$	$c?\{\mathtt{r}_i : l_i(z_i).P_i\}_{i\in I}$	Branch	c ::= $x \mid s[\mathtt{r}]$ (sessions)
$\mid$	$P \mid Q \mid 0$	Parallel, Nil	$s, s', ...$ (session names)
$\mid$	$\mu X.P \mid X$	Recursion	$a, b, ...$ (shared names)
$\mid$	$(\boldsymbol{\nu} a)P \mid (\boldsymbol{\nu} s)P$	Hiding	$x, y, z, ...$ (variables)
$\mid$	$s[\mathtt{r}, \mathtt{r}'] : h$	Queue	

Fig. 6. Syntax of processes

4 Multiparty Asynchronous Session Calculus

Safety and progress are reflected from session graphs onto processes through type conformance. The syntax (Figure 6) is extended from [2], allowing communication with different roles within a single branch. It supports channel mobility and session delegation (i.e. passing and hiding shared/session channels). We summarise the semantics adapted from [2]. ⌊LINK⌋ creates a new session s with bidirectional queues, where $\mathsf{fn}(P)$ is the set of free names of P; ⌊SEL⌋ enqueues and ⌊BRA⌋ dequeues a message. Other rules give the closure under $|$, ν and structural equivalence $\equiv$ (including $(\boldsymbol{\nu} s)(s[\mathtt{r}_1, \mathtt{r}_1'] : \epsilon \mid .. \mid s[\mathtt{r}_n, \mathtt{r}_n'] : \epsilon) \equiv 0$).

⌊LINK⌋ $\overline{a}[\mathtt{r}_1, .., \mathtt{r}_n](x).P_1 \mid a[\mathtt{r}_2](x).P_2 \mid \cdots \mid a[\mathtt{r}_n](x).P_n$
$\longrightarrow (\boldsymbol{\nu} s)(\Pi_{i\in\{1,..,n\}}(P_i[s[\mathtt{r}_i]/x] \mid \Pi_{j\in\{1,..,n\}\setminus i} s[\mathtt{r}_i, \mathtt{r}_j] : \epsilon)) \quad s \notin \mathsf{fn}(P_i)$

⌊SEL⌋ $s[\mathtt{r}]!\,\mathtt{r}' : l\langle v\rangle; P \mid s[\mathtt{r}, \mathtt{r}'] : h \longrightarrow P \mid s[\mathtt{r}, \mathtt{r}'] : h \cdot l\langle v\rangle$

⌊BRA⌋ $s[\mathtt{r}]?\{\mathtt{r}_i' : l_i(z_i).P_i\}_{i\in J} \mid s[\mathtt{r}_j', \mathtt{r}] : l_j\langle v\rangle \cdot h \longrightarrow P_j[v/z_j] \mid s[\mathtt{r}_j', \mathtt{r}] : h$

Conformance replaces the usual endpoint type projection [12]. Type environments use well-formed SGs $\boldsymbol{G}$ and endpoint types T from the previous sections:

$$\Gamma \ ::= \ \emptyset \mid \Gamma \cdot u{:}\boldsymbol{G} \mid \Gamma \cdot X{:}\Delta \qquad \Delta \ ::= \ \emptyset \mid \Delta \cdot c{:}T$$

SG/endpoint type messages are injectively mapped to pairs of process labels $l_1, l_2, \ldots$ and $\boldsymbol{G}$ or T, e.g. $?\{\mathtt{r}_i\langle l_i\langle S_i\rangle\rangle.T_i\}_{i\in I}$ where each S is either $\boldsymbol{G}$ (shared channel passing) or T (session delegation). $X : \Delta$ types a recursive process. $\Gamma \vdash P \rhd \Delta$ is a typing judgement.

Figure 7 lists the key rules, adapted from [2], for typing conformant endpoint processes in the session net setting; the omitted rules are as in [2]. Rule [REQ] types a session initiation request by checking that the endpoint type for the session body conforms to the $\boldsymbol{G}$ associated to the shared channel for role $\mathtt{r}_1$; [ACC] types an initiation accept in the dual manner. Rules [SEL] and [BRA] type selection and branching with shared channel passing (i.e. passing SG-typed messages). Rules [SSEL] and [SBRA] similarly type selection and branching with session delegation (i.e. linear communication of endpoint-typed messages).

Without explicit subsumption typing rules, conformance still enables the typing of processes with branch/select and recursive subtype behaviours [8] and

$$[\text{Req}]\frac{T_{\mathtt{r}_1} \asymp \boldsymbol{G} = \langle P,T,F,f,g\rangle \quad \Gamma \vdash u : \boldsymbol{G} \quad \mathtt{range}(f) = \{\mathtt{r}_1,..,\mathtt{r}_n\} \quad \Gamma \vdash Q \triangleright \Delta, x : T_{\mathtt{r}_1}}{\Gamma \vdash \overline{u}[\mathtt{r}_1,..,\mathtt{r}_n](x).Q \triangleright \Delta} \qquad [\text{Acc}]\frac{T_{\mathtt{r}_i} \asymp \boldsymbol{G} \quad \Gamma \vdash u : \boldsymbol{G} \quad \Gamma \vdash Q \triangleright \Delta, x : T_{\mathtt{r}_i} \quad i \neq 1}{\Gamma \vdash u[\mathtt{r}_i](x).Q \triangleright \Delta}$$

$$[\text{Sel}]\frac{j \in I \quad \Gamma \vdash P \triangleright \Delta, c : T_j \quad \Gamma \vdash u : \boldsymbol{G}_j}{\Gamma \vdash c!\,\mathtt{r}_j : l_j\langle u\rangle; P \triangleright \Delta, c :!\{\mathtt{r}_i\langle l_i\langle \boldsymbol{G}_i\rangle\rangle.T_i\}_{i\in I}}$$

$$[\text{Bra}]\frac{\forall i \in I \quad \Gamma, z_i : \boldsymbol{G}_i \vdash P_i \triangleright \Delta, c : T_i}{\Gamma \vdash c?\{\mathtt{r}_i : l_i(z_i).P_i\}_{i\in I} \triangleright \Delta, c :?\{\mathtt{r}_i\langle l_i\langle \boldsymbol{G}_i\rangle\rangle.T_i\}_{i\in I}}$$

$$[\text{SSel}]\frac{j \in I \quad \Gamma \vdash P \triangleright \Delta, c : T_j}{\Gamma \vdash c!\,\mathtt{r}_j : l_j\langle c'\rangle; P \triangleright \Delta, c :!\{\mathtt{r}_i\langle l_i\langle T_i'\rangle\rangle.T_i\}_{i\in I}, c' : T_j'}$$

$$[\text{SBra}]\frac{\forall i \in I \quad \Gamma \vdash P_i \triangleright \Delta, c : T_i, z_i : T_i'}{\Gamma \vdash c?\{\mathtt{r}_i : l_i(z_i).P_i\}_{i\in I} \triangleright \Delta, c :?\{\mathtt{r}_i\langle l_i\langle T_i'\rangle\rangle.T_i\}_{i\in I}}$$

Fig. 7. Process typing for conformant endpoints

permutation of selections [15], via parallel expansion. By Theorem 3.1, we have the following subject reduction theorem, from which the safety properties for processes are derived as a corollary [12].

Theorem 4.1. *Suppose* $\Gamma \vdash P \triangleright \emptyset$ *and* $P \longrightarrow^* P'$. *Then* $\Gamma \vdash P' \triangleright \emptyset$.

Session net progress (Theorem 2.2) corresponds to the following progress property for processes within a single session [12] (a session net, as any individual global type, models a single protocol). We say $P_0 = \overline{a}[\mathtt{r}_1,..,\mathtt{r}_n](x).P_1 \mid a[\mathtt{r}_2](x).P_2 \mid \cdots \mid a[\mathtt{r}_n](x).P_n$ is *simple* if $a : \boldsymbol{G} \vdash P_0 \triangleright \emptyset$, P_i does not contain session delegation, accept, request and hiding, and $\boldsymbol{G} = \langle P,T,F,f,g\rangle$ where $\mathtt{range}(f) = \{\mathtt{r}_1,..,\mathtt{r}_n\}$.

Theorem 4.2 (Progress). *Let* $a : \boldsymbol{G} \vdash P_0 \triangleright \emptyset$ *and let* P_0 *be simple. Then for all* P *such that* $P_0 \longrightarrow^* P$, *either* $P \equiv 0$ *or* $P \longrightarrow P'$, *for some* P'.

Thus safety and progress of a well-formed net ensure those of the conforming, well-typed processes. Progress across separate sessions can be obtained by using advanced typing systems, e.g. [2], on top of the typing systems in Figure 7.

5 Implementation and Related Work

Implementation. We have implemented Java APIs for validating session graph well-formedness and endpoint type conformance to demonstrate the tractability of our framework. The code and implementations of all the examples in this paper and [19] are available at [18]. We plan to integrate this framework into an extension of Session Java [13], using these well-formedness and conformance APIs to extend the type system following § 3.

Related Work. Workflow nets [20] (WFNs) are a class of Petri nets originally introduced to describe the operation of business processes. A WFN is an abstraction of a global system on which Petri net techniques are used to verify properties such as dead-lock freedom and proper termination. Session nets differ firstly by specifying multiparty role and message details that WFNs are not concerned with. A sound WFN is a good single, self-contained system, whereas a well-formed session net further ensures that the global protocol, given by the configuration of roles and messages on the structure of the net, is safely realisable as a set of independent, distributed endpoints. Secondly, as an MPST framework, session nets bridge from the global graph to syntactic endpoint specifications (via conformance), that are then used to type-check endpoint code.

Open WF-nets (oWFNs) [14,22] are an endpoint-oriented adaptation of WF-nets to distributed systems, that starts from constructing a separate net for each endpoint. In contrast, session nets start from the global-oriented SG model of a protocol against which each endpoint is checked for conformance. In oWFNs, the final system properties depend on the specific endpoint composition (effectively treating the complete system as a standalone WF-net), whereas in session nets, any endpoints that are independently conformant to an SG are guaranteed to give a good composition. Like basic WFNs, oWFNs do not explicitly specify or validate multiparty protocol details.

Although Petri nets classes such as WFNs can be interpreted in a communications setting (e.g. in [21], the validation of a sequence of I/O action sequences is subsumed under the general task of accepting traces of fired transitions), they do not explicitly describe communication protocols. The multiparty protocol information captured by an SG and their associated well-formedness is crucial in the design of session nets, allowing us to validate the safe decomposition of the global system into distributed endpoints. Without these concerns, it is not necessary to consider as many structural constraints for WFNs as for well-formed SGs. (A basic WFN requires only (1) one initial and one terminal place, and (2) that any transition is contained in a path from the initial to the terminal place; an SG with a single terminal node is thus a WFN.) As an example, the following shows a SG whose underlying Petri net satisfies safety and progress, but not the conditions on role labelling (specifically, Def. 2.3 (`L1`)).

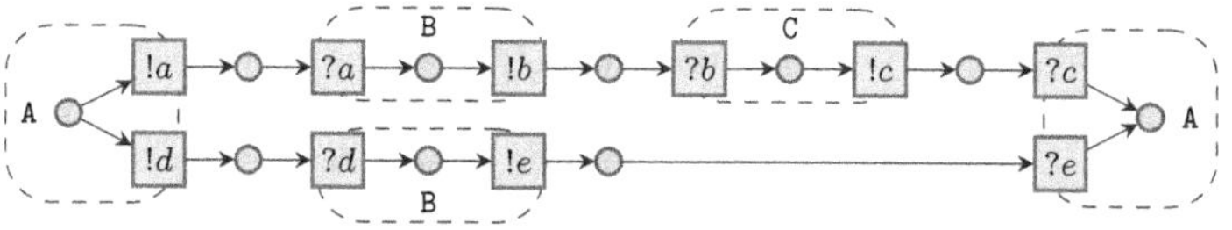

This global protocol cannot be safely realised between the distributed endpoints at the implementation level. If an `A` endpoint chooses to send d in an instance of this protocol, the `C` endpoint will not receive any message. However, this means `C` cannot locally determine whether `A` has indeed selected $!d$, or whether `A` actually selected $!a$ and `C` should wait (indefinitely) to do $?b$. A simple way to amend this SG is to ensure that `C` is also present along the lower branch (not necessarily in the same order), so that the initial internal choice by `A` is explicitly communicated to `C` in all eventualities. Other cases of incoherent message labelling, but otherwise safe in terms of the underlying Petri net, are similarly ruled out by well-formedness, e.g. race conditions in parallel protocol flows.

In [21], WF-nets are used to implement tools for checking the conformance of an executed process to a BPEL specification. Their conformance checking, however, is done at run-time and is used to verify the execution trace of a process, via e.g. a logging service or runtime monitor. Our notion of conformance is different, as it is used to statically check the local correctness of each endpoint type by relating them all to an agreed SG. A well-typed system of endpoint processes is guaranteed to behave safely for all executions.

Session nets, as in [2,4,9,12] and other type structures for Web services (e.g. [1,5,11]), abstract from specific data types so that data typing can be integrated orthogonally. Recently there have been several works to bridge communicating automata with choreographies or session types [1,9]. The main focus of [1,4,9] are projectability conditions for more general forms of global specifications. The unit of their specifications is an input-output relation between two roles (i.e. $\mathtt{A} \to \mathtt{B}$), whereas a main new feature of session nets is the explicit representation of the internal decision structures of participants to produce outputs in response to inputs. This enables more flexible well-formed global types than those in [1,4,9]. None of these works proposed conformance as we have developed for session nets.

Acknowledgments. We thank Luca Aceto and Kohei Honda for their comments and encouragements. The work has been partially sponsored by EPSRC EP/K034413/1 and EP/K011715/1, and EU project FP7-612985 UpScale.

References

1. Basu, S., Bultan, T., Ouederni, M.: Deciding choreography realizability. In POPL, pp. 191–202. ACM (2012)
2. Bettini, L., Coppo, M., D'Antoni, L., De Luca, M., Dezani-Ciancaglini, M., Yoshida, N.: Global progress in dynamically interleaved multiparty sessions. In: van Breugel, F., Chechik, M. (eds.) CONCUR 2008. LNCS, vol. 5201, pp. 418–433. Springer, Heidelberg (2008)
3. Business Process Model and Notation. http://www.bpmn.org
4. Castagna, G., Dezani-Ciancaglini, M., Padovani, L.: On global types and multiparty sessions. Logical Methods in Computer Science **8**(1) (2012)
5. Castagna, G, Gesbert, N., Padovani, L.: A theory of contracts for web services. In POPL, pp. 261–272. ACM (2008)
6. Chen, T.-C., Honda, K.: Specifying stateful asynchronous properties for distributed programs. In: Koutny, M., Ulidowski, I. (eds.) CONCUR 2012. LNCS, vol. 7454, pp. 209–224. Springer, Heidelberg (2012)
7. CPN Homepage. http://cpntools.org/
8. Demangeon, R., Honda, K.: Full abstraction in a subtyped pi-calculus with linear types. In: Katoen, J.-P., König, B. (eds.) CONCUR 2011. LNCS, vol. 6901, pp. 280–296. Springer, Heidelberg (2011)

9. Deniélou, P.-M., Yoshida, N.: Multiparty session types meet communicating automata. In: Seidl, H. (ed.) Programming Languages and Systems. LNCS, vol. 7211, pp. 194–213. Springer, Heidelberg (2012)
10. Desel, J., Esparza, J.: Free Choice Petri Nets (Cambridge Tracts in Theoretical Computer Science). Cambridge University Press (1995)
11. Hallé, S., Bultan, T., Hughes, G., Alkhalaf, M., Villemaire, R.: Runtime verification of web service interface contracts. Computer **43**(3), 59–66 (2010)
12. Honda, K., Yoshida, N., Carbone, M.: Multiparty asynchronous session types. In POPL, pp. 273–284. ACM (2008)
13. Hu, R., Yoshida, N., Honda, K.: Session-Based Distributed Programming in Java. In: Vitek, J. (ed.) ECOOP 2008. LNCS, vol. 5142, pp. 516–541. Springer, Heidelberg (2008)
14. Lohmann, N., Massuthe, P., Stahl, C., Weinberg, D.: Analyzing interacting BPEL processes. In: Dustdar, S., Fiadeiro, J.L., Sheth, A.P. (eds.) BPM 2006. LNCS, vol. 4102, pp. 17–32. Springer, Heidelberg (2006)
15. Mostrous, D., Yoshida, N., Honda, K.: Global principal typing in partially commutative asynchronous sessions. In: Castagna, G. (ed.) ESOP 2009. LNCS, vol. 5502, pp. 316–332. Springer, Heidelberg (2009)
16. Murata, T.: Petri nets: properties, analysis and applications. Proceedings of the IEEE **77**(4), 541–580 (1989)
17. OMG. Unified Modelling Language, Version 2.0 (2004)
18. Java APIs for session nets. http://www.doc.ic.ac.uk/~rhu/session_nets.html
19. Technical Report, Department of Computing, Imperial College London, May 2014. 2014/5
20. van der Aalst, W.M.P.: Verification of workflow nets. In: Azéma, Pierre, Balbo, Gianfranco (eds.) ICATPN 1997. LNCS, vol. 1248. Springer, Heidelberg (1997)
21. van der Aalst, W.M.P., Dumas, M., Ouyang, C., Rozinat, A., Verbeek, H.M.W.: Choreography conformance checking: An approach based on bpel and petri nets. In: The Role of Business Processes in Service Oriented Architectures. IBFI (2006)
22. van der Aalst, W.M.P., et al.: Multiparty contracts: Agreeing and implementing interorganizational processes. Comput. J. **53**(1), 90–106 (2010)
23. Vasconcelos, V.T., Honda, K.: Principal typing scheme for polyadic π-calculus. In: Best, Eike (ed.) CONCUR 1993. LNCS, vol. 715. Springer, Heidelberg (1993)
24. Workflow Patterns homepage. http://www.workflowpatterns.com/

Interaction and Causality in Digital Signature Exchange Protocols

Jonathan Hayman(✉)

Computer Laboratory, University of Cambridge, Cambridge, UK
jonathan.hayman@cl.cam.ac.uk

Abstract. Causal reasoning is a powerful tool in analysing security protocols, as seen in the popularity of the strand space model. However, for protocols that branch, more subtle models are called for to capture the ways in which they can interact with a possibly malign environment. We study a model for security protocols encompassing causal reasoning and interaction, developing a semantics for a simple security protocol language based on concurrent games played on event structures. We show how it supports causal reasoning about a protocol for secure digital signature exchange. The semantics paves the way for the application of more sophisticated forms of concurrent game, for example including symmetry and probability, to the analysis of security protocols.

1 Introduction

The use of models that explicitly represent *causality* has proved highly useful in the analysis of security protocols, as seen in the importance of the strand space model [1]. Through the representation of causal dependency, it is possible to perform an analogue of Paulson's inductive method [2] to establish safety properties by deriving a contradiction to the existence of an earliest violating event, and analyses of causal dependency clarify the specification and proof of authentication properties.

Strand spaces as originally presented represent processes as sets of traces, thereby losing information on branching; this led to Crazzolara and Winskel's development of the semantics based on event structures and Petri nets of a security protocol language called SPL [3]. For the analysis of kinds of security protocol other than authentication protocols, and in particular for the analysis of digital signature exchange protocols, the ability of participants to choose between different forms of behaviour is at the core of the protocols. A key issue then becomes the representation of which participant forces the interaction down different branches: whether it is the process following the protocol or an adversary is of central importance, and this leads to the natural specification of their correctness properties in *game-based* models [4], albeit in past work at the price of no longer representing causality.

The support of the ERC through the Advanced Grant ECSYM is gratefully acknowledged.

M. Maffei and E. Tuosto (Eds.): TGC 2014, LNCS 8902, pp. 128–143, 2014.
DOI: 10.1007/978-3-662-45917-1_9

In this paper, we study the application of *concurrent games* [5] in reasoning about a digital signature exchange protocol, demonstrating how the model supports *both* causal and game-based reasoning. This represents an exciting starting point where other features from the more abstract world of concurrent games, such as probability [6] and symmetry [7], might be brought to bear.

In more detail, we modestly extend SPL and use it to present the Asokan-Shoup-Waidner protocol [8] for digital signature exchange. We then present the semantics of SPL using concurrent games, showing how adversarial behaviour is constrained to the Dolev-Yao model. We conclude by studying the key correctness properties of the protocol.

2 SPL: A Security Protocol Language

SPL, standing for Security Protocol Language, is introduced in [3] along with a semantics based on Petri nets. The work shows how a causal semantics, using a well-known model for concurrency, can be given to syntactically-represented processes that supports the kind of causal reasoning important in the strand space model. As is common when reasoning about security protocols, the language assumes asynchronous communication over a network where we assume messages to persist (for the benefit of any attacker). The language was initially designed for authentication protocols, so it is necessary to extend it slightly for the later study of digital signature exchange protocols by allowing nondeterministic choice and conditionals on input pattern matching.

We begin by assuming the following sets:

- the set **Entity** of *entities* or *participants*, ranged over by X,
- the set **Key** of *encryption keys*, ranged over by k. We assume that for every participant X there is a key $Sig(\mathsf{X})$ representing the signing key of X,
- the set **Hash** of *hash values*,
- the set **New** of *nonces*, representing long (secure pseudo-)randomly generated numbers, ranged over by n, and
- a set of *basic strings* ranged over by m, including for example the message to be signed and any control instructions to be sent to the third party.

We shall assume that the sets above are disjoint: though in principle a nonce value may be equal to a key, the probability of any encountered key being equal to a generated nonce is negligible.

Input in SPL will involve pattern matching: processes specify that they will accept a message matching a pattern, by which variables in the pattern are resolved to messages. We therefore define the set of *message patterns*, ranged over by M, which follow the grammar

$$M := m \mid \mathsf{X} \mid k \mid n \mid (M_1, M_2) \mid \{M\}_k \mid h(M) \mid \psi \mid x.$$

Above, $\{M\}_k$ represents the encryption of M using key k. The message $h(M)$ represents the application of a first -and second-preimage resistant cryptographic hash function [9] to M. The symbols ψ and x range over *message variables*; we shall tend to use the former in patterns, explained next, where any message can match and the latter to suggest that we expect the message to be a nonce or hash value. We say that a message pattern is *closed*, or more simply is a *message*, if it contains no message variables.

We assume that we are given a function associating to every key k its inverse denoted by k^{-1}. Given the key k^{-1}, the message M can be recovered from $\{M\}_k$.

Processes are ranged over by p and b ranges over simple boolean expressions, with the standard definition of when a boolean holds where the atoms are equalities of (closed) messages, following the grammar

$$p := \mathsf{done}(\mathsf{X}) \mid \mathsf{out\,new}\ x\ M.p \mid \mathsf{in\ pat}\ \boldsymbol{\psi}\ M\ \mathsf{where}\ b.p \mid \big\Vert_{i\in I} p_i \mid p + p \mid P$$

$$b := M = M' \mid b \wedge b \mid \neg b.$$

Above, $\boldsymbol{\psi}$ is a finite sequence of distinct message variables. In $\mathsf{out\,new}\ x\ M.p$, we view the variable x as bound, and in $\mathsf{in\ pat}\ \boldsymbol{\psi}\ M\ \mathsf{where}\ b.p$ we view the variables in $\boldsymbol{\psi}$ as bound. We require the free variables in M to be equal to the the variables in ψ, and write $M[\boldsymbol{N}/\boldsymbol{\psi}]$ for the substitution of each message N_i for free occurrences of ψ_i in M.

- $\mathsf{done}(\mathsf{X})$ is included for convenience in proofs, and indicates that the entity X has completed its role in the protocol.
- $\mathsf{out\,new}\ x\ M.p$ generates a new nonce n and then outputs the message $M[n/x]$ (using the newly generated nonce for x) before resuming as $p[n/x]$.
- $\mathsf{in\ pat}\ \boldsymbol{\psi}\ M\ \mathsf{where}\ b.p$ inputs, for any sequence of messages $\boldsymbol{N}$ the same length as $\boldsymbol{\psi}$, the message $M[\boldsymbol{N}/\boldsymbol{\psi}]$ providing the message is available on the network and the proposition $b[\boldsymbol{N}/\boldsymbol{\psi}]$ holds. The process then resumes as $p[\boldsymbol{N}/\boldsymbol{\psi}]$.
- $\Vert_{i\in I}\, p_i$ is the parallel composition of processes indexed by the set I.
- $p_1 + p_2$ is the non-deterministic sum of p_1 and p_2: if p_1 can act to become the resumption p_1' then so can $p_1 + p_2$, and similarly for p_2.
- $P(\boldsymbol{M})$ is a process identifier predicated by a set of messages, and we assume a set of process definitions $Q(\boldsymbol{\psi}) = q$ allowing recursive definition of processes.

In the sequel, we adopt the notation $p_1 \parallel p_2$ for $\Vert_{i\in\{1,2\}}\, p_i$ and write *nil* for the empty parallel composition. When the vector $\boldsymbol{\psi}$ is the set of free variables in M, we write $\mathsf{in}\ M\ \mathsf{where}\ b.p$ for $\mathsf{in\ pat}\ \boldsymbol{\psi}\ M\ \mathsf{where}\ b.p$, and when the condition b is a tautology we simply write $\mathsf{in}\ M.p$. When the variable x is not free in M or p, we write $\mathsf{out}\ M.p$ for $\mathsf{out\,new}\ x\ M.p$.

3 Optimistic Signature Exchange and the ASW Protocol

A digital signature on a message by an entity indicates that the entity has seen and agreed to sign the message. For example, the message *"I agree to sell my house to Bob in exchange for £50"* may be signed by Alice by encrypting it using her private key. Assuming that Alice has kept her private key safe and that everybody has access to her public key, Bob can prove to an arbiter than Alice has seen (and implicitly agreed to) this message.

Contracts require the *exchange* of messages, and this has to be done in a fair way: were Alice simply to send her signature directly to Bob, he could wait an indeterminate amount of time and then decide not to proceed. In the meantime, Alice would be left in limbo, unable to sell her house to anybody else.

Digital signature exchange protocols provide the means to fairly exchange signatures without giving either party an advantage. There are two classes of approach: *incremental* approaches in which the parties gradually release their signature to each other [10] and those based on a *trusted third party.*

With access to an entity that both parties trust to act in a prescribed way, the problem becomes much simpler: the two participants can simply send their signatures to the third party which only exchanges them once both are received. Though it can be shown that there is no non-incremental approach to signature exchange that does not involve a third party [11], the third party is potentially a bottleneck and represents a single point of failure; *optimistic* protocols, such as the Asokan-Shoup-Waidner (ASW) protocol, aim to do better, by only using the third party when necessary.

3.1 The ASW Protocol in SPL

We now introduce the ASW protocol as given in [8], to which we refer the reader for a fuller account. The protocol begins after the two parties, say O acting as the originator and R acting as the responder, have agreed on the message m that they both wish to sign and that an entity T will act as a trusted third party. SPL terms representing both the originator, $\mathit{orig}(m, \mathsf{O}, \mathsf{R}, \mathsf{T})$, and responder, $\mathit{resp}(m, \mathsf{O}, \mathsf{R}, \mathsf{T})$, are presented in Figure 1.

The protocol begins with O sending to R the message M_1 defined in Fig. 1. The message is signed by O and acts as a promise to provide R with O's signature on m providing R follows the protocol. We specify now how the promise of O's signature can be fulfilled:

Definition 1. *A signature by* O *acting as originator for* R *on* m *is a pair of messages* n *and* $\{\mathsf{O}, \mathsf{R}, \mathsf{T}, m, h(n)\}_{\mathit{Sig}(\mathsf{O})}$.

In particular, the initial message M_1 can be translated to a signature by O when accompanied by the nonce x. Importantly, the pre-image resistance of the hash function h accompanied by the fact that x is a nonce (i.e. a long randomly-generated number) means that this translation of the promise to the signature causally depends on O revealing x.

If the protocol proceeds normally (the possibility of *aborting* or *resolving* is discussed below), after O has revealed its promise, the entity R then responds by sending O a message constituting a promise to provide O with R's signature. (Note that second preimage resistance of h prevents O from taking this to be the signature on some other message.)

Let $M_1 = \{\mathsf{O}, \mathsf{R}, \mathsf{T}, m, h(x)\}_{\mathit{Sig}(\mathsf{O})}$ and $M_2 = \{\mathsf{O}, \mathsf{R}, \mathsf{T}, m, z\}_{\mathit{Sig}(\mathsf{O})}$ in

$$\begin{array}{l}
\mathit{orig}(m, \mathsf{O}, \mathsf{R}, \mathsf{T}) \stackrel{\text{def}}{=} \\
\quad \mathsf{out\ new}\ x\ M_1. \\
\quad \mathit{abort}(M_1, \mathsf{O}, \mathsf{T}) + \\
\qquad \mathsf{in}\ \{h(M_1), z\}_{\mathit{Sig}(\mathsf{R})}. \\
\qquad \mathsf{out}\ x. \\
\qquad \mathit{resolve}(M_1, \{h(M_1), z\}_{\mathit{Sig}(\mathsf{R})}, \mathsf{O}, \mathsf{T}, \mathsf{O}) \\
\qquad + \quad \mathsf{in}\ y\ \mathsf{where}\ h(y) = z.\mathsf{done}(\mathsf{O})
\end{array}$$

$$\begin{array}{l}
\mathit{resp}(m, \mathsf{O}, \mathsf{R}, \mathsf{T}) \stackrel{\text{def}}{=} \\
\quad \mathsf{in}\ M_2. \\
\quad \mathsf{out\ new}\ y\{h(M_2), h(y)\}_{\mathit{Sig}(\mathsf{R})}. \\
\qquad \mathsf{in}\ x\ \mathsf{where}\ h(x) = z. \\
\qquad\quad \mathsf{out}\ y.\mathsf{done}(\mathsf{R}) \\
\quad + \ \mathit{resolve}(M_2, \{h(M_2), h(y)\}_{\mathit{Sig}(\mathsf{R})}, \mathsf{O}, \mathsf{T}, \mathsf{R})
\end{array}$$

$$\begin{array}{l}
\mathit{abort}(M, \mathsf{O}, \mathsf{T}) \stackrel{\text{def}}{=} \\
\quad \mathsf{out}\{\mathtt{abort}, M\}_{\mathit{Sig}(\mathsf{O})}. \\
\quad \mathsf{in}\ \{\mathtt{aborted}, \{\mathtt{abort}, M\}_{\mathit{Sig}(\mathsf{O})}\}_{\mathit{Sig}(\mathsf{T})}.\mathsf{done}(\mathsf{O}) \\
\quad + \mathsf{in}\ \{M, \{h(M), z\}_{\mathit{Sig}(\mathsf{R})}\}_{\mathit{Sig}(\mathsf{T})}.\mathsf{done}(\mathsf{O})
\end{array}$$

$$\begin{array}{l}
\mathit{resolve}(M, M', \mathsf{O}, \mathsf{T}, \mathsf{X}) \stackrel{\text{def}}{=} \\
\quad \mathsf{out}(\mathtt{resolve}, M, M'). \\
\qquad \mathsf{in}\ \{\mathtt{aborted}, \{\mathtt{abort}, M\}_{\mathit{Sig}(\mathsf{O})}\}_{\mathit{Sig}(\mathsf{T})}. \\
\qquad\quad \mathsf{done}(\mathsf{X}) \\
\quad + \ \mathsf{in}\ \{M, M'\}_{\mathit{Sig}(\mathsf{T})}.\mathsf{done}(\mathsf{X})
\end{array}$$

Fig. 1. SPL terms for the originator and responder

Definition 2. *A signature by* R *acting as responder for* O *on* m *is a triple of messages* n *and* $M = \{\mathsf{O}, \mathsf{R}, \mathsf{T}, m, n'\}_{\mathit{Sig}(\mathsf{O})}$ *and* $\{h(M), h(n)\}_{\mathit{Sig}(\mathsf{R})}$.

The promise by O is then fulfilled by sending R the nonce n chosen for x; this acts as proof that O either has received R's signature or can do so via the third party. Finally, R sends to O its nonce that allows conversion of its promise to an actual signature.

Let

$$\begin{array}{rcr}
M_2 &=& \{\mathsf{O}, \mathsf{R}, \mathsf{T}, m, z\}_{\mathit{Sig}(\mathsf{O})} \\
M_a &=& \{\mathtt{abort}, M_2\}_{\mathit{Sig}(\mathsf{O})} \\
M_r &=& (\mathtt{resolve}, M_2, \{h(M_2), w\}_{\mathit{Sig}(\mathsf{R})})
\end{array}$$

in

$$\mathit{TTP}(\mathsf{T}) = \mathop{\Big\|}_{\mathsf{O},\mathsf{R} \in \mathbf{Entity}} \ \mathop{\Big\|}_{m \in \mathbf{Message}} \ \mathop{\Big\|}_{z \in \mathbf{Hash}} \mathit{TTP}_0(\mathsf{T}, \mathsf{O}, \mathsf{R}, m, z)$$

where

$$\mathit{TTP}_0(\mathsf{T}, \mathsf{O}, \mathsf{R}, m, z) \stackrel{\text{def}}{=} \begin{array}{l} \mathsf{in}\ M_a.\ \ \mathsf{out}\{\mathtt{aborted}, M_a\}_{\mathit{Sig}(\mathsf{T})}.\ \ \mathit{TTP}_a(\mathsf{T}, \mathsf{O}, \mathsf{R}, m, z) \\ + \ \mathsf{in}\ M_r.\ \ \mathsf{out}\{M_r\}_{\mathit{Sig}(\mathsf{T})}.\ \ \mathit{TTP}_r(\mathsf{T}, \mathsf{O}, \mathsf{R}, m, z, M_r) \end{array}$$

$$\mathit{TTP}_a(\mathsf{T}, \mathsf{O}, \mathsf{R}, m, z) \stackrel{\text{def}}{=} \mathsf{in}\ M_r.\ \ \mathsf{out}\{\mathtt{aborted}, M_a\}_{\mathit{Sig}(\mathsf{T})}.\ \ \mathit{TTP}_a(\mathsf{T}, \mathsf{O}, \mathsf{R}, m, z)$$

$$\mathit{TTP}_r(\mathsf{T}, \mathsf{O}, \mathsf{R}, m, z) \stackrel{\text{def}}{=} \begin{array}{l} \mathsf{in}\ M_r.\ \ \mathsf{out}\{M_r\}_{\mathit{Sig}(\mathsf{T})}.\ \ \mathit{TTP}_r(\mathsf{T}, \mathsf{O}, \mathsf{R}, m, z) \\ + \ \mathsf{in}\ M_a.\ \ \mathsf{out}\{M_r\}_{\mathit{Sig}(\mathsf{T})}.\ \ \mathit{TTP}_r(\mathsf{T}, \mathsf{O}, \mathsf{R}, m, z) \end{array}$$

Fig. 2. SPL terms for the TTP

The ASW protocol allows both the originator and responder to contact the trusted third party if their counterparty fails to respond in the expected way. This could, for example, be due to network failure or due to the other participant (maliciously or not) failing to follow the protocol. The TTP handles two forms of request as part of the *abort* and *resolve* subprotocols. SPL terms for the TTP are presented in Figure 2.

The abort subprotocol is called by the originator if it fails to receive a promise from the responder after it has sent its promise to the responder. The resolve subprotocol can be called by either participant once it has received the promise from its counterparty.

The subprotocols' behaviour is subtle: it depends on whether there has been any prior request to abort or resolve. If the resolve subprotocol is invoked and the abort subprotocol has not earlier been invoked, the third party responds by providing a signature generated on behalf of the counterparty.

Definition 3. *A signature generated by* T *on behalf of either the originator* O *or responder* R *on message* m *is a message of the form*

$$\{\mathtt{resolve}, M, \{h(M), n'\}_{Sig(\mathsf{R})}\}_{Sig(\mathsf{T})}$$

for some hash value n' *and* $M = \{\mathsf{O}, \mathsf{R}, \mathsf{T}, m, n\}_{Sig(\mathsf{O})}$ *for some hash value* n.

If, however, the abort subprotocol has been invoked prior to the resolve request, the third party simply informs the participant that neither party shall receive a signature from it and therefore that the participant can safely assume that its counterparty shall receive no form of signature; it does so by sending the message $\mathtt{out}\{\mathtt{aborted}, M_a\}_{Sig(\mathsf{T})}$, where M_a is the earlier message requesting that the exchange be aborted.

If the abort subprotocol is invoked by the originator and the resolve subprotocol for the message has not earlier been invoked, the TTP responds with a message informing the participant that the transaction has, as above, been aborted. If, otherwise, the other participant has earlier resolved the transaction, the TTP responds with a signature generated on its counterparty's behalf.

It is assumed that interaction with the TTP takes place over *resilient* communication channels: a communication channel is resilient if any message sent over it will eventually be received. An adversary can, however, observe messages sent over the channel and temporarily delay them. We note here that communication between the participants and the TTP is not encrypted; we have adhered to the original presentation since it is unnecessary for the correctness properties studied later. Encrypted communication could easily be added, and would address 'attacks' that are not normally considered where, for example, where the first two messages in a normal exchange are intercepted and then sent as a resolve request, meaning that the exchange certainly goes ahead.

4 Concurrent Games

We now turn to giving a semantics to SPL, representing terms as concurrent strategies. Concurrent strategies are founded upon *event structures* [12].

Definition 4. *An event structure comprises three components* $(E, \leq, \text{Con})$, *where* E *is the set of* events, $\leq \subseteq E \times E$ *is a partial order representing* causal dependency *and the non-empty set* $\text{Con} \subseteq \mathcal{P}_{\text{fin}}(E)$ *represents* consistency, *which jointly satisfy:*

1. $\{e' : e' \leq e\}$ *is finite for all* $e \in E$,
2. $\{e\} \in \text{Con}$ *for all* $e \in E$,
3. *if* $X \in \text{Con}$ *and* $Y \subseteq X$ *then* $Y \in \text{Con}$, *and*
4. *if* $X \in \text{Con}$ *and* $e \in X$ *and* $e' \leq e$ *then* $\{e'\} \cup X \in \text{Con}$.

Events are viewed as atomic and can only occur once. A *configuration* of an event structure is a subset of events $x \subseteq E$ that is down-closed, meaning that $e \in x \;\&\; e' \leq e \implies e' \in x$, and consistent, meaning that, for all subsets $X \subseteq x$, if X is finite then $X \in \text{Con}$. Write $\mathcal{C}^{\infty}(ES)$ for the configurations of an event structure ES, write $\mathcal{C}(ES)$ for its finite configurations, and write $x \overset{e}{\longrightarrow\!\!\subset}$ if $e \notin x$ and $x \in \mathcal{C}^{\infty}(ES)$ and $x \cup \{e\} \in \mathcal{C}^{\infty}(ES)$. An event structure is *elementary* if $\text{Con} = \mathcal{P}_{\text{fin}}(E)$.

We often make use of the binary relations of immediate causal dependency and conflict between events. Immediate causal dependency $e \rightarrowtriangle e'$ means that $e \neq e'$ and $e \leq e'$, and for any u such that $e \leq u \leq e'$ either $e = u$ or $e' = u$. Often, the consistency of a set of events can be determined just by examining pairs of events. In such a case, the consistency relation can be replaced by a *conflict* relation placing two events in conflict, written $e \# e'$, if there is no configuration containing them both. Finally, we say that an event e of an event structure ES is said to be *initial* if $e' \leq e$ implies $e' = e$.

Given a subset of events $V \subseteq E$ of an event structure $ES = (E, \leq, \text{Con})$, the *projection* $(V, \leq_V, \text{Con}_V)$ of ES to V has events V, causal dependency $e \leq_V e'$ iff $e \leq_{ES} e'$ and $X \in \text{Con}_V$ iff $X \in \text{Con}$ for any finite $X \subseteq V$.

Morphisms on event structures will be used to exhibit how the behaviour in one event structure can be simulated by another.

Definition 5. *A (partial)* morphism *from an event structure* $ES = (E, \leq, \text{Con})$ *to an event structure* $ES' = (E', \leq', \text{Con}')$ *is a partial function* $f : E \rightharpoonup E'$ *such that* $fx \in \mathcal{C}(ES')$ *for all configurations* $x \in \mathcal{C}(ES)$, *and*

$$\textit{if } e, e' \in x \textit{ and } f(e), f(e') \textit{ both defined then } f(e) \neq f(e').$$

The latter condition enforces the view that events are indivisible. A morphism is said to be *total* if f is total and *rigid* if it is total and preserves causal dependency in the sense that $f(e) \leq' f(e')$ whenever $e \leq e'$. A *rigid inclusion*, written $\hookrightarrow$, is a rigid map that is also an inclusion.

When defining event structures, it is necessary to ensure that every event has a unique causal history. This aspect can be lightened by building event structures out of *rigid families*.

Definition 6. *A rigid family* $\mathcal{F}$ *is a non-empty set of finite partial orders that are down-closed under rigid inclusions: if* $q' \in \mathcal{F}$ *and* $q \hookrightarrow q'$ *is a rigid inclusion, viewing* q *and* q' *as elementary event structures, then* $q \in \mathcal{F}$.

Concretely, down-closure of $\mathcal{F}$ stipulates that for any $q \in \mathcal{F}$, if e is maximal in q then $q \setminus e \in \mathcal{F}$, where $q \setminus e$ is the partial order with e removed.

Clearly, any event structure determines a rigid family where the orders are its finite configurations ordered by causal dependency; we call the elements of this family *ordered configurations* of the event structure. Conversely, an event structure can be obtained from a rigid family by taking its events to be primes i.e. the partial orders with a *unique* maximal element. Causal dependency between primes $p \leq p'$ is determined by whether there is a rigid inclusion $p \hookrightarrow p'$. A set of primes X is consistent in the event structure if it is finite and it has a supremum, with respect to the partial order of rigid inclusion, in the rigid family.

Example 1. Let the rigid family $\mathcal{F}$ be the down-closure (w.r.t. rigid inclusions) of the two partial orders on the left below. Their corresponding event structure is drawn on the right, where the arrows represent causal dependency and the wavy line represents conflict. The event c_1 is the prime partial order ⓐ⟶ⓒ and c_2 is the prime partial order ⓒ⟵ⓑ.

We make use of a number of constructions on event structures. Given an event structure ES, we now adopt the convention of writing E for its set of events, $\leq$ for its conflict relation and Con for its consistency relation. When ES has a subscript, we add the subscript to its components.

Firstly, the simple parallel composition of event structures $||_{i\in I} ES_i$ has events $\bigcup_{i\in I}\{i\} \times E_i$, causal dependency $(i, e) \leq (i', e')$ iff $i = i'$ and $e \leq_i e'$ and a set of events X is consistent iff $\{e : (i, e) \in X\} \in \text{Con}_i$ for every $i \in I$. The event structure $!ES$ consists of countably-many copies of ES placed in parallel with each other, $!ES = ||_{i\in\mathbb{N}} ES$.

The *augmentation* of an event structure $\text{aug}(ES)$ is defined via a rigid family. A partial order q is in the rigid family if its underlying set $|q|$ is a member of $\mathcal{C}(ES)$ and the order is an extension of the order on the configuration in ES: it satisfies $e \leq e' \implies e \leq_q e'$ for all $e, e' \in |q|$.

Note that there are total functions from the events of $\text{aug}(ES)$ and $!ES$ to the events of ES taking any event in either $\text{aug}(ES)$ or $!ES$ to the event that generated it.

4.1 Concurrent Games and Winning Strategies

An *event structure with polarity* is an event structure with a total function $\text{pol} : E \to \{+, -\}$ attaching a polarity, either $+$ for player or $-$ for opponent, to every event. The intuition is that the state of an interaction between the player and the opponent is a configuration of an event structure with polarity called the *game*. The player can extend the configuration by playing any of the enabled $+$ events and the opponent can extend the configuration by playing any of the enabled $-$ events. The occurrence of any event can affect what the other player

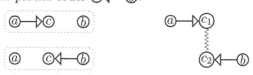

can do: it can enable events in the game that causally depend upon it and it prohibits the occurrence of events that are inconsistent with it.

The constructions on event structures above extend straightforwardly to event structures with polarity, with polarity being inherited from the event structures from which they are constructed. A further important operation is the dual $ES^{\perp}$, which is $(E, \leq, \mathrm{Con}, \mathrm{pol}')$ where $\mathrm{pol}'(e) = +$ iff $\mathrm{pol}(e) = -$.

We now introduce *strategies* on event structures with polarity as introduced in [5], which are potentially non-deterministic specifications of how the player is to act. Their definition is guided by properties that are desired when strategies are composed; we briefly mention an application of composition in the conclusion.

Definition 7. *A strategy for the player is a total morphism $\sigma : S \to A$ between event structures with polarity s.t.*

- *(Polarity preservation)* $\mathrm{pol}_S(e) = \mathrm{pol}_A(\sigma(e))$ *for all* $e \in E_S$,
- *(Receptivity) for any* $x \in \mathcal{C}^\infty(S)$, *if* $\sigma(s) \overset{e}{\longrightarrow\!\!\subset}$ *and* $\mathrm{pol}(e) = -$ *then there exists unique* s *such that* $x \overset{s}{\longrightarrow\!\!\subset}$ *and* $\sigma(s) = e$, *and*
- *(Innocence) if* $e \rightarrowtriangle e'$ *in* S *then either* $\sigma(e) \rightarrowtriangle \sigma(e')$ *in* A *or* $\mathrm{pol}(e) = -$ *and* $\mathrm{pol}(e') = +$

Correctness properties shall be expressed with reference to *winning strategies* [13].

Definition 8. *Consider a strategy* $\sigma : S \to A$. *With reference to a set* $W \subseteq \mathcal{C}^\infty(A)$ *of* winning configurations, *the strategy* σ *is* winning *if every* $+$*-maximal configuration of* S *(i.e. every configuration* $x \in \mathcal{C}^\infty(S)$ *for which there is no* s *satisfying* $x \overset{s}{\longrightarrow\!\!\subset}$ *and* $\mathrm{pol}(s) = +$*) has* $\sigma x \in W$.

4.2 Semantics of SPL

The semantics of a closed SPL term shall be given as a strategy on a game denoted by *SPL*, in which players perform *actions* successively and potentially repeatedly. Let **Msg** denote the set of all (closed) messages and let the set of actions be

$$\begin{aligned} Act =& \{\mathsf{in}\, M : M \in \mathbf{Msg}\} \cup \{\mathsf{out}\, M : M \in \mathbf{Msg}\} \\ & \cup \{\mathsf{done}(X) : X \in \mathbf{Entity}\} \cup \{\mathsf{new}\, n : n \in \mathbf{New}\}. \end{aligned}$$

Given an event structure Y and $p \in \{+, -\}$, let Y^p denote the event structure with polarity where the underlying event structure is Y and all events have polarity p. Viewing Act as an event structure with trivial causal dependency and consistency relations, we define the game $SPL_0 = \mathrm{aug}(!Act^-) \parallel \mathrm{aug}(!Act^+)$. Let the function sending an event of SPL_0 to its image in Act be denoted by $act : SPL_0 \to Act$. The game SPL is specified as a rigid family: its partial order configurations are configurations x in $\mathcal{C}(SPL_0)$ inheriting order from SPL_0 for which, for any $n \in \mathbf{New}$, there is at most one $e \in x$ such that $act(e) = \mathsf{new}\, n$.

Actions of the process to which we give semantics are represented by events with positive polarity. Events with negative polarity represent any other process that may act in parallel with the process to which we give semantics. The definition of the game *SPL* allows the player to have strategies that successively perform actions in response to those of the opponent; in particular, the use of augmentation is necessary for the strategy to be innocent. The difference between the games SPL_0 and *SPL* is that, in *SPL*, a nonce can be generated only once.

We now proceed to give the semantics of SPL terms. We omit the formal definition of recursion, which is a straightforward adaption of the recursive definition of event structures [14]. By induction on the size (the number of actions) of terms, we shall define an event structure with polarity S_p and strategy $\sigma_p : S_p \to SPL$. In each case, the set of negative events in S_p shall be equal to the set of negative events in *SPL*. Any two negative events in S_p are causally dependent iff they are causally dependent in *SPL*. For any finite set of negative events X of S_p, we shall have $X \in \mathrm{Con}_p$ iff X is consistent in *SPL*.

A first useful operation is *prefixing* by a positive action. Given a strategy $\sigma_p : S_p \to SPL$ and $\alpha \in Act$, and assuming first that $\alpha \neq \mathsf{new}\ n$ for $n \in \mathbf{New}$, we define $\alpha.\sigma_p : \alpha.S_p \to SPL$ to have domain $\alpha.S_p$ formed with events the disjoint union of those from S_p and a new event, say a, with positive polarity. Causal dependency in $\alpha.S_p$ extends that of S_p with $a \leq e$ for all events e with positive polarity. A subset of events X of $\alpha.S_p$ is consistent iff $X \setminus \{a\}$ is consistent in S_p. Let a' be the first[1] initial positive α-event in *SPL* and let $SPL \uparrow a'$ be the projection of *SPL* to all negative events along with positive events that causally depend on but are not equal to a'. There is an isomorphism $\phi : SPL \cong SPL \uparrow a'$ that acts as the identity on events with negative polarity. The morphism $\alpha.\sigma_p$ sends a to a' and $e \neq a$ to $\phi(e)$.

Now, if $\alpha = \mathsf{new}\ n$, it is necessary to remove from $\alpha.S_p$ all positive events u for which there exists $e \leq u$ satisfying $e \neq a$ and $\mathrm{pol}(e) = +$ and $act(e) = \mathsf{new}\ n$. A subset of events X of $\alpha.S_p$ is consistent iff $X \setminus \{a\}$ is consistent in S_p and there is no $e \in X$ such that $\mathrm{pol}(e) = -$ and $act(e) = \mathsf{new}\ n$.

A second convenient operation is the *generalized sum* of strategies as described above (*i.e.* strategies with negative events those from *SPL*). Given a non-empty family of strategies $\sigma_i : S_i \to SPL$ for $i \in I$ where $S_i = (E_i, \leq_i, \mathrm{Con}_i, \mathrm{pol}_i)$, their sum $\sum_i \sigma_i : \sum_i S_i \to SPL$ is defined as follows. The event structure $\sum_i S_i = (E, \leq, \mathrm{Con}, \mathrm{pol})$ has negative events and causality dependency within them, as specified above, from *SPL*. The positive events form the set $\{(i,e) : i \in I \;\&\; e \in E_i\}$. No negative event depends on any positive event (as required for innocence), but for a positive event (i,e) we have $u \leq (i,e)$ iff either u is positive and there exists e' s.t. $u = (i,e')$ and $e' \leq_i e$ or u is negative and $u \leq_i e$. For a subset of events $X \subseteq E$, we have $X \in \mathrm{Con}$ iff there exists $i \in I$ and $Y \in \mathrm{Con}_i$ such that $X = \{e \in Y : \mathrm{pol}_i(e) = -\} \cup \{(i,e) : e \in Y \;\&\; \mathrm{pol}_i(e) = +\}$.

Input. The strategy for $\mathsf{in\ pat}\ \psi\ M\ \mathsf{where}\ b.p$ is as follows. Let A be the set of events e in *SPL* with negative polarity for which there exists M_0 such that

[1] This choice is arbitrary and can be alleviated by adding symmetry: see the conclusion.

$act(e) = \mathsf{out}\, M_0$ and there exists a sequence of messages $\boldsymbol{N}$ the same length as $\boldsymbol{\psi}$ satisfying $M_0 = M[\boldsymbol{N}/\boldsymbol{\psi}]$ and $b[\boldsymbol{N}/\boldsymbol{\psi}]$ holds. Note that any such sequence is unique for e. For any $e \in A$, by prefixing we form the strategy in $M_0.\sigma_{p[\boldsymbol{N}/\boldsymbol{\psi}]}$ where $\sigma_{p[\boldsymbol{N}/\boldsymbol{\psi}]}$ is the strategy inductively obtained for $p[\boldsymbol{N}/\boldsymbol{\psi}]$. From this strategy, we obtain a strategy σ_e by adding a single immediate causal dependency $e \twoheadrightarrow a$, where a is the event for the initial input, the least positive event in in $M_0.S_{p[\boldsymbol{N}/\boldsymbol{\psi}]}$. Finally, we define $\sigma = \sum_{e \in A} \sigma_e$.

Output. Considering $\mathsf{out\,new}\; x\, M.p$, let n be any nonce. By induction, we have a strategy $\sigma_{p[n/x]}$ and so, by prefixing twice, a strategy $\sigma_{\mathsf{new}\; n\,.\,\mathsf{out}\; M[n/x].p[n/x]}$. The strategy for $\mathsf{out\,new}\; x\, M.p$ is defined to be $\sum_{n \in \mathbf{New}} \sigma_n$.

Parallel Composition. The strategy for the parallel composition $||_{i \in I}\, p_i$ is relatively simple: we do not at this stage introduce any causal dependencies between the processes since we do now know with which other processes $||_{i \in I}\, p_i$ shall be composed. Formally, we define the strategy $\sigma : S \to SPL$ where $S = (E, \leq, \mathrm{Con})$ as follows. For $i \in \{I\}$, let $\sigma_i : S_i \to SPL$ be the strategy strategy for p_i where $S_i = (E_i, \leq_i, \mathrm{Con}_i, \mathrm{pol}_i)$, and let $SPL = (E_{SPL}, \leq_{SPL}, \mathrm{Con}_{SPL}, \mathrm{pol}_{SPL})$.

$$E = \{e \in E_{SPL} : \mathrm{pol}_{SPL}(e) = -\} \cup \bigcup_{i \in I}(\{i\} \times \{e : e \in E_i \;\&\; \mathrm{pol}_i(e) = +\})$$

$$\begin{aligned} e \leq e' \iff & \mathrm{pol}(e) = - \;\&\; \mathrm{pol}(e') = - \;\&\; e \leq_{SPL} e' \\ \text{or } & \mathrm{pol}(e) = - \;\&\; \mathrm{pol}(e') = + \;\&\; \exists i, u' : e' = (i, u') \;\&\; e \leq_i u' \\ \text{or } & \mathrm{pol}(e) = + \;\&\; \mathrm{pol}(e') = + \;\&\; \exists i, u, u' : e = (i, u) \;\&\; e' = (i, u) \;\&\; u \leq_i u' \end{aligned}$$

$$\begin{aligned} X \in \mathrm{Con} \iff & \{e \in X : \mathrm{pol}(e) = -\} \in \mathrm{Con}_{SPL} \text{ and for all } i \in I : \\ & \{u : (\mathrm{pol}(u) = - \;\&\; u \in X) \text{ or } ((i, u) \in X \;\&\; \mathrm{pol}(i, u) = +)\} \in \mathrm{Con}_i \end{aligned}$$

Nondeterministic sum The sum $p_1 + p_2$ has strategy $\sum_{i \in \{1,2\}} \sigma_i$, where σ_i is the strategy for p_i.

Theorem 1. *σ_p, as defined above, is a strategy for any closed term p.*

There is an asymmetry in the semantics above that warrants explanation: Any player input event in the strategy causally depends on an opponent event that outputs the same message, but there are no causal dependencies of the opponent events on player events (such dependencies would, indeed, violate the innocence condition). Causal dependency of opponent events on those of the process are central to reasoning about security protocols: for example, an initially secret message may be replayed but not guessed by an attacker, so any attacker event that outputs the secret message causally depends on some output by the process. As we proceed to describe, these causal dependencies are introduced after we have inductively obtained the strategy σ_p on SPL; the reason why it is not defined as we give the semantics for each term is that we do not know with which other processes the processes under consideration shall be composed and therefore what messages it will be possible for the attacker to output.

4.3 Constraining the Attacker

We now move from from strategies that can be composed to form semantics to ones that are used to reason about the behaviour of adversaries.

The key principle is that any message that the attacker outputs has to be justified, in the sense of the Dolev-Yao [15] model, from messages to which it has access. For a set of messages s, we write $s \vdash M$ if M is justified by s, defined to be the least relation satisfying the following rules:

$s \vdash M$ if $M \in s$ $\qquad\qquad\qquad\qquad$ $s \vdash (M_1, M_2)$ if $s \vdash M_1$ and $s \vdash M_2$

$s \vdash M_1$ and $s \vdash M_2$ if $s \vdash (M_1, M_2)$ $\qquad$ $s \vdash M$ if $s \vdash k^-1$ and $s \vdash \{M\}_k$

$s \vdash \{M\}_k$ if $s \vdash M$ and $s \vdash k$ $\qquad\qquad$ $s \vdash h(M)$ if $s \vdash M$

We write $M \prec M'$ if M is a sub-message of M', the least reflexive transitive relation such that $M_1 \prec (M_1, M_2)$ and $M_1 \prec \{M_1\}_k$. Given a set of messages s that is initially on the network, we now refine the game SPL so that all opponent outputs are justified and all opponent inputs of messages not in s depend on on corresponding outputs. We also ensure that any generated nonce is not a submessage in s. The game, denoted by $ASPL(s)$, is defined to be the event structure obtained from the following rigid family of configurations (inheriting polarity from SPL):

Definition 9. *For any configuration x of an event structure with polarity, subset of messages $s \subseteq \mathbf{Msg}$ and $\alpha : x \to Act$, the configuration x is defined to be secured w.r.t. α iff for any e such that $\text{pol}(e) = -$ and there exists M such that $\alpha(e) = \text{out}\, M$, we have $s \cup \{N : \exists e' \le e\ \&\ \text{pol}(e') = -\ \&\ act(e') = \text{in}\, N\} \vdash M$. A source map for x and α is a partial function $\kappa : x \rightharpoonup x$ that is defined on an event e iff $\text{pol}(e) = -$ and there exists $M \notin s$ such that $e = \text{in}\, M$, in which case we require that $act(f(e)) = \text{out}\, M$.*

The rigid family defining $ASPL(s)$ consists of finite partial orders $\le$ over configurations $x \in \mathcal{C}(SPL)$ that contain no event e such that $act(e) = \text{new}\, n$ for any $n \in \mathbf{New}$ if $n \prec M \in s$, that are secured w.r.t. $act : x \to Act$ and for which there exists a source map κ such that $\le$ is the transitive closure of $(\le_{SPL} \cap (x \times x)) \cup \{(\kappa(e), e) : e \in x\ \&\ \kappa(e)\ defined\}$.

There is a morphism of event structures $\hat{s} : ASPL(s) \to SPL$. Given a strategy $\sigma_p : S_p \to SPL$ representing the semantics of p, we can form a strategy $\hat{\sigma}_p : \hat{S}_p \to ASPL(s)$ by pullback as drawn to the right, since the pullback of a strategy against a morphism that preserves polarity is also a strategy [6]. Concretely, the strategy $\hat{\sigma}_p$ only has opponent events that are justified by what the opponent may have intercepted according to the Dolev-Yao model. The pullback can be viewed as minimally modifying the domain S_p so that it meets the additional causal constraints in $ASPL(s)$. From now on, we denote by $(\!|p|\!)_s$ the strategy $\hat{\sigma}_p : \hat{S}_p \to ASPL(s)$. A particular instance of the pullback is obtained as follows.

$$\begin{array}{ccc} \hat{S}_p & \longrightarrow & S_p \\ \hat{\sigma}_p \downarrow & \lrcorner & \downarrow \sigma_p \\ ASPL(s) & \xrightarrow{\ \hat{s}\ } & SPL \end{array}$$

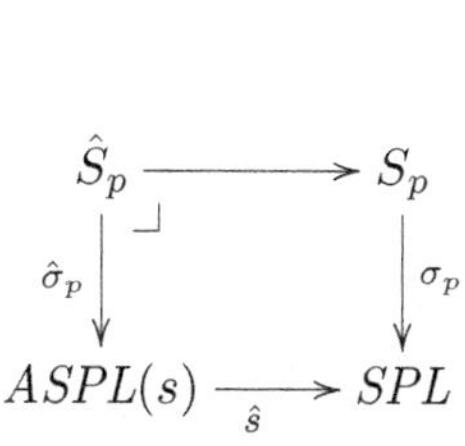

Theorem 2. *A finite partial order $\le_x \subseteq x \times x$ is an order configuration of $\hat{S}_p$ iff there is no $e \in x$ such that $act(e) = \text{new}\, n$ and $n \prec M \in s$, there exists an order*

configuration $\leq_y \subseteq y \times y$ *of* S_p *such that* y *is secured w.r.t.* $act \circ \sigma_p : y \to Act$ *and there exists a source map* $\kappa : y \rightharpoonup y$ *such that* $\leq_x$ *is the transitive closure of the following relation:* $\leq_y \cup \{(\kappa(e), e) : e \in y \;\&\; \kappa(e) \text{ defined}\}$.

Note that the configurations are required to be partial orders: if the source map creates a cyclic dependency, it will not result in an order configuration.

The pullback construction has the effect of introducing causal dependencies of negative events on positive ones. For example, an order configuration of S_p of the form on the left below (where we label events with their actions) gives rise to the configuration in $\hat{S}_p$ on the right.

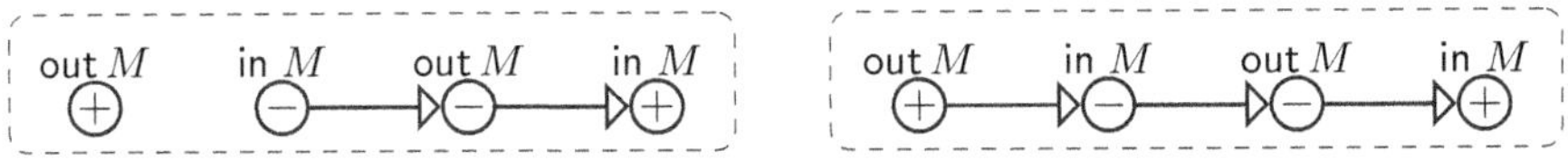

This kind of pattern is always encountered when one player event outputs a message that the attacker does not initially know and another player event receives it. It has the correct causal dependency of the player input on the player output. The intermediate opponent events are useful: they mean that we give the attacker the ability to intercept or delay messages.

5 Correctness Properties

We now use the semantics to formulate correctness properties for the ASW protocol. The properties that we consider are expressed in terms of strategies being winning with respect to particular sets of winning configurations.

It is in the formulation of correctness properties that we capture the notion of resilient communication between the third party and the participants: the protocol will win by default if the resilience assumption is not satisfied. Since we do not explicitly represent channels of communication, we directly characterize the messages intended to be between participants and the third party T as those either under the key $Sig(\mathsf{T})$ or containing either `abort` or `resolve`.

The following predicates on configurations x of $ASPL(s)$ will be useful.

- $x \models \mathsf{Sig}^p_{\mathsf{Orig}}(\mathsf{X},\mathsf{Y},\mathsf{T},m)$ if $\{M : \exists e \in x : act(x) = \mathsf{in}\ M \;\&\; \mathrm{pol}(e) = p\}$ contains a signature by X acting as originator for Y on m with TTP T
- $x \models \mathsf{Sig}^p_{\mathsf{Resp}}(\mathsf{X},\mathsf{Y},\mathsf{T},m)$ if $\{M : \exists e \in x : act(x) = \mathsf{in}\ M \;\&\; \mathrm{pol}(e) = p\}$ contains a signature by Y acting as responder for X on m with TTP T
- $x \models \mathsf{Sig}^p_{\mathsf{TTP}}(\mathsf{X},\mathsf{Y},\mathsf{T},m)$ if $\{M : \exists e \in x : act(x) = \mathsf{in}\ M \;\&\; \mathrm{pol}(e) = p\}$ contains a signature by TTP T on behalf of X or Y
- $x \models \mathsf{Resil}(\mathsf{T})$ if for all events $e \in x$ such that $\mathrm{pol}(e) = +$ and $act(e) = \mathsf{out}\ M$ and M is a message to/from the third party T, there exists $e' \in x$ such that $\mathrm{pol}(e') = -$ and $act(e') = \mathsf{out}\ M$

The first property is *effectiveness*: that whenever the protocol completes without invoking the third party, each party has the signature of the other.

Theorem 3 (Effectiveness). *Let s be any set of messages such that $s \not\vdash \mathit{Sig}(\mathsf{O})$ and $s \not\vdash \mathit{Sig}(\mathsf{R})$ and $s \not\vdash \{\mathsf{O}, \mathsf{R}, \mathsf{T}, m, M\}_{\mathit{Sig}(\mathsf{O})}$ for any message M. The strategy $(\!| \mathit{orig}(m, \mathsf{O}, \mathsf{R}, \mathsf{T}) \parallel \mathit{resp}(m, \mathsf{O}, \mathsf{R}, \mathsf{T}) \parallel \mathit{TTP}(\mathsf{T}) |\!)_s$ is winning with respect to winning configurations x of $\mathit{ASPL}(s)$ that satisfy either:*

- $x \models \mathsf{Sig}^{+}_{\mathsf{Orig}}(\mathsf{O}, \mathsf{R}, \mathsf{T}, m)$ *and* $\mathsf{Sig}^{+}_{\mathsf{Resp}}(\mathsf{O}, \mathsf{R}, \mathsf{T}, m)$,
- *there exists* $e \in x$ *and* M *such that* $\mathrm{pol}(e) = +$ *and* $\mathit{act}(e) = \mathsf{out}\, M$ *but there is no* $e' \in x$ *such that* $\mathrm{pol}(e') = -$ *and* $\mathit{act}(e') = \mathsf{out}\, M$, *or*
- *there exists* $e \in x$ *such that* $\mathrm{pol}(e) = +$ *that carries a message containing either* `abort` *or* `resolve`.

Note that, since we trust how the third party will behave, it is included in the process being considered. The proof of the theorem is omitted, but it makes use of causal reasoning: the key aspect is that no attacker can interfere with the protocol since any such action would causally depend on some process event that outputs the signing key for either O or T, of which there is none.

The statement of effectiveness makes use of the notion of winning strategy to ensure that the environment (assumed to be hostile) does not indefinitely block transmission of a message. In particular, a configuration is winning if the process outputs a message but there is no corresponding negative event outputting the same message. The same kind of definition is used later to ensure that the attacker always releases messages to/from the third party: the other correctness properties do not require *all* messages eventually to get through.

Two further correctness properties for the ASW protocol are *fairness* and *timeliness*. Fairness asserts that if one party gains a signature of the other then the other party will gain a signature of the first if it continues with the protocol. Timeliness asserts that each party can proceed with the protocol no matter how the other party acts: it will not be stuck indefinitely waiting for the other. It is convenient to prove fairness and timeliness together. The properties for the originator and responder are stated separately since they hold even when the other party is dishonest (*i.e.* doesn't follow the protocol), and we only present them for the originator; those for the responder are similar.

Theorem 4 (Fairness and timeliness for the originator). *Let s be any set of messages such that $s \not\vdash \mathit{Sig}(\mathsf{O})$ and $s \not\vdash \mathit{Sig}(\mathsf{T})$ and $s \not\vdash \{\mathsf{O}, \mathsf{R}, \mathsf{T}, m, M\}_{\mathit{Sig}(\mathsf{O})}$ for any M. The strategy $(\!| \mathit{orig}(m, \mathsf{O}, \mathsf{R}, \mathsf{T}) \parallel \mathit{TTP}(\mathsf{T}) |\!)_s$ is winning with respect to the set of winning configurations x of $\mathit{ASPL}(s)$ that satisfy either $x \not\models \mathsf{Resil}(\mathsf{T})$ or both*

1. *if* $x \models \mathsf{Sig}^{-}_{\mathsf{Orig}}(\mathsf{O}, \mathsf{R}, \mathsf{T}, m) \vee \mathsf{Sig}^{-}_{\mathsf{TTP}}(\mathsf{O}, \mathsf{R}, \mathsf{T}, m)$ *then* $x \models \mathsf{Sig}^{+}_{\mathsf{Resp}}(\mathsf{O}, \mathsf{R}, \mathsf{T}, m) \vee \mathsf{Sig}^{+}_{\mathsf{TTP}}(\mathsf{O}, \mathsf{R}, \mathsf{T}, m)$, *and*
2. *x contains a player event* $\mathsf{done}(\mathsf{O})$.

Fairness is the first point above and timeliness the second. Again, causal reasoning comes to the fore in their proofs. The key properties for fairness are that the key $\mathit{Sig}(\mathsf{O})$ is never available to the adversary, as before, and that if the adversary gains a signature either by O or on behalf of O then the signature must have come from either the O or the third party, and these events causally depend on other events that allow the generation of R's signature.

6 Conclusion and Related Work

We have given a semantics for SPL using concurrent games and used this to apply causal reasoning when studying correctness of the ASW protocol, providing what we feel are more intuitive and direct proofs than those obtained by inductive techniques based on interleaving structures. The work provides a starting point for application of concurrent games and their extensions to provide a rich foundation for the semantics of security protocols, where both interaction and causality are explicitly represented.

Formal methods have been applied previously to analyse the ASW and GJM protocols in [4,16,17]. [16] describes the use of the Murφ model checker, and implicitly assumes the fairness of runs (in the sense that it is assumed that the entities terminate) to study protocol fairness and other correctness properties. [4] introduced the idea of specifying fairness through the use of strategies and used the MOCHA model checker to study them. Notably, their games are played over interleaving structures, and fairness constraints on runs have to be added to deal, for example, with resilience. Finally, [17] studies the GJM (Garay-Jakobbsson-MacKenzie) protocol using a combination of inductive methods and interleaved tree structures to represent the game.

There has not been space to present the details here, but the semantics can also be applied to give an account of the GJM protocol [18], which uses a cryptographic primitive called private contract signatures to provide a property called *abuse freeness*: that there is no reachable configuration where one entity can prove to an external entity that it has to ability to choose unilaterally either to exchange signatures or to abort the protocol. In previous work [16,17], this has been simplified to considering *balance*, which is that there is no reachable configuration where one entity can choose between exchange of signatures or aborting. Balance can be formulated in the framework presented here by saying that there is no configuration where there are two counterstrategies [13] to either the originator or responder in parallel with the third party, where one counterstrategy wins if it obtains the signature and the other counter strategy wins if it or the TTP do not reveal its signature.

There are a number of variations on the basic game structures that we intend to study. Firstly, rather than directly representing input moves in the game, we can model them using 'neutral' events in a 'partial strategy' [19]. Composition of partial strategies (such as those for the originator and responder) then has neutral events representing a global session type [20]. Composition may also play a role when probabilistic strategies [6] are studied, using probability to discuss the likelihood of either breaking a key or being able to do no better than simply guessing what value is encrypted beneath a key. Finally, the current work motivates the study of multiplayer games to allow us to reason about TTP accountability and to study multiparty exchange in the GJM protocol.

References

1. Thayer, F.J., Herzog, J.C., Guttman, J.D.: Strand spaces: Proving security protocols correct. Journal of Computer Security **7**(1), 191–230 (1999)
2. Paulson, L.C.: Proving properties of security protocols by induction. In: Proc. 10th IEEE Workshop on Computer Security Foundations, CSFW (1997)
3. Crazzolara, F., Winskel, G.: Events in security protocols. In: ACM Conference on Computer and Communications Security (2001)
4. Kremer, S., Raskin, J.F.: Game analysis of abuse-free contract signing. In: Proc. 15th IEEE Workshop on Computer Security Foundations, CSFW (2002)
5. Rideau, S., Winskel, G.: Concurrent strategies. In: Proc. LICS, pp. 409–418. IEEE Computer Society (2011)
6. Winskel, G.: Distributed probabilistic and quantum strategies. In: Proc. MFPS. ENTCS, vol. 298 (2013)
7. Castellan, S., Clairambault, P., Winskel, G.: Symmetry in concurrent games. In: Proc. LICS (2014)
8. Asokan, N., Shoup, V., Waidner, M.: Asynchronous protocols for optimistic fair exchange. In: Proc. 1998 IEEE Symp. on Security and Privacy, pp. 86–99 (May 1998)
9. Menezes, A., van Oorschot, P., Vanstone, S.: Handbook of Applied Cryptography. CRC Press (2001)
10. Even, S., Goldreich, O., Lempel, A.: A randomized protocol for signing contracts. Commun. ACM **28**(6) (June 1985)
11. Pagnia, H., Gärtner, F.C.: On the impossibility of fair exchange without a trusted third party. Technical report. Darmstadt University of Technology (1999)
12. Winskel, G.: Event structures. In: Brauer, W., Reisig, W., Rozenberg, G. (eds.) Petri Nets: Applications and Relationships to Other Models of Concurrency. LNCS, vol. 255, pp. 325–392. Springer, Heidelberg (1986)
13. Clairambault, P., Gutierrez, J., Winskel, G.: The winning ways of concurrent games. In: Proc. LICS, IEEE (2012)
14. Winskel, G.: Event structure semantics for CCS and related languages. In: Nielsen, M., Schmidt, E.M. (eds.) ICALP. LNCS, vol. 140, pp. 561–576. Springer, Heidelberg (1982)
15. Dolev, D., Yao, A.C.C.: On the security of public key protocols. IEEE Transactions on Information Theory **29**(2), 198–207 (1983)
16. Shmatikov, V., Mitchell, J.C.: Finite-state analysis of two contract signing protocols. TCS **283**(2), (2002)
17. Chadha, R., Kanovich, M., Scedrov, A.: Inductive methods and contract-signing protocols. In: ACM Conference on Computer and Communications Security (2001)
18. Garay, J.A., Jakobsson, M., MacKenzie, P.D.: Abuse-free optimistic contract signing. In: Wiener, M. (ed.) CRYPTO 1999. LNCS, vol. 1666, p. 449. Springer, Heidelberg (1999)
19. Castellan, S., Hayman, J., Winskel, G.: Strategies as concurrent processes. In: Proceedings of the 30th Conference on the Mathematical Foundations of Programmings Semantics (MFPS XXX), vol. 308, pp. 1–328 (Ocotober 29, 2014)
20. Takeuchi, K., Honda, K., Kubo, M.: An interaction-based language and its typing. In: Halatsis, C., Philokyprou, G., Maritsas, D., Theodoridis, S. (eds.) PARLE 1994. LNCS, vol. 817. Springer, Heidelberg (1994)

Session Types with Gradual Typing

Peter Thiemann(✉)

University of Freiburg, Georges-Köhler-Allee 079, 79110 Freiburg, Germany
thiemann@acm.org

Abstract. Session types enable fine-grained static control over communication protocols. Gradual typing is a means to safely integrate statically and dynamically typed program fragments.

We propose a calculus for synchronous functional two-party session types, augment this calculus with a dynamically typed fragment as well as coercion operations between statically and dynamically typed parts, and establish its basic metatheory: type preservation and progress. A technical novelty is the notion of coercions for the choice operator in session types which is related to coercions of sum types.

Keywords: Session types · Gradual typing · Coercion calculus

1 Introduction

Session types enable fine-grained static control over communication protocols. They evolved from a structuring scheme for two-party communication in π-calculus [11] over calculi embedded in functional languages [6,7,19] to a powerful means of describing multi-party orchestration of communication [13]. There are various embeddings in object-oriented languages [2,8] as well as uses in the context of scripting languages [12,14]. Their logical foundations have been investigated with interpretations in intuitionistic and classical linear logic [1,20].

Gradual types [16], on the other hand, were conceived to improve the efficiency of dynamically typed programs by imposing static typing where possible and by resorting to dynamic checking where necessary. However, gradual types have further applications. For example, the blame calculus [21] explores the safe interaction of statically and dynamically typed program fragments on the basis of gradual typing. There are also gradual versions of type systems for information flow [3,5] and typestate [22].

Our work explores the safe interplay of statically and dynamically typed program fragments in the context of session types. We start from a session-typed functional calculus with synchronous communication and augment it with a type D (dynamic) along with coercions into and out of that type. The resulting calculus has interesting applications inspired by recent work on applying session types in connection with scripting languages [12,14]. In particular, in the cited work, program stubs in a dynamically typed language are generated for clients (and servers) from a session type specification. Our calculus can be used for

M. Maffei and E. Tuosto (Eds.): TGC 2014, LNCS 8902, pp. 144–158, 2014.
DOI: 10.1007/978-3-662-45917-1_10

dynamically ensuring type safety when such a stub is used in connection with a statically typed server (client).

In session types, the choice operations on the sender and receiver side naturally generate a subtyping relation[6]: a receiver may accept more alternatives than provided by a sender. Our calculus comes with a new, dynamically checked notion of sender and receiver choice coercions, which allow a receiver to accept *fewer* alternatives than provided by the sender. These coercions are useful to manage prototyping situations, where a communication peer initially implements only parts of a protocol or where the peer implements a protocol extension before it becomes part of the agreed upon protocol specification. Choice coercions are closely related to gradual typing for sum types, which has not be investigated in the literature so far.

Our calculus allows the application of coercions to all communications in a channel, but it does not allow the coercion of an entire session type to type D. We leave this additional step to future work because it requires a closer look at the interaction between dynamic types and linear/affine types as investigated by prior work [4,18,22]. In any case, our calculus seems to be a good fit for the intended scenario of ensuring type safety for programs that are elaborations of generated program stubs. In the dynamic part, the generated code guarantees adherence to the message sequencing constraints imposed by the session typing. Our calculus guarantees the type checking for the transmitted values on both ends of the communication.

Furthermore, the work on gradual types for improving the efficiency of dynamically typed programs [16] imposes a type discipline on an underlying untyped calculus and then specifies a type-driven transformation that introduces coercions. Our calculus follows the approach of the blame calculus [21] and considers what can be seen as the target language of the transformation after coercion introduction. This latter choice is appropriate when considering programs composed of statically and dynamically typed fragments where the programmer uses explicit coercions to demarcate the fragments.

Overview. Sec. 2 introduces the session calculus with gradual types with examples. Sec. 3 contains the syntax, semantics, and typing of the calculus. Sec. 4 proves type soundness. Sec. 5 discusses related work.

2 Sessions Between Static and Dynamic Peers

Consider a client-server system that implements the web interface of a weather forecast system. For this system, a simple protocol between client and server might look like this: The client first sends its location as a number (postcode or GPS coordinate, type `num`). Next, it may either request the current temperature measurement (m) or a comprehensive report including historic data and forecasts (r). After sending an m-request the client expects the current measurement as a number. After sending an r-request the client expects a `num->num` function that returns measurements according to its input. Zero corresponds to

```
client(p, location, single) {
  cl = request p
  cs = send (location, cl)
  if (single) { ca = select m cs
                (n:num, ca') = receive ca
                displayCurrent (n)
                close ca'
  } else {      cb = select r cs
                (f:num->num, cb') = receive cb
                display14DayAverage (f)
                close cb'
}}
```

Fig. 1. Statically typed client code

present, negative arguments return past measurements, positive arguments yield forecasts. Results are meaningful only in a certain, undetermined range.[1]

This protocol is expressed as a session type on the port p providing the service with $\oplus\langle\ldots\rangle$ denoting a sender choice between sessions starting with label m or r, $!t.s$ ($?t.s$) sending (receiving) an item of type t and continuing with s, and END indicating the end of the connection:

$$p : [!\,\mathtt{num}.\oplus\langle \mathtt{m} : ?\,\mathtt{num}.\mathtt{END}, \mathtt{r} : ?\,(\mathtt{num} \rightarrow \mathtt{num}).\mathtt{END}\rangle]$$

Figure 1 contains code for statically typed client. It performs a request on the port and obtains a channel typed with the session type associated to the port. It then runs the protocol on the channel using the usual primitives of sessions types: `send` and `receive` for simple messages, `select x c` for selecting alternative `x` on connection `c`, and `close` for closing a connection. The assignment notation in the code abbreviates sequences of let-expressions.

At the other end, the server may be written in a dynamically typed language (Figure 2).[2] Although the server can accept a connection on port `p`, it cannot directly communicate on the connection obtained from it because the channel does not accept dynamic values. For that reason, the server first coerces the connection to process dynamically typed values.

The session type of the accepted connection is the dual of the client's session type: $?\,\mathtt{num}.\&\langle \mathtt{m} : !\,\mathtt{num}.\mathtt{END}, \mathtt{r} : !\,(\mathtt{num} \rightarrow \mathtt{num}).\mathtt{END}\rangle$. The cast applied to it is expressed using a coercion calculus with # standing for coercion application and ; for left-to-right sequential composition of coercions. For each (session-) type constructor, there is a corresponding coercion constructor that takes a coercion that is applied to each constituent type of the constructor. The example code uses the coercion operator for receiving choice, which fits to the type of the accepted connection. The m compartment of the coercion contains a coercion for

[1] The protocol does not transmit the range to keep it simple.

[2] The code makes all coercions explicit, including those that need not be written by the programmer.

```
server(p) {
  cl = accept p #
    ?(num↑).&⟨m : !(num↓^{b.1}).END, r : !((D → D)↓^{b.2} ; (num↑ → num↓^{b.3})).END⟩
  (location, cd) = receive cl
  case cd of {
  m : fun ca => ca' = send (24.3 # num↑, ca)
                close ca'
  r : fun cb => cb' = send (
        fun z => (24.3 + (z # num↓^b)*0.1) # num↑ #(D → D)↑, cb)
                close cb'
  }
}
```

Fig. 2. Dynamically typed server code

the value before it is sent to the client: num $\downarrow^{b.1}$ checks that a value of type dynamic is indeed a num and extracts it. The annotation $b.1$ is a *blame label* that identifies the source of the (potential) run-time error when the types do not match. The coercion in the r compartment first checks that its argument is a function and then applies a function coercion that transforms that argument and result type to the desired target types. Assuming a code generator for session types, all of this code except the boxed fragments would be generated.

2.1 Coercions as Proxies

Applying the coercion to the accepted session creates a proxy process that mediates between the existing connection and the new connection. This proxy maintains a new channel of the desired target type of the coercion. The proxy forwards the operations between the channels as prescribed by the session types. It applies the cast operations from the session coercion before writing to the other end of a channel. It also retains the blame labels. Conceptually, the construction of the proxy could be done by a program transformation before execution as demonstrated with the transformed server program in Fig. 3.

2.2 Choice Coercions

There are two kinds of choice operators in session types, the internal choice $\oplus\langle\ldots\rangle$ where the program selects a particular outcome and the external choice where the program reacts and makes a case distinction driven by the label it receives. The coercion operator corresponding to choice supplies a coercion for each case mentioned in the type.

As a novel feature, a coercion may also add or remove cases from the set of labels on which the session type branches. This flexibility is achieved by only restricting the argument type of a coercion to match on the common branch labels. The result type of the coercion specifies the branches in the coerced

```
server_eager(p) {
  cs' = accept p
  p' = new port [?num.&⟨m : ! D.END, r : ! D.END⟩]
  cl = pipe p' (proxy cs') (fun cl => cl)
  (loc, cd) = receive cl
  ...
}
proxy = fun cl cl' {
  (dl : D, cp) = receive cl
  cp' = send (dl # num↑, cl')
  case cp of {
  m : fun ca => (df : D, ca1) = receive ca
                ca2 = send (df # num↓^{b.1} , ca1)
                close ca2
  r : fun cb => (df : D, cb1) = receive cb
                cb2 = send (df # (D → D)↓^{b.2} ; (num↑ → num↓^{b.3}), cb1)
                close cb2
}}
```

Fig. 3. Transformed server with proxy implementation of session coercion

```
partial_server(p) {
  cl = accept p # ?(num↑).&^{r↦b.0}_{{m,r}}⟨m : !(num↓^{b.1}).END⟩
  (loc, cd) = receive cl
  case cd of {
    m : fun ca => close (send ([24.3], ca))
}}
```

Fig. 4. Partial server code

session type. The branches which are not specified by the coercion result in blame, but this blame may depend on the particular label. Thus, each choice coercion is annotated with a blame map β indicating the blame $\beta(l)$ which is raised if a non-existing branch labeled l is addressed. If this blame map is a constant function, then a single blame annotation suffices.

As an example, consider a partial implementation of the server protocol that just serves the current temperature (Fig. 4). If a client sends an r-request, then the choice coercion intercepts this request and triggers blame with label $b.0$. This label abbreviates a second branch in the choice: $\mathtt{r} : 0\#\bot^{b.0}$, a failure coercion that always triggers blame, applied to an arbitrary value. The proxy that implements the "restricting" choice coercion is defined accordingly.

```
case cp of {
  m : fun ca => (df : D, ca1) = receive ca
                ca2 = send (df # num↓^{b.1} , ca1)
                close ca2
  r : 0 # ⊥^{b.0}
}
```

$$
\begin{aligned}
s &::= \mathtt{END} \mid\, !t.s \mid ?t.s \mid \oplus\langle l : s, \ldots\rangle \mid \&\langle l : s, \ldots\rangle \\
t &::= s \mid * \mid t \otimes t \mid t \multimap t \mid t \rightarrow t \mid [s] \\
k &::= * \mid c\{s\} \mid n\{s\} \mid \mathtt{req} \mid \mathtt{accept} \mid \mathtt{send} \mid \mathtt{receive} \mid \mathtt{close} \\
e &::= x \mid k \mid e \otimes e \mid \mathtt{let}\, x \otimes x = e\, \mathtt{in}\, e \mid \mathtt{rec}\, x(x) e \mid \lambda x.e \mid e\, e \mid \\
&\quad\;\; \mathtt{sel}\, l\, e \mid \mathtt{case}\, e\, \mathtt{of}\, \{l : e, \ldots\} \mid \mathtt{fork}\, e\, e \mid \mathtt{pipe}\, s\, e\, e \\
p &::= \mathbf{0} \mid e \mid p \,\|\, p
\end{aligned}
$$

Fig. 5. Syntax of sessions, types, constants, expressions, and processes

The server may also implement alternatives that are not required by the protocol, but these extra alternatives require no special handling because the server type is a subtype of the protocol type, in this case.

Dually, the programmer of the client may apply a sender-choice coercion to develop and type check future extensions of a protocol. For example, introducing a new x-request into the client code in Fig. 1 would require adding a line like the following.[3]

```
cl0 = request p
cl = cl0 # ! (ι_num). ⊕^{x↦b}_{x,m,r} ⟨m : ι_? num.END, r : ι_? num→num.END⟩
cs = send (loc, cl)
...
cx = select x cs
```

An execution that reaches `select x cs` would raise an exception after reducing to `cx #` $\bot^b$. This execution is impossible with the protocol on `p`.

The final case, where a sender-choice coercion removes an alternative, is dual to the addition of a receiver-choice alternative.

3 Session Calculus with Gradual Types

This section introduces syntax and semantics of the functional calculus with synchronous session types and gradual types. The first subsection explains the fragment without gradual types. It is inspired by Gay and Vasconcelos's calculus for asynchronous functional session types [7]. Our calculus differs from theirs by being synchronous and by describing the semantics with a labeled transition system, which simplifies our proofs. The second subsection introduces coercions and gradual typing; the third subsection defines coercion typing.

3.1 Functional Session Calculus

Fig. 5 defines the syntax of the calculus. A session type s indicates the protocol that can be run on a connection of this type: END means that the connection can only be closed, $?t.s$ receiving a value of type t and continue according to s ,

[3] The coercion ι_t is the identity coercion at type t. The notation $\mathtt{x} \mapsto b$ denotes a one-element blame map.

$$\begin{array}{rcl} v & ::= & k \mid v \otimes v \mid \mathtt{rec}\, x(x)e \mid \lambda x.e \\ \mathcal{E} & ::= & \square \mid \mathcal{E} \otimes e \mid v \otimes \mathcal{E} \mid \mathtt{let}\, x \otimes x = \mathcal{E}\, \mathtt{in}\, e \mid \\ & & \mathcal{E}\, e \mid v\, \mathcal{E} \mid \mathtt{sel}\, l\, \mathcal{E} \mid \mathtt{case}\, \mathcal{E}\, \mathtt{of}\ \{l : e, \dots\} \\ \mathcal{P} & ::= & \square \mid p \,\|\, \mathcal{P} \mid \mathcal{E} \\ \alpha & ::= & \tau \mid \mathit{req}\ c\{s\} \mid \mathit{acc}\ c\{s\} \mid \mathit{sel}(l, c) \mid \mathit{case}(l, c) \mid \\ & & !(v, c) \mid ?(v, c) \mid \mathit{close}(c) \end{array}
\qquad
\begin{array}{rcl} \overline{\mathtt{END}} & = & \mathtt{END} \\ \overline{!\,t.s} & = & ?\,t.\bar{s} \\ \overline{?\,t.s} & = & !\,t.\bar{s} \\ \overline{\&\langle l : s, \dots\rangle} & = & \oplus\langle l : \bar{s}, \dots\rangle \\ \overline{\oplus\langle l : s, \dots\rangle} & = & \&\langle l : \bar{s}, \dots\rangle \end{array}$$

Fig. 6. Values, evaluation contexts, process contexts, actions, dual of a session type

$!\,t.s$ sending a value of type t and continue, $\&\langle l : s, \dots\rangle$ and $\oplus\langle l : s, \dots\rangle$ receive or send a choice with each alternative indexed by a label l and then continuing according to s in that alternative.

A standard type t is either a session type s, a unit type $*$, a linear product $t \otimes t$, a linear function $t \multimap t$, a standard function $t \to t$, or a port $[s]$ which may be used to create connections that use the protocol s.

A constant k is either a unit value $*$, a connection token $c\{s\}$, a port token $n\{s\}$, or a built-in operation involving a connection: `req` and `accept` both take a port argument and produce a connection as described in the reduction rules in Fig. 7. The operations `receive`, `send`, and `close` act on connections in the obvious way. Both connection (channel) and port tokens are special symbols which are adorned with a session type. Connection tokens never show up in source programs and must be handled linearly.

Expressions e are constants, variables, introduction $e \otimes e$ and elimination $\mathtt{let}\, x \otimes x = e\, \mathtt{in}\, e$ of pairs where the latter form is required because the pair type is linear. There are recursive functions $\mathtt{rec}\, x(x)e$, linear functions $\lambda x.e$, function application $e\, e$, as well as $\mathtt{sel}\, l\, e$ to send a label indicating a particular alternative in a sender choice, $\mathtt{case}\, e\, \mathtt{of}\ \{l : e, \dots\}$ to perform a choice based on the label received, $\mathtt{fork}\, e_1\, e_2$ to fork e_1 as a new process, and $\mathtt{pipe}\, s\, e_1\, e_2$ to create a channel of type s, fork e_1, and pass the channel ends to e_1 and e_2.

Process expressions p are either the null process $\mathbf{0}$, single expressions e or two processes running in parallel $p \,\|\, p$. Process expressions are identified up to commutativity and associativity of parallel composition $\|$ with the null process $\mathbf{0}$ serving as an identity.

We specify the semantics in small-step operational style using a labeled transition system. Fig. 6 specifies values v as a subset of expressions (constants, pairs of values, and functions), evaluation contexts $\mathcal{E}$ for expressions where $\square$ is the empty evaluation context (standard strict left-to-right evaluation), and evaluation contexts $\mathcal{P}$ for processes. The latter are understood up to associativity and commutativity of $\|$ so that $p \,\|\, \mathcal{P}$ selects either the left or right subprocess.

Reductions are adorned with actions α, where τ is the silent action (i.e., no interaction), $\mathit{req}\ c\{s\}$ and $\mathit{acc}\ c\{s\}$ signal that a `req` or `accept` operation has been performed on channel $c\{s\}$, similarly, the *sel*, *case*, ?, !, and *close* actions signal that the corresponding operation has been performed on the indicated channel. We usually omit the silent action τ.

$$\begin{array}{lcll}
\mathcal{P}[\mathtt{let}\, x_1 \otimes x_2 = (v_1 \otimes v_2)\,\mathtt{in}\, e] & \longrightarrow & \mathcal{P}[e[x_1, x_2 \mapsto v_1, v_2]] & \\
\mathcal{P}[(\mathtt{rec}\, x_1(x_2) e_1)\, v] & \longrightarrow & \mathcal{P}[e_1[x_1, x_2 \mapsto (\mathtt{rec}\, x_1(x_2)e_1), v]] & \\
\mathcal{P}[(\lambda x.e)\, v] & \longrightarrow & \mathcal{P}[e[x \mapsto v]] & \\
\\
\mathcal{P}[v] & \longrightarrow & \mathcal{P}[\mathbf{0}] & \\
\mathcal{P}[\mathbf{0} \parallel p] & \longrightarrow & \mathcal{P}[p] & \\
\mathcal{P}[\mathtt{fork}\, e_1\, e_2] & \longrightarrow & e_1 \parallel \mathcal{P}[e_2] & \\
\mathcal{P}[\mathtt{pipe}\, s\, e_1\, e_2] & \longrightarrow & e_1\,(c\{\bar{s}\}) \parallel \mathcal{P}[e_2\,(c\{s\})] & c\{s\} \notin \mathit{fc}(\mathcal{P}, e_1, e_2) \\
\mathcal{P}[\mathtt{req}\, n\{s\}] & \xrightarrow{req\ c\{s\}} & \mathcal{P}[c\{s\}] & \\
\mathcal{P}[\mathtt{accept}\, n\{s\}] & \xrightarrow{acc\ c\{s\}} & \mathcal{P}[c\{\bar{s}\}] & \\
\mathcal{P}[\mathtt{sel}\, l_j\, c\{\oplus\langle l_i : s_i, \dots\rangle\}] & \xrightarrow{sel(l_j,c)} & \mathcal{P}[c\{s_j\}] & \\
\mathcal{P}[\mathtt{case}\, c\{\&\langle l_i : \bar{s}_i, \dots\rangle\}\,\mathtt{of}\,\{l_i : e_i, \dots\}] & \xrightarrow{case(l_j,c)} & \mathcal{P}[e_j\, c\{\bar{s}_j\}] & \\
\mathcal{P}[\mathtt{send}\,(v \otimes c\{!\,t.s\})] & \xrightarrow{!(v,c)} & \mathcal{P}[c\{s\}] & \\
\mathcal{P}[\mathtt{receive}\, c\{?\,t.\bar{s}\}] & \xrightarrow{?(v,c)} & \mathcal{P}[v \otimes c\{\bar{s}\}] & \\
\mathcal{P}[\mathtt{close}\, c\{\mathtt{END}\}] & \xrightarrow{close(c)} & \mathcal{P}[*] &
\end{array}$$

RClose

$$\frac{p_1 \xrightarrow{close(c)} p_1' \qquad p_2 \xrightarrow{close(c)} p_2'}{\mathcal{P}[p_1 \parallel p_2] \to \mathcal{P}[p_1' \parallel p_2']}$$

RSingle

$$\frac{p_1 \xrightarrow{!(v,c)} p_1' \qquad p_2 \xrightarrow{?(v,c)} p_2'}{\mathcal{P}[p_1 \parallel p_2] \to \mathcal{P}[p_1' \parallel p_2']}$$

RChoice

$$\frac{p_1 \xrightarrow{sel(l,c)} p_1' \qquad p_2 \xrightarrow{case(l,c)} p_2'}{\mathcal{P}[p_1 \parallel p_2] \to \mathcal{P}[p_1' \parallel p_2']}$$

RConnect

$$\frac{p_1 \xrightarrow{req\ c\{s\}} p_1' \qquad p_2 \xrightarrow{acc\ c\{s\}} p_2' \qquad c\{s\} \notin \mathit{fc}(\mathcal{P}[p_1 \parallel p_2])}{\mathcal{P}[p_1 \parallel p_2] \to \mathcal{P}[p_1' \parallel p_2']}$$

Fig. 7. Evaluation rules

Fig. 7 specifies the top-level reduction relation $\to$ which relies on an auxiliary labeled reduction relation where the label specifies a communication action α. The context rules RClose, RSingle, RChoice, and RConnect guarantee that these labeled reductions always pair up one producer action and one consumer action. The RConnect rule guarantees that the newly created connection token is fresh, using $\mathit{fc}(p)$ for the set of connection tokens in process p. The labeled reduction rules are *not* intended to run at the top-level. For each of them, there is a context rule that matches it up with a corresponding labeled reduction (labeled with the complementary action on the same channel) in another process.

The reduction rules for let, rec, and lambda are standard. A process that has been reduced to a value turns into the null process. The null process in parallel to some p is eliminated. The $\mathtt{fork}\, e_1\, e_2$ expression starts e_1 as a new process. The $\mathtt{pipe}\, s\, e_1\, e_2$ expression creates a fresh channel $c\{s\}$, passes the server end to e_1 and the client end to e_2, and then starts the server $e_1(c\{\bar{s}\})$ as a new process. The labeled reductions for `request` and `accept` work together with the RConnect rule to create a new connection. The RConnect rule makes sure that the same connection token is used with the same session type in both contracta. Additionally, the `accept` rule emits the server end of the channel where the session type is inverted (dualized). This inversion is indicated by the function $\bar{s}$ (see Figure 7). It exchanges the read and write operations in a protocol to generate the server view from the client view.

The reductions for `select` and `case` work together with RCHOICE to select an alternative in a session choice. They update the session type of the connection token accordingly. The reductions for `send` and `receive` work together with RSINGLE in the same way. The `send` operation takes a linear pair and the `receive` operation returns one because these pairs contain a connection token, which is a linear value.

The reduction for `close` consumes the connection token at returns the unit value. The RCLOSE rule guarantees that exactly two processes perform a close step on both ends of the same connection.

Figure 8 contains the definition of the type system. It first defines symbol environments Σ that associate channel names with session types and typing environments Γ that map identifiers to types. The use of Γ_x in the definition indicates that x does not occur in Γ_x. In contrast, a symbol environment may contain multiple identical associations for the same channel. The predicate $unr(t)$ specifies unrestricted types, which need not be treated linearly, along with its extension $unr(\Gamma)$ to typing environments. The splitting operator $+$ for environments is defined as usual to avoid the duplication and weakening of linearly typed values. We also use splitting for symbol environments.

The calculus contains type and session type indexed families of constants for the operations request, accept, send, receive, and close. The function $hd(s)$ describes the next possible communication on a channel of type s. It may be a set of labels, with the empty set denoting that the channel may only be closed, or the type of the next value that may be transmitted on the channel.

The typing rules are standard for a lambda calculus with linear types. The rule for a channel makes sure its type is specified by the symbol environment. The rules for the `select` and `case` constructs are standard for the session choice operators in a calculus with session types. Because connections are represented by type-carrying connection tokens, the typing judgment for processes does not require a typing environment, but the symbol environment is required to ensure consistent use of channels.

3.2 Gradual Typing

Gradual typing adds a type D "dynamic" to the type language, introduces a type cast operation of the form $e\#\gamma$, and a blame signal $\Uparrow^b$ to the expression language. A cast checks the actual type of a value of type dynamic at run time. A value of dynamic type has the form $D_{tc}(v)$, which is a pair of a type constructor and a ground type value v of type $tc(\overrightarrow{D})$. The new syntactic form γ is a coercion defined along with the other syntactic extensions by the grammar in Figure 9. Type constructors (except session types) are ranged over by tc, each with an associated arity. Ground types g are applications of a type constructor to all dynamic arguments.

Symbol environments, variable environments, unrestricted types

$$\Sigma ::= \cdot \mid \Sigma, c : s \qquad \Gamma ::= \cdot \mid \Gamma_x, x : t \qquad unr(*) \qquad unr(t \to t) \qquad unr([s])$$

Unrestricted environments

$$unr(\cdot) \qquad \frac{unr(\Gamma) \qquad unr(t)}{unr(\Gamma, x : t)}$$

Environment splitting

$$\cdot + \cdot = \cdot \qquad \frac{unr(t) \qquad \Gamma_1 + \Gamma_2 = \Gamma}{x : t, \Gamma_1 + x : t, \Gamma_2 = x : t, \Gamma}$$

$$\frac{\Gamma_1 + \Gamma_2 = \Gamma}{x : t, \Gamma_1 + \Gamma_2 = x : t, \Gamma} \qquad \frac{\Gamma_1 + \Gamma_2 = \Gamma}{\Gamma_1 + x : t, \Gamma_2 = x : t, \Gamma}$$

Typing of constants

$$\mathtt{req} : [s] \to s \qquad \mathtt{accept} : [s] \to \bar{s}$$

$$\mathtt{send} : t \otimes (!\,t.s) \to s \qquad \mathtt{receive} : (?\,t.s) \to t \otimes s \qquad \mathtt{close} : \mathtt{END} \to *$$

Head of session type

$$hd(\mathtt{END}) = \emptyset \qquad hd(?\,t.s) = hd(!\,t.s) = t$$

$$hd(\&\langle l : s, \dots \rangle) = hd(\oplus\langle l : s, \dots \rangle) = \{l, \dots\}$$

Typing rules for expressions

$$\frac{unr(\Gamma)}{\cdot, \Gamma + x : t \vdash x : t} \qquad \frac{unr(\Gamma)}{\cdot, \Gamma \vdash * : *} \qquad \frac{unr(\Gamma)}{c : s, \Gamma \vdash c\{s\} : s} \qquad \frac{unr(\Gamma)}{\cdot, \Gamma \vdash n\{s\} : [s]}$$

$$\frac{\Sigma_1, \Gamma_1 \vdash e_1 : t_1 \qquad \Sigma_2, \Gamma_2 \vdash e_2 : t_2}{\Sigma_1 + \Sigma_2, \Gamma_1 + \Gamma_2 \vdash e_1 \otimes e_2 : t_1 \otimes t_2}$$

$$\frac{\Sigma_1, \Gamma_1 \vdash e_1 : t_1 \otimes t_2 \qquad \Sigma_2, \Gamma_2 + x_1 : t_1, x_2 : t_2 \vdash e : t}{\Sigma_1 + \Sigma_2, \Gamma_1 + \Gamma_2 \vdash \mathtt{let}\, x_1 \otimes x_2 = e_1 \,\mathtt{in}\, e : t}$$

$$\frac{unr(\Gamma) \qquad \cdot, \Gamma + x_1 : t_2 \to t, x_2 : t_2 \vdash e : t}{\cdot, \Gamma \vdash \mathtt{rec}\, x_1(x_2)e : t_2 \to t} \qquad \frac{\Sigma, \Gamma + x : t_1 \vdash e : t_2}{\Sigma, \Gamma \vdash \lambda x.e : t_1 \multimap t_2}$$

$$\frac{\Sigma_1, \Gamma_1 \vdash e_1 : t_2 \to t \qquad \Sigma_2, \Gamma_2 \vdash e_2 : t_2}{\Sigma_1 + \Sigma_2, \Gamma_1 + \Gamma_2 \vdash e_1\, e_2 : t} \qquad \frac{\Sigma_1, \Gamma_1 \vdash e_1 : t_2 \multimap t \qquad \Sigma_2, \Gamma_2 \vdash e_2 : t_2}{\Sigma_1 + \Sigma_2, \Gamma_1 + \Gamma_2 \vdash e_1\, e_2 : t}$$

$$\frac{\Sigma, \Gamma \vdash e : \oplus\langle l : s, \dots \rangle}{\Sigma, \Gamma \vdash \mathtt{sel}\, l\, e : s} \qquad \frac{\Sigma_1, \Gamma_1 \vdash e : \&\langle l_i : s_i, \dots \rangle \qquad \Sigma_2, \Gamma_2 \vdash e_i : s_i \multimap t}{\Sigma_1 + \Sigma_2, \Gamma_1 + \Gamma_2 \vdash \mathtt{case}\, e \,\mathtt{of}\, \{l_i : e_i, \dots\} : t}$$

$$\frac{\Sigma_1, \Gamma_1 \vdash e_1 : * \qquad \Sigma_2, \Gamma_2 \vdash e_2 : t_2}{\Sigma_1 + \Sigma_2, \Gamma_1 + \Gamma_2 \vdash \mathtt{fork}\, e_1\, e_2 : t_2} \qquad \frac{\Sigma_1, \Gamma_1 \vdash e_1 : \bar{s} \multimap * \qquad \Sigma_2, \Gamma_2 \vdash e_2 : s \multimap t_2}{\Sigma_1 + \Sigma_2, \Gamma_1 + \Gamma_2 \vdash \mathtt{pipe}\, s\, e_1\, e_2 : t_2}$$

Typing rules for processes

$$\cdot \vdash \mathbf{0} \qquad \frac{unr(t) \qquad \Sigma, \cdot \vdash e : t}{\Sigma \vdash e} \qquad \frac{\Sigma_1 \vdash p_1 \qquad \Sigma_2 \vdash p_2}{\Sigma_1 + \Sigma_2 \vdash p_1 \parallel p_2}$$

Fig. 8. Typing rules and auxiliary definitions

$$\begin{array}{ll} t ::= \cdots \mid D & tc ::= * \mid \otimes \mid \multimap \mid \rightarrow \mid [s] \\ e ::= \cdots \mid e\#\gamma \mid \Uparrow^b & g ::= * \mid D \otimes D \mid D \multimap D \mid D \rightarrow D \mid [s] \\ \mathcal{E} ::= \cdots \mid \mathcal{E}\#\gamma & \gamma ::= \sigma \mid \iota_t \mid g\uparrow \mid g\downarrow^b \mid \gamma\,;\gamma \mid \gamma \otimes \gamma \mid \gamma \multimap \gamma \mid \gamma \rightarrow \gamma \mid \bot^b \\ v ::= \cdots \mid D_{tc}(v) & \sigma ::= \mathtt{END} \mid !\,\gamma.\sigma \mid ?\,\gamma.\sigma \mid \oplus^{\beta}_{\mathfrak{L}}\langle l : \sigma, \ldots\rangle \mid \&^{\beta}_{\mathfrak{L}}\langle l : \sigma, \ldots\rangle \end{array}$$

Fig. 9. Syntax extensions for gradual typing: types, expressions, evaluation contexts, values, type constructors, ground types, coercions, and session coercions

A coercion term γ is either a session coercion σ, an identity coercion ι_t indexed by a type, an injection of a ground type into type D, a projection from D into a ground type, diagrammatic (left-to-right) composition of coercions $\gamma;\gamma$, functorial coercions that apply coercions under the type constructors for pair, linear function, and function, or a coercion $\bot^b$ that always fails. It is indexed with the blame label b that is raised when the coercion is executed. The projection is also indexed with a blame label that is raised if the underlying dynamic value does not match the expected ground type.

Session type coercions σ mimic the syntax of session types, but with coercions in place of types. As with subtyping, sending type positions in session types and coercions are covariant whereas receiving positions are contravariant. The choice coercions carry a blame map b and their range index set $\mathfrak{L}$ as annotations. They facilitate the addition and removal of alternative choices.

The send choice coercion $\oplus^{\beta}_{\mathfrak{M}}\langle l : \sigma \mid l \in \mathfrak{L}\rangle$ applies to a channel with alternatives at least $\mathfrak{L}$ and it provides a channel with alternatives $\mathfrak{M}$. Only the coercions for the $\mathfrak{L}$ continuations need to be provided, the others generate blame according to the blame map β. The domain of β is $\mathfrak{M} \setminus \mathfrak{L}$. Dually, the receive choice coercion $\&^{\beta}_{\mathfrak{M}}\langle l : \sigma \mid l \in \mathfrak{L}\rangle$ applies to a connection with at most $\mathfrak{M}$ alternatives and it provides a channel with $\mathfrak{L}$ alternatives. Only labels in $\mathfrak{L}$ are forwarded, the others generate blame according to β. The domain of β is again $\mathfrak{M} \setminus \mathfrak{L}$.

3.3 Coercion Typing

Coercions come with their own type system which derives judgments of the form $\gamma : t \Rightarrow t$. Figure 10 contains the typing rules for coercions along with expression typing rules for coercion application and the blame expression. It remains to define the semantics of the coercions in Figures 11 and 12.

Applying a composed coercion gets reduced to a nested application of the components. We split a composed coercion in this way to simplify the creation of proxies: they only have to deal with simple, non-composed coercions at the top-level. The identity coercion leaves its argument unchanged. The injection of a ground type into D adds the type tag to the value. The projection from dynamic checks the type constructor and either yields the value if the type constructors coincide or raises a blame exception, otherwise. Applying the failure coercion directly raises blame. A functorial coercion expands its argument and applies the constituent coercions to the constituents of the argument. A session coercion

Typing rules for coercion terms

$$\iota_t : t \Rightarrow t \qquad g\!\uparrow\, : g \Rightarrow D \qquad g\!\downarrow^b : D \Rightarrow g \qquad \frac{\gamma_1 : t_0 \Rightarrow t_1 \qquad \gamma_2 : t_1 \Rightarrow t_2}{\gamma_1 \,;\, \gamma_2 : t_0 \Rightarrow t_2}$$

$$\frac{\gamma : t_1' \Rightarrow t_1 \qquad \gamma' : t_2 \Rightarrow t_2'}{\gamma \rightarrow \gamma' : t_1 \rightarrow t_2 \Rightarrow t_1' \rightarrow t_2'} \qquad \frac{\gamma : t_1' \Rightarrow t_1 \qquad \gamma' : t_2 \Rightarrow t_2'}{\gamma \multimap \gamma' : t_1 \multimap t_2 \Rightarrow t_1' \rightarrow t_2'}$$

$$\frac{\gamma_i : t_i \Rightarrow t_i'}{\gamma_1 \otimes \gamma_2 : t_1 \otimes t_2 \Rightarrow t_1' \otimes t_2'} \qquad \bot^b : t \Rightarrow t'$$

Typing rules for session coercions

$$\iota_s : s \Rightarrow s \qquad \frac{\gamma : t \Rightarrow t' \qquad \sigma : s \Rightarrow s'}{!\,\gamma.\sigma : \,!\,t.s \Rightarrow \,!\,t'.s'} \qquad \frac{\gamma : t' \Rightarrow t \qquad \sigma : s \Rightarrow s'}{?\,\gamma.\sigma : \,?\,t.s \Rightarrow \,?\,t'.s'}$$

$$\frac{(\forall l \in \mathfrak{L})\sigma_l : s_l \Rightarrow s_l' \qquad dom(\beta) = \mathfrak{M} \setminus \mathfrak{L}}{\oplus^{\beta}_{\mathfrak{M}}\langle l : \sigma_l \mid l \in \mathfrak{L}\rangle : \oplus\langle l : s_l \mid l \in \mathfrak{L}\rangle \Rightarrow \oplus\langle l : s_l' \mid l \in \mathfrak{M}\rangle}$$

$$\frac{(\forall l \in \mathfrak{L})\sigma_l : s_l \Rightarrow s_l' \qquad dom(\beta) = \mathfrak{M} \setminus \mathfrak{L}}{\&^{\beta}_{\mathfrak{M}}\langle l : \sigma_l \mid l \in \mathfrak{L}\rangle : \&\langle l : s_l \mid l \in \mathfrak{M}\rangle \Rightarrow \&\langle l : s_l' \mid l \in \mathfrak{L}\rangle}$$

Expression typing rules

$$\frac{\Sigma, \Gamma \vdash e : t \qquad \gamma : t \Rightarrow t'}{\Sigma, \Gamma \vdash e\#\gamma : t'} \qquad \frac{}{\Sigma, \Gamma \vdash \Uparrow^b : t}$$

Fig. 10. Coercion typing

creates a new connection of the target type of the coercion and it forks a new process running the expression generated by the meta-function $Proxy(\mathbf{x}, \sigma, \mathbf{y})$ from the coercion σ. This process serves as a proxy between the source-typed connection $\mathbf{x}$ and the target-typed connection $\mathbf{y}$.

The generation of the proxy expression is straightforward (Fig. 12) except for two special twists. One point is the generation of code from an identity coercion ι_s. It continues by mapping the type into the corresponding eta-expanded identity coercion $\hat{s}$: $\widehat{!\,t.s} = \,!\,\iota_t.\hat{s}$, $\widehat{\oplus\langle l : s_l \mid l \in \mathfrak{L}\rangle} = \oplus^{\emptyset}_{\mathfrak{L}}\langle l : \hat{s}_l \mid l \in \mathfrak{L}\rangle$, and analogously for the remaining session type constructors.

The other point is the consumption of the two linearly typed channels in the choice coercions that discard alternatives. In these cases, the proxy code bundles the channels into a linear pair and applies a failure coercion to the pair.

4 Type Preservation and Progress Properties

This section considers the interplay between the operational semantics and the type system. We show that reduction of expressions and processes preserves their types. We further characterize the conditions under which typed expressions and processes make progress. We only consider the extended calculus with gradual types and start by establishing preservation and progress for expressions.

$$\begin{array}{lll} v\#(\gamma\,;\gamma') \rightarrow (v\#\gamma)\#\gamma' & D_{tc}(v)\#tc\downarrow^b \rightarrow v & \\ v\#\iota_t \quad\; \rightarrow v & D_{tc}(v)\#tc'\downarrow^b \rightarrow \Uparrow^b & tc \neq tc' \\ v\#tc\uparrow \quad \rightarrow D_{tc}(v) & v\#\bot^b \quad\; \rightarrow \Uparrow^b & \end{array}$$

$$\begin{array}{ll} v\#(\gamma \otimes \gamma') & \rightarrow \texttt{let}\, x_1 \otimes x_2 = v\, \texttt{in}\, (x_1\#\gamma) \otimes (x_2\#\gamma') \\ v\#(\gamma \rightarrow \gamma') & \rightarrow \texttt{rec}\, f(y)(v\,(y\#\gamma))\#\gamma' \\ v\#(\gamma \multimap \gamma') & \rightarrow \lambda y.(v\,(y\#\gamma))\#\gamma' \\ v\#\sigma & \rightarrow \texttt{pipe}\, s'\,(\lambda y.\mathit{Proxy}(v,\sigma,y))\,(\lambda y.y) \\ & \quad \mathit{if}\ \sigma : s \Rightarrow s' \end{array}$$

Fig. 11. Eager cast reduction (in context $\mathcal{P}$ or $\mathcal{E}$)

$$\begin{array}{ll} \mathit{Proxy}(\mathbf{x}, \iota_s, \mathbf{y}) & = \mathit{Proxy}(\mathbf{x}, \hat{s}, \mathbf{y}) \\ \mathit{Proxy}(\mathbf{x}, \texttt{END}, \mathbf{y}) & = \texttt{close}\,\mathbf{x}; \texttt{close}\,\mathbf{y} \\ \mathit{Proxy}(\mathbf{x}, ?\,\gamma.\sigma, \mathbf{y}) & = \texttt{let}\, x_1 \otimes x_2 = \texttt{receive}\,\mathbf{x}\,\texttt{in}\,\texttt{let}\, y = \texttt{send}\,((x_1\#\gamma) \otimes \mathbf{y})\,\texttt{in} \\ & \qquad \mathit{Proxy}(x_2, \sigma, y) \\ \mathit{Proxy}(\mathbf{x}, !\,\gamma.\sigma, \mathbf{y}) & = \mathit{Proxy}(\mathbf{y}, ?\,\gamma.\bar{\sigma}, \mathbf{x}) \\ \mathit{Proxy}(\mathbf{x}, \&^{\beta}_{\mathfrak{M}}\langle l : \sigma_l \mid l \in \mathfrak{L}\rangle, \mathbf{y}) & \\ & = \texttt{case}\,\mathbf{x}\,\texttt{of}\,\{\, l : \lambda x.\texttt{let}\, y = \texttt{sel}\, l\, \mathbf{y}\,\texttt{in}\, \mathit{Proxy}(x, \sigma_l, y) \mid l \in \mathfrak{L}, \\ & \qquad l : \lambda x.(x \otimes \mathbf{y})\#\bot^{\beta(l)} \mid l \in \mathfrak{M} \setminus \mathfrak{L} \,\} \\ \mathit{Proxy}(\mathbf{x}, \oplus^{\beta}_{\mathfrak{M}}\langle l : \sigma_l \mid l \in \mathfrak{L}\rangle, \mathbf{y}) & = \mathit{Proxy}(\mathbf{y}, \&^{\beta}_{\mathfrak{M}}\langle l : \bar{\sigma}_l \mid l \in \mathfrak{L}\rangle, \mathbf{x}) \end{array}$$

Fig. 12. Coercion proxies

Lemma 1 (Preservation I). *Suppose that $\Sigma, \cdot \vdash e : t$ and that $e \xrightarrow{\alpha} e'$. Then there exists some Σ' such that $\Sigma', \cdot \vdash e' : t$.*

Lemma 2 (Progress I). *If $\Sigma, \cdot \vdash e : t$, then one of the following holds: 1. e is a value; 2. $e = \Uparrow^b$ raises blame; 3. $\exists e'$ such that $e \rightarrow e'$; 4. $e = \mathcal{E}[\texttt{fork}\, e_1\, e_2]$; 5. $e = \mathcal{E}[\texttt{pipe}\, s\, e_1\, e_2]$; 6. $e = \mathcal{E}[\texttt{req}\, n\{s\}]$; 7. $e = \mathcal{E}[\texttt{accept}\, n\{s\}]$; 8. $e = \mathcal{E}[\texttt{sel}\, l_j\, c\{\oplus\langle l_i : s_i, \dots\rangle\}]$; 9. $e = \mathcal{E}[\texttt{case}\, c\{\&\langle l_i : \bar{s}_i, \dots\rangle\}\, \texttt{of}\, \{l_i : e_i, \dots\}]$; 10. $e = \mathcal{E}[\texttt{send}\,(v \otimes c\{!\,t.s\})]$; 11. $e = \mathcal{E}[\texttt{receive}\, c\{?\,t.\bar{s}\}]$; 12. $e = \mathcal{E}[\texttt{close}\, c\{\texttt{END}\}]$.*

Preservation for expressions extends to processes.

Lemma 3 (Preservation II). *Suppose that $\Sigma \vdash p$ and $p \rightarrow p'$. Then there exists some Σ' such that $\Sigma' \vdash p'$.*

Lemma 4 (Progress II). *Suppose that $\Sigma \vdash p$. Then one of the following holds: 1. $p = \mathbf{0}$; 2. $p = \Uparrow^b$; 3. $\exists p'$ such that $p \rightarrow p'$; 4. $p = p_1 \parallel p_2 \parallel p_3$ where*
- $p_1 = \mathcal{E}[\texttt{req}\, n_1\{s\}] \parallel \dots \parallel \mathcal{E}[\texttt{req}\, n_{k_2}\{s\}]$,
- $p_2 = \mathcal{E}[\texttt{accept}\, n_{k_2+1}\{s\}] \parallel \dots \parallel \mathcal{E}[\texttt{accept}\, n_{k_2+k_3}\{s\}]$
- $\{n_1, \dots, n_{k_1}\} \cap \{n_{k_1+1}, \dots, n_{k_1+k_2}\} = \emptyset$,
- $p_3 = \mathcal{E}[N_1[c_1\{s\}]] \parallel \dots \parallel \mathcal{E}[N_{k_4}[c_{k_4}\{s\}]]$ *where all c_j are distinct and*

$N ::= \texttt{sel}\, l_j\, \square \mid \texttt{case}\, \square\, \texttt{of}\, \{l_j : e_j, \dots\} \mid \texttt{send}\,(v \otimes \square) \mid \texttt{receive}\, \square \mid \texttt{close}\, \square$ *It is understood that $p_1 = \mathbf{0}$ if $k_1 = 0$ and analogously for p_2, p_3, and p_4.*

All proofs for the preservation results (Lemmas 1 and 3) proceed by induction on the reduction relation. The progress results (Lemma 2 and 4) are by induction on the typing derivation. The proof of the last lemma exploits associativity and commutativity of the $\|$ operator as well as the neutrality of $\mathbf{0}$.

Typing does not guarantee progress. The creation of a connection via request and accept guarantees that the two ends of a channel start of in different processes. However, this interaction may never happen (p_1 and p_2). Furthermore, due to the presence of higher-order channels, a process may receive the other end of a channel that it already works with. Any action on one of the ends leads to deadlock according to p_5 in Lemma 4.

5 Related Work

The introduction gives an overview of a small fraction of the work on session types. This work is the first to explore the connection of session types with gradual types. A further novelty is the exploration of gradual typing in the presence of choice types.

Gradual types are also briefly explored in the introduction. Here, we offer some additional perspective on the use of coercions in such a calculus. Henglein [9] introduced the coercion calculus to investigate the foundations of dynamic typing and in particular the optimization possibilities from manipulating type tagging and untagging operations. Early work on gradual types [16] did not use coercions, however, the need for space efficient representations [10] required a normalization procedure for compositions of casts. This effort culminated in the discovery of threesomes[17], roughly casts with an intermediate type, which are a compressed representation of arbitrary sequences of simple casts. The same paper also shows that threesomes are intertranslatable with coercions.

6 Conclusions and Future Work

We define the first calculus with session types and gradual types. The calculus provides useful insights for interlanguage programs, where one end of a protocol is run by a statically typed program and the other end by a dynamically typed one. It introduces a novel, liberal notion of cast between session types. We establish its basic metatheory and explore an eager implementation casts with proxies. In future work, we want to consider a different, lazy implementation of casts with commuting conversions as well as further extensions to the calculus.

References

1. Caires, L., Pfenning, F.: Session types as intuitionistic linear propositions. In: Gastin, P., Laroussinie, F. (eds.) CONCUR 2010. LNCS, vol. 6269, pp. 222–236. Springer, Heidelberg (2010)
2. Dezani-Ciancaglini, M., Drossopoulou, S., Mostrous, D., Yoshida, N.: Objects and session types. Information and Computation **207**(5), 595–641 (2009)
3. Disney, T., Flanagan, C.: Gradual information flow typing. In: STOP (2011)

4. Fennell, L., Thiemann, P.: The blame theorem for a linear lambda calculus with type dynamic. In: Loidl, H.-W., Peña, R. (eds.) TFP 2012. LNCS, vol. 7829, pp. 37–52. Springer, Heidelberg (2013)
5. Fennell, L., Thiemann, P.: Gradual security typing with references. In: Cortier, V., Datta, A. (eds.) CSF, pp. 224–239. IEEE, New Orleans (2013)
6. Gay, S.J., Hole, M.: Types and subtypes for client-server interactions. In: Swierstra, S.D. (ed.) ESOP 1999. LNCS, vol. 1576, pp. 74–90. Springer, Heidelberg (1999)
7. Gay, S.J., Vasconcelos, V.T.: Linear type theory for asynchronous session types. J. Funct. Program. **20**(1), 19–50 (2010)
8. Gay, S.J., Vasconcelos, V.T., Ravara, A., Gesbert, N., Caldeira, A. Z.: Modular session types for distributed object-oriented programming. In: POPL 2010 [15], pp. 299–312
9. Henglein, F.: Dynamic typing: Syntax and proof theory. Science of Computer Programming **22**, 197–230 (1994)
10. Herman, D., Tomb, A., Flanagan, C.: Space-efficient gradual typing. In: Trends in Functional Programming (TFP) (2007)
11. Honda, K.: Types for dyadic interaction. In: Best, E. (ed.) CONCUR 1993. LNCS, vol. 715, pp. 509–523. Springer, Heidelberg (1993)
12. Honda, K., Mukhamedov, A., Brown, G., Chen, T.-C., Yoshida, N.: Scribbling interactions with a formal foundation. In: Natarajan, R., Ojo, A. (eds.) ICDCIT 2011. LNCS, vol. 6536, pp. 55–75. Springer, Heidelberg (2011)
13. Honda, K., Yoshida, N., Carbone, M.: Multiparty asynchronous session types. In: Wadler, P. (eds.) Proc. 35th ACM Symp. POPL, pp. 273–284. ACM Press, San Francisco (2008)
14. Hu, R., Neykova, R., Yoshida, N., Demangeon, R., Honda, K.: Practical interruptible conversations. In: Legay, A., Bensalem, S. (eds.) RV 2013. LNCS, vol. 8174, pp. 130–148. Springer, Heidelberg (2013)
15. Proc. 37th ACM Symp. POPL. ACM Press, Madrid (January 2010)
16. Siek, J.G., Taha, W.: Gradual typing for objects. In: Ernst, E. (ed.) ECOOP 2007. LNCS, vol. 4609, pp. 2–27. Springer, Heidelberg (2007)
17. Siek, J.G., Wadler, P.: Threesomes, with and without blame. In: POPL 2010 [15], pp. 365–376
18. Tov, J.A., Pucella, R.: Stateful contracts for affine types. In: Gordon, A.D. (ed.) ESOP 2010. LNCS, vol. 6012, pp. 550–569. Springer, Heidelberg (2010)
19. Vasconcelos, V.T., Ravara, A., Gay, S.J.: Type checking a multithreaded functional language with session types. Theoretical Computer Science **368**(1–2), 64–87 (2006)
20. Wadler, P.: Propositions as sessions. In: Findler, R.B. (ed.) ICFP 2012, pp. 273–286. ACM, Copenhagen, Denmark (2012)
21. Wadler, P., Findler, R.B.: Well-typed programs can't be blamed. In: Castagna, G. (ed.) ESOP 2009. LNCS, vol. 5502, pp. 1–16. Springer, Heidelberg (2009)
22. Wolff, R., Garcia, R., Tanter, É., Aldrich, J.: Gradual typestate. In: Mezini, M. (ed.) ECOOP 2011. LNCS, vol. 6813, pp. 459–483. Springer, Heidelberg (2011)

Corecursion and Non-divergence in Session-Typed Processes

Bernardo Toninho[1,2](✉), Luis Caires[1], and Frank Pfenning[2]

[1] Universidade Nova de Lisboa, Lisboa, Portugal
[2] Carnegie Mellon University, Pittsburgh, USA
btoninho@cs.cmu.edu

Abstract. Session types are widely accepted as an expressive discipline for structuring communications in concurrent and distributed systems. In order to express infinitely unbounded sessions, session typed languages often include general recursion which may introduce undesirable divergence, e.g., infinite unobservable reduction sequences. In this paper we address, by means of typing, the challenge of ensuring non-divergence in a session-typed π-calculus with general (co)recursion, while still allowing interesting infinite behaviors to be definable. Our approach builds on a Curry-Howard correspondence between our type system and linear logic extended with co-inductive types, for which our non-divergence property implies consistency. We prove type safety for our framework, implying protocol compliance and global progress of well-typed processes. We also establish, using a logical relation argument, that well-typed processes are compositionally non-divergent, that is, that no well-typed composition of processes, including those dynamically assembled via name passing, can result in divergent behavior.

1 Introduction

We live in an age of concurrent and distributed software, meant to run not only as local applications but as cooperating parts of larger, distributed and mobile services, meant to run indefinitely with multiple independent clients, which are hard to build and ensure correct. Process models combined with techniques for precisely characterizing and analyzing system behavior have been used to verify properties such as deadlock freedom, protocol compliance, and availability in distributed and service based systems.

Among type-based approaches to verification, a rather successful technique has been that of *session types* [1–3]. Session types structure message-based concurrency based on the notion of a session, which is a precise description of the interaction patterns of two (or more) communicating agents with an intrinsic notion of protocol state (e.g. input a string and then output an integer) and duality. Thus, session types are a form of protocol descriptions that can be statically checked for compliance. The recent discovery of a correspondence between session types and linear logic in the style of Curry-Howard [4], linking proofs with typed processes and proof reduction with communication, has

M. Maffei and E. Tuosto (Eds.): TGC 2014, LNCS 8902, pp. 159–175, 2014.
DOI: 10.1007/978-3-662-45917-1_11

sparked a renewed interest in session types and their foundations [5], and in the idea of exploiting logically motivated approaches for providing powerful reasoning techniques about concurrent and distributed systems. This line of work has addressed concepts such as value-dependent types [6], proof-carrying code [7], behavioural polymorphism [8], and higher-order computation [9], approaching a general type theory for session-based concurrency, with strong typing guarantees such as deadlock freedom and session fidelity.

Although in the untyped setting infinite behavior is encodable using (π-calculus) replication, more "practical" session typed languages often introduce general recursion at both the program and type level [2]. In a typed setting, replication can only capture *finite* session behaviors, even if replicated arbitrarily often. It is insufficient to model *infinite session behavior*, or repeating behavioral patterns depending on evolving state.

Unfortunately, existing session type systems for languages equipped with general recursion do not avoid validating systems exhibiting undesirable *internal divergence*, e.g., infinite sequences of unobservable internal reduction steps. While this issue already arises at the level of individual systems, it becomes more serious when one needs to consider dynamically linked systems. For example, plugging together subsystems, e.g. as a result of dynamic channel passing or of linking higher-order code, may undesirably result in a system unable to offer its intended services due to divergent behavior, even if the subsystems are independently well-typed and divergence-free.

In this work, we tackle the challenge, within a session typed framework, of reconciling general recursion, enabling potentially infinite behavior to be expressed, with local termination (non-divergence), strong normalization, and compositionality (i.e. any well-typed process composition is non-divergent).

We illustrate our language with a toy example: consider a Twitter web service offering a replicated session *trends* which is intended to produce a stream of current trends, according to some custom metrics. The service is parametrized by a filter session that given a stream of tweets produces a stream of trends. The session types involved are ($\multimap$ and $\wedge$ denote session data input and data output, respectively, and ! service offering):

$$\mathsf{TrendService} \triangleq\ !(\mathsf{Filter} \multimap \mathsf{Trends}) \qquad \mathsf{Filter} \triangleq \mathsf{Tweets} \multimap \mathsf{Trends}$$
$$\mathsf{Tweets} \triangleq \nu X.(\mathsf{tweet} \wedge X) \qquad \mathsf{Trends} \triangleq \nu Y.(\mathsf{trend} \wedge Y)$$

Type $\mathsf{TrendService}$ specifies a replicated service that given an appropriate filter process providing the trend metrics specified by the client, transforms a stream of tweets (a recursive session that outputs tweets) into a stream of trends (a recursive session that outputs trends), produces the stream of trends the client wishes to measure. A possible client for the service is the following process (we write $\mathsf{corec}\ Z.P$ for a corecursive definition of P with recursion variable Z):

$$\mathsf{Client} \triangleq (\boldsymbol{\nu} x)\mathit{trends}\langle x\rangle.(\boldsymbol{\nu} k)x\langle k\rangle.(\mathsf{F}_k \mid (\mathsf{corec}\ Z.x(y).p\langle y\rangle.Z))$$

The Client process invokes the shared server, resulting in a fresh session on channel x, sends a handle k to the analytics package F_k, and then sits in a loop printing out (on session p) each trend received from the server on session x. In our type system, we may derive the typing judgment: $\mathit{trends}{:}\mathsf{TrendService} \vdash \mathsf{Client} :: p{:}\mathsf{Trends}$. We follow the formulation of linear logic based session types of [4], where typing judgments have the form $\Gamma; \Delta \vdash P :: x{:}U$. Such a judgment states of process P that it provides a session of type U at x, when composed with services / sessions as specified by $\Gamma; \Delta$. We may compose the client and the trend service (offered by a process Serv) into a closed system $\mathsf{Sys} \triangleq (\boldsymbol{\nu}\mathit{trends})(\mathsf{Serv} \mid \mathsf{Client})$. Sys will (unboundedly) print out trends on channel p. Although it generates an infinite stream of trends at p, involves higher-order name passing, dynamic linking, and occurrences of recursive calls, Sys will never get into internal divergence, as a result of being well-typed in our type system.

It is challenging to obtain an expressive and flexible typing discipline for general co-recursion (provably) ensuring the compositional non-divergence property, as we do in this work. For instance, consider the similar looking processes:

$$\mathsf{Loop} \triangleq \mathsf{corec}\ L(c).c(x).(\boldsymbol{\nu}d)(L(d) \mid d\langle n\rangle.[d \leftrightarrow c])$$
$$\mathsf{Good} \triangleq \mathsf{corec}\ G(c).c\langle x\rangle.(\boldsymbol{\nu}d)(G(d) \mid c\langle n\rangle.[d \leftrightarrow c])$$

Both processes do not autonomously diverge. It is possible to type Good in our system, ensuring that it will never diverge, even when composed with arbitrary (well-typed) processes. However, this is not the case for Loop which produces an infinite reduction sequence after the first communication on c (see Section 4), and is not well-typed.

Our typing discipline eliminates *unproductive* internal behavior, ensuring together with global progress (actually, lock-freedom) and protocol fidelity, the *compositional non-divergence* of infinite behaviors (i.e. there is no well-typed process context under which a well-typed process will evolve to a divergent behavior), an important property out of the scope of existing session type systems with recursive types. We summarize the contributions of our work:

- We introduce a session type system for our process calculus based on linear logic with coinductive types, associating corecursive process definitions with coinductive session types which encode potentially infinite session behavior.
- We show that well-typed processes enjoy very strong safety properties such as type preservation (or session fidelity) and progress, even in the presence of corecursion.
- We prove that well-typed processes are *compositionally non-divergent* by employing a logical relations argument, extended to coinductive session types, ensuring that any well-typed service implemented in our calculus may never become unavailable through divergent behavior.

2 Process Model

In this section we introduce our process calculus, essentially consisting of a (synchronous) π-calculus with basic data types for convenience, input-guarded replication, labelled choice and selection and corecursion. The syntax of processes is given below:

$$\begin{array}{lll} M, N & ::= \ldots & \text{(basic data constructors)} \\ P, Q & ::= & x\langle M\rangle.P \mid x(y).P \mid x\langle y\rangle.P \mid (\boldsymbol{\nu}y)P \mid !x(y).P \mid P \mid Q \\ & \mid & x.\mathsf{case}(\overline{l_j \Rightarrow P_j}) \mid x.l_i;P \mid (\mathsf{corec}\ X(\overline{y}).P)\ \overline{c} \mid X(\overline{c}) \mid [x \leftrightarrow y] \mid \mathbf{0} \end{array}$$

$$
\begin{array}{ll}
x \notin fn(P) \Rightarrow P\,|\,(\boldsymbol{\nu}x)Q \equiv (\boldsymbol{\nu}x)(P\,|\,Q) & P \equiv_\alpha Q \Rightarrow P \equiv Q \\
P \mid (Q\,|\,R) \equiv (P\,|\,Q) & \\
R & P\,|\,Q \equiv Q\,|\,P \\
(\boldsymbol{\nu}x)(\boldsymbol{\nu}y)P \equiv (\boldsymbol{\nu}y)(\boldsymbol{\nu}x)P & [y \leftrightarrow x] \equiv [x \leftrightarrow y] \\
P\,|\,\mathbf{0} \equiv P & (\boldsymbol{\nu}x)\mathbf{0} \equiv \mathbf{0}
\end{array}
$$

Fig. 1. Structural Congruence

$$
\begin{array}{ll}
c\langle V\rangle.P \mid c(x).Q \longrightarrow P \mid Q\{V/x\} & c\langle y\rangle.P \mid c(x).Q \longrightarrow P \mid Q\{y/x\} \\
c\langle y\rangle.P \mid !c(x).Q \longrightarrow P \mid Q\{y/x\} \mid !c(x).Q & c.\mathsf{case}(\overline{l_i \Rightarrow P_i}) \mid c.l_i;Q \longrightarrow P_i \mid Q \\
(\nu x)(P \mid [y \leftrightarrow x]) \longrightarrow P\{y/x\} \;\; (x \neq y) & \text{If } Q \longrightarrow Q' \text{ then } P \mid Q \longrightarrow P \mid Q' \\
(\mathsf{corec}\ X(\overline{y}).P)\ \overline{c} \longrightarrow P\{\overline{c}/\overline{y}\}\{(\mathsf{corec}\ X(\overline{y}).P)/X\} & \text{If } P \longrightarrow Q \text{ then } (\boldsymbol{\nu}y)P \longrightarrow (\boldsymbol{\nu}y)Q \\
\text{If } P \equiv P' \text{ and } P' \longrightarrow Q' \text{ and } Q' \equiv Q \text{ then } P \longrightarrow Q &
\end{array}
$$

Fig. 2. Reduction

We range over basic data with M, N and processes with P, Q. We write $\overline{y}$ and $\overline{c}$ for a list of variables and channels, respectively. We write $fn(P)$ for the free names of process P. Basic data type constructors include the typical constructs for manipulating data such as numbers, strings and lists. The process language is a synchronous π-calculus with term input $x(y).P$ and output $x\langle M\rangle.P$, channel output $c\langle y\rangle.P$, input-guarded replication $!x(y).P$, n-ary labelled choice $x.\mathsf{case}(\overline{l_j \Rightarrow P_j})$ and selection $x.l_i; P$, channel forwarding $[x \leftrightarrow y]$ and, crucially, a parametrized *corecursion* operator $(\mathsf{corec}\ X(\overline{y}).P)\ \overline{c}$, enabling corecursive process definitions (the variables $\overline{y}$ are bound in P). The parameters are used to instantiate channels (and values) in recursive calls accordingly.

The operational behavior of processes is given in terms of reduction and labelled transitions, both defined modulo structural congruence (written $\equiv$) which captures basic structural identities of processes (Fig. 1). Reduction $P \longrightarrow Q$ is defined by the rules in Fig. 2. Term communication is only done in value form, meaning that all terms are reduced to values – written as V – before communication takes place (the reduction rules for terms and the compatible closure rules are omitted). We note the standard unfolding semantics for corecursion. We write $\Rightarrow$ for the reflexive transitive closure of $\longrightarrow$ and $P \Downarrow$ iff P is non-divergent (i.e. no infinite reduction sequence starting with P).

To define the interactions of a process with its environment we adopt the early labelled transition system for the π-calculus [10] extended with the appropriate labels and rules for choice, value communication, forwarding and corecursion. A transition $P \xrightarrow{\alpha} Q$ denotes that process P may evolve to Q by performing the action represented by label α. Transition labels are defined as:

$$\alpha ::= \tau \mid x(y) \mid x(V) \mid x.l \mid \overline{x\,y} \mid \overline{x\,V} \mid \overline{x\langle y\rangle} \mid \overline{x.l}$$

Actions are channel input $x(y)$, value input $x(V)$, the offer of a labelled choice $x.l$ and their matching co-actions, respectively the channel output $\overline{x\,y}$, value output $\overline{x\,V}$ and bound output $\overline{x\langle y\rangle}$ actions, and the selection $\overline{x.l}$. The bound output $\overline{x\langle y\rangle}$ denotes extrusion of a fresh name y along x. Internal action is denoted by τ. For conciseness we highlight only the transition rules for forwarding and corecursion, which are given a silent transition semantics:

$$(\nu x)(P \mid [y \leftrightarrow x]) \xrightarrow{\tau} P\{y/x\} \ (y \neq x) \quad (\mathsf{corec}\ X(\overline{y}).P)\ \overline{c} \xrightarrow{\tau} P\{\overline{c}/\overline{y}\}\{(\mathsf{corec}\ X(\overline{y}).P)/X\}$$

The remaining rules for the labelled transitions semantics are identical to those in [4].

3 Type System

In this section we motivate and present our type system based on intuitionistic linear logic. The syntax of types is given below:

$$\begin{array}{ll} \tau, \sigma & ::= \mathtt{nat} \mid \mathtt{string} \mid \ldots \\ A, B, C & ::= \tau \supset A \mid \tau \wedge A \mid A \multimap B \mid A \otimes B \mid \mathbf{1} \mid \&\{\overline{l_j{:}A_j}\} \mid \oplus\{\overline{l_j{:}A_j}\} \mid {!A} \mid \nu X.A \mid X \end{array}$$

We distinguish the types of data τ, σ from sessions A, B, C. The language of session types covers the standard session constructs: data input and output ($\tau \supset A$ and $\tau \wedge A$), session input and output ($A \multimap B$ and $A \otimes B$), termination ($\mathbf{1}$), labelled choice and selection ($\&\{\overline{l_j{:}A_j}\}$ and $\oplus\{\overline{l_j{:}A_j}\}$), replication ($!A$) and coinductive sessions ($\nu X.A$).

From General Recursion to Corecursion. While both recursive and coinductive session types denote potentially infinite session behavior, the fundamental distinction is that general recursion might generate an infinite sequence of *internal* actions and thus cause divergence, whereas a valid coinductive definition of a session typed process is guaranteed to always have a finite sequence of internal actions before offering some observable behavior – i.e. be *productive* – and thus cannot diverge. It is this *external*, observable behavior that may be infinite in a coinductively defined, session typed process. Moreover, this non-divergence result is *compositional*: well-typed coinductive sessions may be safely composed, ensuring that the resulting system is itself non-divergent.

To rule out divergence we impose a discipline on the occurrence of the recursion variable in processes, in line with the work on coinductive definitions in dependent type theories such as that of Coq [11] or Agda [12], but here mapped to a concurrent setting, where types describe *behavior* that is produced by processes rather than *data* that is constructed by functions, making many of the more recent type-based termination methods [13] based on indexing constructors for coinductive data types not immediately applicable. Essentially, we require that a corecursive process definition be *productive* – there is always a finite sequence of internal actions between *observable* actions.

Observable actions are those that take place on the session channel that is being *offered* by a given process, whereas internal actions are those generated through interactions with ambient sessions. Given our notion of productivity, a natural restriction is to require an action on the offered channel before allowing recursive calls to take place (i.e. recursive calls must be *guarded* by an observable action). However, guardedness alone is not sufficient to ensure productivity. Process Loop from Section 1 is guarded but produces divergent behavior when composed with a process that provides it with an output. The issue is that after

$$(\wedge R)\ \frac{\Psi \vdash M{:}\tau \quad \Psi; \Gamma; \Delta \vdash_\eta P :: c{:}A}{\Psi; \Gamma; \Delta \vdash_\eta c\langle M\rangle.P :: c{:}\tau \wedge A} \qquad (\wedge L)\ \frac{\Psi, x{:}\tau\ ;\ \Gamma; \Delta, c{:}A \vdash_\eta Q :: d{:}D}{\Psi\ ;\ \Gamma; \Delta, c{:}\tau \wedge A \vdash_\eta c(x).Q :: d{:}D}$$

$$(\mathbf{1}L)\ \frac{\Psi; \Gamma; \Delta \vdash_\eta P :: d{:}D}{\Psi; \Gamma; \Delta, c{:}\mathbf{1} \vdash_\eta P :: d{:}D} \qquad (\otimes R)\ \frac{\Psi; \Gamma; \Delta_1 \vdash_\eta P_1 :: x{:}A \quad \Psi; \Gamma; \Delta_2 \vdash_\eta P_2 :: c{:}B}{\Psi; \Gamma; \Delta_1, \Delta_2 \vdash_\eta (\boldsymbol{\nu} x)c\langle x\rangle.(P_1 \mid P_2) :: c{:}A \otimes B}$$

$$(\otimes L)\ \frac{\Psi; \Gamma; \Delta, x{:}A, c{:}B \vdash_\eta Q :: d{:}D}{\Psi; \Gamma; \Delta, c{:}A \otimes B \vdash_\eta c(x).Q :: d{:}D} \qquad (\multimap R)\ \frac{\Psi; \Gamma; \Delta, x{:}A \vdash_\eta P :: c{:}B}{\Psi; \Gamma; \Delta \vdash_\eta c(x).P :: c{:}A \multimap B}$$

$$(\multimap L)\ \frac{\Psi; \Gamma; \Delta_1 \vdash_\eta Q_1 :: x{:}A \quad \Psi; \Gamma; \Delta_2, c{:}B \vdash_\eta Q_2 :: d{:}D}{\Psi; \Gamma; \Delta_1, \Delta_2, c{:}A \multimap B \vdash_\eta (\boldsymbol{\nu} x)c\langle x\rangle.(Q_1 \mid Q_2) :: d{:}D} \qquad (\mathbf{1}R)\ \frac{}{\Psi; \Gamma; \cdot \vdash_\eta \mathbf{0} :: c{:}\mathbf{1}}$$

$$(\& R)\ \frac{\Psi; \Gamma; \Delta \vdash_\eta P_1 :: c{:}A_1 \ \ldots\ \Psi; \Gamma; \Delta \vdash_\eta P_n :: c{:}A_n}{\Psi; \Gamma; \Delta \vdash_\eta c.\mathsf{case}(\overline{l_j \Rightarrow P_j}) :: c{:}\ \&\ \{\overline{l_j{:}A_j}\}} \qquad (\& L)\ \frac{\Psi; \Gamma; \Delta, c{:}A_i \vdash_\eta Q :: d{:}D}{\Psi; \Gamma; \Delta, c{:}\ \&\ \{\overline{l_j{:}A_j}\} \vdash_\eta c.l_i; Q :: d{:}D}$$

$$(\nu L)\ \frac{\Psi; \Gamma; \Delta, c{:}A\{\nu X.A/X\} \vdash_\eta Q :: d{:}D}{\Psi; \Gamma; \Delta, c{:}\nu X.A \vdash_\eta Q :: d{:}D} \qquad (\textsc{var})\ \frac{\eta(X(\overline{y})) = \Psi; \Gamma; \Delta \vdash d{:}Y \quad \rho = \{\overline{z}/\overline{y}\}}{\rho(\Psi); \rho(\Gamma); \rho(\Delta) \vdash_\eta X(\overline{z}) :: \rho(d){:}Y}$$

$$(\nu R)\ \frac{\Psi; \Gamma; \Delta \vdash_{\eta'} P :: c{:}A \quad \eta' = \eta[X(\overline{y}) \mapsto \Psi; \Gamma; \Delta \vdash c{:}Y]}{\Psi; \Gamma; \Delta \vdash_\eta (\mathsf{corec}\ X(\overline{y}).P\{\overline{y}/\overline{z}\})\ \overline{z} :: c{:}\nu Y.A} \qquad (\textsc{id})\ \frac{}{\Psi; \Gamma; d{:}A \vdash_\eta [d \leftrightarrow c] :: c{:}A}$$

$$(\textsc{cut})\ \frac{\Psi; \Gamma; \Delta_1 \vdash_\eta P :: x{:}A \quad \Psi; \Gamma; \Delta_2, x{:}A \vdash_\eta Q :: d{:}D}{\Psi; \Gamma; \Delta_1, \Delta_2 \vdash_\eta (\boldsymbol{\nu} x)(P \mid Q) :: d{:}D} \qquad (\textsc{cut}^!)\ \frac{\Psi; \Gamma; \cdot \vdash_\eta P :: x{:}A \quad \Psi; \Gamma, u{:}A; \Delta \vdash Q :: d{:}D}{\Psi; \Gamma; \Delta \vdash_\eta (\boldsymbol{\nu} u)(!u(x).P \mid Q) :: d{:}D}$$

Fig. 3. Typing Rules (abridged)

the input along c, we have an occurrence of the recursion variable in parallel with a process that *interacts* with the recursive occurrence locally, destroying the productivity of the original definition.

Thus, ensuring non-divergence in a compositional way requires not only guardedness but also disallowing interactions with corecursive calls within corecursive definitions, a property we call *co-regular recursion*. To this end, we must impose that processes that are placed in parallel with corecursive calls may not communicate with the corecursive call, although they may themselves perform other actions. As we discuss at the end of this section, our type system ensures this form of non-interference by not exposing the communication interface of corecursive calls, ensuring that processes composed with corecursive calls may perform communication, but *not* with the corecursive call itself.

3.1 Typing Coinductive Sessions

Having made the informal case for the kinds of restrictions on general recursion that are needed in order to eliminate divergent computation, we now present the type system for our language, essentially made up of the rules of linear logic plus the rules that pertain to corecursive process definitions, coinductive session types and the corecursion variable.

We define the typing judgment: $\Psi; \Gamma; \Delta \vdash_\eta P :: z{:}A$ denoting that process P offers the session behavior typed with A along channel z, when composed with the (linear) session behaviors specified in Δ, with the (unrestricted, or shared) session behaviors specified in Γ and where η is a mapping from (corecursive) type variables to typing contexts (we detail this further below). We note that the names in Γ, Δ and z are all pairwise distinct. We assume typing to be defined modulo structural congruence by definition. Context Ψ tracks the free variables in P that pertain to basic data values that are to be sent and received. We make use of judgment $\Psi \vdash M{:}\tau$ to denote that term M, denoting a value that is to be communicated, is well typed under the assumptions in Ψ.

The rules that define our type system are given in Fig. 3, consisting essentially of those of [4] with the identity rule, value input and output (present in [9]) and coinductive types, which are associated with corecursion in the process calculus. We note that coinductive types have strictly positive occurrences of the type variable, also excluding coinductive types that have no associated session behavior before the type variable occurrence (such as $\nu X.X$). Moreover, we require coinductive types to mention the type variable. These restrictions are standard and thus enforced implicitly. As usual, in the presence of type annotations, typechecking is decidable.

We refrain from a detailed presentation of every rule for the sake of conciseness, highlighting instead the rules pertaining to corecursive processes and coinductive session types. We begin with the right rule for coinductive sessions, which types (parameterized) corecursive process definitions:

$$\frac{\Psi; \Gamma; \Delta \vdash_{\eta'} P :: c{:}A \quad \eta' = \eta[X(\overline{y}) \mapsto \Psi; \Gamma; \Delta \vdash c{:}Y]}{\Psi; \Gamma; \Delta \vdash_\eta (\mathsf{corec}\ X(\overline{y}).P\{\overline{y}/\overline{z}\})\ \overline{z} :: c{:}\nu Y.A}\ (\nu\mathsf{R})$$

In the rule above, the process P may use the recursion variable X and refer to the parameter list $\overline{y}$, which is instantiated with the list of (distinct) names $\overline{z}$ which may occur in Ψ, Δ, Γ or c. Moreover, we keep track of the contexts Ψ, Γ and Δ in which the corecursive definition is made, as well as the channel name along which the coinductive behavior is offered and the type variable associated with the corecursive behavior, by extending the mapping η with a binding for X with the appropriate information. This is necessary because, intuitively, each occurrence of the corecursion variable stands for P itself (modulo the parameter instantiations) and therefore we must check that the necessary ambient session behaviors are available for P to execute in a type correct way, respecting linearity. P itself simply offers along channel c the session behavior A (which is an open type). To type the corecursion variable we use the following rule:

$$\frac{\eta(X(\overline{y})) = \Psi; \Gamma; \Delta \vdash d{:}Y \quad \rho = \{\overline{z}/\overline{y}\}}{\rho(\Psi); \rho(\Gamma); \rho(\Delta) \vdash_\eta X(\overline{z}) :: \rho(d){:}Y}\ (\text{VAR})$$

We type a process corecursion variable X by looking up in η the binding for X, which references the typing environments Ψ, Γ and Δ under which the corecursive definition is well defined, the coinductive type variable Y associated with the corecursive behavior and the channel name d along which the behavior is offered. The corecursion variable X is typed with the type variable Y if the parameter instantiation is able to satisfy the typing signature (by renaming available linear and exponential resources or term variables). We also allow for the offered session channel to be a parameter of the corecursion. Finally, the left rule for coinductive session types simply unfolds the type:

$$\frac{\Psi; \Gamma; \Delta, c{:}A\{\nu X.A/X\} \vdash_\eta Q :: d{:}D}{\Psi; \Gamma; \Delta, c{:}\nu X.A \vdash_\eta Q :: d{:}D} \ (\nu \mathsf{L})$$

While the rules look fairly straightforward, they turn out to introduce quite subtle restrictions on what constitutes a well-formed (i.e. well-typed) corecursive process definition. First, observe that the introduction form for corecursive definitions does not directly unfold the coinductive type in its premise and thus references an *open* type, which means that the (corecursive) definition of P provides the behavior specified in A up to occurrences of the coinductive type variable Y. On the other hand, using a coinductive session type (which is achieved by the left rule $\nu\mathsf{L}$) entails unfolding the coinductive type as expected, and so a user of a coinductive behavior may use as many unfoldings of $\nu Y.A$ as required.

Up to this point, we have yet to discuss how our type system enforces the necessary restrictions to ensure non-divergence. It turns out that these restrictions are imposed by the variable rule in quite subtle ways, due to its interaction with the $\nu\mathsf{R}$ rule. While we do not syntactically exclude processes without terminal recursion (for instance, process Good from Section 1), a well-typed corecursive definition crucially *cannot* interact with its corecursive calls (which could potentially destroy productivity). To see why this is the case, consider how such an interaction might be allowed in our type system: in order for a corecursive definition to interact with its own corecursive call in a well-typed manner, the system would require some form of parallel composition where we obtain a handle to the corecursive call. That is, we need to obtain a typing where the channel of the corecursive call is in the context, which is only possible through a cut.

However, since the coinductive type is never unfolded when *offering* a coinductive definition, the session interface of the corecursive occurrence is not visible internally. Thus, a cut of the corecursion variable with some other process Q will generate a fresh channel c that offers the coinductive type variable, but not the *coinductive type*, meaning that no left rules that interact with the unfolding of the recursive definition can be applied. In fact, the only rule that can use $c{:}X$ is the identity rule, which will forward the corecursively defined session. This does not prohibit Q from having additional behavior besides forwarding, it simply excludes (potentially) problematic internal interactions with corecursive calls.

4 Examples

Excluding Unobservable Divergence. Elaborating on the process Loop given in Section 1, we show how it can result in divergent behavior when interacting with a client and why Loop is not typeable in our system.

The intended behavior of Loop is to continuously input along the channel c, which is represented by the session type $\nu X.\mathsf{nat} \supset X$. Consider a process P

that provides an output along c, composed with Loop. We have the following reduction(s):

$$(\boldsymbol{\nu} c)(\mathsf{Loop}(c) \mid P) \Rightarrow (\boldsymbol{\nu} c)(\boldsymbol{\nu} d)(\mathsf{Loop}(d) \mid d\langle n\rangle.[d \leftrightarrow c] \mid P')$$

In the process to the right of the arrow, there is an internal synchronization between the output along d and the input along the unfolding of Loop, resulting in the following:

$$\Rightarrow (\boldsymbol{\nu} c)(\boldsymbol{\nu} d)((\boldsymbol{\nu} d')(\mathsf{Loop}(d') \mid d'\langle n\rangle.[d' \leftrightarrow d]) \mid [d \leftrightarrow c] \mid P')$$

The infinite internal reduction is now made clear, where regardless of the behavior of P' there is always an internal reduction that produces an additional unfolding of Loop and may repeat this behavior an unbounded number of times.

It is easy to see that Loop is not well-typed: if we try to type the process bottom-up, we first apply the $\nu\mathsf{R}$ rule, followed by the $\supset\mathsf{R}$ rule. We are then left with the following:

$$(\mathsf{cut})\ \frac{\vdash L(d) :: d{:}X \quad d{:}X \vdash d\langle n\rangle.[d \leftrightarrow c] :: c{:}X}{\vdash (\boldsymbol{\nu} d)(L(d) \mid d\langle n\rangle.[d \leftrightarrow c]) :: c{:}X}$$

It is immediate that the right premise of the cut cannot be typed, since all that is known about session d is that it has type X, so no communication along d can be well-typed.

The fundamental motivation for excluding these forms of unobservable divergence is that morally a process must offer some observable behavior in order to be useful. Realistically, even a divergent process should be receptive to a "kill" signal, which is encodable in our setting using choice and $\mathbf{1}$.

Little Endian Bit Counter. We illustrate how our framework can express fairly general process networks with nodes interacting according to structured session protocols. We consider the implementation of a binary counter, where each bit of a (arbitrary length) binary numeral is implemented by a process node which can only communicate with its neighboring processes in the network (in [9] we discussed a similar example, but expressed using non co-regular recursion, and not typeable in our system. We present here a version using co-regular recursion, and requiring more sophisticated handshaking). The network implements a protocol offering three operations: poll the counter for its current integer value; increment the counter value, or terminate the counter. The corresponding session type is: $\mathsf{Counter} \triangleq \nu X.\ \&\{\mathsf{val{:}int} \wedge X, \mathsf{inc}{:}X, \mathsf{halt}{:}\mathbf{1}\}$

Our implementation of $\mathsf{Counter}$ is based on a coordinator process that keeps a (linear) network of communicating processes, representing the counter value in little endian form (the tail process in the network holds the least significant bit). Each network node communicates with its two adjacent bit representations, whereas the coordinator communicates with the most significant bit process (and with the counter's external client), spawning new bits as needed. Overall, the coordinator works as follows: To halt the counter, the coordinator halts every node and then terminates. To provide the value of the counter, the coordinator

$$\begin{aligned}\mathsf{Node}(b,x,n) \triangleq\ & \mathsf{corec}\ X(b,x,n).n.\mathsf{case}(\\ & \mathsf{val} \Rightarrow x.\mathsf{val}; n(m).x\langle(2*m+b)\rangle.x(v).n\langle v\rangle.X(b,x,n),\\ & \mathsf{inc} \Rightarrow x.\mathsf{inc}; x.\mathsf{case}(\mathsf{carry} \Rightarrow \mathsf{if}\ (b=1)\ \mathsf{then}\ n.\mathsf{carry}; X(0,x,n)\\ & \qquad \mathsf{else}\ n.\mathsf{done}; X(1,x,n), \mathsf{done} \Rightarrow X(1,x,n)),\\ & \mathsf{halt} \Rightarrow x.\mathsf{halt}; \mathbf{0})\ (b,x,n)\end{aligned}$$

Fig. 4. Node Process

propagates a val message along the network, which will compute the value as an integer and forward it back to the coordinator. To increment the counter, the coordinator injects an inc message into the network, which will be propagated to the least significant bit process, and, in a second phase, propagated back as a carry message, incrementing each bit (modulo 2) as needed. If the carry message, instead of a done message, reaches the coordinator, a new bit process will be spawned.

The behavior of each node is as follows. When a node receives a val message it receives the integer value computed by all the nodes encoding more significant bits, updates it with its own contribution and propagates the val message to the less significant bit nodes, from which it will receive the total counter value and send it forward to the coordinator. When an inc message is received, a node forwards it to its less significant bit neighbor, and waits for it to send back either a carry or done message. In the latter case, it will just forward the done message network along the most significant bit node up to the coordinator, signaling that nothing more needs to be done. In the former case, it will flip its value and either send a carry or a done message to its most significant bit neighbor. When a carry message reaches the coordinator, it generates a new bit, as mentioned above. The type for $\mathsf{Node}(b,x,n)$ is given by $x{:}\mathsf{CImpl} \vdash \mathsf{Node}(b,x,n) :: n{:}\mathsf{CImpl}$ with

$$\mathsf{CImpl} \triangleq \nu X.\ \&\,\{\mathsf{val}{:}\mathsf{int} \supset \mathsf{int} \wedge X, \mathsf{inc}{:} \oplus \{\mathsf{carry}{:}X, \mathsf{done}{:}X\}, \mathsf{halt}{:}\mathbf{1}\}$$

In $\mathsf{Node}(b,x,n)$, b holds the bit value, x is the session channel connecting to the less significant node (or to the terminal node) and n is the channel connecting to the most significant node (or to the coordinator). Code for $\mathsf{Node}(b,x,n)$ is given in Fig. 4.

The coordinator process code interfaces with clients and wraps the bit process network, generating new bit nodes as needed.

$$\begin{aligned}\mathsf{Coord}(x,z) \triangleq\ & \mathsf{corec}\ X(x,z).z.\mathsf{case}(\mathsf{val} \Rightarrow x.\mathsf{val}; x\langle 0\rangle.x(n).z\langle n\rangle.X(x,z),\\ & \mathsf{inc} \Rightarrow x.\mathsf{inc}; x.\mathsf{case}(\mathsf{carry} \Rightarrow (\boldsymbol{\nu} n')(\mathsf{Node}(1,x,n') \mid \mathsf{Coord}(n',z)),\\ & \qquad \mathsf{done} \Rightarrow X(x,z)), \mathsf{halt} \Rightarrow x.\mathsf{halt}; \mathbf{0})\ (x,z)\end{aligned}$$

To complete the system we provide the implementation of the empty bit string epsilon, which will be a closed process of type CImpl. For the val branch, it ping pongs the received value. For incrementing, it emits the (first) carry message:

$$\begin{aligned}\mathsf{epsilon}(x) &\triangleq \mathsf{corec}\ X(x).x.\mathsf{case}(\mathsf{val} \Rightarrow x(n).x\langle n\rangle.X(x), \mathsf{inc} \Rightarrow x.\mathsf{carry}; X(x),\\ &\qquad \mathsf{halt} \Rightarrow \mathbf{0})\ x\\ \mathsf{Counter}(c) &\triangleq (\boldsymbol{\nu} e)(\mathsf{epsilon}(e) \mid \mathsf{Coord}(e,c))\end{aligned}$$

The system (offering $c{:}\mathsf{Counter}$) is then produced by composing epsilon and Coord.

5 Results

In this section, we establish type safety for our calculus, entailing session fidelity and deadlock freedom. We also develop our main result of compositional non-divergence by extending the linear logical relations of [8,14] to the coinductive setting, restoring the connection of our framework with the logical interpretation.

Type Safety. Following [4], our proof of type preservation relies on a simulation between reductions in the session-typed π-calculus and proof reductions from logic.

Theorem 1 (Type Preservation). *If* $\Psi; \Gamma; \Delta \vdash_\eta P :: z{:}A$ *and* $P \rightarrow Q$ *then* $\Psi; \Gamma; \Delta \vdash_\eta Q :: z{:}A$.

The proof of progress also follows the lines of [4], but with some additional caveats due to the presence of corecursive definitions. The key technical aspects of the proof are a series of inversion lemmas and a notion of a *live* process, consisting of a process that has not yet fully carried out its ascribed session behavior, and thus is a parallel composition of processes where at least one is a non-replicated process, guarded by some action. We define $live(P)$ if and only if $P \equiv (\boldsymbol{\nu}\tilde{n})(\pi.Q \mid R)$, for some process R, sequence of names $\tilde{n}$ and a non-replicated guarded process $\pi.Q$.

Theorem 2 (Progress). *If* $\Psi; \Gamma; \Delta \vdash P :: z{:}A$ *and* $live(P)$ *then there is some* Q *with* $P \rightarrow Q$ *or one of the following holds:*

(a) $\Delta = \Delta', y{:}B$, *for some* Δ' *and* $y{:}B$. *There exists* R *s.t.* $\Psi; \Gamma; \Delta'' \vdash R :: y{:}B$, $R \not\rightarrow$ *and* $(\boldsymbol{\nu}y)(R \mid P) \rightarrow Q$.
(b) *There exists* R *s.t.* $\Psi; \Gamma; z{:}A, \Delta' \vdash R :: w{:}C$, $R \not\rightarrow$ *and* $(\boldsymbol{\nu}z)(P \mid R) \rightarrow Q$.
(c) $\Gamma = \Gamma', u{:}B$, *for some* Γ' *and* $u{:}B$. *There exists* $\Psi; \Gamma; \cdot \vdash R :: x{:}B$ *s.t.* $(\boldsymbol{\nu}u)(!u(x).R \mid P) \rightarrow Q$.

Our notion of progress states that well-typed processes never get stuck even in the presence of infinite session behavior. Either the process progresses outright via internal computation, awaits on an interaction with its environment ((*a*) or (*c*)) or is waiting for an interaction along its offered channel ((*b*)).

Compositional Non-Divergence. To prove the key property of compositional non-divergence, we develop a (linear) logical relations argument for coinductive session types. As in prior work for languages without recursion [8,14], we build on Girard's technique of reducibility candidates: sets of non-divergent, well-typed terms, closed under reduction and (typed) expansion, adapted to the setting of our process calculus.

Definition 1 (Reducibility Candidates). *Given a type A and name z, a reducibility candidate at $z{:}A$, written $\mathcal{R}[z{:}A]$ is a set of closed, well-typed processes offering $z{:}A$ that satisfy the following:*

1. *If $P \in \mathcal{R}[z{:}A]$ then $P \Downarrow$.*
2. *If $P \in \mathcal{R}[z{:}A]$ and $P \Rightarrow P'$ then $P' \in \mathcal{R}[z{:}A]$*
3. *If for all P_i such that $P \Rightarrow P_i$ we have $P_i \in \mathcal{R}[z{:}A]$ then $P \in \mathcal{R}[z{:}A]$.*

We refer to $\mathbb{R}[-{:}A]$ as the collection of all sets of reducibility candidates at (closed) type A. Our definition of the logical predicate identifies processes up to the compatible extension of structural congruence with the well-known *sharpened replication axioms* [10], written $\equiv_!$. The replication axioms express strong behavioral equivalences in our typed setting [14].

Definition 2. *We write $\equiv_!$ for the least congruence relation on process expressions resulting from extending structural congruence $\equiv$ with the following axioms:*

1. $(\nu u)(!u(z).P(\nu y)(QR)) \equiv_! (\nu y)((\nu u)(!u(z).PQ)(\nu u)(!u(z).PR))$
2. $(\nu u)(!u(y).P(\nu v)(!v(z).QR)) \equiv_! (\nu v)((!v(z).(\nu u)(!u(y).P|Q))(\nu u)(!u(y).P|R))$
3. $(\nu u)(!u(y).QP) \equiv_! P \quad \textit{if } u \notin \textit{fn}(P)$

Intuitively, axioms (1) and (2) represent the distribution of shared servers among "client" processes, and (3) garbage collects shared servers which can no longer be invoked.

We define a logical predicate on processes by induction on types and the size of typing contexts. The predicate captures the computational behavior of non-divergent processes, as defined by their typing. In the development below, we make use of $\mathcal{L}[\tau]$, which denotes the logical interpretation of the values exchanged in communication (i.e. sets for well-typed values of the appropriate type). We omit this definition due to its simplicity and for the sake of conciseness.

Definition 3 (Logical Predicate - Open Process Expressions). *Given $\Psi; \Gamma; \Delta \vdash_\eta T$ with a non-empty left hand side environment, we define $\mathcal{L}^\omega[\Psi; \Gamma; \Delta \vdash_\eta T]$, where ω is a mapping from type variables to reducibility candidates, as the set of processes inductively defined as:*

$$
\begin{array}{lll}
P \in \mathcal{L}^\omega[\Psi, x{:}\tau; \Gamma; \Delta \vdash_\eta T] & \textit{iff} & \forall M \in \mathcal{L}[\tau].P\{M/x\} \in \mathcal{L}^\omega[\Psi; \Gamma; \Delta \vdash_\eta T] \\
P \in \mathcal{L}^\omega[\Gamma; \Delta, y{:}A \vdash_\eta T] & \textit{iff} & \forall R \in \mathcal{L}^\omega[y{:}A].(\nu y)(R \mid P) \in \mathcal{L}^\omega[\Gamma; \Delta \vdash_\eta T] \\
P \in \mathcal{L}^\omega[\Gamma, u{:}A; \Delta \vdash_\eta T] & \textit{iff} & \forall R \in \mathcal{L}^\omega[y{:}A].(\nu u)(!u(y).R \mid P) \in \mathcal{L}^\omega[\Gamma; \Delta \vdash_\eta T]
\end{array}
$$

The definition of the logical interpretation for open processes inductively composes the process with the appropriate witnesses in the logical interpretation at the types specified in the three contexts, following [14].

The key part of our development is the definition of the logical predicate for closed processes. Similar to the treatment of type variables in logical relations for polymorphic languages (c.f. [8]), we employ a mapping from type variables to candidates at a given type. More precisely, we map type variables to candidates at the appropriate coinductive type, representing the unfolding of coinductive types.

$$
\begin{array}{ll}
\mathcal{L}^{\omega}[z{:}\nu X.A] & \triangleq\ \bigcup\{\Psi \in \mathbb{R}[-{:}\nu X.A] \mid \Psi \subseteq \mathcal{L}^{\omega[X \mapsto \Psi]}[z{:}A]\} \\
\mathcal{L}^{\omega}[z{:}X] & \triangleq\ \omega(X)(z) \\
\mathcal{L}^{\omega}[z{:}\mathbf{1}] & \triangleq\ \{P \mid \forall P'.(P \Longrightarrow P' \wedge P' \not\longrightarrow) \Rightarrow P' \equiv_{!} \mathbf{0}\} \\
\mathcal{L}^{\omega}[z{:}A \multimap B] & \triangleq\ \{P \mid \forall P' y.(P \stackrel{z(y)}{\Longrightarrow} P') \Rightarrow \forall Q \in \mathcal{L}^{\omega}[y{:}A].(\nu y)(P' \\
Q) \in \mathcal{L}^{\omega}[z{:}B]\} & \\
\mathcal{L}^{\omega}[z{:}A \otimes B] & \triangleq\ \{P \mid \forall P' y.(P \stackrel{\overline{(\nu y) z\langle y\rangle}}{\Longrightarrow} P') \Rightarrow \\
 & \quad \exists P_1, P_2.(P' \equiv_{!} P_1 \\
P_2 \wedge P_1 \in \mathcal{L}^{\omega}[y{:}A] \wedge P_2 \in \mathcal{L}^{\omega}[z{:}B])\} & \\
\mathcal{L}^{\omega}[z{:}!A] & \triangleq\ \{P \mid \forall P'.(P \Longrightarrow P') \Rightarrow \exists P_1.(P' \equiv_{!} !z(y).P_1 \wedge P_1 \in \mathcal{L}^{\omega}[y{:}A])\} \\
\mathcal{L}^{\omega}[z{:}\ \&\ \{\overline{l_i \Rightarrow A_i}\}] & \triangleq \{P \mid \bigwedge_i\ (\forall P'.(P \stackrel{z.l_i}{\Longrightarrow} P') \Rightarrow P' \in \mathcal{L}^{\omega}[z{:}A_i])\} \\
\mathcal{L}^{\omega}[z{:} \oplus \{\overline{l_i \Rightarrow A_i}\}] & \triangleq\ \{P \mid \bigwedge_i\ (\forall P'.(P \stackrel{\overline{z.l_i}}{\Longrightarrow} P') \Rightarrow P' \in \mathcal{L}^{\omega}[z{:}A_i])\} \\
\mathcal{L}^{\omega}[z{:}\tau \wedge A] & \triangleq\ \{P \mid \forall P'.(P \stackrel{z\langle M\rangle}{\Longrightarrow} P') \Rightarrow (M \in \mathcal{L}[\tau] \wedge P' \in \mathcal{L}^{\omega}[z{:}A])\} \\
\mathcal{L}^{\omega}[z{:}\tau \supset A] & \triangleq\ \{P \mid \forall P', M.(M \in \mathcal{L}[\tau] \wedge P \stackrel{z(M)}{\Longrightarrow} P') \Rightarrow P' \in \mathcal{L}^{\omega}[z{:}A]\}
\end{array}
$$

Fig. 5. Logical Predicate - Closed Processes

We interpret a coinductive session type $\nu X.A$ as the union of all reducibility candidates ψ of the appropriate coinductive type that are in the interpretation of the *open* type A, when X is mapped to ψ itself, enabling a principle of proof by coinduction.

Definition 4 (Logical Predicate - Closed Process Expressions). *For any type $T = z{:}A$ we define $\mathcal{L}^{\omega}[T]$ as the set of all processes P such that $P\Downarrow$ and $\cdot;\cdot;\cdot \vdash_{\eta} P :: T$ satisfying the rules of Fig. 5.*

We elide several technical aspects and focus mainly on the intuitions behind the development. The key observation is that for *open types*, we may view our logical predicate as a mapping between sets of reducibility candidates, of which the interpretation for coinductive session type turns out to be a greatest fixpoint (Theorem 3).

Definition 5. *Let $\nu X.A$ be a strictly positive type. We define: $\phi_A(s) \triangleq \mathcal{L}^{\omega[X \mapsto s]}[z{:}A]$*

Theorem 3 (Greatest Fixpoint). *$\mathcal{L}^{\omega}[z{:}\nu X.A]$ is a greatest fixpoint of ϕ_A.*

The combination of these results enables us to obtain our main result (Theorem 4): all well-typed processes are in the logical predicate, from which follows that all well-typed processes are compositionally non-divergent.

Theorem 4. *If $\Psi; \Gamma; \Delta \vdash_{\eta} P :: z{:}A$ then $P \in \mathcal{L}[\Psi; \Gamma; \Delta \vdash_{\eta} z{:}A]$.*

Proof. e proceed by induction on typing. The most interesting case is the one for the $\nu\mathsf{R}$ rule. Since the interpretation of coinductive types $\nu X.A$ is a greatest fixpoint (Theorem 3), we proceed by coinduction: we produce a set of processes $\mathcal{C}_{P'}$, containing the body of the corecursive definition P' where the corecursion variable has been instantiated with an unfolding of the corecursive definition (let us refer to this process as P''), closed under reduction and (typed) expansion. We show that $\mathcal{C}_{P'}$ is a reducibility candidate at $\nu X.A$ and that $\mathcal{C}_{P'} \subseteq \mathcal{L}^{\omega[X \mapsto \mathcal{C}_{P'}]}[z{:}A]$. This is a sufficient condition since $\mathcal{L}[c{:}\nu X.A]$ is the largest such set. We need essentially to focus on P''.

Showing this property relies crucially on the fact that type variables are ultimately offered by the unfolding of the corecursive definition. The key points are the occurrences of the corecursion variable in P', which in P'' are instantiated with P' itself: if its a terminal occurrence the property is immediate, since the corecursion variable is typed with the type variable X, which is mapped to $\mathcal{C}_{P'}$, containing P'. If the corecursion variable occurs in the left branch of a cut, we know that the only possible use of the fresh channel (typed with the type variable) by the right branch of the cut is to eventually forward it, potentially after a number of internal reductions or observable actions as specified by the session A. When the forwarder is triggered, we must necessarily be at the type variable X and we can conclude since the resulting process is P', in $\mathcal{C}_{P'}$. We remark that if the corecursion variable is guarded in the left branch of a cut, these guards must be consumed by the right branch of the cut (this follows by well-typedness and progress) through internal reductions.

Corollary 1 (Non-Divergence). *If* $\Psi; \Gamma; \Delta \vdash_\eta P :: z{:}A$ *then* $P \Downarrow$

Combining type safety (Theorems 1 and 2) and non-divergence (Corollary 1) we conclude that typing enables strong guarantees on processes written in our calculus. A well-typed process is always be able to fulfil its protocol: no divergence can take place, nor can any deadlocks occur. Moreover, these properties are *compositional*, ensuring that any (well-typed) service composition produces a deadlock-free, non-divergent service.

6 Related Work and Concluding Remarks

Expressiveness relationships between replication and recursion in the context of π-calculi have been investigated (e.g, [15]); in general such constructs are not reducible to each other, in particular in the presence of name scoping constructs. In our context, replication codifies behavior that may be repeated arbitrarily often on independent channels, whereas recursion denotes potentially infinite behavior on the same channel.

Forms of general recursion have been often introduced in session typed languages, but without much concern on how to conciliate unbounded behaviour with local termination (e.g, [2,16]). From the perspective of more traditional work on session typed languages, [17] establishes a strong normalization result for action types, which are similar to session types, but without addressing recursive types. Still within the logic based approach to session typed programming, our work is related to [5], which develops a logical interpretation of session types using second-order classical linear logic and a polymorphic session-typed functional language similar to that of [18], but does not consider coinductive sessions.

In prior work, we have studied strong normalization for session types based on linear logic, including extensions to behavioral polymorphism [8,14], however, this work is the first to address general corecursion in the framework. While there are works that address termination by typability in the π-calculus, they either do not have explicit recursion [19] or consider simpler type systems [20] without notions of session fidelity or lock freedom and impose more intricate syntactic restrictions on processes.

The particular issues related to coinductive session types have to the best of our knowledge been overlooked in the traditional literature, which typically deals with general recursive types and definitions [2,3,18], including divergence by construction. More recently, [21] considers least and greatest fixpoints in classical linear logic (in the sense of [22]) as primitive recursors and corecursors in a session typed calculus, respectively. Since, in their setting, a corecursor can only synchronize with a recursor, it is not straightforward how to encode transducers that transform one coinductive session into another. This is a common programming pattern, where a service is offered through composition and transformation of a collection of other coinductive sessions. Moreover, their work does not develop a logical relation proof technique nor establish a non-divergence result, as we do.

In this regard our work is closer to that on termination for λ-calculi with inductive and coinductive types [23]. For instance, [24] develops a strong normalization result for the second-order λ-calculus with explicit inductive and coinductive types using logical relations. The restrictions imposed by our type system to ensure non-divergence are related to those developed in [25] for the Coq proof assistant, but with obvious distinctions given the very different settings. Our interpretation of coinductive types as greatest fixed points is also related to the work of Baelde [22]. The main differences are that his work uses classical linear logic and does not consider a proof term assignment. The former makes the system and logical relation techniques substantially different since they rely on orthogonality, whereas ours do not; the latter leads Baelde's work towards proof search related techniques, which is in sharp contrast to our work.

The work on type-based methods for ensuring termination has been generalized to include inductive and coinductive definitions in the style of Coq [26] (although the proof of strong normalization is substantially more complex due to the expressive power of CIC and type annotations). It is not clear how to adapt these type-based methods to our setting since type annotations are a measure of the size of "values", which do not immediately apply to processes. Similar difficulties arise when considering copatterns [13], which seem to be inherently tied to the term structure.

Concluding Remarks. We have developed a theory of coinductive definitions for a synchronous π-calculus with corecursion, establishing a logical foundation based on intuitionistic linear logic which provides guarantees of deadlock freedom, session fidelity and, crucially, compositional non-divergence by typing. Thus, services implemented in our calculus do not "get stuck", nor become unavailable due to divergent behavior.

Our type system ensures termination by eliminating unproductive internal behavior in corecursive process definitions. While the restrictions we impose are not particularly oppressive, they naturally still exclude processes that are non-divergent (for instance, the binary counter example of [9]), as often is the case in these settings given that productivity is undecidable in general. Having set forth a first significant benchmark, it is certainly a challenge for future work to find less restrictive or more general conditions for guaranteeing productivity in this setting, potentially adapting type-based termination techniques (viz. [13,26]).

By establishing a logical foundation for coinductive session-typed processes, the work set forth in this paper is an important stepping stone towards the development of a dependent type theory rich enough to allow us to express and reason about session-based concurrency. These concurrent programs are often coinductive in nature, and are typically studied using coinductive proof techniques. Since we establish typed processes as coinductive objects, we may be able to use processes as witnesses to coinductive proofs. A sound (wrt an extensional typed equivalence, c.f. [8,14]) notion of definitional equality of corecursive processes is also part of future work.

References

1. Honda, K.: Types for dyadic interaction. In: Best, E. (ed.) CONCUR 1993. LNCS, vol. 715, pp. 509–523. Springer, Heidelberg (1993)
2. Honda, K., Vasconcelos, V.T., Kubo, M.: Language primitives and type discipline for structured communication-based programming. In: Hankin, C. (ed.) ESOP 1998. LNCS, vol. 1381, pp. 122–138. Springer, Heidelberg (1998)
3. Honda, K., Yoshida, N., Carbone, M.: Multiparty asynchronous session types. In: POPL, pp. 273–284 (2008)
4. Caires, L., Pfenning, F.: Session types as intuitionistic linear propositions. In: Gastin, P., Laroussinie, F. (eds.) CONCUR 2010. LNCS, vol. 6269, pp. 222–236. Springer, Heidelberg (2010)
5. Wadler, P.: Propositions as sessions. In: ICFP 2012, pp. 273–286 (2012)
6. Toninho, B., Caires, L., Pfenning, F.: Dependent session types via intuitionistic linear type theory. In: PPDP 2011, pp. 161–172 (2011)
7. Pfenning, F., Caires, L., Toninho, B.: Proof-carrying code in a session-typed process calculus. In: Jouannaud, J.-P., Shao, Z. (eds.) CPP 2011. LNCS, vol. 7086, pp. 21–36. Springer, Heidelberg (2011)
8. Caires, L., Pérez, J.A., Pfenning, F., Toninho, B.: Behavioral polymorphism and parametricity in session-based communication. In: Felleisen, M., Gardner, P. (eds.) Programming Languages and Systems. LNCS, vol. 7792, pp. 330–349. Springer, Heidelberg (2013)
9. Toninho, B., Caires, L., Pfenning, F.: Higher-order processes, functions, and sessions: A monadic integration. In: Felleisen, M., Gardner, P. (eds.) Programming Languages and Systems. LNCS, vol. 7792, pp. 350–369. Springer, Heidelberg (2013)
10. Sangiorgi, D., Walker, D.: The π-calculus: A Theory of Mobile Processes. Cambridge University Press (2001)
11. The Coq Development Team: The Coq Proof Assistant Reference Manual (2013)
12. Norell, U.: Towards a practical programming language based on dependent type theory. PhD thesis, Chalmers University of Technology (2007)
13. Abel, A., Pientka, B.: Wellfounded recursion with copatterns: A unified approach to termination and productivity. In: LICS (2013)
14. Pérez, J.A., Caires, L., Pfenning, F., Toninho, B.: Linear logical relations for session-based concurrency. In: Seidl, H. (ed.) Programming Languages and Systems. LNCS, vol. 7211, pp. 539–558. Springer, Heidelberg (2012)

15. Aranda, J., Di Giusto, C., Palamidessi, C., Valencia, F.: On recursion, replication and scope mechanisms in process calculi. In: de Boer, F.S., Bonsangue, M.M., Graf, S., de Roever, W.-P. (eds.) FMCO 2006. LNCS, vol. 4709, pp. 185–206. Springer, Heidelberg (2007)
16. Gay, S., Hole, M.: Subtyping for Session Types in the Pi Calculus. Acta Informatica **42**(2–3), 191–225 (2005)
17. Yoshida, N., Berger, M., Honda, K.: Strong normalisation in the pi -calculus. Inf. Comput. **191**(2), 145–202 (2004)
18. Gay, S., Vasconcelos, V.T.: Linear type theory for asynchronous session types. J. Funct. Programming **20**(1), 19–50 (2010)
19. Deng, Y., Sangiorgi, D.: Ensuring Termination by Typability. In: Levy, J.-J., Mayr, E.W., Mitchell, J.C. (eds.) TCS 2004. IFIP, vol. 155, pp. 619–632. Springer, Boston (2004)
20. Sangiorgi, D.: Termination of processes. Math. Struct. in Comp. Sci. **16**(1), 1–39 (2006)
21. Morris, J.G., Lindley, S., Wadler, P.: The least must speak with the greatest (2014) Draft
22. Baelde, D.: Least and greatest fixed points in linear logic. TOCL 13(1) (January 2012)
23. Abel, A.: Strong normalization and equi-(co)inductive types. In: Della Rocca, S.R. (ed.) TLCA 2007. LNCS, vol. 4583, pp. 8–22. Springer, Heidelberg (2007)
24. Mendler, N.P.: Inductive types and type constraints in the second-order lambda calculus. Annals of Pure and Applied Logic **5**(12), 159–172 (1991)
25. Giménez, E.: Structural recursive definitions in type theory. In: Larsen, K.G., Skyum, S., Winskel, G. (eds.) ICALP 1998. LNCS, vol. 1443, pp. 397–408. Springer, Heidelberg (1998)
26. Grégoire, B., Sacchini, J.L.: On strong normalization of the calculus of constructions with type-based termination. In: Fermüller, C.G., Voronkov, A. (eds.) LPAR-17. LNCS, vol. 6397, pp. 333–347. Springer, Heidelberg (2010)

Trust-Based Enforcement of Security Policies

Roberto Vigo[1(✉)], Alessandro Celestini[2], Francesco Tiezzi[3], Rocco De Nicola[3], Flemming Nielson[1], and Hanne Riis Nielson[1]

[1] DTU Compute, Technical University of Denmark, Kongens Lyngby, Denmark
{rvig,fnie,hrni}@dtu.dk
[2] Istituto per le Applicazioni del Calcolo, IAC-CNR, Rome, Italy
a.celestini@iac.cnr.it
[3] IMT, Institute for Advanced Studies Lucca, Lucca, Italy
{francesco.tiezzi,rocco.denicola}@imtlucca.it

Abstract. Two conflicting high-level goals govern the enforcement of security policies, abridged in the phrase "high security at a low cost". While these drivers seem irreconcilable, formal modelling languages and automated verification techniques can facilitate the task of finding the right balance. We propose a modelling language and a framework in which security checks can be relaxed or strengthened to save resources or increase protection, on the basis of trust relationships among communicating parties. Such relationships are automatically derived through a reputation system, hence adapt dynamically to the observed behaviour of the parties and are not fixed a priori. In order to evaluate the impact of the approach, we encode our modelling language in StoKlaim, which enables verification via the dedicated statistical model checker SAM. The overall approach is applied to a fragment of a Wireless Sensor Network, where there is a clear tension between devices with limited resources and the cost for securing the communication.

Keywords: Security policies · Probabilistic aspects · Reputation systems · Stochastic verification

1 Introduction

Security policies are usually formalised as fixed rules concerning actions that have to be executed whenever given conditions are met. Nonetheless, the scenarios in which security policies operate are often open and highly dynamic, and decisions may depend on external factors, not entirely known at design-time: this is for example the case when human agents play a role in the system, or when systems components have limited resources that need be used carefully.

The challenge of modelling security policies in an uncertain world has been first addressed by AspectKP [1], where policies are implemented as probabilistic aspects: when the triggering conditions are met, an aspect (i.e., a policy) is enforced with a given probability. This approach is suitable for taking into account a great many real concerns, including the possibility that some undertaken security measures are eluded.

M. Maffei and E. Tuosto (Eds.): TGC 2014, LNCS 8902, pp. 176–191, 2014.
DOI: 10.1007/978-3-662-45917-1_12

In a more complex scenario, the probabilistic enforcement of security policies can account for relaxing or strengthening a security check, aiming at saving resources or increasing protection. In order to react to a dynamic environment, the probability to undertake, relax, or strengthen a given security measure cannot be fixed a priori, as in [1], but depends on our knowledge of the past and on our expectations for the future. In a distributed system, knowledge and expectation can be interpreted as the opinion we have formed about the parties we are interacting with, hence they can be connected to the *trust* we put on our peers.

Probabilistic reputation systems [2,3] offer a framework for quantifying trust in probabilistic terms. In a reputation system, communicating parties rate each other when an interaction is completed, and then use such rates to compute a reputation score, which is levered to decide about future interactions. The main advantage of reputation systems is that they permit computing the probability that a policy is enforced as the system evolves and according to its observed behaviour. This leads to the notion of *trust-based enforcement of security policies*.

The trust we put on the involved parties at a given time can be used to determine the actual enforcement of security polices. A policy can be relaxed with the aim of saving resources: in case enforcing the prescribed checks is expensive (in terms of time, energy, etc.), they can be skipped or relaxed when interacting with parties who exhibited fair behaviour in the past. On the contrary, we can strengthen a security check when interacting with a party we do not trust, or dually we can exchange critical information only with highly-trusted parties. In this view, the enforcement or relaxation of security policies becomes (probabilistically) optional with respect to a default mode, which is to be followed when we do not have enough information to take meaningful decisions.

In order to tackle the challenge of modelling and reasoning about systems where security policies are enforced on a trust basis, we propose TESP (Trust-based Enforcement of Security Policies), a calculus inspired by [1], that enriches the StoKlaim [4] formalism with probabilistic aspects for security policies and with primitives for managing reputation scores. The transformational semantics of TESP associates to each TESP term a StoKlaim one, thus enabling the verification of properties specified in MoSL (Mobile Stochastic Logic) [5] by means of the model checker SAM [6]. The main technical challenge addressed in this work is the integration of all these elements (in particular, probabilistic aspects, security policies, and reputations) in a uniform framework. The key role in this integration is played by the policy evaluation described in Sect. 2.3.

The choice of a stochastic process calculus seems natural once one considers that trust relationships vary over time. Moreover, also resource usage is conditioned temporally: batteries deplete and may recharge, and for instance we might wonder whether the probability of disclosing some information to a third party within the average life-span of a component meets a given threshold.

The flexibility of the framework is demonstrated on the example of a Wireless Sensor Network, where the need for securing the communication in an open environment coexists with "lazy" components that have limited resources and thus want to perform as few operations as possible.

Related Work. Aspects Oriented Programming (AOP) [7] focuses on separation of concerns in developing software systems, and has been extensively studied in connection with the enforcement of security policies [8–10]. TESP extends and combines two lines of research, putting reputation systems to use in the development of security policies through aspects. On the one hand, the integration of aspects into a coordination language in the KLAIM family [11] has been explored in [10]. On the other hand, STOKLAIM has been used in [12] to model and verify properties of reputation systems, aiming at providing a formal understanding of such objects. The statistical model checker [13] SAM is presented in [14].

The relationship of TESP with respect to its inspiring languages, namely AspectKP and STOKLAIM, can be summarised as follows. On the one hand, our language is essentially a superset of AspectKP, and can certainly model all the systems expressible with AspectKP. In fact, one of our aims is to loosen the rigidity of the latter, where policies are applied with fixed probabilities. On the other hand, we have that our language is fully encodable in STOKLAIM, as argued throughout Sect. 2, and we can thus exploit the statistical model checker SAM, that works on STOKLAIM models, to check properties expressed in MOSL.

Statistical inference offers a formal framework for analysing historical observation and synthesising probability distributions. Whilst probabilistic reputation systems surely relies on the applications of statistical methods, they have the specific merit of defining a framework where trust scores are adjusted dynamically, as the system evolves. We consider here reputation systems based on probabilistic trust [15], whose basic postulate is that the behaviour of each player in the system can be modelled as a probability distribution over a given set of interaction *outcomes*. Once this postulate is accepted, the task of computing reputation scores reduces to inferring the *true* distribution parameters for a given player. A study of reputation systems in the realm on WSNs is presented in [16].

In this work we stick to basic mechanisms for managing policies, focusing instead on their trust-based enforcement. For more elaborate approaches to policy selection and combination the reader may refer to XACML [17].

Outline. We present TESP syntax in Sect. 2, showing how to encode the new constructs in STOKLAIM. The developments of the language is demonstrated on a running example, showing how reputation management and policy enforcement seamlessly integrate in the basic calculus. Some quantitative properties of interest are verified by means of statistical model checking and simulation in Sect. 3. Finally, Sect. 4 concludes and sketches a line for future work.

2 TESP: Syntax and Informal Semantics

TESP (Trust-based Enforcement of Security Policies) is a distributed process calculus which can be used to model security policies and their probabilistic enforcement, relying on a reputation system to infer probabilities. The calculus, displayed in Table 1, enriches (a subset of) STOKLAIM with primitives for handling reputations and inherits the aspect-oriented mind-set of AspectKP for the design of security policies.

A system is rendered as a network whose nodes represent the communicating parties (referred to also as *players* in the following). As customary in KLAIM [18], each node is equipped with a tuplespace, modelling a local memory. Communication between nodes is asynchronous and point-to-point: sending is modelled as storing a tuple in the receiver's locality space, whereas receiving is modelled as reading a tuple from the local tuplespace. However, other forms of interaction typical of tuplespace-based communication are allowed: e.g., receiving can be rendered as reading a tuple from the sender's locality. With respect to KLAIM-like calculi we refrain from allowing process mobility. We deem that this simplification facilitates focusing on the novelty of our work, and that the technical developments needed to encompass the full-fledged version of STOKLAIM would provide little additional insight into our approach.

In the following we present the syntax and the intended semantics of the calculus. The formal semantics of STOKLAIM is introduced in [4]; we provide the semantics of the new constructs by means of a translation into STOKLAIM processes.

2.1 Basic Calculus

The top-level entities of the calculus are networks. A network is a collection of nodes $l ::^{\pi} (P, \mathcal{T})$ combined with the parallel operator $||$. Each node represents a player, which is uniquely identified by its locality l, and is characterised by a list of policies π, a running process P, and a tuplespace $\mathcal{T}$.

Given a process P, the special locality self denotes the locality where P is executing. A process is either the parallel composition of processes (i.e., threads), the guarded sum of action-prefixed processes, or the invocation of a process identifier. We assume that each process identifier A has a unique definition of the form $A \triangleq P$, visible from any locality of a network. The terminated process **nil** is obtained as the empty sum. For the sake of writing more readable processes, we introduce the conditional statement $\mathsf{if}\ e\ \mathsf{then}\ P_1\ \mathsf{else}\ P_2$, which is is not pure STOKLAIM syntax but can be easily encoded in the language and is available in the model checker SAM together with Boolean expressions e, that can check locality equality or compare integers.

An action has the form $a@u\!:\!\lambda$, denoting that action a has target locality u and a stochastic duration governed by a negative exponential distribution with rate λ. We write $l\!::\!a@u\!:\!\lambda$ to stress that a is attempted from locality l.

An action can be an output to or an input from a tuplespace. Tuples t are communicable objects consisting of sequences of data elements u. Such elements can be constant locality values l[1] and applied occurrences of variables v. Templates T consist of sequences of data element u and defining occurrences of variables $v?$. Prefixes $\mathsf{in}(\ldots, v?, \ldots)@u : \lambda.P$ and $\mathsf{read}(\ldots, v?, \ldots)@u : \lambda.P$ bind

[1] For the sake of simplicity we consider here only localities as communicable values. Observe however that Boolean, integer, and string values can be encoded with ad hoc localities.

Table 1. Syntax: Networks, Processes and Actions

$N ::= N_1 \| N_2 \quad \| \quad l ::^{\pi} (P, \mathcal{T})$	(Network)
$P ::= P_1 \| P_2 \quad \| \quad \sum_i a_i @ u : \lambda_i . P_i \quad \| \quad A \quad \| \quad \textsf{if } e \textsf{ then } P_1 \textsf{ else } P_2$	(Process)
$a ::= \textsf{out}(t) \quad \| \quad \textsf{in}(T) \quad \| \quad \textsf{inp}(T) \quad \| \quad \textsf{read}(T) \quad \| \quad \textsf{readp}(T) \quad \| \quad \textsf{rate}(res)$	(Action)
$res ::= \textsf{true} \quad \| \quad \textsf{false}$	(Interaction result)
$\mathcal{T} ::= \{\!\{\}\!\} \quad \| \quad \mathcal{T} \uplus \langle t \rangle$	(Tuplespace)
$u ::= l \quad \| \quad v \qquad t ::= u \quad \| \quad t_1, t_2 \qquad T ::= u \quad \| \quad v? \quad \| \quad T_1, T_2$	(Data)

variable v in P. Operator $\uplus$ increments tuplespaces, modelled as multi-sets of tuples.

As for communication, input works by pattern-matching on tuples: the process $\textsf{in}(T)@u:\lambda.P$ looks for a tuple t matching the template T in the tuplespace located at u, and whenever such a t is found it is removed from u and the process evolves to $P\sigma$, where σ is a substitution containing the bindings of variables defined in T and instantiated as in t. If t is not found, then $\textsf{in}(T)@u:\lambda.P$ is blocked until a matching tuple is available. The input action $\textsf{read}(T)@u:\lambda$ behaves like $\textsf{in}(T)@u:\lambda$, except that t is not removed from u. A process $\textsf{out}(t)@u:\lambda.P$ puts tuple t in the tuplespace at locality u and proceeds as P.

For convenience, we inherit from Linda and some versions of KLAIM the distinction between blocking and non-blocking input actions, the latter being denoted $\textsf{inp}(T)@u:\lambda$ and $\textsf{readp}(T)@u:\lambda$, for destructive and non-destructive input, respectively. These are *predicate* operations that returns true if a matching tuple is found, false otherwise. As inp, readp always allow progressing with the computation, some defining occurrence of variable might have not received a value after such an operation is consumed. There are different approaches to handle a non-bound variable in a continuation process. In Linda, where non-blocking input operations have been first introduced, the intention was to check the boolean result of the operation, so as to split the continuation process in two branches, and use such variables only in the branch related to a successful input [19, pg. 2-25]. However, no enforcement mechanism is provided which guarantees that a variable is accessed only if it carries some information. A more elegant approach has been recently proposed in [20], where the notion of option data type is exploited to differentiate an input variable possibly carrying no value from one actually bound to some value. Whilst this would be an interesting development, it is independent from the use of reputation systems, and thus in the following we resort to Linda style, to avoid overly complicating the syntax. Finally, a third possibility consists in restricting the syntax of inp, readp not to range on binding occurrences of variables, hence writing $\textsf{inp}(t)@u:\lambda$.

As usual, in the following we consider closed processes (no free variable).

Running Example 1/3. Consider a hierarchical Wireless Sensor Network in which a number of *sensors* monitor environmental parameters (e.g., temperature, pressure, etc.) and communicate them to *base stations*, in charge of validating the data and forwarding them to a *central server*. Since sensors and stations are generally powered by batteries and have limited computational capabilities, communication between them is not encrypted but relies on signatures appended to messages, so as to enable stations to verify the integrity of received sensor readings. Due to cheap hardware, unreliable wireless communication, and active attackers it may indeed be the case that the message received by a station gets corrupted.

A possibly faulty sensor can be modelled by the following process:

$$\mathsf{sensor}_i \triangleq \mathsf{sensor}_i^{sound} \mid \mathsf{sensor}_i^{faulty}$$

$$\mathsf{sensor}_i^{sound} \triangleq \mathsf{in}(\text{“token”})@\mathsf{self}:\lambda_{sound}.\,\mathsf{out}(\text{“reading”}, m, \mathsf{self}, \mathsf{self})@\mathsf{station}_j:\lambda_1.\\ \mathsf{out}(\text{“token”})@\mathsf{self}:\lambda_2.\,\mathsf{sensor}_i^{sound}$$

$$\mathsf{sensor}_i^{faulty} \triangleq \mathsf{in}(\text{“token”})@\mathsf{self}:\lambda_{faulty}.\,\mathsf{out}(\text{“reading”}, m, n, \mathsf{self})@\mathsf{station}_j:\lambda_1.\\ \mathsf{out}(\text{“token”})@\mathsf{self}:\lambda_2.\,\mathsf{sensor}_i^{faulty}$$

where the first parallel component ($\mathsf{sensor}_i^{sound}$) models the case in which the sensor issues a reading with the correct message signature, and the second component ($\mathsf{sensor}_i^{faulty}$) describes the case in which the message is corrupted. The choice is modelled by two concurrent withdrawals (in) of a local ($@\mathsf{self}$) shared tuple (“token”), whose rates (λ_{sound} and λ_{faulty}) determine the frequency with which a message is delivered intact or corrupted, respectively. Sending a sensor reading to the parent $\mathsf{station}_j$ corresponds to storing (out) a tuple in its tuplespace ($@\mathsf{station}_j$), containing the string “reading” as first field, the content of the reading m (assumed to be a fresh constant), the signature, and the source locality. For the sake of simplicity, a signed message is ideally described by a pair (m, l), where m is the message payload and l the signature (second and third fields, respectively), represented as the locality that generated the message[2]. If the delivered message is not corrupted, at $\mathsf{station}_j$ the third and fourth fields of the tuple will be identical (declared and actual source coincide), otherwise they will not (n is a fresh constant). Once the sensor reading is sent, the component releases the token ($\mathsf{out}(\text{“token”})@\mathsf{self}$) and restarts.

A base station is then in charge of receiving readings and forwarding them to the central server. A sensor reading is forwarded only after the signature check is successfully passed. A station can modelled by the following process:

$$\mathsf{station}_j \triangleq \mathsf{in}(\text{“reading”}, v_m?, v_s?, v_{source}?)@\mathsf{self}:\lambda_3.\\ \mathsf{out}(\text{“check\_req”}, v_m, v_s, v_{source})@\mathsf{self}:\lambda_4.\\ \mathsf{in}(\text{“check\_res”}, v_{res}?)@\mathsf{self}:\lambda_5.\\ \mathsf{if}\ (v_{res})\ \mathsf{then}\ \mathsf{out}(\text{“reading”}, v_m)@\mathsf{server}:\lambda_7.\,\mathsf{station}_j\ \mathsf{else}\ \mathsf{station}_j$$

The retrieval of a reading from the local tuplespace binds variables v_m, v_s, v_{source} to the reading measure, the corresponding signature, and the sensor's locality,

[2] Modelling cryptographic primitives and keys falls outside the scope of this work. The presence of the sender locality in the signed message accounts for the usage of a private key in a more precise encoding.

respectively. The signature check is then performed by a check service local to each base station, rendered as the following parallel process:

$$\begin{aligned}\mathsf{check}_j \triangleq\ & \mathsf{in}(\text{"check\_req"}, v_m?, v_s?, v_{source}?)@\mathsf{self}:\lambda_8.\\ & \mathsf{if}\ (v_s = v_{source})\ \mathsf{then}\ \mathsf{out}(\text{"check\_res"}, \mathsf{true})@\mathsf{self}:\lambda_9.\,\mathsf{check}_j\\ & \qquad\qquad\qquad\quad \mathsf{else}\ \mathsf{out}(\text{"check\_res"}, \mathsf{false})@\mathsf{self}:\lambda_9.\,\mathsf{check}_j\end{aligned}$$

This process consumes a check request, compares[3] the signature with the source locality and sends a Boolean value representing the result of the comparison to the requester. In case the check fails, i.e., the message is corrupted, the base station discards it, otherwise it is forwarded to the server.

2.2 Reputations

The novelty of TESP consists in coupling networks with reputation systems; specifically, we focus on probabilistic reputation systems [2], where players' behaviour is modelled as a probability distribution over a set of interaction outcomes.

We assume that each locality l (i.e., player) has an associated reputation value $rep(l) \in [0, 1]$, representing the trust that the system puts on l, namely 0 denoting a completely distrusted player and 1 a completely trusted one. A new action is introduced to deal with reputations: $\mathsf{rate}(res)@u:\lambda$ updates $rep(u)$ according to the outcome res of an interaction involving the process located at u. We shall see in Sect. 2.3 how reputation scores are levered to enforce policies probabilistically.

In the StoKlaim implementation, the reputation score of a player is modelled as a set of tuples stored in some tuplespace. Accordingly, $\mathsf{rate}(res)@u$ would take the form of one or more output actions, whose values and target tuplespaces are defined by the reputation model.

For the sake of simplicity, in the grammar of Table 1 the outcome of an interaction between processes is a Boolean value, ideally denoting whether or not the interaction took place as expected. We refrain from discussing more complex choices (e.g., using Boolean expressions as argument of rate), as they would provide no additional insight into our approach. The specification of a system, finally, requires defining the initial reputation of each locality. This is an application-dependent task: in our running example we make a conservative choice and start with $rep(l) = 0$ for all localities.

Running Example 2/3. As a base station is connected to a great many sensors, it is the bottle-neck on the way to the server in charge of transforming sensed data into information. In order to save time and energy, the behaviour of stations can be revised so that they check signatures probabilistically, on a trust basis. In fact, together with communication, checking a signature is the most demanding

[3] In a real-world application this consists in hashing the message plain-text, decrypting the signature with the source's public key, and comparing the two bit-strings.

operation performed by stations. The first step consists in coupling processes with a reputation system, where sensors are rated by stations according to their behaviour. In the base station process the last line is replaced by:

$$\text{if } (v_{res}) \text{ then rate(true)}@v_{source}:\lambda_6.\,\text{out(“reading”}, v_m)@\text{server}:\lambda_7.\,\text{station}_j$$
$$\text{else rate(false)}@v_{source}:\lambda_6.\,\text{station}_j$$

The base station exploits the result of the signature check to rate sensors: in case the check succeeds, the sensor receives a positive score (rate(true)$@v_{source}$), otherwise if the message is corrupted the sensor receives a negative score.

As for the reputation system, in the implementation of the example we chose the ML model [3], where the reputation score of a sensor is given by the number of positive interactions (i.e., successful signature checks) over the total number of interactions. rate is thus implemented as an output performed by the base station to its own locality, recording for each sensor the number of positive and negative interactions. In case more base stations were considered, each one would have its own opinion about the reputation of connected sensors, even if a sensor were communicating with more than one station, hence obtaining a local view of reputations. A global perspective would be implemented with a unique tuplespace (e.g., at the server) where all the reputation scores were stored and retrieved from.

2.3 Policies

We assume that each locality l is annotated with a list of policies $\pi_1.\pi_2.\pi_3\ldots$, denoted $\pi(l)$. According to the syntax displayed in Table 2, a list of policies consists of a sequence of aspects followed by allow or block, which stand for policies allowing and denying everything, respectively.

A policy $[?_{rep(u)} rec \text{ if } cut : cond]$ is applied when an action $l :: a@u$ is executed which matches the aspect trigger *cut*. On the contrary, allow and block apply to every action. The selection mechanism scans policy lists from left to right and selects the first policy that applies, disregarding other relevant policies that may occur later in the list. First, the local policies $\pi(l)$ are scanned, and only upon local approval by the action source l the policies at the target u are scanned. This approach is suitable to combine optimisation with security concerns: while the source l may deny the execution of an action to save resources or to ensure security, the target u implements access control on its local tuplespace and thus has the last word. Therefore, it is always the case that two policies are enforced, one at source and one at the target of an action, as the last policy of a list suits every action. In the example, we assume $\pi(l) =$ allow for every location l if not otherwise specified.

The matching between an action $l :: a@u$ and an aspect trigger *cut* works via pattern-matching and produces a substitution from variables that occur free in *cut* to terms in corresponding positions in a. We shall feel free to use the wild-card symbol _ (obtained by matching a variable never used in the policy.)

Assume that the execution of a process located at l reaches a point $a@u:\lambda.Q$, and that $[?_{rep(u')} rec \text{ if } cut : cond]$ is the policy to be enforced. If the predicate

Table 2. Syntax: Aspects and Policies

$\pi ::= \mathsf{allow} \mid \mathsf{block} \mid [?_{rep(u)} rec \ \mathsf{if} \ cut : cond].\pi$	(Policy)
$cut ::= l :: a@u$	(Aspect trigger)
$cond ::= \mathsf{true} \mid \mathsf{false} \mid d_1 = d_2 \mid \mathsf{readp}(T)@u : \lambda$ $\mid \neg cond \mid cond_1 \wedge cond_2 \mid cond_1 \vee cond_2$	(Applicability condition)
$rec ::= \mathsf{skip} \mid \mathsf{do} \mid P$	(Recommendation)

specified by the condition *cond* evaluates to true then the probabilistic recommendation $?_{rep(u')} rec$ is evaluated. The condition *cond* can either test the presence of a tuple in a given tuplespace (and thus generates a substitutions that applies to the whole policy), check locality equality, or be the Boolean combination of simpler conditions.

A recommendation can prescribe to skip the triggering action $l :: a@u$, to execute $a@u$, or to replace *$a@u$ and its continuation* with a *closed* process P. Recommendations behave probabilistically, levering trust relationships. $?_{rep(u)} rec$ enforces *rec* with probability $rep(u)$, while with probability $1 - rep(u)$ the recommendation is not enforced and $a@u$ is executed according to the default plan. Hence, the enforcement of policies relies on reputation scores rather than fixed probabilities (that can however be introduced seamlessly).

Running Example 3/3. We can now show how a base station exploits reputation scores to enforce checking signatures probabilistically: the higher reputation a sensor has, the less wary the station will be when interacting with it.

A base station is instrumented with a policy triggered by the output requesting to check a signature. The policy allows or denies such request according to the reputation of the message source, as prescribed by the probabilistic recommendation:

$$\mathsf{Pol}_{check} \triangleq \left[\begin{array}{l} ?_{rep(v_{source})} \ \mathsf{out}(\text{“reading”}, v_m)@\mathsf{server}: \lambda_7.\,\mathsf{station}_j \\ \mathsf{if} \ \mathsf{self} :: \mathsf{out}(\text{“check\_req”}, v_m, \_, v_{source})@\mathsf{self} : \mathsf{true} \end{array} \right]$$

Whenever an output matching $\mathsf{out}(\text{“check\_req”}, v_m, \_, v_{source})$ is attempted by the base station, the probabilistic recommendation is evaluated (the condition being true). The higher the reputation of the source v_{source}, the higher the probability to enforce the recommendation, which simply replaces the output and its continuation with a new process that directly forwards the message to the server skipping the signature check and the emission of the rating, and then restarts the original process. Pol_{check} is followed by allow in the policy list.

It is worth noticing that another way to obtain similar (or better) results in reducing the computational overhead of sensors is by redesigning and modifying the system using checks less expensive than those based on digital signatures (e.g., based on Message Authentication Codes). However, refactoring the system is much more costly than deploying new aspects, which are independent from the implementation once the binding mechanism is in place.

Semantics. Our policy selection mechanism leads to replace an action $l_i :: a@u : \lambda$ with a conditional structure testing which local policy applies to the action and, in case the action is granted, which remote policy applies to the action. In particular, the more interesting latter check translates as follows:

```
if(u = l1) then
   select the first π in π(l1) s.t. π applies to a;
   evaluate(π);
else if (u = l2) then ...
```

where $l_1, \ldots, l_n$ are all the localities in the network, allow and block apply to every action, and an aspect applies if its *cut* matches a (yielding another conditional structure). Assuming that $a@u : \lambda$ triggered the policy and that Q is its continuation, the evaluation of π is defined as follows:

$$\mathsf{evaluate}(\pi) = \begin{cases} a@u : \lambda.Q & \text{if } \pi = \mathsf{allow} \\ Q & \text{if } \pi = \mathsf{block} \\ \ldots & \text{if } \pi = [?_{rep(u)} rec \text{ if } cut : cond] \end{cases}$$

(the last case is detailed below). Observe that we can only achieve this behaviour in closed systems, where nodes know each other's policies. As the lists of policies are fixed, the translation can be automatically generated. The machinery necessary to remove this restriction would imply fairly elaborate technical developments that falls outside the scope of this work (basically, code mobility and reflection capabilities). Similarly, more complex look-up criteria can be considered, well-beyond the sequential priority we resort to (which is however motivated by implementations common in firewalls). Nonetheless, such elaborate mechanisms are independent from our usage of reputation, hence we point the curious reader to [1] for further details on policy combination in an aspect-oriented mind-set.

It is worthwhile noticing that block allow ignoring an action and going on with the continuation process, whereas in [1] the failure of a policy leads to entering a busy waiting state where the action might be attempted at a later time. Obviously, due care has to be paid in the continuation process, as variables bound by an action that might be skipped cannot be used freely. This issue advocates for a programming style similar to the one prescribed with predicate input actions inp and readp. Other actions do not return a Boolean value denoting success or failure, but this behaviour can be encoded initialising variables with a default value not used elsewhere (e.g., $\perp$) and check whether or not they have been modified after the evaluation of the policy and before accessing them. This would result in replacing $a@u : \lambda.Q$ with $Q[\perp/v_1, \ldots, \perp/v_n]$ in the definition of evaluate for the case $\pi =$ block, the v_i's being the variables bound by action a.

It remains to show how aspects are translated. Consider the policy $\pi \triangleq [?_{rep(u)} rec \text{ if } cut : cond]$, and assume that the matching between the action a

and the trigger *cut* yields substitution θ_1, under which *cond* yields substitution θ_2. Then, $\mathsf{evaluate}(\pi)$ is defined as

$$\begin{array}{l}\texttt{if}(\theta_1(cond))\ \texttt{then}\\ \quad \texttt{if}([\![(\theta_2 \circ \theta_1)(?_{rep(u)}rec)]\!])\ \texttt{then enforce}(rec,\ a@u:\lambda.Q)\ \texttt{else}\ Q\\ \texttt{else}\ a@u:\lambda.Q\end{array}$$

where $\theta_2 \circ \theta_1$ denotes the composition of substitutions, and its application to the probabilistic recommendation can only determine the location u whose reputation is being considered, as skip, do, P are closed.

The translation relies on the auxiliary functions $[\![\cdot]\!]$ and $\mathsf{enforce}$, for evaluating probabilistic recommendations and the outcome of their enforcement. The probabilistic enforcement of a recommendation translates to a Boolean guard:

$$[\![?_{rep(u)}\mathsf{skip}]\!] = ((rand(0,1) > rep(u)) \vee (rep(u) = 0)) = [\![?_{rep(u)}P]\!]$$
$$[\![?_{rep(u)}\mathsf{do}]\!] = ((rand(0,1) < rep(u)) \vee (rep(u) = 1))$$

where $rand(x, y)$ picks a number randomly[4] in the interval $[x, y]$. For instance, with $?_{rep(u)}\mathsf{skip}$ we obtain false, i.e., the action governed by the policy is skipped, with probability $rep(u)$: the higher the trust, the higher the chances to skip executing the action governed by the policy. Conversely, with $?_{rep(u)}\mathsf{do}$ we obtain true, i.e., the action governed by the policy is executed, with probability $rep(u)$: the higher the trust, the higher the chances to execute the action.

The result of enforcing a recommendation is defined as follows:

$$\mathsf{enforce}(\mathsf{skip}, a@u:\lambda.Q) = \mathsf{enforce}(\mathsf{do}, a@u:\lambda.Q) = a@u:\lambda.Q$$
$$\mathsf{enforce}(P, a@u:\lambda.Q) = P$$

Finally, observe that $?_{rep(u)}\mathsf{skip}$ and $?_{rep(u)}\mathsf{do}$ may be both used to relax or strengthen probabilistically a security measure, depending on the application. For example, by enforcing to encrypt a message by default sent as plain-text, or by skipping outputting it at all when possible, we are heightening the overall security of the system either way.

3 Analysing TESP

The stochastic nature of TESP specifications inherently calls for a quantitative verification approach. Quantitative techniques allow determining the probability that a given event will occur, and thus checking whether or not such value meets a threshold of interest.

In Sect. 2.3 we showed how a system in TESP can be translated into StoKlaim. Once a StoKlaim specification is obtained for the system under study, we can express the properties of interest in the temporal stochastic logic MoSL, and then verify whether or not a property holds by means of SAM, a statistical

[4] Function $rand(x, y)$ is implemented in StoKlaim as a selection among a number of tuples representing the interval values. In fact, the semantics of StoKlaim chooses with uniform probability among all matching tuples.

Table 3. Results of the analysis of the formula $true\ U^{\leq t}\phi_{FwdCorrupted}$

Behaviour θ	Time t	Threshold th	Probabilities	Time t	Probabilities
0.2	20	1%	0.6534	40	0.8894
0.2	20	5%	0.4693	40	0.6087
0.2	20	10%	0.2378	40	0.2565
0.5	20	1%	0.8974	40	0.9869
0.5	20	5%	0.7256	40	0.8584
0.5	20	10%	0.3747	40	0.4010
0.8	20	1%	0.9279	40	0.9928
0.8	20	5%	0.5535	40	0.6151
0.8	20	10%	0.1379	40	0.1382

model checker that determines the probability associated to a path formula after a set of independent observations. The model checking algorithm is parametrised on a given tolerance threshold ϵ and error probability p, and guarantees that the difference between the computed values and the exact ones exceeds ϵ with a probability that is less than p.

In order to carry out a quantitative analysis on a StoKlaim network, we first have to specify the value of the rates characterising the actions. As an illustrative example, we show how the rate λ_1 of action $\mathsf{out}(\text{"reading"}, m, \mathsf{self}, \mathsf{self})@\mathsf{station}_j$ can be determined. The rate specifies the duration of a communicating action: assuming that the sensors are relying on an wireless connection providing 250 Kbit/s transfer rate, and that sending a reading requires transferring 20KB, we obtain $\lambda_1 = \frac{1}{(20\times 8)/250} = 1.5$ actions per unit of time.

3.1 Experimental Results

The implementation of the example is available at

`http://www.imm.dtu.dk/~rvig/reputation-policies-WSN.zip`

The first property we investigate tests whether the probability that *the number of corrupted messages forwarded by a base station is greater than a fixed fraction of the total number of forwarded messages.* This property is expressed in MoSL by the formula

$$\phi_{FwdCorrupted} = \langle \text{"forwarded\_corrupted"} \rangle @\mathsf{server} \rightarrow true$$

This formula relies on the *consumption* operator $\langle T \rangle @l \rightarrow \phi$ [4], which is satisfied whenever a tuple matching template T is located at l and the remaining part of the system satisfies ϕ. Hence, the formula $\phi_{FwdCorrupted}$ is satisfied if and only if a tuple $\langle \text{"forwarded\_corrupted"} \rangle$ is stored in the server tuplespace. Notice that the TESP model of the example has been enriched with some outputs: the base station takes note of the numbers of corrupted and forwarded messages, and uses this information to produce a service tuple in case the number of corrupted forwarded is greater than the fixed percentage.

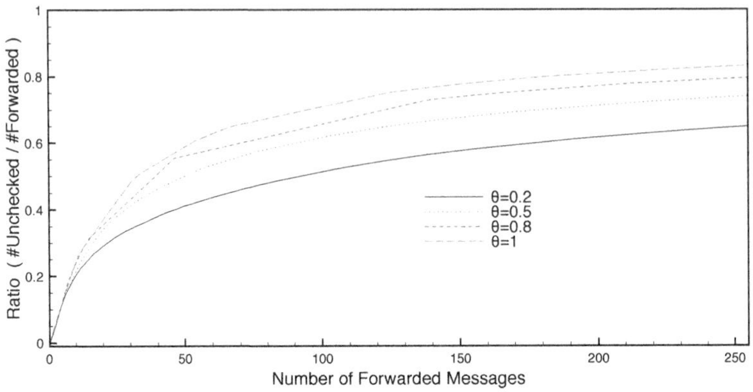

Fig. 1. Ratio between unchecked and forwarded messages

Exploiting the previous formula, we can specify the more interesting property whether the number of corrupted messages forwarded by a base station is greater than a fixed percentage of the total number of forwarded messages *within time* t, defined as $true\ U^{\leq t}\phi_{FwdCorrupted}$, where the *until* formula $\phi_1 U^{\leq t}\phi_2$ is satisfied by all the runs that reach within t time units a state satisfying ϕ_2 while only traversing states that satisfy ϕ_1. The model checking analysis estimates the total probability of the set of runs satisfying such formula. Table 3 reports the results of the analysis with respect to the following parameters: ϵ and p are both set to 0.05; in the network there are four sensors and one base station; three sensors always send correct messages while one behaves according to a parameter θ; three possible sensor's behaviours θ, with $\theta \in \{0.2, 0.5, 0.8\}$ being the probability of sending a correct message; two time limits t, with $t \in \{20, 40\}$; three threshold percentages th, with $th \in \{1\%, 5\%, 10\%\}$.

Inspecting the table, we observe that the probability of satisfying the formula is strictly related to the sensor's behaviour and to the threshold value. In particular, it is not always true that the better the behaviour of the sensor, the lower the probability of forwarding corrupted messages, as one might expect. For $th = 1\%$ the best result - that is, the lowest probability of sending more than 1% corrupted messages - is achieved when the sensor's behaviour is the worst ($\theta = 0.2$). This is due do to the fact that messages from trusted parties are seldom checked, yielding a higher number of forwarded messages.

Figures 1 and 2 show the ratio between the number of unchecked and forwarded messages, and the number of corrupted and forwarded messages, respectively. These results have been obtained thanks to the simulation engine provided with SAM. As expected (see Fig. 1) we observe that the better the sensor behaviour, the higher the ratio of unchecked messages, and thus the higher the quantity of saved resources. On the contrary, Fig. 2 seems not to confirm the results of the model checking analysis: the ratio of corrupted messages over the forwarded is lower for $\theta = 0.8$ than for $\theta = 0.2$. Nonetheless, mind to observe that the simulation computes an average value, while the model checking

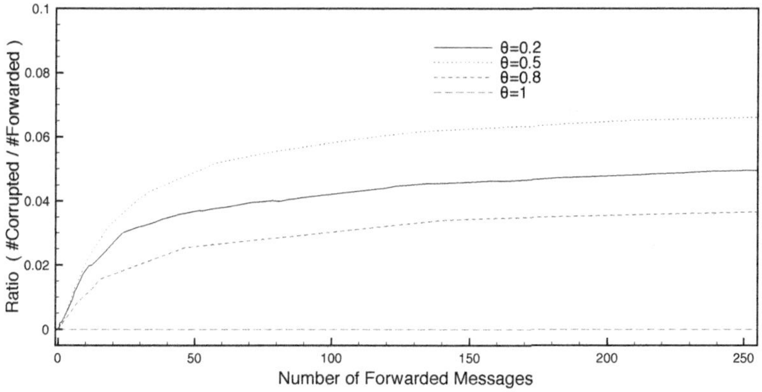

Fig. 2. Ratio between corrupted and forwarded messages

algorithm estimates the probability of exceeding a threshold. Hence, we can conclude that on average the ratio between corrupted and forwarded messages is lower for $\theta = 0.8$, but the probability that the number of corrupted messages exceeds a percentage of the forwarded messages is lower for $\theta = 0.2$. This is due to the decreasing number of checks that are performed for $\theta = 0.8$, and to the fact that the model checking analysis has a temporal horizon: for a fixed time limit t, the total number of messages processed by the system is higher for $\theta = 0.8$ than for $\theta = 0.2$ (less checks, more time for processing new messages).

Hence, the analysis facilitates determining the best trade-off between saving resources (skipping checks) and guaranteeing security (enforcing them, thus forwarding only correct messages). Comparing the number of saved checks with the number of wrong messages that are forwarded we are indeed studying the effect of the policy in terms of resource optimisation and security relaxation, that should match an utility function defined by the system administrator.

4 Conclusions

This work combines two lines of research, showing how aspects and reputation systems can be used to obtain trust-based enforcement of security policies, where trust relationships are determined as the system evolves and according to the behaviour of the parties. Moreover, it shows how the notion of trust can be exploited to optimise resources or increase security, skipping controls if peers are trustworthy or enforcing additional checks when they are not, thus adapting to the environment.

In order to reason about trust-based enforcement of security policies in a natural way we have defined TESP, a stochastic process calculus that extends StoKlaim with primitives for reputation management and aspects. By means of a translation to the original StoKlaim we can verify quantitative properties of interest via statistical model checking and simulation. The expressiveness of the framework has been demonstrated on the simple yet meaningful example of a WSN, where reputations are used to balance the need for security with the shortage of computational resources and power supply.

A promising direction for future work is to investigate the impact of trust-based enforcement of policies on a more optimisation-oriented framework, where explicit optimisation goals are given. This is a challenging task, as even in our simple example multiple conflicting criteria need be considered. At the implementation level, a more succinct translation of TESP into StoKlaim would seem desirable. Moreover, concerning the translation, we also intend to provide a formal proof of its correctness.

Acknowledgements. This work is supported by the IDEA4CPS project, granted by the Danish Research Foundations for Basic Research (DNRF86-10). The work is also partially supported by the EU projects ASCENS (257414) and QUANTICOL (600708), and by the MIUR PRIN project CINA (2010LHT4KM).

References

1. Hankin, C., Nielson, F., Nielson, H.R.: Probabilistic Aspects: Checking Security in an Imperfect World. In: Wirsing, M., Hofmann, M., Rauschmayer, A. (eds.) TGC 2010. LNCS, vol. 6084, pp. 348–363. Springer, Heidelberg (2010)
2. Jøsang, A., Ismailb, R., Boyd, C.: A survey of trust and reputation systems for online service provision. Decision Support Systems 43(2), 618–644 (2007)
3. Despotovic, Z., Aberer, K.: P2P reputation management: Probabilistic estimation vs. social networks. Computer Networks **50**(4), 485–500 (2006)
4. De Nicola, R., Loreti, M.: A modal logic for mobil agents. ACM Trans. Comput. Log. **5**(1), 79–128 (2004)
5. De Nicola, R., Katoen, J.P., Latella, D., Loreti, M., Massink, M.: Model checking mobile stochastic logic. Theoretical Computer Science **382**(1), 42–70 (2007)
6. Loreti, M.: Stochastic Analyser for Mobility (2010). http://rap.dsi.unifi.it/SAM/
7. Kiczales, G., Lamping, J., Mendhekar, A., Maeda, C., Lopes, C., Loingtier, J.-M., Irwin, J.: Aspect-Oriented Programming. In: Akşit, M., Matsuoka, S. (eds.) ECOOP 1997. LNCS, vol. 1241, pp. 220–242. Springer, Heidelberg (1997)
8. Georg, G., Ray, I., France, R.B.: Using Aspects to Design a Secure System. In: IEEE 8th International Conference on Engineering of Complex Computer Systems (ICECCS 2002) (2002)
9. Win, B.D., Joosen, W., Piessens, F.: Developing Secure Applications through Aspect-Oriented Programming. In: Aspect-Oriented Software Development, pp. 633–650 (2004)
10. Hankin, C., Nielson, F., Riis Nielson, H., Yang, F.: Advice for Coordination. In: Lea, D., Zavattaro, G. (eds.) COORDINATION 2008. LNCS, vol. 5052, pp. 153–168. Springer, Heidelberg (2008)
11. Bettini, L., Kannan, R., De Nicola, R., Ferrari, G.-L., Gorla, D., Loreti, M., Moggi, E., Pugliese, R., Tuosto, E., Venneri, B.: The Klaim Project: Theory and Practice. In: Priami, C. (ed.) GC 2003. LNCS, vol. 2874, pp. 88–150. Springer, Heidelberg (2003)
12. Celestini, A., De Nicola, R., Tiezzi, F.: Specifying and Analysing Reputation Systems with a Coordination Language. In: 28th Annual ACM Symposium on Applied Computing (SAC 2013), pp. 1363–1368. ACM (2013)

13. Legay, A., Delahaye, B.: Statistical Model Checking : An Overview. ArXiv (2010)
14. Calzolai, F., Loreti, M.: Simulation and Analysis of Distributed Systems in Klaim. In: Clarke, D., Agha, G. (eds.) COORDINATION 2010. LNCS, vol. 6116, pp. 122–136. Springer, Heidelberg (2010)
15. Gambetta, D.: Can We Trust Trust? Basil Blackwell (1988)
16. Alzaid, H., Alfaraj, M., Ries, S., Jøsang, A., Albabtain, M., Abuhaimed, A.: Reputation-based trust systems for wireless sensor networks: A comprehensive review. In: Fernández-Gago, C., Martinelli, F., Pearson, S., Agudo, I. (eds.) Trust Management VII. IFIP AICT, vol. 401, pp. 66–82. Springer, Heidelberg (2013)
17. OASIS: eXtensible Access Control Markup Language (XACML) Version 3.0 (2013). http://docs.oasis-open.org/xacml/3.0/xacml-3.0-core-spec-os-en.html
18. De Nicola, R., Ferrari, G.L., Pugliese, R.: KLAIM: A Kernel Language for Agents Interaction and Mobility. IEEE Trans. Software Eng. **24**(5), 315–330 (1998)
19. Linda: User's Guide and Reference Manual. Scientific Computing Associates (1995)
20. Nielson, H.R., Nielson, F., Vigo, R.: A Calculus for Quality. In: Păsăreanu, C.S., Salaün, G. (eds.) FACS 2012. LNCS, vol. 7684, pp. 188–204. Springer, Heidelberg (2013)

Author Index

Printed in the United States
By Bookmasters